ANARCHISM

NOMOS
XIX

NOMOS

NOMOS XIX

Yearbook of the American Society for Political and Legal Philosophy

ANARCHISM

Edited by

J. Roland Pennock, *Swarthmore College*

and

John W. Chapman, *University of Pittsburgh*

New York: New York University Press · 1978

. *Anarchism: Nomos XIX*
edited by J. Roland Pennock and John W. Chapman

Copyright © 1978 by New York University

Library of Congress Cataloging in Publication Data
Main entry under title:
Anarchism.
    (Nomos ; 19)
    Bibliography: p.
    Includes index.
    1. Anarchism and anarchists—Addreses, essays,
lectures. I. Pennock, James Roland, 1906-
II. Chapman, John William, 1923-   III. Series.
HX833.A568   335′.83   77-84158
ISBN 0-8147-6572-6

Printed in the United States of America

PREFACE

When the membership of the American Society for Political and Legal Philosophy was called upon to select a topic for their annual meetings to be held in Washington, D.C. in December 1974, they voted overwhelmingly for "anarchism." Judging by the unusually large attendance and the lively discussions, it was a popular choice. At a time when government is in low esteem and when democracies and nondemocracies alike are characterized by ever growing and powerful bureaucracies, it is not suprising that anarchism should experience one of its periodic waves of popularity. It will be of more than academic interest to see whether this current revival proves to be more than a passing phase. In any case, it will almost certainly have some impact on political and constitutional developments. One sees the new emotional climate reflected today in certain regimes in a growing demand for greater respect for human rights and in our own country in the election of a president who ran on an anti-big-government platform. To the best of our knowledge, no one has called Jimmy Carter an anarchist, although his political style is certainly populistic. But the difference between opposition to big government and opposition to all government can be seen as one of degree. These moods have common roots in both philosophy and historical experience. And those roots are the democratic concerns for liberty and equality. Perhaps the difference between anarchy and democracy is to be found in the fact that, while democracy seeks a balance between these two sources of its strength, anarchists tend to divide sharply between "libertarians" and "egalitarians."

We are inclined to view this division among the self-proclaimed anarchists as a sign and a portent. Within the past few years the case for liberty has been given powerful statements, in Michael Oakeshott's *On Human Conduct* and Friedrich Hayek's *The Mirage of Social Justice*. And the case for equality has found an equally worthy representative in Roberto Mangabeira Unger's *Knowledge and Politics*. Behind the present debate stands the great issue, perhaps the greatest of all issues in political philosophy, of whether to run society on the basis of impersonal rules or to organize for the pursuit of common objectives. We hope that our examination of "anarchism" will contribute to this debate.

The Society and the editors of this volume are indebted to Robert Paul Wolff, of the University of Massachusetts, for his service as chairman of the program committee for the meetings out of which the book has grown. The contributions by De George, Mazor, Newton, Ritter, Rothbard, Stone, Wasserstrom, Wertheimer, and Wieck were all derived directly from that program. The other chapters were submitted to the editors subsequent to the Society's meeting. Although two of our authors criticize the work of Robert Paul Wolff, he declined our suggestion that he take this opportunity to reply to them or to add to his well-known work on the subject at this time. To all the contributors the editors express their thanks; and also to Eleanor Greitzer, invaluable assistant to the editor.

The organization of *Nomos XIX* owes much to Gerald F. Gaus, a graduate student at the University of Pittsburgh. For the very comprehensive bibliography, we are indebted to Robert Kocis, also a graduate student at Pittsburgh.

Finally, our Society wishes to thank the John Dewey Foundation for a most generous grant in support of its activities. The first application of these funds has made possible the publication of the present volume at this time, the third volume of the series to appear within a twelve-month period. The grant will also contribute to the furtherance of the Society's objectives in other ways, including assurance that NOMOS volumes will continue the process of catching up with our normal publication schedule.

J. R. P.
J. W. C.

CONTENTS

xi

THE MORAL PSYCHOLOGY OF ANARCHISM

CONTRIBUTORS

JAMES M. BUCHANAN
Economics, Virginia Polytechnic Institute

APRIL CARTER
Political Science, Somerville College, Oxford

JOHN W. CHAPMAN
Political Science, University of Pittsburgh

JOHN P. CLARK
Philosophy, Loyola University

RICHARD T. De GEORGE
Philosophy, University of Kansas

RICHARD FALK
Political Science, Princeton University

GERALD F. GAUS
Political Science, University of Pittsburgh

ROBERT A. KOCIS
Political Science, University of Pittsburgh

ERIC MACK
Philosophy, Newcomb College, Tulane University

REX MARTIN
Philosophy, University of Kansas

LESTER J. MAZOR
Law, Hampshire College

DONALD McINTOSH
Political Science, Windsor, Massachusetts

LISA NEWTON
Philosophy, Fairfield University

PATRICK RILEY
Political Science, University of Wisconsin

ALAN RITTER
Political Science, Indiana University

MURRAY N. ROTHBARD
Economics, Polytechnic Institute of New York

CHRISTOPHER D. STONE
Law, University of Southern California

GRENVILLE WALL
Philosophy, Middlesex Polytechnic at Enfield, U.K.

RICHARD WASSERSTROM
Law and Philosophy, University of California, Los Angeles

ALAN WERTHEIMER
Political Science, University of Vermont

DAVID WIECK
Philosophy, Rensselaer Polytechnic Institute

ANARCHISM AND POLITICAL PHILOSOPHY: AN INTRODUCTION

GERALD F. GAUS and JOHN W. CHAPMAN

In *Nomos XIX* we set out to examine the nature of anarchism. But as soon as we try to clarify the meaning of anarchism we encounter widely disparate views. It refracts into a spectrum of doctrines. Individualist anarchists occupy one end of the spectrum, collectivists the other. Some individualists base their case for freedom on natural rights, perhaps understood as historical entitlements, against which the legitimacy of political authority is to be appraised. Others look to the power of rational calculation to integrate interests. They oppose the state more as superfluous than as immoral. Both these brands of individualism are based on confidence in the market as the source of spontaneously generated social order. Adam Smith would not feel uncomfortable in the presence of these descendants of classical liberalism. On the other hand, the communal anarchists are wont to emphasize the strength of social sentiment. And they envisage society as based on shared or common purposes, the existence or legitimacy of which the individualists are inclined to deny. Manifestly different conceptions of human nature and of the good for man are at issue. Are we rights-endowed, rational calculators; or are we designed for, and do we crave after, the warmth of emotional unification? Are we like Schopenhauer's porcupines, or are we destined for life in organic groups?

Further lines of differentiation show up among the anarchists. Some hold anarchism to be the complete absence of political authority; others see it as compatible with a minimal form of government. For still others anarchism is essentially a moral attitude, an emotional climate, or even a mood, rather than a prescription for specific social, economic, or political arrangements. Again, with reference to the individualist-communalist distinction, we find arguments that only one among the competing conceptions of the humanly valuable can be truly anarchist, while others, perhaps more tolerantly, conceive of anarchism as consisting of many species, extending from the strictly individualist to the expressivist communitarian. Hence, throughout the volume the reader may expect to meet significant disagreement as to both the nature and the institutional implications of anarchism.

After an overview of the volume's central themes we shall attempt to identify some of the critical issues that arise in the analysis of anarchism, viewed both historically and theoretically, and so to place the various doctrines in the perspective of Western political philosophy.

PERSPECTIVES ON ANARCHY

Part I recognizes diversity of thinking appropriately by offering several contrasting perspectives on anarchism. We open with John P. Clark's effort at definition. He discerns a theme common to all varieties of anarchist thought. "In both social and individualist anarchism . . . the view prevails that people have a great potential for voluntaristic action, and ability to overcome the use of violence and coercion." Of particular concern to Clark is that a definition take account of historical movements as well as theoretical formulations. By considering both theory and practice, he says, the error of treating anarchist doctrines as inherently unrealistic and utopian is avoided. "The distinctive characteristic of anarchist programs is that they institute an immediate movement in the direction of voluntarism and antiauthoritarianism." Central to Clark's definitional analysis, then, is the idea that anarchism is just as much a call to action as it is a critique of the established order.

In the next chapter, James M. Buchanan presents quite a different interpretation. In apparent contradistinction to Clark's thesis, Buchanan thinks human nature too frail for genuine anarchy to be a real possibility. Therefore, we must move "one stage down" from utopia to "ordered anarchy," which he contemplates in straightforwardly constitutional and market terms. Buchanan sees concord between anarchists and liberal constitutionalists on "the primary value premise of individualism," that is, on the moral equality of free men. The two part company, though, when this moral outlook is translated into political and social precepts.

This concern with the alternatives of minimal stateness and pure or total anarchy is continued in Eric Mack's contribution, in which he disputes Robert Nozick's proposition that a "minimal state" is a morally legitimate corrective for the inconveniences of the "state of nature." Starting from Lockean postulates, Mack affirms that it is logically impossible for any "protection agency" legitimately to impose its conception of fair procedures on those who prefer otherwise. Since consent and not coercion must be the rule, no state, however minimal, can justifiably arise.[1] Moral principle points only to some kind of voluntary "accommodation" among a multiplicity of private "protection agencies." Perhaps the contributions of Buchanan and Mack license us to distinguish between anarchists and near-anarchists.

The last essay in Part I, Richard A. Falk's "Anarchism and World Order," extends the anarchists' complaints against the state and politics to the global level. Falk, like Clark, perceives anarchism as the living alternative to what he calls "statism" and "bureaucratic centralism." Indeed, he contends that anarchism's emphases on communal consciousness and transterritorial organization render it far more suitable than the national state for dealing with both community and planetary problems. Falk looks toward "libertarian socialism," toward ". . . a minimalist governing structure in a setting that encourages the full realization of human potentialities for cooperation and happiness."

AUTHORITY AND ANARCHISM

The chapters of Part II address the issue: Is anarchism opposed to authority as such? Richard De George begins the discussion by maintaining, despite all claims to the contrary, that the doctrine does not preclude the legitimacy of every type of authority, rather only that "imposed from above." "The root problem is to provide organization without authoritarianism." This thought leads him to conclude that anarchist principles are compatible with authoritative institutions, including minimal, responsive government. Richard Wasserstrom, in his comment on De George's analysis, holds that both the spirit and the substance of anarchism are violated by even "nonauthoritarian exercises of authority." The true anarchist regards "all forms of coercive authority" as oppressive.

However, De George's thesis is upheld by Rex Martin in the following paper, in which he seeks to demonstrate that De George's controverted conclusion comes from a tension intrinsic to anarchist thought. Martin advances the logical notion that anarchists' use of moral arguments to criticize established authorities as illegitimate is inconsistent with their denial of the possibility of legitimate authority. Moral criticism presumes the possibility of corrective measures. Either, Martin contends, the consistent anarchist must hold that the concept of rightful authority is absurd and abandon moral talk about it, or he must build his case on moral foundations, thus admitting implicitly that rightful authority is at least conceivable. De George's proposal that there can be valid anarchistic authority derives from his appreciation of this implicit admission.

In the final contribution to this debate, Alan Ritter accepts De George's distinction between legitimate and illegitimate anarchist authority, but alleges he has misdescribed the distinguishing criterion. In connection with authority as ordinarily understood, Ritter says, ". . . even the most limited authority impedes deliberation, thus damaging what anarchists most cherish as a source of human worth." According to Ritter, for true anarchists, "justified authority must be shared by all." Hence genuine anarchist authority allows a maximum of "rational deliberation" while still preserving the peace. Moreover, ". . . anarchist authority, being intimate, particular and internal cannot issue directives of a legal sort." This commitment to ethical discretion as opposed to the rule of law runs contrary to the political tradition of the West, understood as freedom under rationally acceptable laws. A "startling conclusion," says Ritter. Here we come upon a critical issue on which communitarian anarchists diverge from the mainstream of Western political philosophy, whether to organize for the pursuit of communal values or to pursue individual interests within a framework of impersonal law.[2]

ANARCHISM AND THE RULE OF LAW

This issue of anarchists' attitude toward the rule of law is the focus of Part III. Lester J. Mazor asserts that American law is an instrument of "dominance" and hence ought to be "disrespected" and disparaged as a "means to justice." "The legal process is loaded with devices that cause it to operate primarily to the benefit of those who approach it from a position of superiority." Contempt for law is on the increase, Mazor goes on to say, and ". . . the ultimate result of lack of respect for law is anarchy." In her comment, Lisa Newton questions whether it is the rule or the abuse of law to which anarchists object. Holding it to be the latter, Newton then finds similarities in the anarchist and Aristotelian conceptions of community. She says the "realistic anarchist" is an "Aristotelian" who values human "autonomy" in a civic setting as distinguished from a playful "otterdom."

Alan Wertheimer, again speaking to Mazor's position, believes that he merely describes disobedience to law, which does not necessarily entail contempt for it. People break laws for purely instrumental as well as for moral or civil reasons. Moreover, provision of "public goods" is squarely dependent on coercive law, as Rousseau full well knew. "I believe it is this argument which presents the greatest difficulty for the defender of anarchy." Given the uncertainties and potential instabilities that pervade society, Wertheimer concludes that simple prudence dictates that human relations be legally grounded.

ANARCHIST THEORIES OF JUSTICE

Consideration of Mazor's attitude toward law leads naturally to an examination of anarchistic conceptions of justice. For Murray N. Rothbard, a founder of the Libertarian party, the state is nothing but a "protection racket," a "Great Company" writ large.[3] Accordingly, "Anarchism advocates the dissolution of the state into social and market arrangements. . . ."[4] He opens Part IV by outlining a system of arbitration whereby disputes over violations of person and property may be settled without resort to the courts. In Rothbard's scheme, to which, he says, there are historical analogues, arbitration firms yield decisions enforceable by private police agencies. A radical individualist, he desires heavy reliance on market forces to

further "anarchistic values of peaceful cooperation and agreement."
In reflecting on Rothbard's plan, Christopher D. Stone finds a
number of difficulties likely to arise in anarcho-capitalism. Of these
perhaps the most critical have to do with activities injurious to the
general community rather than to specified individuals; for example, environmental pollution. His argument at this point coincides
with that of Alan Wertheimer. Rothbard's adversary-arbitration
model seems ill-designed to cope with such collective depradations.
Nevertheless, Stone believes, ". . . the idea of offering arbitration as
a substitute for present criminal law enforcement ought to be
explored further."

    In the eyes of David Wieck, however, Rothbard's brand of
anarcho-capitalism is just "one more bourgeois ideology" that serves
to justify a "libertarian state," but has no bearing on anarchist
justice properly understood. Wieck's conception of anarchy is one in
which ". . . freedom is defined not by rights and liberties but by the
functioning of society as a network of voluntary cooperation."
Although highly individualistic, this society, Wieck argues, would
certainly not be characterized by what he calls Rothbard's "severe
individualism." For Wieck, anarchistic justice is not a matter of
rationally calculating marketmen submitting their affairs to private
arbitrations. Rather it integrates individual freedom and social
interdependence through spirited concern for both individual
independence and communal well-being.[5] "Anarchism represents,
as I understand it, a kind of intransigent effort to conceive of and to
seek means to realize a *human* liberation from every power structure,
every form of domination and hierarchy."[6] In Wieck's opinion,
". . . anarchism represents, finally, not a specific social design but a
moral commitment."[7]

THE MORAL PSYCHOLOGY OF ANARCHISM

    Wieck's exposition of the spirit of anarchism takes us on to
questions of moral psychology, the subject of Part V. Donald
McIntosh says that anarchism is "inherently collectivistic," and so is
in basic agreement with Wieck on this point. However, McIntosh
presents an entirely different interpretation of the emotional and
moral climate of an anarchist society. Anarchism is not the outcome
of deep respect for individual independence and freedom. Rather,

according to McIntosh, a "passion for equality" inspires anarchist morality. This passion determines attitudes toward authority. "The core of anarchism is the rejection of all political authority whatsoever." But the egalitarian mentality does sanction intense "peer authority" to induce both unanimity and conformity. "The psychological prototype of the anarchist community is an adolescent gang. . . ."[8] Hence anarchism is not rightly conceived as a radical form of liberalism. "Those who have espoused anarchism on individualistic grounds are in error." Rather, McIntosh concludes, it is a species of moral collectivism, peculiar to which is "government without politics," based on an absence of personal independence, coupled with revulsion against hierarchical authority. These are the psychodynamics that McIntosh discerns at the heart of the anarchist quest for fraternal unanimity.

Whereas McIntosh denies that anarchism is grounded in respect for freedom and individuality, Grenville Wall's contribution submits that it is the logical implication of what he refers to as "ethical individualism." In his appraisal of Robert Paul Wolff's defense of anarchism, he contends that Wolff moves from a mistaken conception of moral autonomy to the false conclusion that all political authority is incompatible with moral freedom. According to Wall, "ethical individualism" implies that all values are personal and subjective, and this belief, he thinks, taints Wolff's conception of moral autonomy. But given "public rule-governed activities and practices and public criteria of correctness in judgment," moral reasoning and political activity cannot be conceived as entirely lacking in objective reference. In this light, "ethical individualism," based as it is on the privateness of criteria of judgment, is "just a special case of philosophical individualism," and as such is fully as absurd as the notion of a private language.[9] "Autonomy and authority are really just two sides of the same coin."

Patrick Riley continues the analysis of Wolff's anarchism. He holds that Wolff's idea of moral autonomy is not Kantian, but rather "quasi-existentialist." On Riley's reading of Kant, "autonomy is a hypothetical 'property' or 'attribute' of free will, not a substantive moral duty," as Wolff would have it. Not surprisingly, therefore, "There is no trace of anarchism in his (Kant's) political and legal theory." Indeed, a republic is required to provide the requisite security for men to perform their moral duties. Both Wall and Riley agree, then, that moral autonomy, rightly conceived, provides no support for anarchy.[10]

The volume concludes with April Carter's examination of the ambiguous position of "propaganda by the deed" in the anarchist tradition. She finds in anarchism an incongruity between pacifist attitudes and a heroic yearning that both condones and encourages violence. The history of anarchism reveals a persisting struggle between rationalism and romanticism. Indeed, this struggle may be inherent in anarchism, as Carter comes to see romantic violence as an "emotive necessity." This moral ambiguity may lead one to reflect back to John P. Clark's essay and to wonder whether his objective, a definition of anarchism that logically unites theory and practice, is attainable. Perhaps, at least so far as communitarian anarchism is concerned, both the felt coherence and the attraction of the doctrine ultimately derive from contrary yearnings fostered in modern society.

AUTHENTIC ANARCHISM

This overview confirms our initial observation that very different doctrines march together under the black flag of anarchism. Our authors clearly reveal a deep rift between the libertarian individualists and the egalitarian communalists. Moreover, there is striking contrast between the classical anarchists of the nineteenth century and the neo-anarchists who have recently erupted in universities around the world. The middle-class students who gave expression to patently anarchistic moods and impulses in the 1960s seem far removed from those Russians, Spaniards, and Italians who rebelled against political oppression and the vicissitudes of industrialization.[11] Is anarchism merely a label we attach to doctrines, movements, and moods so inchoate that their only unifying theme is emotive opposition to authority and hierarchy?[12] Or is there a distinctively anarchist vision of how men ought to stand in relation to their societies? Should it be the former, then thinking about anarchism in general would make no more sense than lumping together all theories that call for a state. We might have to be content with appraising anarchisms but not anarchism.

For the purpose of analytical clarification we intend to distinguish anarchism, properly so called, from those doctrines that possess an anarchistic flavoring such as Murray Rothbard's "anarcho-capitalism," "anarcho-syndicalism," [13] and "anarcho-Maoism." [14] Putting these to one side, we are left with an understanding of anarchism that is well presented by David Wieck. Within its own terms, his authentic anarchism has both psychological and moral coherence. In the first place, it represents an intelligible response to the condition of modern man, faced, as he feels himself to be, with barely tolerable constraints upon self-expression and realization.[15] And secondly, authentic anarchism looks toward self-fulfillment through both heightened individuality and communal solidarity. Of paramount importance to an evaluation of anarchism is an analysis of these ideals and their mutual consistency.

POPULISM, EXPRESSIONISM, AND ANARCHISM

The authentically anarchist way of thinking about human being and relations first appears explicitly, in modern times anyway, in Herder's "populism" and "expressionism." According to Sir Isaiah Berlin, his populism consisted in ". . . the belief in the value of belonging to a group or a culture . . . ," and his expressionism amounted to the conviction that ". . . human activity in general, and art in particular, express the entire personality of the individual or the group, and are intelligible only to the degree to which they do so." [16] Berlin goes on to say Herder's ". . . conception of a good society is closer to the anarchism of Thoreau or Proudhon or Kropotkin, and to the conception of a culture *(Bildung)* of which such liberals as Goethe and Humboldt were proponents, than to the ideals of Fichte or Hegel or political socialists." [17]

Expressionism and populism also appear in Marx's notion of man as a "species being," whose destiny it is to assume collective direction and control of his creative activities.[18] In Marx's philosophy of man social guidance of productive activity transforms work into a vehicle for self-affirmation and creation, thus permitting full release of human potentialities and the overcoming of "alienation." Human relations become reciprocal and cooperative instead of competitive. As a result, the distinction between the private and the public, embedded in Hegel's division between "civil society" and "state," disappears. Men become both more deeply individualized and socialized.

As is well known, Marx did not present a systematic institutional-ization of his vision. Lenin, however, in his *State and Revolution* did present a blueprint of the good society, one which he would later repudiate as "syndicalist nonsense." As John Plamenatz remarked, "Slavs rush in where Germans fear to tread." [19]

Our view is that this conception of the good of man attempts to override the principles of balance and compromise central to Western political philosophy. Despite the inspiration that anarchists draw from Rousseau, they try to ignore his most fundamental principle: that the moral development of men depends decisively on political neutralization of their drives for power and superiority. At the core of authentic anarchism we discern a romantic and monolithic ideal of human perfectibility quite at odds with the pluralistic view of man on which Western moral and political philosophy is built.

ALTERNATIVE PHILOSOPHIES OF MAN

Running through Western thinking is a contrast between two, apparently alternative, philosophies of man. In one, man is conceived as an independent agent, freely choosing and pursuing his own ends. Each person is responsible for constructing his plan of life. Law provides the framework within which individuals may seek their objectives without undue interference from others on a basis of mutual indifference. Society is nothing more than these indi-vidualized and interdependent life plans; no common human enterprise exists. In Oakeshott's words, genuinely human conduct presupposes a state that articulates the principle of *societas,* not the corporate principle of *universitas.* [20] The alternative philosophy portrays men as intrinsically social; they are designed for life in society conceived as a common enterprise. On this view, there are indeed purposes proper to men as such. Life is thought of as indelibly teleological, as it was by the theorists of natural law. More recently common purposes have ranged from maximizing welfare and securing social justice to the pursuit of national grandeur and advantage.

One of our great philosophies of man, that which is at the foundation of liberalism, depicts society as a collection of rights-bearing persons, order among whom arises more or less spontaneously. Today the social philosophy, in a radically egalitarian form, is upheld by Roberto Mangabeira Unger. He thinks that human nature can flourish only through organic groups united by a corporate state.[21] We shall deal more fully with his ideals later on.

It would be mistaken to regard these two conceptions of man and his good as mutually exclusive. Indeed, much social and political thought revolves around the issue as to what mobilelike balancing of the polar images best exhibits our nature. This balancing or blending of the individual and social visions depends upon pushing neither to an extreme. If one starts out an individualist, recognition of the strengths of the social conception forces modification of one's original position. Locke's acceptance of social obligations places natural limitations on the range of legitimate life plans. Classical liberals like Hayek and Oakeshott would have human sociability express itself through voluntary associations.[22] The British Hegelians, T. H. Green and Bernard Bosanquet, who give priority to a common good, never completely dissolve human autonomy in that good, any more than did Hegel. From Locke to the present theorists have sought to reconcile the morality of social utility and the morality of individual rights.[23]

Thus the ambivalent and pluralistic nature of man has steadily pressed political and moral theorists toward mutual dilution of the paradigmatic images. Few have been willing to follow Plato or Max Stirner in adopting one at the total expense of the other. However, there is yet a third possibility: intensification and integration of the social and individual bents of human nature. The authentic anarchists concur with Herder and Marx in advocating such an "expressivist synthesis." [24]

THE IMPLICATIONS OF EXPRESSIVISM

Distinctive to anarchism, as we see it, is the conviction that full and free expression of personality will generate feelings of unity and mutual responsibility that issue in moral solidarity.[25] In these circumstances differences of interest and status are either minimized or disappear entirely. Expansion of selves is no longer divisive. These beliefs inform Kropotkin's ideal of ". . . individuality which attains the greatest individual development possible through practicing the highest communist sociability in what concerns both its primordial needs and its relationship with others in general." [26] His idea is that expressive freedom and communal dedication are equally necessary for man to be truly human, to exhibit what Marx called a "human morality." As Richard A. Falk puts it, an anarchist society would be a "libertarian socialism." For Michael Bakunin there is no dissonance between these ideals, because "frank and human egotism" [27] is fully in accord with justice and human welfare.

Of course, anarchists differ as to the optimum intensity of social feeling and cohesion. Proudhon, of whom Michael Oakeshott speaks with approval, clearly desires a less solidary society than David Wieck, who characteristically insists upon the reinforcing nature of individuality and community. There are also questions as to the size and diversity of anarchic societies. Both Bakunin and Kropotkin think of federalisms of rather homogeneous groupings, whereas the libertarian "near-anarchist," Robert Nozick, situates his rugged individualists in a variety of like-minded "utopias." [28] Unger leaves open the question whether a division of labor will occur within or among his "organic groups." [29]

It is easy to see how the anarchist ideal of man is averse to law and the state. As Alan Ritter says, its conception of freedom and human worth prescribes resolution of differences through delibera-tion on communal purposes. Harmony, so achieved, is felt to be much more fully in accord with the high value placed on selves than would be their exposure to the rule of law, which Unger associates with "the disintegration of community." [30] Indeed, even Rous-seauistic moral freedom, based upon inwardly acceptable rules, does not meet the anarchist ideal of a life worth living.[31] Even Plato, who took a thoroughly social view of man, never entertained the possibility of entirely displacing law and government by ethical agreement deriving from spontaneous sociability. Other proponents of social man, such as Aristotle and St. Thomas, found it necessary to organize the common good by legal institutions and to protect men against their asocial inclinations. And Kant, supremely concerned for ethical freedom, founded morality in the republic of law. But the authentic anarchist has no place for either law or the state, not even when inspired by a general will for justice or devotion to the common good.

The anarchist philosophy of man, in which the individual and social paradigms of our nature are both intensified and fused, entails that we are truly human only when freely seeking to lead a consensual existence. His experiences with anarchistically minded students leads Donald G. MacRae to the conclusion that their "... ideal man is collective, he is social, but not social in terms of the state or any social organization. He is social in terms of spontaneous cooperation and of consensual feeling because everyone ... knows what is good, and hence all must, in their heart, think alike." [32] All the classical anarchists, of course, had held that the great institutions of state and property frustrate our sociability and hide our natural goodness.

ROMANTICISM AND MODERNITY

Charles Taylor has shown that the wish to synthesize "expressive unity," which we have identified as an inflation of the social theory of man, with "radical autonomy" is the defining feature of all forms of romanticism. Taylor holds that the anarchists, like the other romantics, disdain modern society because public life is ruled by inhuman utilitarianism and romantic expressivism is banished to privacy.[33] But, as Anthony Giddens argues, anarchism does seem more rigorous than other romanticisms; it simply refuses to put up with schizophrenic compromises imposed on men by a technocratic and meritocratic society.[34] Whereas socialists and Marxists, except for the advocates of self-management, compromise with the imperative of rationally structured authority, the authentic anarchist stands adamant against what he takes to be personal subordination.[35]

Unlike Rousseau, however, anarchists generally do not repudiate modernity. They simply insist that industrialized societies need not be run by political and economic hierarchies inimical to expressivist selves. This attitude is displayed by Bakunin and Kropotkin,[36] as well as by the near-anarchist, Frederick C. Thayer, who offers some operational alternatives to the supposedly dysfunctional principles of competition and hierarchy. In an anarchistic spirit, Thayer calls for new forms of organization that would somehow articulate without compromise the "integrity of the individual" and the "integrity of the community." In his view, anarchism becomes the operational ideal of modernity, failure to implement which will bring on anarchy. After the coming revolution, ". . . the world of organizations will be one of innumerable small face-to-face groups characterized by openness, trust, and intensive interpersonal relations." [37]

HISTORICAL AND SOCIAL CONTEXTS

If we put aside the anarchistic moods and movements of the ancient and medieval worlds,[38] the first great outburst of anarchist feeling comes during the nineteenth century in those countries that were being sharply but unevenly transformed into industrial societies, namely, France, Italy, and Spain. In Russia, antagonism to patrimonial absolutism gave birth to populism from which the anarchism of Bakunin and Kropotkin derives.[39] Because all these countries were late starters, industrialization, when it came, was more painful and disruptive than it had been in England. There, neither William Godwin's rationalistic anarchism nor anarchistic sentiments ever took root. Moreover, the other countries lacked both the discipline and the resources to sustain the pace of development that Germany and the United States were to achieve. The workshop form of capitalism being bypassed, their populations encountered directly intensive industrial regimentation, the consequence of which was cultural trauma of an especially severe kind.[40]

The source of this trauma was the clash between the agrarian attitudes of these peasant workers and the logic of their new situation in which they were, as naked individuals, pitted against their employers and one another. Bakunin deplored both this laissez-faire individualism as well as the smothering of the individual in the countryside. Capitalism meant competitive individualism, whereas the rural emotional climate had been deeply corporate. Anarchism promised personal liberation from both of these environments. Hence Bakunin's slogan: "Liberty without socialism is privilege, injustice; socialism without liberty is slavery and brutality." [41]

Bakunin's ideal of libertarian socialism has not been attained in any modern society. The strain between an essentially romantic individualism and inapposite cultures continues. The conception of self implied in the "expressivist synthesis" has been largely relegated to private life while public existence has become dominated by

Weberian rationality. In this light, the resurgence of anarchist feeling we have witnessed in the last decade may well be interpreted as a renewed rejection of the psychic compartmentalization imposed on modern man. This interpretation of recent anarchic attitudes is supported by David E. Apter's analysis of the "New Left's" hatred of "roles." [42] Expansive selves experience the university as a "sausage-machine." [43] The new anarchism, Apter says, is not aimed at the restructuring of roles, rather at their obliteration. Standardized lives are anathema to romantic personalities.

Despite a radical difference in social and economic context, then, the new and the old anarchism seem to share a common psychodynamic that leads to a mood of resentful rebellion against disciplined complexity. Somehow, it is felt, life should be both more receptive to individual impulse and more gratifyingly unitary.

THEORETICAL TRENDS

What is the outlook for the anarchist synthesis? We notice a trend toward polarization in recent political thinking. Some liberals become libertarians, rather stridently individualistic. The "Lockean" Robert Nozick is a case in point. Classical liberals like Oakeshott and Hayek look upon the very notion of "social justice" as nonsensical and pernicious. [44] On the other hand, institutionalized individualism and pluralism come under fire from egalitarians such as Brian Barry and Steven Lukes. [45] And even the self-professed anarchists themselves divide, as we have seen, into libertarians and egalitarian communalists. Individualism and socialism tend to become stark alternatives, and integral anarchism dissolves into competing ideals. Certainly no support for an "expressivist synthesis" is to be found in the work of those who would build society on the foundations of moral freedom and justice, the centrist liberals, if we may so call them, the late John Plamenatz, Sir Isaiah Berlin, and John Rawls.

It would be rash, however, to conclude that expressivism is being abandoned. Indeed it has just received impressive formulation in Unger's *Knowledge and Politics*. His work warrants our attention not only because it presents a comprehensive critique of liberal psychology and institutions but also because it constitutes a unique statement as to how expressivist ideals could be institutionalized.

UNGER'S EXPRESSIVISM

Strictly speaking, Unger is not an anarchist, or at least he does not announce himself as such. It does not feel inappropriate to us, however, to refer to his theoretical posture as that of modified anarchism. He is a near-anarchist, an advocate of "expressivist democracy."

Like all expressivists, Unger deplores the bifurcation of life into a private world, in which the wholeness of self is intimated, and a public domain regulated by rules and fragmented into roles.[46] "Disintegration is the defining experience of the culture of modernism." [47] It is his thesis that cleavage and disintegration have their origin in a fundamental error of liberalism, its presumed subjectivity of value.

Liberal moral psychology, Unger maintains, assumes that all values are inherently individualized and hence subjective and arbitrary. "The political doctrine of liberalism does not acknowledge communal values." [48] That is to say, the only goods for liberals are the capricious desires of unrelated persons. There are no social values. But, Unger tells us, this poses a serious problem for liberalism. If society is not to be rent by incessant conflict, somebody must have power to maintain order.[49] However, to hand anyone power over others, given the assumed subjectivity of value, is to permit him to impose his personal values on them. The logic of the situation seems to require that the man in command not only pacifies but dominates the rest. Liberalism tries to avoid "domination" by placing power under the rule of law. Liberal legalism purports to offer fair and impartial public order.[50] Personal "domination" is prevented, and all are equally free to lead their lives as they see fit.

Unger charges that the impartiality of law is a liberal illusion.[51] An attempt to legislate purely rational rules, which do not favor anyone's special interests, is doomed. Kant's "categorical imperative" is an empty criterion; it yields maxims that are vacuous and so cannot guide conduct. Rules are of use only when infused with specific values, that is, only when they operate to the advantage of some against others. "Domination" returns.

Utilitarianism is also biased. For there can be no way to aggregate private ends into some public measure of value. Somebody's desires will always achieve priority. Unger's argument is that "domination" is inescapable in any attempt to unify intrinsically arbitrary values. Neither impersonal law nor social utility offers a way out of the impasse of liberalism. In a liberal society there can be no genuine authority, at best only "tranquil exercise of power, which men call authority." [52]

In both theory and practice liberalism separates private from public man. This separation is morally and psychologically devastating. "The self is split in two, each half finding the other incomprehensible, then mad." [53] Insanity is the price of liberal illusion.

How can "domination" and madness be overcome? Clearly, on Unger's view, only when preferences of some cease to prevail and selves are reunified. Unger argues that for society to be organized without "domination" it must be based upon values that emanate from human nature itself.[54] The values expressive of human nature are to be discovered through the practice of anarchistic democracy. According to Unger, this practice will demonstrate, given time, the existence of a greater and greater area of shared values and purposes. These will be recognized as valid indicators of the objectively human good.

Democracy reveals the good only under certain conditions.[55] The presence of dominance results in distortions; truly human values are obscured by the wills of the powerful. "Domination" must be gotten rid of before human nature can show itself. Notice the circularity. Dominance can be extirpated only when objective values are found, but a truly human morality is possible only when relations of superiority and inferiority no longer exist. But, Unger contends, the circle may be transformed into a spiral. By this, he means that once the more obvious forms of "domination" are rooted out, some unifying aspirations will take hold of people. This experience will permit further eradications of power, and so on and on.

Unger believes that the society which articulates the human nature revealed by the democratic process will approach the expressivist ideal. He says:

> The more these shared ends express the nature of humanity rather than simply the preferences of particular individuals and groups, the more would one's acceptance of them become an affirmation of one's own nature; the less it would have to represent the abandonment of individuality in favor of assent

and recognition. Thus, it would be possible to view others as complementary rather than opposing wills; furtherance of their ends would mean the advancement of one's own. The conflict between the demands of individuality and sociability would disappear.[56]

Not only is subjective individualism thus avoided, but, argues Unger, this conception of the humanly good also defeats authoritarian collectivism, the notion that some objective purpose in life may rightfully be imposed on the blind or recalcitrant. Only through free deliberation and choice can genuinely shared values come into consciousness.[57] The truly human society would attain very considerable, though never complete, harmony between the singular and social natures of men.[58] For Unger, society is best conceived in terms of concrete universality. In the language of British Hegelianism, the expressivist ideal of human relations is that of an "identity in difference."

EXPRESSIVIST DEMOCRACY

How might this vision be institutionalized? Unger shows us a picture of a society composed of "organic groups." Each group is to be small enough that all members know each other. Moreover, people are to relate to one another in a variety of ways, not merely by way of a single role as in contemporary business and government organizations. Thus organic groups will unite the public and the private dimensions of life. As Unger puts it, ". . . the oneness of personality is reaffirmed." [59]

The paramount objective of these organic communities is to destroy all forms of "domination." In consequence, considerations of ability and merit are to have no weight in the groups' deliberations. Meritocracy is the final bastion of unjustified power. Only egalitarian democrats can take this bastion and begin to exhibit what human nature really is. Only under total democracy do men face each other as concrete individuals, rather than as abstract role occupants.[60] Again we are reminded of Alan Ritter's emphasis on deliberation in the anarchist ideal of freedom.

The upshot of "expressivist democracy" is intense politicization of life.[61] All other values, including economic efficiency, are to give way to the supreme criterion of anarchic equality.[62]

A division of labor will remain in the society of organic groups, but it will not serve as a basis for differential rewards; the criterion of need will be the sole distributive principle.[63] The purpose of occupational specialization is to foster development of some aspect of men's many-sided selves to the fullest possible extent. Specialization promotes romantic expression, not rationalistic regimentation. Thus respect for human differences is preserved without the moral costs of meritocratic "domination."

People in Unger's democracy would be allowed to move from one organic group to another if they could no longer subscribe to a group's purposes. Since there will be a multiplicity of groups, Unger foresees a need for a statelike agency to coordinate and harmonize their activities. He leaves open the issue of the nature of this authority. Given his lack of reliance on market processes, we may surmise that this authority will have a good deal to do.

UNGER AND AUTHENTIC ANARCHISM

The anarchist ideal permeates Unger's thinking. Liberalism is dismissed for its presumed atomistic individualism, collectivism for submersion of the individual in the group. Moreover, like the authentic anarchists, Unger sees the expressivist synthesis arising out of life in small communal settings. And at the center of his thought is preoccupation with inequalities that are translated into forms of "domination." As with David Wieck, Unger's primary purpose is to cleanse human relations of all unjustified power. Neither the rule of law nor of the market, nor both in combination, can accomplish this purpose. In the good society the only morally acceptable function of authority is to protect and to advance those values found to be constituent of human nature. Authority cannot be permitted to reflect human inequalities and personal preferences.

There is, then, broad agreement between Unger's expressivism and what we have called authentic anarchism. Common to both is the conviction that apparently impersonal and rational law does not, and can not, secure true justice. The liberal rule of law, Unger claims, is not a remedy for partiality; it is actually the rule of men. We deceive ourselves if we think that freedom under law is a morally defensible ideal. Without expressivist democracy, our humanity will remain thwarted and deformed by inegalitarian "domination." The final unfolding of human nature depends decisively on defeating the arrogance of merit, presently disguised by liberal theories of justice. In the end the moral defect of liberalism is the presumption that justice can be had ". . . without it being necessary to establish the precise ends for which power ought to be exercised." [64]

INSTITUTIONALIZED EXPRESSIVISM

We cannot, of course, here enter into a full appraisal of Unger's institutionalized expressivism. Rather we shall attempt to make explicit some of its major assumptions and implications.

Unger speaks immediately above of "precise ends," although he never really specifies them. It is obvious, however, that the ends he has in mind are both communal and latent in human nature. Moreover, he asserts that they have been suppressed by an essentially procedural civilization. The implication is that we should go over to a new society, one far more appropriate to our nature. This proposal collides head-on with the liberal conception of the good for man. In Friedrich Hayek's words, "A Great Society has nothing to do with, and is in fact irreconcilable with 'solidarity' in the true sense of unitedness in the pursuit of known common goals." [65] Indeed, from Hayek's standpoint, Unger's proposal is a regression to "tribal" morality.

Unger's aversion to procedural civilization, based on the rule of law and the open market, entails drastic politicizing of life. In his view, this poses no threat to individuality and freedom. Although he relies on majority rule in his "organic groups" to elicit objective ends and values, there is no "domination." For he assumes the values so uncovered to be universal, and so to live according to them involves no arbitrary subjection to the will of another. Again, Unger's thinking runs completely contrary to the liberal's belief in the diversity of human purposes. According to Hayek, ". . . in the Great Society the different members benefit from each other's efforts not only in spite of but often even because of their several aims being different." [66]

Finally, it may be asked why does not Unger's expressivism culminate in full-fledged anarchism? The answer is that we are flawed. He refers to a ". . . hypothetical condition in which the greatest individuality is allied with the greatest sociability, and realized through it, [as] the ideal of sympathy." [67] And our sympathy is not unlimited. Therefore, the expressivist synthesis can never fully be achieved on earth, only approximated to. Since harmony of men cannot ever be entirely spontaneous, there will always be need for a harmonizing authority, a state. Again, the fundamental divergence between communal anarchism and liberalism appears: Should society be organized for pursuit of common purposes, or should we continue to rely as far as possible upon our procedural heritage?

THE FUTURE OF ANARCHISM

Unger believes the society of "organic groups" is emerging from the present social order. "The conflicts within its dominant types of social consciousness and order push the liberal state in the direction of the welfare-corporate state." [68] We are depending less and less on market criteria of distribution as we take account of the welfare criterion of need.[69] Furthermore, society has become a web of intermediate organizations, the sign of incipient corporatism. Thus the welfare-corporate state is growing naturally out of liberal proceduralism. Already occupational and voluntary associations foretell the coming of the organic-grouped society.[70] And universal affirmation of welfare confirms the death of ethical subjectivism. Here is a value objectively grounded in human nature. The ideals common to expressivism and anarchism would seem to be coming within our reach.

Other readings of our situation are less sanguine for their future. According to Hayek, we are living through an upsurge of divisive, tribal sentiment, totally inconsistent with the impersonal morality required to sustain an open society. "The submergence of classical liberalism under the inseparable forces of socialism and nationalism is the consequence of a revival of those tribal sentiments." [71] In a similar vein, Oakeshott remarks on "the masses" and on ". . . their incapacity to sustain an individual life and their longing for the shelter of a community." He goes on to say, "Their numbers have fluctuated greatly in modern times although they are now proportionately greater than ever before, mainly because of the policies of governments." [72] These great trends bode no less ill for anarchist expressivism than they do for liberalism.

Observers of more recent developments find an intensification of
competition. Raymond Boudon discovers an "aggregation paradox," by which he means that increasing equality of opportunity
drives people into ever more severe competition for income and
status. Paradoxically, they have to run even harder merely to retain
position in the Hobbesian race.[73] Fred Hirsch writes of "social
congestion" and "positional competition." [74] Affluence turns attention to goods the supply of which, as a matter of logic, cannot be
increased to meet demand. In other words, a new form of scarcity,
having to do with social rank, is the unexpected outcome of
economic freedom and success. What are its implications? Hirsch
thinks that we will become more occupied with distributional issues,
and this will move us, if reluctantly, in a collectivist direction.

In any event, the coming of "social scarcity" is bound to cause
romantic irritation and dismay. Yet this very scarcity will make
more sober those whose dreams of self-realization and expression
were based on the prospect of abundance. Simultaneous inflaming
and dampening of expressivist aspirations may well influence the
prospects of anarchism in a countervailing manner. While we may
anticipate anarchistic attitudes to become chronic, the probability
of serious anarchist movements would seem to be small. Jean
Baechler says, "Assuming that anarchism has a purpose, it must lie
within local and limited counter-societies. At the very best, anarchism can only be a kind of flight from society." [75]

Perhaps, however, anarchist thought and feeling, if moderated,
will have a more constructive role to play. Freedom may be
enhanced by exploring new modes of association along lines
suggested by the near- and neo-anarchists. May not the real future
of anarchism be that of both a safety valve and a benign influence
on the alienated condition of man? [76] Anyway, neither the long-run
trends nor recent developments, on which we have touched, augur
well for the institutionalization of romantic expressivism in a
pristine form.

PERSONALITY AND SOCIETY

Anarchism has flowed from a sense of oppression and outrage, as
in the nineteenth century and earlier, and flows today from feelings
of discomfort with the inner compromises and institutional balances

of our society. The authentic anarchists are acutely sensitive to the limits on solidarity and equality required by the dualistic nature of men and their public situation. The final question for them is whether these discomforts and constraints can be eliminated or only mitigated; whether men, given human dynamics, could exemplify their ideals of self and society. Is the "expressivist synthesis" humanly possible?

One wonders how the processes through which people become individuated could operate effectively in an intensely communal setting. Individuation, that is, acquiring a sense of independence and inner authority, dictates that a person experience the distinction between self and others. He cannot, as Hume would say, entirely "kindle in the common blaze." Becoming a person involves resisting pressures that arise from within the group even as one remains in empathetic identification with it. It may well be only through mutual opposition and correction that people obtain capacity for self-direction and self-affirmation. Only emotionally dependent and acquiescent personalities could fully identify with their fellows.[77] Even Unger worries about the dangers of communalism. "By its very nature, community is always on the verge of becoming oppression."[78]

These considerations surely must concern the egalitarian expressivists who exalt social sentiment as the mark of true individuality. The issue for individualistic anarchism, including piggyback "anarcho-capitalism," is social solidarity. Could the highly individualized creatures envisaged ever establish enduring, stable relations? Social disintegration might follow upon the growth of contractarian attitudes toward the family and the state. According to David Gauthier, in the past these institutions functioned to contain market impulses; they served as the framework of the liberal economy. "Bereft of its framework, the bargaining order will collapse into competitive chaos."[79] Unbalanced men would seem destined for "Hobbism," as Jean-Paul Sartre has well said.[80]

ANARCHISM AND POLITICAL PHILOSOPHY

What we wish to suggest, by way of conclusion, is that a genuine person must always feel less than perfectly in accord with society; a sense of separateness is integral to being human. To appreciate that

"I" am distinct from, as well as interdependent with, "others" one cannot think and feel always as "we." To hold that one may be thoroughly an'individual and also immersed in community seems to misunderstand the dynamics of individuality. Could it not be that anarchists are working with an ideal of personhood that verges on self-contradiction?

Perhaps the expressivists have erred in deriving a philosophy of man from natural but incompatible cravings that arise in disorienting circumstances. If so, then we are led away from the anarchistic goal of synthesis and toward balance and compromise. And the state reappears to offset the weight of community. As Unger rightly says, "The basic liberties of membership, expression, and work require protection by a body other than the very one whose powers they restrict." [81] Our investigation of anarchism brings us back to political philosophy.

NOTES

1. Coercion, of course, played a central part in the formation of the modern state as men sought to protect themselves against the gangs that were ravaging Europe in the late middle ages. See Michael Howard, *War in European History* (London: Oxford University Press, 1976), Chapter 2, "The Wars of the Mercenaries."

2. According to Roberto Mangabeira Unger, all who have "communitarian aspirations" ". . . will look for an alternative to legality in the notion of a community bound together by a shared experience and capable of developing its own self-revising customs or principles of interaction." *Law in Modern Society* (New York: The Free Press, 1976), pp. 202-3.

3. The "Great Company" was ". . . a band nearly ten thousand strong and totally international in membership which persisted for fifteen years between 1338 and 1354 and ran what would now be called a protection racket on a very large scale." Howard, *War in European History,* p. 25.

4. According to Norman Macrae, "Many services now provided by governments will need to be 'recompetitioned' and reprivatized." "The Coming Entrepreneurial Revolution: A Survey," 261 *The Economist* (25 December 1976), 41-65, p. 41. Comment on Macrae and his response

may be found in the issues of 8 January 1977 and 5 and 12 March 1977.

5. Compare Wieck's conception of justice with Kropotkin's as expounded by David Miller in his *Social Justice* (Oxford: Clarendon Press, 1976), Chapter VII.

6. Forms of "domination" are dealt with in Alkis Kontos, ed., *Domination* (Toronto: University of Toronto Press, 1975). The concept of personal "domination" is crucial to Unger's indictment of the rule of law and liberalism in general. In addition to *Law in Modern Society,* see his *Knowledge and Politics* (New York: The Free Press, 1975). "Domination" is central to these recent critiques of liberalism: C. B. Macpherson, *Democratic Theory: Essays in Retrieval* (Oxford: Clarendon Press, 1973); Paul N. Goldstene, *The Collapse of Liberal Empire: Science and Revolution in the Twentieth Century* (New Haven: Yale University Press, 1977); and Robert Paul Wolff, *Understanding Rawls* (Princeton: Princeton University Press, 1977).

7. Compare Hampshire's statement that "For me socialism is not so much a theory as a set of moral injunctions. . . ." Leszek Kolakowski and Stuart Hampshire, eds., *The Socialist Idea: A Reappraisal* (London: Weidenfeld and Nicolson, 1974), "Epilogue," 245-49, p. 249.

8. On the impulse to humiliate authorities, see Edward Shils, "Plenitude and Scarcity: The Anatomy of an International Cultural Crisis," in his *The Intellectuals and the Powers and Other Essays* (Chicago: University of Chicago Press, 1972), 265-97, p. 293. On attitudes toward personal dignity and integrity, see Adam Ulam, *The Fall of the American University* (New York: The Library Press, 1972), pp. 129-33.

9. Unger says, "The individuality of values is the very basis of personal identity in liberal thought, a basis the communal conception of value destroys." *Knowledge and Politics,* p. 76.

10. See also Jeffrey H. Reiman, *In Defense of Political Philosophy* (New York: Harper & Row, 1972), and Wolff's "A Reply to Reiman," in his *In Defense of Anarchism* (New York: Harper & Row, 1976), pp. 83-113.

11. On "classical" anarchism, see James Joll, *The Anarchists* (New York: Grosset & Dunlap, 1964), and Eric Voeglin, *From Enlightenment to Revolution,* edited by John H. Hallowell (Durham: Duke University Press, 1975). On Russian populism and anarchism, see Franco Venturi, *Roots of Revolution* (New York: Grosset & Dunlap, 1966); Richard Pipes, *Russia Under the Old Regime* (London: Weidenfeld and Nicolson, 1974); and Adam Ulam, *In the Name of the People* (New York: Viking, 1977).

12. About anarchists, Jean Baechler says: "They must inevitably draw their recruits from a very narrow field. The only sizeable groups they could possibly attract make up the rabble, the social category that, by its very nature, plays no part in society and is conspicuous for its utter

fragmentation. Hence, in the normal course of events, anarchism comes as the climax of a personal destiny. It follows that there are, in the final analysis, as many forms of anarchism as there are anarchists." *Revolution,* trans. Joan Vickers (New York: Harper & Row, 1975), p. 115.

13. On French anarchism and syndicalism, see F. F. Ridley, *Revolutionary Syndicalism in France: The Direct Action of Its Time* (Cambridge: Cambridge University Press, 1970).

14. The anarchistic elements in Mao's thought are examined by Benjamin Schwartz, "Thoughts of Mao Tse-tung," XX *The New York Review of Books* (8 February 1973), 26-31.

15. Ortega y Gasset refers to two fundamental traits of the "mass-man of today": ". . . the free expansion of his vital desires, and therefore, of his personality; and his radical ingratitude towards all that has made possible the ease of his existence." *The Revolt of the Masses,* Authorized Translation from the Spanish (New York: Mentor Books, 1952), pp. 41-42.

16. Berlin, "Herder and the Enlightenment," in his *Vico and Herder: Two Studies in the History of Ideas* (London: The Hogarth Press, 1976), p. 153.

17. Ibid., p. 181.

18. See John Plamenatz, *Karl Marx's Philosophy of Man* (Oxford: Clarendon Press, 1975), Chapter III, and Shlomo Avineri, *The Social and Political Thought of Karl Marx* (Cambridge: Cambridge University Press, 1968), pp. 86-95.

19. Plamenatz, *Karl Marx's Philosophy of Man,* p. 458. According to P. J. D. Wiles, it is mistaken to think that Marx ignored questions of institutionalization; at scattered places in his writings, for example, one can find discussions of nationalization of industry, agricultural cooperatives and equality of pay. *The Political Economy of Communism* (Cambridge: Harvard University Press, 1962), pp. 56-61.

20. See Michael Oakeshott, *On Human Conduct* (Oxford: Clarendon Press, 1975), Part II. The other great contemporary exponent of classical liberalism is Friedrich A. Hayek. See his *Law, Legislation and Liberty,* 2 vols. (Chicago: University of Chicago Press, 1973 and 1976).

21. Unger, *Knowledge and Politics,* Chapters 4-6.

22. See Hayek, *Law, Legislation and Liberty,* Vol. II, *The Mirage of Social Justice,* pp. 150-52, and Oakeshott, *On Human Conduct,* p. 319 n.

23. A recent example is David Lyons, "Human Rights and the General Welfare," 6 *Philosophy & Public Affairs* (Winter 1977), 113-29.

24. The notion of an "expressivist synthesis" is taken from Charles Taylor, *Hegel* (New York: Cambridge University Press, 1975), p. 49 and elsewhere. Taylor's concept descends from Berlin's understanding of Herder's "populism" and "expressionism."

25. In one Christian perspective "expressivism" amounts to a glorification of self and society. It is a manifestation of what Eric Voegelin refers to as "the pneumatic disease." Indeed, it is nothing other than a branch of the "Religion of social Satanism." *From Enlightenment to Revolution,* pp. 220 & 71, and throughout.

26. As quoted in Martin A. Miller, *Kropotkin* (Chicago: University of Chicago Press, 1976), p. 197.

27. From *Bakunin on Anarchy,* edited and translated by Sam Dolgoff (London: Allen and Unwin, 1971), p. 119.

28. Nozick, *Anarchy, State, and Utopia* (New York: Basic Books, 1974), Part III.

29. Unger, *Knowledge and Politics,* p. 285.

30. Unger, *Law in Modern Society,* p. 58.

31. In this respect they are in tune with the present emotional climate. According to Plamenatz, "It is self-realization rather than moral freedom that is by way of becoming a popular idea." *Karl Marx's Philosophy of Man,* p. 341.

32. MacRae, "Students in Orbit," in G. R. Urban, *Hazards of Learning: An International Symposium on the Crisis of the University* (La Salle, Ill.: Open Court, 1977), 19-38, pp. 37-38.

33. Taylor, *Hegel,* pp. 541-42.

34. According to Unger, "The self is split in two, each half finding the other incomprehensible, then mad." *Knowledge and Politics,* p. 27.

35. Giddens, *The Class Structure of the Advanced Societies* (London: Hutchinson University Press, 1973), pp. 293-94.

36. See Dolgoff, *Bakunin on Anarchy,* pp. 225-42 and 356-79; and Miller, *Kropotkin,* pp. 189-95.

37. Thayer, *An End to Hierarchy! An End to Competition!* (New York: New Viewpoints, 1973), p. 5. He admires the McDonald's organization, but not without reservation. "When no one is compelled to fight to obtain and preserve status, prestige, or success, the atmosphere may become more erotic and sensual, and even office sex may be a natural thing. The operational restriction on McDonald's water-bed room may be a casualty of the overarching social revolution we must experience." Ibid., p. 6.

38. On medieval anarchism, see Joll, *The Anarchists,* Chapter I.

39. According to Miller, "The link between Russian Populism and European anarchism was Bakunin, who incorporated aspects of both ideologies.... Kropotkin assimilated Bakunin's dedication to the abolition of the European state ... and merged it with the populists' feeling of moral responsibility toward the Russian masses." *Kropotkin,* p. 252.

40. Giddens, *The Class Structure,* pp. 212-13.

41. Dolgoff, *Bakunin on Anarchy,* p. v.

42. Apter, "The Old Anarchism and the New—Some Comments," in Apter and James Joll, eds., *Anarchism Today* (New York: Anchor Books, 1972), 1-13, pp. 10-12.

43. Daniel and Gabriel Cohn-Bendit, *Obsolete Communism: The Left Wing Alternative,* trans. Arnold Pomerans (New York: McGraw-Hill, 1968), p. 27.

44. Hayek, *The Mirage of Social Justice,* Chapters 9 and 11.

45. See Barry, *The Liberal Theory of Justice* (Oxford: Clarendon Press, 1973), and Lukes, "Socialism and Equality," in Kolakowski and Hampshire, *The Socialist Idea,* pp. 74-95.

46. Unger, *Knowledge and Politics,* pp. 173-74.

47. Ibid., p. 26.

48. Ibid., p. 76.

49. Ibid., p. 64.

50. Ibid., pp. 67-69.

51. Ibid., pp. 83-88.

52. Ibid., p. 64.

53. Ibid., p. 27.

54. Ibid., pp. 238-48, 267-74.

55. Ibid., pp. 242-53.

56. Ibid., p. 220.

57. Ibid., pp. 76-78, 238-42.

58. Ibid., p. 285.

59. Ibid., p. 263.

60. Ibid., p. 264.

61. Ibid., p. 268. "The democracy of ends in the organic group consists in the progressive replacement of meritocratic by democratic power in the ordinary institutions of society and, above all, in its occupational groups."

62. Ibid., pp. 265-68, 273.

63. Ibid., pp. 271-72.

64. Ibid., p. 168.

65. Hayek, *The Mirage of Social Justice,* p. 111. He says, "The possibility of men living together in peace and to their mutual advantage without having to agree on common concrete aims, and bound only by abstract rules of conduct, was perhaps the greatest discovery mankind ever made." Ibid., p. 136.

66. Ibid., p. 110.

67. Unger, *Knowledge and Politics,* p. 217.

68. Ibid., p. 174.

69. According to Hayek, "There is no reason why in a free society

government should not assure to all protection against severe deprivation in the form of an assured minimum income, or a floor below which nobody need to descend." *The Mirage of Social Justice,* p. 87.

70. Unger, *Knowledge and Politics,* pp. 264-65. Hayek thinks that "It is the great merit of the spontaneous order concerned only with means that it makes possible the existence of a large number of distinct and voluntary value communities serving such values as science, the arts, sports and the like." *The Mirage of Social Justice,* p. 151.

71. Ibid., p. 134. In his opinion, "At a time when the great majority are employed in organizations and have little opportunity to learn the morals of the market, their intuitive craving for a more humane and personal morals corresponding to their inherited instincts is quite likely to destroy the Open Society." Ibid., p. 146.

72. Oakeshott, *On Human Conduct,* p. 276.

73. Boudon, *Education, Opportunity, and Social Inequality: Changing Prospects in Western Society* (New York: John Wiley, 1973), pp. 198-99.

74. Hirsch, *Social Limits to Growth* (Cambridge: Harvard University Press, 1976), Chapter I.

75. Baechler, *Revolution,* p. 128.

76. On the inevitability of alienation, see Morton A. Kaplan, *Alienation and Identification* (New York: The Free Press, 1976).

77. See Zevedei Barbu, *Problems of Historical Psychology* (London: Routledge and Kegan Paul, 1960), pp. 74-96.

78. Unger, *Knowledge and Politics,* p. 266. See also Richard E. Flathman, *The Practice of Rights* (New York: Cambridge University Press, 1976), Chapter 9, "Rights and Community"; and Richard Sennett, *The Fall of Public Man* (Cambridge: Cambridge University Press, 1976).

79. Gauthier, "The Social Contract as Ideology," 6 *Philosophy & Public Affairs* (Winter 1977), 130-64, p. 163.

80. According to Maurice Cranston, ". . . just as Hobbes is haunted by fear of political society relapsing into the intolerable condition of the state of nature where no man is safe, Sartre gives grim warnings about the danger of the group's relapsing into an intolerable condition of seriality." "Sartre and Violence," in his *The Mask of Politics and Other Essays* (London: Allen Lane, 1973), 77-110, p. 108.

81. Unger, *Knowledge and Politics,* p. 282.

PERSPECTIVES ON ANARCHY

1

WHAT IS ANARCHISM?

JOHN P. CLARK

Much of the recent philosophical discussion of anarchism exhibits a disturbing lack of clarity because of widespread failure on the part of political theorists to define terms such as "anarchy," "anarchist," and "anarchism" with sufficient care. This failure results, I believe, from neglect of a number of topics relevant to the subject, including (to mention the most important of these) the nature of classical anarchist theory, the history of the anarchist movement, and numerous endeavors to apply anarchist theory and practice to contemporary realities. In this essay an attempt will be made to formulate a definition which takes into account all significant aspects of anarchism: both theory and practice, both past historical forms and contemporary manifestations. At the same time, those concepts of anarchism which disregard any of these important elements, or which misrepresent the anarchist position, will be criticized.

I. OVERSIMPLIFICATIONS OF ANARCHISM

According to George Woodcock, one of the most judicious historians of anarchism, "the first thing to guard against" in discussing the topic is simplicity.[1] Unfortunately, most commentators on the subject, far from guarding against oversimplification, eagerly grasp at the most simplistic and nontechnical senses of the term, and seem to have little interest in analyzing the phenomenon to which it refers. Thus, it is not unusual for scholars to gather no more evidence about the nature of anarchism than the derivation of the term, after which they can ascend to the heights of abstraction, paying attention neither to social history nor to the history of ideas. Since anarchy means "without rule," it is said, an anarchist is one who advocates a society in which ruling is abolished, and anarchism is the theory that such a society is necessary. In almost every case the conclusion drawn from this superficial analysis is that such a goal is obviously beyond our reach, and that anarchism should therefore be dismissed as naive utopianism. This will not do. As I hope to show, such an approach fails abysmally to do justice to anarchism, as, in fact, does any definition which attempts to define the term by one simple idea. I would like to discuss such simple definitions further before pointing out additional difficulties in analyzing anarchism.

The assumption which underlies the sort of definition I am criticizing is that anarchism can be identified through one essential characteristic that distinguishes it from all other social and political positions. Most definitions of this type characterize anarchism in terms of some principle or some institution that it opposes. One such definition would see anarchism as a movement that is defined by its complete rejection of government. A great deal of evidence from the anarchist tradition could be pointed out in support of this view. Thus, in his *Encyclopaedia Britannica* article on anarchism, Kropotkin defines it is "a principle or theory of life and conduct in which society is conceived without government." [2] Emma Goldman, in her essay, "Anarchism," defines it as "the theory that all forms of government rest on violence, and are therefore wrong and harmful, as well as unnecessary." [3] A well-known contemporary anarchist, Colin Ward (editor of the first series of the journal *Anarchy*), defines anarchy as "the absence of government," [4] and anarchism as "the idea that it is possible and desirable for society to organize itself without government." [5] In some definitions, that which is rejected is identified, not as government, but rather as the power that controls government. In support of this position, one could cite Proudhon, who defines anarchy as "the absence of a ruler or a sovereign." [6] A number of writers would take the essence of anarchism to be its attack on the state, which is often distinguished from government, as will be discussed in detail later. This can be supported by Bakunin's statement that "the system of Anarchism . . . aims at the abolition of the State," [7] to mention just one of many such statements by major anarchist theorists. Woodcock asserts that "the common element uniting all its forms" is its aim of "the replacement of the authoritarian state by some form of non-governmental cooperation between free individuals." [8] Other writers hold that it is not merely the state or political authority, but in fact authority itself which anarchism opposes. Sebastien Faure proclaims that "whoever denies authority and fights against it is an anarchist." [9] Malatesta accepts the view that anarchy means "without government" but he expands the definition to mean "without any constituted authority." [10] Recently, Ward has said that anarchists oppose the "principle of authority," [11] while Runkle, in his attack on anarchism, maintains that it "opposes authority in all its forms." [12] While Daniel Guérin is in most cases a perceptive commentator on anarchism, at one point he characterizes it in a way which is reminiscent of the most superficial and uncritical views. He goes so far as to suggest that the anarchist is one who "rejects society as a whole." [13] A negative characterization which is probably the most adequate of all, if any is to be taken in isolation, is made by Malatesta, who holds that anarchists desire "the complete destruction of the domination and exploitation of man by man." [14] Recently, Murray Bookchin has described anarchism in terms of its opposition to all forms of domination and all types of hierarchical organization.[15]

While fewer theorists (and especially nonanarchists) have attempted to define anarchism in terms of its positive side, there are examples of generalizations about its proposals. It might be seen, for example, as a theory of voluntary association. Kropotkin describes anarchism as seeking social order "by free agreements between the various groups, territorial and professional, freely constituted for the sake of production and consumption." [16] Proudhon says that in anarchism "the notion of Government is succeeded by that of Contract." [17] This idea of voluntary association is also included in Woodcock's reference, cited above, to "cooperation between free individuals." [18] Anarchism might also be defined as a theory of decentralization. Paul Goodman notes that if anarchy means "lack of order and planning," then "most Anarchists, like the anarcho-syndicalists or the community-anarchists, have not been 'anarchists' either, but decentralists." [19] A closely related concept descriptive of anarchism is federalism. Bakunin holds that anarchism proposes "an organization from below upward, by means of a federation." [20] Another way of defining anarchism is by its advocacy of freedom. Runkle holds that "the essence of anarchism is individual liberty." [21] A more specific but related conception is suggested by Bookchin, who describes the goal as "a situation in which men liberate not only 'history,' but all the immediate circumstances of their everyday lives." [22]

Thus, anarchism can be described not only as a theory that opposes such things as government, the state, authority, or domination, but also as a theory that proposes voluntarism, decentralization, or freedom. Yet to define anarchism in terms of its opposition or support for any or all of these would be inadequate. In fact, the anarchists who have been cited, while they sometimes present ill-considered, simplistic definitions, are aware of the complexity of the theory that they espouse, and their works, when taken as a whole, point to the necessity of a more comprehensive definition.[23]

Of all those who have attempted to define anarchism, to my knowledge only one, Woodcock, clearly and concisely indicates the elements that will be taken here to constitute a minimum definition of anarchism. According to Woodcock, "historically, anarchism is a doctrine which poses a criticism of existing society; a view of a desirable future society; and a means of passing from one to the other." [24] In this discussion, the nature of these three criteria for anarchist theory will be elaborated upon, and a fourth, which is only implied by Woodcock, will be added. At this point, it will merely be pointed out that any definition which reduces anarchism to a single dimension, such as its critical element, must be judged seriously inadequate.

II. MISINTERPRETATIONS OF ANARCHISM

Not all misunderstanding of the nature of anarchism results from oversimplification. As was mentioned earlier, one of the most serious faults of most discussions of anarchism is neglect of historical anarchist thought and practice. The paradoxical result is that we find political theorists attacking an anarchism that has existed primarily as a fiction in the minds of its opponents, and we find philosophers defending an anarchism that would be unrecognizable to the vast majority of anarchists throughout history (including the present). For example, Benjamin Barber, in his essay "Poetry and Revolution: The Anarchist as Reactionary," repeats the cliché of the irrationally utopian nature of anarchism. "The anarchists" he says, "manage to stand the naturalistic fallacy on its head: not that natural man, as he is, is what he ought to be; but that utopian man, as the anarchist conceives he ought to be, is in fact what man is." [25] Barber contends further that anarchism has no idea of political realities, and is concerned instead with a romanticist exhortation to revolution. "It must reject political theory itself in favor of poetry and revolution." [26] Isaac Kramnick develops Barber's viewpoint further in his article "On Anarchism and the Real World: William Godwin and Radical England." Kramnick holds that "what replaces politics for the anarchist is either education or theater," [27] and that, again, anarchists are totally out of touch with reality.[28] Runkle, in his book *Anarchism: Old and New,* asserts that "the student left, the radical right, and existentialism seem, at least superficially, to be contemporary forms of anarchism." [29] Runkle devotes half his book to the development of this view, which he correctly sees as superficial.

The writings of Barber, Kramnick, and Runkle exhibit very well the consequences of an ignorance of many elements of the anarchist tradition, and of the selective use of evidence about that tradition to construct misleading generalizations. Barber's charge of utopianism overlooks the many concrete and practical proposals that anarchists have presented, while his belief that the anarchist view of human nature is naively optimistic is a perennial half-truth that deserves to be critically examined. Kramnick's view that anarchist strategy has been limited primarily to education and theatrics shows an almost inconceivable disregard for the history of the anarchist movement. Finally, Runkle's careless attribution of relations between anarchism and recent political and philosophical tendencies is coupled with an apparent unawareness of the existence of a true "new anarchism," which has sought to synthesize the insights of classical anarchism with developments such as advanced technology and ecological theory.

While these various attacks on anarchism do a great deal to confuse the issue, some of its philosophical defenders succeed only in increasing the chaos. The work that has done most to retard meaningful analysis and criticism of the anarchist position is Wolff's *In Defense of Anarchism.*[30] As his critics have rightly pointed out, Wolff's argument that autonomy and moral authority are incompatible constitutes neither a defense of anarchism as a political theory nor a proof of the unjustifiable nature of the state and government.[31] Whatever support Wolff's ethical position might give to anarchism is effectively undermined by his statement that he sees no practical proposals that follow from his theoretical acceptance of anarchism.[32] Anarchists have differed greatly on the issue of the degree of activism demanded by their position, but never before to my knowledge has any theorist claiming to be an anarchist presented no proposals for action at all.

III. ANARCHISM AND GOVERNMENT

The widespread misunderstanding of the nature of anarchism points to the need for a clear definition of the term, and this will be attempted shortly. First, however, two subjects about which there is particularly widespread confusion must be considered. The first of these concerns the anarchist view of government. As has been indicated, many writers about anarchism have taken opposition to government to be the most distinctive characteristic of the theory. This is, in fact, probably the most popular means of defining the term. Much of the present discussion brings into question the adequacy of a definition of anarchism that conceives of it exclusively in terms of its relation to one social institution, even if that institution is held to be the most important one. However, there is further reason for questioning such a characterization: the distinction that some anarchists have themselves made between government and the state. While there runs through all anarchist writings an unmitigated contempt for the state, the anarchist position on government is far from unequivocal hostility.

A case in point is the thought of the American individualist anarchist, Albert Jay Nock. In Nock's book *Our Enemy the State,* he distinguishes sharply between the state and government. Government, he says, consists of "strictly negative intervention" to secure the natural rights of the individual.[33] By this he means protection of life, liberty, and property in the strictest Lockean sense. When society acts to prevent one individual from aggressing against a second individual who has acted peacefully, such government is perfectly justifiable. It is important to realize that Nock is not supporting governmental protection of huge concentrations of wealth, property, or economic power. In fact he argues quite vehemently that unless special interests are given favorable treatment and protection through political means, there can be no amassing of vast wealth. Much of his book, which shows individualist anarchism at its best, is dedicated to an analysis of state power in American history, and to a demonstration of the ways in which the state has supported certain mercantile interests, especially through land grants and protective tariffs. The state, according to Nock, arises when political means are used for the protection of exclusive interests. Following Franz Oppenheimer, he contends that the state originated historically as the tool of a dominant class.[34] According to this view, state power began with the conquest of a weaker (probably agrarian) tribe by a stronger (probably herding) tribe, the latter of which established a system of class rule in order to use the former for its labor power. The state, Nock says, has always maintained this class character, and state power has always been seen by special interests as an alluring means of gaining advantage over other groups in society.

Nock's use of the term "government" is quite atypical of that of anarchists in general, since most have not hesitated to use the term to refer to the abuses they attribute to the state. However, his ideas are seen to fit well into the mainstream of anarchist thought when examined in terms of the scale of the two systems he compares. He contends that if the state were replaced by "government" (in his unusual, limited sense of the term), this would result in something very close to Jefferson's proposal for "ward" government. Under such a system, the fundamental political unit would be the local township (for which I think we might also substitute the urban neighborhood), which would be "the repository and source of political authority and initiative." [35] Action on a larger scale should be carried out, Nock says, through a voluntary federation of communities for their common purposes. He believes that the essential protective functions of government can be achieved through such a system, while avoiding the dangers of exploitation that exist in a centralized, large-scale state.

While Nock is not one of the most widely known anarchist theorists (although he is one of the most eloquent of the individualists), ideas similar to his can be found in the writings of the foremost exponent of anarchist communism, Kropotkin. While it is true that Kropotkin holds that anarchism aims at the production of a society "without government," [36] nevertheless he sometimes praises a condition of society in which some elements of government remain, while the state is not present. In his essay *The State: Its Historic Role,* Kropotkin distinguishes sharply between the state and government. "Since there can be no State without government, it has sometimes been said that one must aim at the absence of government and not the abolition of the state." [37] Kropotkin correctly sees this strategy as unrealistic in relation to practical political possibilities. The state in particular should be the object of immediate attention, for it entails not only political power but additional elements, such as large territorial areas, centralization and the concentration of power in the hands of a few, hierarchical relationships, and class domination.[38] To such an institution, Kropotkin contrasts the medieval city, which he takes to be the best polity developed historically.[39] While these cities were not part of the nation-state, they certainly had governments; but far from lamenting their existence, Kropotkin has great praise for these governmental institutions. He enthusiastically approves of their assemblies, elected judges, and local militias, which are in accord with his own ideas about decentralized, participatory institutions. He also praises their belief in arbitration as opposed to authority without consent, and the subordination of military power to civil authority.[40] Thus, while he always kept in mind the ultimate goal of dispensing with government entirely, he was realistic enough to see that from an anarchist perspective decentralized community government was a considerable advance beyond the empires of ancient times, and would constitute progress beyond the modern nation-state. In view of this more complex view of government, it can be seen that a simple conception of anarchism as "opposition to government" does not accurately represent its position.

IV. GOALS AND STRATEGIES IN ANARCHISM

There is a further problem which, perhaps more than any other, underlies the widespread confusion about the nature of anarchism. It deals with the distinction between anarchism's vision of the ideal society and its view of immediate action. Stated differently, it is the question of the relation between utopian goals and practical possibilities. Several difficulties arise in regard to this question. Some would define an anarchist entirely in terms of the acceptance of a noncoercive, nonauthoritarian utopia as the moral ideal. Thus, one who can describe what the ideal society might be like, express a belief that it might in some way be possible, and judge this ideal to be the only system which can be fully justified morally is called an anarchist.

I believe that this is a rather bad misuse of terminology, if traditional distinctions are to be maintained and contradiction avoided. Under such a definition it is clear that many (perhaps most) Marxists would qualify as anarchists, since they accept the ideal of the withering away of the state.[41] As many anarchists (for example, Bakunin) have pointed out, it is on the question of practical strategies that anarchists and Marxists part company, rather than on their visions of the ideal society. In many ways, Kropotkin's description of communism is similar to that of Marx and Engels. The anarchist's point is not necessarily that the Marxists' goal is wrong, but that given the methods they advocate, they can be certain never to reach it. Methods of achieving change must therefore be considered if anarchism is not to be confused with Marxism (not to mention other socialist, and perhaps even liberal, positions that could, without contradiction, set up the same long-range goal).

It is true that we often come across articles on Marx's anarchism, but we find that they do not reveal new information showing that Marx advocated decentralization, self-management, and voluntary association, nor that he was a secret admirer of Bakunin. Rather, they discuss one limited aspect of his position: his view of the final utopia. Robert Tucker's discussion of Marxism and anarchism in *The Marxian Revolutionary Idea* may be taken as an example. Tucker holds that Marxism is anarchist in the sense mentioned, but "if we consider Anarchism not as an abstract political philosophy but as a revolutionary movement associated with a political philosophy, then we are confronted with the fact that Marxism was deeply at odds with it." [42] This view of the matter is much superior to those which exhibit no awareness of the relevance of anarchism to social realities. Yet it is still inadequate, for there is no need to look for two anarchisms—one a political theory, and the other a social practice. Tucker does this when he asks how it is "that classical Marxism, while embracing anarchism as a political philosophy, disagreed with Anarchism as a socialist ideology." [43] This shows a misunderstanding of the relation between theory and practice in anarchism. It is essential to anarchism that ends not be separated from means, and there can be no "anarchism" in a full sense which does not as an integral part of its theoretical framework make distinctive proposals concerning practice, and take account of real historical conditions. Anarchist political philosophy implies anarchist activity in society.

It should be apparent from the discussion thus far that the interpretation of anarchism as the belief that utopia can be achieved immediately is erroneous. Because anarchists have accepted the ideal of a noncoercive, nonauthoritarian society, some have assumed that they automatically must reject anything short of the ideal as unjustifiable, and therefore deserving of immediate destruction. The result is that anarchism is sometimes seen as implying a desire to destroy all established social institutions, preferably through violence. Yet none of the major anarchist theories from Godwin to the present has held such an extreme view, and no anarchist popular movement has presented such a proposal as part of its program. In spite of such lack of evidence, we often find even students of political theory confusing anarchism and nihilism, and scholars attending conferences on political philosophy questioning whether anarchist theory has any necessary link with bomb-throwing.

V. A DEFINITION OF ANARCHISM

In hopes of clarifying the meaning of anarchism, I would like to propose a definition that is specific enough to be recognizable as a reasonable characterization of historical anarchism and to distinguish it from political positions that have not traditionally been denominated "anarchist," and that is also general enough to take account of the wealth of diversity contained within the anarchist tradition. It is hoped that this definition will lay the groundwork for further clarification of the concept by others.

There are four elements to this proposed definition, and I believe that for one to be described as an anarchist in a full sense, all four criteria should be met. The founders of anarchist theory (Godwin, Proudhon, Bakunin, and Kropotkin) all fit this paradigm, and the principles embodied therein are implicit in the programs of the anarcho-syndicalist and anarcho-communist movements, which constitute the mainstream of historical anarchist activism. Individualist anarchism in most forms also falls under the definition (although there are a few borderline cases).

In order for a political theory to be called "anarchism" in a complete sense, it must contain: (1) a view of an ideal, noncoercive, nonauthoritarian society; (2) a criticism of existing society and its institutions, based on this antiauthoritarian ideal; (3) a view of human nature that justifies the hope for significant progress toward the ideal; and (4) a strategy for change, involving immediate institution of noncoercive, nonauthoritarian, and decentralist alternatives. This definition would allow for use of the term "anarchist" in both a strong and in several weaker senses. Obviously, an anarchist in the strongest sense would exhibit all four characteristics. Yet, one, for example, who advocated anarchistic tactics without an explicit commitment to the anarchist ideal, or one who accepted the ideal but proposed different strategies, could only be called an "anarchist" in a more limited sense.

VI. THE IDEAL OF ANARCHISM

"Anarchy" is the term usually applied to the ideal society for which the anarchist strives, and believes to be fully moral. It is true that many anarchists are rather vague about the nature of this ideal. This is the case for several reasons. One, which De George mentions, is that free, autonomous individuals will work out solutions that we can hardly, in the context of present society, foresee. Furthermore, the anarchist does not want to bind anyone to one vision of the ideal, since the acceptance of pluralism implies that various groups will create numerous variations on the general goal. However, this argument concerning the authoritarianism inherent in such prescriptions can be overstated. There is certainly no contradiction in the idea of an anarchist setting forth a fairly specific description of a society would live up to the anarchist criteria for moral justification, so long as it is clear that the model is subject to criticism and modification, and that other models might be found to conform at least as adequately to those criteria. As has been mentioned, the criteria are that such a society be noncoercive and nonauthoritarian, and that all forms of domination be eliminated. To describe such a society, one would have to show how institutions might be designed that would, at a minimum, eliminate the need for the use of physical force, government, and the state. In view of the third criterion, this ideal must be at least plausible in relation to the anarchist conception of human nature, which includes speculation about what people are capable of becoming, in addition to a description of what they are. The most convincing anarchist theories, while accepting the noncoercive, nongovernmental, and, of course, nonstatist nature of anarchy, deduce further characteristics of a society that has abolished domination. Examples often mentioned by anarchists include economic, social, racial, sexual, and generational equality, mutual aid, cooperation, and communalism.

The working out of a consistent view of anarchy is an important problem for the anarchist theorist. However, it is necessary to realize that work on this problem makes a theorist an "anarchist" only in a very limited sense, as has already been noted. Thus, the Marxist political philosopher might take on this task as an integral part of the development of a theory of transition from capitalism and socialism to full communism. It might also be undertaken by a utopian novelist who enjoys dreaming about ideal societies, or by a political philosopher who has a merely academic interest in the nature of the morally justifiable society.

VII. THE ANARCHIST CRITIQUE OF THE PRESENT

An anarchist has a distinctive view of the present state of things. This view is, in a sense, the link between the vision of the ideal and those political and social proposals that are typical of anarchism. It consists of a distinctive critique of existing social institutions, the core of which deals with coercion and authoritarianism. The anarchist finds many institutions to be unacceptable from a moral standpoint because they are based on force and externally imposed authority. It is, of course, the state and centralized political authority that receive the most destructive analysis on these grounds. It is therefore reasonable to accept as fulfilling this criterion any theory that on an antiauthoritarian basis questions the moral foundations of the state and government. However, it must be noted that the anarchist almost always proceeds to a further analysis of social institutions. Anarchism has not stopped with a criticism of political organization, but has investigated the authoritarian nature of economic inequality and private property, hierarchical economic structures, traditional education, the patriarchal family, class and racial discrimination, and rigid sex- and age-roles, to mention just a few of the more important topics. In some varieties of anarchism, institutions such as private property and patriarchy are condemned at least as severely as is the state.

It is hardly necessary to dwell on this criterion, since it is the one that has received the most attention, as was mentioned at the beginning of this essay. Most commentators on anarchism are well aware of the anarchist opposition to the forms of political organization existing in the modern nation-state. To a lesser degree, they grasp the anarchist critique of other authoritarian social institutions. What they often do not comprehend is the way in which this opposition to present social conditions fits into the anarchist position as a whole.

VIII. THE ANARCHIST VIEW OF HUMAN NATURE

A central element of anarchism is its view of human nature. The anarchist believes that there are qualities of human beings which enable them to live together in a condition of peace and freedom. Most anarchists go further and describe the human capacity for mutual aid, cooperation, respect, and communal relationships, which are seen as the basis for expectation of social progress. While most anarchists hold a belief in such human solidarity, it is significant that some individualists reject it. Instead, they base their proposals for social organization on contract; on rational self-interest; and, in the extreme case of Stirner, on ruthless egoism.[44] In both social and individualist anarchism, however, there exists the view that people have a great potential for voluntaristic action, and ability to overcome the use of violence and coercion.

This view is the basis for the frequent criticism of anarchism that it is excessively optimistic about human nature. For anarchism to be a coherent theory, it must have a conception of human nature which forms the basis for speculation about the ideal for society and which gives a foundation for those practical proposals that are necessary if the ideal is to have political and social relevance. However, it is false that all the views of human nature that have been put forth by anarchists have been in any meaningful way "optimistic," and that this quality is a necessary characteristic of the theory. It might be argued, in fact, that in some ways anarchists hold a quite realistic if not pessimistic view of human nature. It is the belief that power corrupts and that people easily become irresponsible in their exercise of it that forms the basis for much of their criticism of political authority and centralized power. Power must be dispersed, they say, not so much because everyone is always so *good,* but because when it is concentrated some people tend to become extremely *evil.* The point is made, not only in regard to political power, but also to a variety of other sorts, ranging from concentrated economic power on the level of society to concentrated patriarchal power on the level of the family.

There is, of course, abundant evidence of optimism in the anarchist tradition. Some of the greatest anarchist philosophers (e.g., Kropotkin) have at times expressed a rather naive belief in the capacity of people to act benevolently and to cooperate. Yet such optimism should certainly not be taken as part of the definition of anarchism, as it is by those who dismiss it as "utopian socialism," in the derogatory sense of that term. There is much in the anarchist tradition which would point to a rejection of all dogmatic views of human nature (whether "optimistic," "pessimistic," or "realistic"), and to the acceptance of environmentalism. Godwin's thought is explicitly based on this outlook, and it is implicit in Bakunin's deterministic materialism. In such a view, people are inherently neither good nor evil, but rather they behave and think in radically different ways under different circumstances. The problem for anarchists is to create the social conditions under which the libertarian rather than the authoritarian (or, in some cases, the cooperative rather than the competitive) capacities of people are realized. What all anarchist positions have in common is that they accept this libertarian potential as a constituent of human nature.

IX. THE ANARCHIST PROGRAM FOR CHANGE

The final defining characteristic of anarchism is its practical proposals for change. An anarchist has a distinctive program for action in the present, which constitutes a strategy for movement in the direction of the ideal, which is a response to the failure of existing institutions, and which is consistent with the anarchist view of human potentialities. Anarchism can have no meaning as a social and political theory if it says nothing about praxis, and it can have no clear meaning if it is defined in ways which would confuse its proposals with those of theories known by other names. Thus, as has been mentioned, theories that say nothing about strategies for change, or which advocate centralist, authoritarian, or bureaucratic policies cannot meaningfully be labeled "anarchist," if the theory that has been known by that name since Proudhon (and which has roots, some claim, as far back in history as the thought of Lao-tzu and Diogenes the Cynic, and in the practice of tribal society) is to be considered relevant.

The distinctive characteristic of anarchist programs is that they institute an immediate movement in the direction of voluntarism and antiauthoritarianism. Examples of typical anarchist programs include decentralization of political authority; worker self-management of workplaces; extension of freedom of thought and expression; expansion of sexual freedom; voluntary education; decentralization of economic structures; cooperatives; open access to media; free schools; open education and deschooling; neighborhood government, noninstitutional psychotherapy; nondominating family and personal relationships; and elimination of arbitrary distinctions based on sex, race, age, linguistic usage, and so forth. Such anarchist proposals are practical in two senses. The most ambitious of those mentioned are within the power of a society to institute, were anarchist ideology to become widely accepted within the society (as happened historically during the Spanish Revolution of 1936-39).[45] Furthermore, it is within the reach of anarchists in many societies in which anarchist theory is not yet widely accepted to put some of the proposals into immediate practice among themselves, as an alternative to the dominant institutions. In fact, the greatest energy of anarchists themselves (as opposed to writers about anarchism) has been put into this task, rather than into speculation about minute details of an ideal society.

It should now be clear how erroneous the view is which reduces the anarchist program to an uncritical demand for the immediate abolition of government. What has confused many superficial observers is the demand by anarchists that the state be abolished. In most cases they do not, however, propose that the nation-state be replaced by an ideal anarchic society, but rather by a decentralized system, in which federation from below increasingly displaces centralized authority. It is certainly held to be desirable that the primary groups which federate be as voluntary as is practically possible, but there is no dogmatic demand that all vestiges of government, even in a decentralized form, be immediately destroyed. The guiding principle, to be applied according to historical conditions, is the replacement of coercive and authoritarian institutions by voluntary and libertarian ones.

A consideration of anarchist proposals as analyzed here shows that they differ markedly from those typical of other political ideologies. These proposals emphasize decentralization and voluntarism, while the Marxist, the non-Marxian socialist, the welfare statist, and the modern liberal have quite obviously come to rely increasingly on the state, centralized political authority, and hierarchical bureaucracy as a means toward social change. The anarchist differs from the classical liberal (who has been reincarnated in some elements of American conservatism) in that the former rejects the use of government to protect any interests, including those based on private ownership of the means of production and class differences, while the classical liberal accepts the limited state as a means by which to preserve capitalism. In spite of these distinctions, there are no clear boundaries between the political positions mentioned, and they tend to merge at some points. Thus, leftist Marxism merges into anarcho-syndicalism. Daniel and Gabriel Cohn-Bendit, in their well-known book on the 1968 French revolt, call their position *Linksradicalismus* or *le gauchisme,* and describe it as being both Marxist and anarchist.[46] When leftist Marxists call for workers' councils and attack elitism and bureaucracy, it becomes difficult to distinguish them from the anarcho-syndicalists, who present similar proposals based on a similar class analysis.[47] On the other hand, the position of the individualists merges with that of classical liberals. As Benjamin Tucker, the great American individualist, claimed, "genuine [i.e., individualist] Anarchism is consistent Manchesterism." [48] The individualist anarchists hoped that the abolition of state interference would lead to a free and relatively equal society based on the labor theory of value. In this they have much in common with Locke, Adam Smith, Jefferson, and, above all, Spencer.[49] In view of such similarities, it must be concluded that while most of those who fall within the definition of "anarchist" presented here hold a position which is distinctive, and which constitutes an alternative to the standard political options, it is nevertheless the case that some who fulfill the criteria have viewpoints which are quite close to those of others who fit within other identifiable political traditions. There is no reason why terms in political theory such as "anarchist" and "Marxist" should be mutually exclusive in their denotation, even though their connotations differ considerably.

X. IS ANARCHISM UTOPIAN?

I believe that the definition of anarchism that has been presented and discussed can help avoid certain errors about the anarchist position. One of these is the charge that anarchists *must be* or *always have been* utopians. Some have attempted to demonstrate that anarchists are utopians by including the quality of utopianism in the definition of anarchism. I would suggest a different approach to the question. If we wish to find out whether anarchism is utopian, insofar as that term implies some sort of neglect for reality, we should examine the theories and practical proposals of those who have been conventionally called, and who have called themselves, anarchists. If we do, I do not believe that we will come to De George's conclusion that the anarchist's "threshold of acceptance is so high, his faith in the rationality and morality of the ordinary person so little in accord with what many people experience in their dealings with their fellow man, and his scheme for bringing about his desired anarchist society is as vague that he is not a political realist but an idealistic utopian." [50]

I see no reason why anarchism should be defined as to exclude people who can practically accept, if not be entirely satisfied with, limited progress toward the ideal. Many great anarchists have, in fact, been such "pragmatic libertarians" (for example, Proudhon among the classical anarchists, and Paul Goodman among the recent ones). Thus, Goodman defends "piecemeal change" in his article "The Black Flag of Anarchism." This article drew a ranting, simplistic, and blatantly *ad hominem* reply from Mark Rudd, who interprets anarchism as conservative because it attempts to change a variety of institutions instead of putting all its efforts into toppling the economic structure (assumed to be the sole basis for all the ills of society) at once.[51] Criticism like Rudd's makes De George's first accusation sound strange and suggests that they might each be missing something important about the nature of anarchism.

Problems also arise in connection with De George's second point. As has been noted, anarchists do not have an exclusively optimistic view of human nature. It has, in fact, become popular recently for liberals and unsympathetic socialists to condemn anarchism for the opposite quality: a lack of faith in the capacities of ordinary people. Barber, for example, accuses anarchists of having contempt for the masses and being elitists. Not being totally oblivious to history, he is forced to recognize that anarchists have indeed defended people's ability to determine their own destiny. Rather than questioning the accuracy of his previous contention, or considering the possibility that he is describing two conflicting factions within anarchism, he concludes that anarchists are "egalitarian elitists." [52] Kramnick, who relies heavily on Barber's analysis, goes a step further and depicts anarchism as unmitigated elitism. Through the method of selective quotation (when he bothers to cite evidence at all), he attempts to show that anarchists are extremely pessimistic about the abilities of the average person.[53] While such criticism does little to increase understanding of anarchism, it at least serves to point out that element of anarchist thought which exhibits skepticism about human goodness.

Finally, it should be noted that anarchists are not as vague about their proposals as De George thinks they are, and in fact, must be. Paul and Percival Goodman, for example, present numerous proposals (based on an anarchist outlook) for community planning in their book *Communitas*.[54] Richard Sennett's viewpoint in *The Uses of Disorder,* the second part of which he calls "a new anarchism," is highly suggestive in terms of urban policy issues.[55] A. S. Neill's *Summerhill* presents an educational philosophy which has been closely identified with anarchism, and which has been applied not only at his school for over fifty years but at numerous others which it has influenced.[56] Description of large-scale application of the anarchist program in the collectivised factories and communal farms in which millions participated during the Spanish Revolution can be found in Dolgoff's *The Anarchist Collectives.*[57] In view of such evidence (an abundance of which exists for those who care to investigate), the attribution of vagueness to anarchist proposals must be judged incomplete as a description of the actual performance of anarchism as a whole. Although some anarchists have been vague (whether out of principle or lack of imagination), others have not, especially in regard to immediate strategies for change. The desire not to impose one's will on others does not, as De George contends, demand vagueness. What it demands is that suggestions, which might be fully worked out, perhaps in terms of possible variations, should not be imposed through coercion, or accepted uncritically by the community.

XI. VARIETIES OF ANARCHISM

I would like to discuss one final topic that might help clarify the nature of anarchism. This concerns the various schemes of classifying anarchist positions. One such scheme divides anarchism into those varieties which put the greatest emphasis on personal autonomy and individual freedom, and those which stress participation in communal and intentional groups. In this way a distinction can be made between individualist and social anarchism (although some figures, like Emma Goldman, seem to have an equally strong commitment to both individual freedom and social solidarity).

A more detailed classification based on theories of social organization divides anarchists into individualists, mutualists, syndicalists, and communists. Individualists (whose major theorists include Max Stirner, Josiah Warren, and Benjamin Tucker) are interested not so much in forming associations, as in enabling individuals to pursue their own ends without interference from others. They desire a society of self-reliant and largely self-sufficient individuals, achieving their ends through voluntary agreement, or contracts, with others. The mutualists, following Proudhon, see a greater need for social organization. Since economic and political power are concentrated, people must organize to defend their interests, and especially to eliminate such state-supported abuses as rent, profit, and interest. There is, for that reason, a need for mutual banks and producers' and consumers' cooperatives. The anarcho-syndicalists go one step further and propose large-scale organization of the working class into a single labor union as the essential means toward meaningful social change. Their typical tactic is the general strike, which is to be followed by the reorganization of the means of production on principles of self-management. They are much in the tradition of Bakunin's collectivism. Finally, anarchist communism takes the commune, town, or neighborhood as its basic unit. Decisions are to be made on the basis of communal needs, with production according to ability and distribution according to need. Kropotkin is the classical theorist of this variety of anarchism.

I would like to elaborate somewhat on the distinction between anarcho-syndicalism and anarcho-communism for two reasons. First, these are the two forms of anarchism which have been of the greatest historical importance and have produced the most debate among anarchists themselves concerning practical proposals. Secondly, many observers of anarchism do not realize the fundamental importance of this division to anarchist theory. De George, for example, holds that "the strongest present-day position" consists of "an amalgam" of the two positions mentioned. He takes Guérin as the best exemplar of this position.[58] I believe that Guérin has rendered an enormous service to Marxists, anarchists, and to those interested in either of these theories, in his attempts to effect a synthesis between the two traditions. His outstanding book on anarchism is a notable product of this endeavor. However, it is this synthesis of Marxism and anarchism that is the "amalgam" presented by Guérin, not the one mentioned by De George. There is still a fundamental opposition between the position taken by Guérin and that of anarcho-communists like Murray Bookchin, or of any of those who are in a meaningful sense "communitarian" or "community" anarchists.[59]

While it is true that communitarian anarchism has incorporated many elements of the anarcho-syndicalist position, the converse does not seem to be true. We find in present-day anarchism a perpetuation of a traditional division, in which the communitarians continue in the tradition of the communist anarchists (who did not deny the importance of the syndicalist emphasis on liberating the workplace), while others, like Guérin and Chomsky, preserve an essentially syndicalist approach.[60] The communitarian anarchists do not take the workplace or even the economy as the primary focus (as important as these may be), but rather the total community, with all its interrelated elements, such as work, play, education, communication, transportation, ecology, and so forth. They argue that to isolate problems of production from their social context might lead to the perennial Marxist error of combating economic exploitation while perpetuating and perhaps even expanding other forms of domination. Further, communitarian anarchists argue that the analysis of economics and class on which both classical Marxism and syndicalism are built is outdated, and that anarcho-syndicalism itself is therefore at least partially obsolete.[61] If anarchism is to be fully understood, the nature of this very important dispute must be understood: one alternative focuses on work, the other on life as a whole; one on economic relationships, the other on the totality of human relationships, and on the relationships between humanity and nature.

Although the subject cannot be discussed in detail here, it is my view that the anarcho-communist position as developed by Bookchin and others is the strongest contemporary anarchist position. In fact, it appears to be the sociopolitical position which is best capable of incorporating such developments in modern thought as the theory of the rise of neotechnic civilization,[62] the ecological view of human society and nature,[63] and, on the highest level of generality, the organic and process view of reality, based in part on modern science.[64] If anarchism is to be evaluated, it is this, its strongest and most highly developed form, which should be considered.

It is hoped that the definition presented and the distinctions delineated here can make a contribution to reducing the prevailing confusion concerning the nature of anarchism. If so, it will perhaps become increasingly possible for anarchism to be seen for what it is—a complex and challenging social and political theory—and to be judged according to its merits.

NOTES

1. George Woodcock, *Anarchism* (Harmondsworth, Middlesex: Penguin Books, 1963), p. 7.

2. Peter Kropotkin, *Revolutionary Pamphlets* (New York: Dover, 1970), p. 284.

3. Emma Goldman, *Anarchism and Other Essays* (New York: Dover, 1969), p. 50.

4. Colin Ward, *Anarchy in Action* (London: Allen and Unwin, 1973), p. 11.

5. Ibid., p. 12.

6. Steward Edwards, ed., *Selected Writings of Pierre-Joseph Proudhon* (Garden City: Doubleday Anchor, 1969), p. 89. With his usual penchant for paradox, Proudhon describes this condition as "a form of government."

7. G. P. Maximoff, ed., *The Political Philosophy of Bakunin* (New York: Free Press, 1964), pp. 297-98.

8. Woodcock, p. 11.

9. Ibid., p. 7.

10. Errico Malatesta, *Anarchy* (London: Freedom Press, n.d.), p. 7.

11. Ward, p. 12.

12. Gerald Runkle, *Anarchism: Old and New* (New York: Delta, 1972), p. 3.

13. Daniel Guérin, *Anarchism: From Theory to Practice* (New York: Monthly Review Press, 1970), p. 13.

14. Paul Berman, ed., *Quotations from the Anarchists* (New York: Praeger, 1972), p. 28.

15. See *Post-Scarcity Anarchism* (Berkeley: Ramparts Press, 1971), especially the title essay.

16. Kropotkin, *Revolutionary Pamphlets,* p. 284.

17. Proudhon, p. 98.

18. Woodcock, p. 11.

19. Paul Goodman, *People or Personnel* and *Like a Conquered Province* (New York: Vintage, 1968), p. 6.

20. Bakunin, p. 298.

21. Runkle, p. 3.

22. Bookchin, *Post-Scarcity Anarchism,* p. 41.

23. It might be mentioned that a definition of anarchism which differs from both types mentioned is put forth recently by Robert Wolff. According to Wolff, the distinctive characteristic of what he calls an anarchist is that he or she "will never view the commands of the state as *legitimate,* as having binding moral force." *In Defense of Anarchism* (New York: Harper and Row, 1970), p. 18. The uniqueness of this definition lies in the fact that it commits the anarchist neither to support for, nor to opposition to any social and political institution, at

least in any obvious way. This point will be discussed further below.

24. Woodcock, p. 7.

25. Benjamin Barber, *Superman and Common Men: Freedom, Anarchy, and the Revolution* (New York: Praeger, 1972), p. 18.

26. The text reads "revelation," but presumably this is a misprint. However, those who are interested in the relationship between anarchism and revelation are directed to the *Catholic Worker*.

27. Isaac Kramnick, "On Anarchism and the Real World: William Godwin and Radical England," *American Political Science Review* 66 (March 1972), 114. I have dealt with Kramnick's contentions elsewhere in detail. See "On Anarchism in an Unreal World: Kramnick's View of Godwin and the Anarchists," *American Political Science Review* 69 (March 1975), 162-67, and also Kramnick's comment and my rejoinder, in the same issue. For a more detailed discussion of Godwin's contribution to anarchist thought, see my book, *The Philosophical Anarchism of William Godwin* (Princeton: Princeton University Press, 1977).

28. Kramnick, p. 128. Kramnick concludes that "utopian anarchism" is ultimately reactionary, since it has no effective strategy for change.

29. Runkle, p. 13. The idea of a professor of philosophy suggesting that existentialism might seem to be "a form" of anarchism appears ludicrous beyond belief, and that suggestion is a good hint as to the quality of his book. The relationship between anarchism and existentialism is, however, a topic which deserves serious study (as opposed to Runkle's sensationalistic exploitation). Strangely, in order to find out whether existentialism really is "a form" of anarchism, Runkle examines the thought of Sartre, who until his recent movement toward anarchism had long been much closer to Marxism. At the same time, Runkle overlooks the fact that two well-known existentialists, Martin Buber and Nikolai Berdyaev, have been anarchists. See Buber's *Paths in Utopia* (Boston: Beacon Press, 1955), and Berdyaev's *Dream and Reality* (New York: Collier, 1962), especially the epilogue; *The Beginning and the End* (New York: Harper and Row, 1957), Chapter viii; and *Slavery and Freedom* (New York: Scribners, 1944), Part III, Section IA.

30. Robert Wolff, *In Defense of Anarchism* (New York: Harper and Row, 1970).

31. See Jeffrey Reiman, *In Defense of Political Philosophy* (New York: Harper and Row, 1972).

32. Interview with Robert Wolff, included in a radio broadcast entitled "The Black Flag of Anarchy" (Baltimore: Great Atlantic Radio Conspiracy, 1973). A catalogue of tapes on anarchism and related topics, including interviews with Wolff, Bookchin, and other well-known figures, is available from that group.

33. Albert Jay Nock, *Our Enemy the State* (New York: Free Life Editions, 1973), p. 22.

34. Nock, p. 20. See Franz Oppenheimer, *The State* (New York: Free Life Editions, 1975).

35. Ibid., p. 57.

36. Kropotkin, *Revolutionary Pamphlets,* p. 284.

37. Ibid., p. 10.

38. Ibid., pp. 10-11.

39. Ibid., p. 27. Had he been more familiar with non-Western and tribal societies, he might have judged differently. See Dorothy Lee, *Freedom and Culture* (Englewood Cliffs: Prentice-Hall, 1959); Frederick Engels, *The Origin of the Family, Private Property and the State* (New York: International Publishers, 1973); and any of the many works on stateless societies, including, perhaps most notably, E. E. Evans-Pritchard, *The Nuer* (Oxford: Clarendon Press, 1940).

40. Kropotkin, *Revolutionary Pamphlets,* pp. 26-27.

41. The authenticity of this ideal has been questioned by some. See Richard Adamiak, "The Withering Away of the State: A Reconsideration," *Journal of Politics* 32 (February 1970):

42. Robert Tucker, *The Marxian Revolutionary Idea* (New York: Norton, 1969), p. 87.

43. Ibid., p. 88. As a result, he feels he must use capitalization to distinguish between the two.

44. For a criticism of extreme individualist anarchism, see my book *Max Stirner's Egoism,* (London: Freedom Press, 1976).

45. For descriptions of revolutionary Spain, see Sam Dolgoff's *The Anarchist Collectives: Worker Self-Management in the Spanish Revolution (1936-39)* (New York: Free Life Editions, 1974), Vernon Richards's *Lessons of the Spanish Revolution* (London: Freedom Press, 1972), and Gaston Leval, *Collectives in the Spanish Revolution* (London: Freedom Press, 1975).

46. See their book mistranslated as *Obsolete Communism: The Left-Wing Alternative* (London: Pengui 1968). The correct title, as anarchist reviewers have pointed out, should be something like *Leftism: A Cure for the Senile Disorder of Communism,* which, besides being less confusing, preserves the parody on Lenin's work *Left-Wing Communism: An Infantile Disorder.*

47. De George holds that communist anarchists present a "Marxian analysis." Richard De George, "Anarchism and Authority," this volume, p. 000. This is partially true; however, such an analysis is more typical of anarcho-syndicalism, as will be discussed further.

48. Cited in Leonard Krimerman and Lewis Perry, eds. *Patterns of Anarchy* (Garden City: Doubleday Anchor, 1966), p. 34.

49. The case is perhaps different with the "anarcho-capitalists" of the present, who live in an era of entrenched economic power. Since they have not explained how all can be placed in an equal bargaining position without abolishing present property relationships, it seems likely that what they propose is a system in which the affluent voluntarily associate to use force and coercion against the poor and weak in order to maintain class privilege. The abuses of the state are thus perpetuated after the state is allegedly abolished.

50. De George, p. 37.

51. Paul Goodman, "The Black Flag of Anarchy" (Corinth, Vermont: Black Mountain Press, n.d.). The article originally appeared in the *New York Times Magazine,* July 14, 1968.

52. Barber, p. 25.

53. Kramnick, p. 114.

54. Paul and Percival Goodman, *Communitas* (New York: Random House, 1960).

55. Richard Sennett, *The Uses of Disorder: Personal Identity and City Life* (New York: Vintage, 1970).

56. A. S. Neill, *Summerhill* (Harmondsworth, Middlesex: Penguin, 1968).

57. See especially Bookchin's introductory essay, which is a brief but masterly treatment of the relationship between theory and practice, in historical context.

58. The statements here quoted from De George's original paper were omitted from his revised version. The discussion in this paragraph is nonetheless useful for the exposition of Clark's interpretation of anarchism. (The Editors.)

59. A good example is Karl Hess (a former Goldwater speechwriter, now a community anarchist), who lives in and works with the Adams-Morgan neighborhood community in Washington, D.C. See his articles "Washington Utopia: An Election Eve Dream," *Washington Post/Potomac* (3 November 1974), and "The System has Failed," *Penthouse* (August 1974), which are popular presentations of his communal and decentralist ideas. His Community Technology group publishes a newsletter on decentralized technology, "Science in the Neighborhood."

60. It is the latter who have a Marxian analysis, not so much the communitarians, as De George contends. On this question, see "Syndicalism and Anarchism" in *Freedom* 35 (26 October 1974), 4 and (2 November 1974), 6. The debate between Monatte and Malatesta concerning syndicalism and communism is reproduced. Even more important is George Woodcock's "Chomsky's Anarchism," *Freedom* 35 (16 November 1974), 4, in which the nature of the anarchism of

Chomsky and Guérin is discussed in view of that historical division within anarchism.

61. Again, Bookchin's introduction to *The Anarchist Collectives* is relevant.

62. See Lewis Mumford, *Technics and Civilization* (New York: Harcourt, Brace and World, 1934), especially Chapter viii, "Orientation." The sections entitled "Basic Communism," "Socialize Creation," and "Political Control" are particularly relevant.

63. The most important recent works in this connection are Bookchin's *Limits of the City* (New York: Harper and Row, 1974) and E. F. Schumacher's *Small Is Beautiful: Economics as if People Mattered* (New York: Harper and Row, 1973).

64. The literature on this topic has yet to be written. However, several of the works mentioned above, including those by Lee, Bookchin, Mumford, and Schumacher present evidence related to the subject. See also Geoffrey Ostergaard and Melville Currell, *The Gentle Anarchists* (New York: Oxford University Press), which discuss Gandhian anarchism, which is based on an organic world view. Another source of organicist thinking in anarchism is the work of Kropotkin. See Peter Kropotkin, *Mutual Aid: A Factor of Evolution* (Boston: Porter Sargent, n.d.), and Roel van Duyn, *Message of a Wise Kabouter* (London: Gerald Duckworth, 1972).

2

A CONTRACTARIAN PERSPECTIVE ON ANARCHY

JAMES M. BUCHANAN

I. TWO-STAGE UTOPIA

I have often described myself as a philosophical anarchist. In my conceptualized ideal society individuals with well defined and mutually respected rights coexist and cooperate as they desire without formal political structure. My practical ideal, however, moves one stage down from this and is based on the presumption that individuals could not attain the behavioral standards required for such an anarchy to function acceptably. In general recognition of this frailty in human nature, persons would agree to enact laws, and to provide means of enforcement, so as to achieve the closest approximation that is possible to the ideally free society. At this second level of norms, therefore, I am a constitutionalist and a contractarian: constitutionalist in the sense of recognizing that the rules of order are, and must be, selected at a different level and via a different process from the decisions made within those rules; contractarian in the sense that conceptual agreement among individuals provides the only benchmark against which to evaluate observed rules and actions taken within those rules.

This avowedly normative construction enables me to imagine the existence of an ideal social order inhabited by real persons, by men and women that I can potentially observe. In moving from stage one, where the persons are themselves imaginary beings, to stage two, the persons become real, or potentially so, while the rules and institutions of order become imaginary. But I must ask myself why I consider the second stage to be an appropriate subject for analysis and discussion whereas the first stage seems methodologically out of bounds, or at least beyond my interest. Presumably, the distinction here must rest on the notion that the basic structure of order, "the law," is itself chosen, is subject to ultimate human control, and may be changed as a result of deliberative human action. By contrast, the fundamental character traits of human beings either cannot be, or should not be, manipulated deliberately. In other terms, attempts to move toward an idealized first-stage order may require some modification of human character, an objective that seems contrary to the individualistic value judgments that I make quite explicit. On the other hand, attempts to move toward an idealized second-stage ideal require only that institutions be modified, an objective that seems ethically acceptable.

As a preliminary step, I have called for the adoption of a "constitutional attitude," a willingness to accept the necessity of rules and an acknowledgment that choices among rules for living together must be categorically separated from the choices among alternative courses of action permitted under whatever rules may be chosen. But what happens if I should be forced, however reluctantly, to the presumption that individual human beings, as they exist, are not and may not be capable of taking on such requisite constitutional attitudes. In this case, my treatment of an idealized constitutionalist-contractarian social order becomes neither more nor less defensible than the discourse of those who go all the way and treat genuine anarchy as an ideal. Yet, somehow, I feel that my discussion of idealized social order is more legitimate, more productive, and less escapist, than the comparable discussion of the libertarian anarchists, perhaps best exemplified here by Murray Rothbard.[1] I shall return to this proposition below, and I shall attempt an argument in defense.

II. THE LOGIC OF AUTHORITY?

Before doing so, however, I want to examine one possible consequence of abandoning the constitutionalist-contractarian perspective. If we say that persons are simply incapable of adopting the requisite set of constitutionalist attitudes, which is another way of saying that they are incapable of evaluating their own long-term interests, we are led, almost inexorably, to imposed authority as the only escape from the genuine Hobbesian jungle. Anyone who takes such a position, however, must acknowledge that a "free society," in the meaningful sense of process stability, is not possible. The analysis turns to alternative criteria for authority, both in terms of the basic objectives to be sought and in terms of the efficiency properties of structures designed to accomplish whatever objectives might be chosen. But whose values are to be counted in deriving such criteria? We have, in this setting, already rejected the individualistic base, at least in its universalized sense, from which such criteria might be derived. But if only some persons are to be counted, how do we discriminate? Of necessity, the treatment of the idealized limits to authority must be informed by the explicit or implicit value norms of some subset of the community's membership. In the extreme, the value norms become those of the person who offers the argument and his alone.

Most discussion of social reform proceeds on precisely this fragile philosophical structure, whether or not the participants are aware of it. When an economist proposes that a particular policy measure be taken, for example, that the ICC be abolished, he is arguing that his own authority, backed presumably by some of the technical analysis of his professional discipline which has its own implicit or built-in value norms (in economics, Pareto efficiency), is self-justificatory. But since different persons, and groups, possess different norms, there is no observed consensual basis for discriminating between one authority and another. The linkage between the consent of individuals and the policy outcomes is severed, even at the purely conceptual level and even if attention is shifted back to basic rules of order.

The implication of all this is that the authority which emerges from such a babel of voices, and from the power struggle that these voices inform and motivate, carries with it no legitimacy, even in some putative sense of this term. The authoritarian paradigm for the emergence and support of the state lacks even so much as the utilitarian claims made for the basic Hobbesian contract between the individual and the sovereign, whomever this might be. There can be no moral legitimacy of government in this paradigm, no grounds for obligation to obey law, no reasons for the mutual respect of individuals' boundaries or rights.

If most persons, including most intellectuals-academicians, view government in this perspective, and more importantly, if those who act on behalf of government view themselves in this manner, both the libertarian anarchist and the constitutional-contractarian exert didactic influence in their attempts to expose the absence of moral underpinnings. But does not such activity, in and of itself, reduce to nihilism under the presupposition that universalized individual values are not acceptable bases for moral authority? If individuals are not capable of acting in their own interest in the formulation of social institutions, both the anarchist and the contractarian may be deemed genuinely subversive in their "as if" modeling of society, in their establishment of normative standards for improvement that are empirically nonsupportable. The activity in question weakens the natural subservience to the existing authority, whomever this might be, and may disrupt social order without offering redeeming elements that might be located in some constructive alternative.

III. INDIVIDUALISTIC NORMS

The libertarian anarchist and the contractarian must ask these questions and somehow answer them to their own satisfaction. I pose these questions here in part for their own intrinsic interest and importance but also in part because they place the libertarian anarchist and the constitutionalist-contractarian squarely on the same side of the central debate in political philosophy, the debate that has gone on for several centuries and which promises to go on for several more. Both the libertarian anarchist and the constitutionalist-contractarian work within the *individualistic* rather than the *nonindividualistic* framework or setting.[2] I use the term "nonindividualistic" rather than "collectivist" explicitly here because I want to include in this category the transcendent or truth-judgment paradigm of politics, a paradigm that may produce either collectivist or noncollectivist outcomes at a practical level.

I want to argue first that it is normatively legitimate to adopt the individualistic model, regardless of empirical presuppositions, and secondly, that within this model broadly defined the constitutionalist-contractarian variant is superior to the libertarian-anarchist variant. It is morally justifiable, and indeed morally necessary, to proceed on the "as if" presumption that individuals, by their membership in the human species, are capable of acting in their own interest, which they alone can ultimately define. Empirical observation of human error, evaluated *ex post,* can never provide a basis for supplanting this "as if" presumption; for no acceptable alternative exists. If persons are considered to be incapable of defining and furthering their own interests, who is to define such interests and promote them? If God did, in fact, exist as a suprahuman entity, an alternative source of authority might be acknowledged. But failing this, the only conceivable alternative authority must be some selected individual or group of individuals, some man who presumes to be God, or some group that claims godlike qualities. Those who act in such capacities and who make such claims behave immorally in a fundamental sense; they deny the moral autonomy of other members of the species and relegate them to a value status little different from that of animals.

The primary value premise of individualism is the philosophical equality of men, as men, despite all evidence concerning inequalities in particular characteristics or components. In thinking about men, we are morally obligated to proceed as if they are equals, as if no man counts for more than another. Acceptance of these precepts sharply distinguishes the individualist from the nonindividualist. But we must go one step further to inquire as to the implications of these precepts for social order. It is at this point that the libertarian anarchist and the constitutionalist-contractarian part company, but, philosophically, they have come a long way together, a simple statement but one that is worthy of emphasis.

IV. ANARCHY AND CONTRACTUAL ORDER

The issue that divides the anarchist and the contractarian is "conjecturally empirical." It concerns the conceptually observable structure of social order that would emerge if men could, in fact, start from scratch. Would they choose to live in the idealized anarchy, or would they contractually agree to a set of laws, along with enforcement mechanisms, that would constrain individual and group behavior? This question cannot actually be answered empirically because, of course, societies do not start from scratch. They exist in and through history. And those elements of order that may be observed at any point in time may or may not have emerged contractually.

It is at this point that the constitutionalist-contractarian paradigm is most vulnerable to the criticisms of the anarchist. How are we to distinguish between those elements of social order, those laws and institutions which can be "explained" or "interpreted" (and by inference "justified") as having emerged, actually or conceptually, on contractual precepts and those which have been imposed noncontractually (and hence by inference "illegitimately")? If the contractual paradigm is sufficiently flexible to "explain" all observable institutions it remains empty of discriminant content, quite apart from its possible aesthetic appeal.

Careful usage of the model can, however, produce a classification that will differentiate between these two sets of potentially observable institutions. For example, the existence of unrestricted political authority in the hands of a political majority could never be brought within contractarian principles. Persons who could not, at a time of contract, predict their own positions, would never agree to grant unrestricted political authority to any group, whether this be a duly elected majority of a parliament, a judicial elite, or a military despot. Recognition of this simple point is, of course, the source of the necessary tie-in between the contractarian paradigm and constitutionalism.[3] But what are the constitutional limits here? What actions by governments, within broad constitutional authority, may be thrown out on contractarian precepts?

Arbitrary restrictions or prohibitions on voluntary contractual agreements among persons and groups, in the absence of demonstrable spillover effects on third parties, cannot be parts of any plausible "social contract." For example, minimum-wage legislation, most restrictions on entry into professions, occupations, types of investment, or geographical locations could be rejected, as could all discrimination on racial, ethnic, religious, grounds.

This is not to suggest that the appropriate line is easy to draw and that borderline cases requiring judgment are absent. More importantly, however, the classification step alone does not "justify" the institutions that remain in the potentially allowable set. To conclude that an observed institution may have emerged, conceptually, on generalized contractarian grounds, is not at all equivalent to saying that such an institution did, in fact, emerge in this way. Many, and perhaps most, of the governmental regulations and restrictions that we observe and which remain within possible contractarian limits, may, in fact, represent arbitrary political impositions which could never have reflected generalized agreement.

Consider a single example, that of the imposition of the fifty-five-mile speed limit in 1974. We observe this restriction on personal liberties. Where can we classify this in terms of the contractarian paradigm? Because of the acknowledged interdependencies among individual motorists, in terms of safety as well as fuel usage, it seems clearly possible that general agreement on the imposition of some limits might well have emerged, and fifty-five miles per hour might have been within reasonable boundaries. But whether or not the fifty-five-mile limit, as we observe it, would have, in fact, reflected a widely supported and essentially consensual outcome of some referendum process cannot be determined directly. The observed results could just as well reflect the preferences of members of the governmental bureaucracy who were able to exert sufficient influence on the legislators who took the policy action.

V. CONSTITUTIONAL CONTRACT

If we look too closely at particular policy measures in this way, however, we tend to overlook the necessary differentiation between the constitutional and the postconstitutional stage of political action. Should we think of applying contractarian criteria at the postconstitutional level at all? Or should we confine this procedure to the constitutional level? In reference to the fifty-five-mile limit, so long as the legislature acted within its authorized constitutional powers, which are themselves generally acceptable on contractarian grounds, the observed results in only one instance need not be required to meet conceptual contractarian tests.

At this juncture, the contractarian position again becomes highly vulnerable to the taunts of the libertarian anarchist. If specific political actions cannot be evaluated per se, but must instead be judged only in terms of their adherence to acceptable constitutional process, the basic paradigm seems lacking in teeth. Improperly applied, it may become an apology for almost any conceivable action by legislative majorities or by bureaucrats acting under the authorization of such majorities, and even strict application finds discrimination difficult. This criticism is effective, and the contrasting stance of the uncompromising libertarian anarchist is surely attractive in its superior ability to classify. Since, to the anarchist, all political action is illegitimate, the set of admissible claims begins and remains empty.

The constitutionalist-contractarian can, and must, retreat to the procedural stage of evaluation. If his hypotheses suggest that particular political actions, and especially over a sequence of isolated events, fail to reflect consensus, he must look again at the constitutional authorizations for such actions. Is it contractually legitimate that the Congress and the state legislatures be empowered by the constitution to impose speed limits? What about the activities of the environmental agencies, acting as directed by the Congress? What about the many regulatory agencies? Such questions as these suggest that the constitutionalist-contractarian must devote more time and effort into attempts to derive appropriate constitutional limits, and notably with respect to the powers of political bodies to restrict economic liberties. Furthermore, the many interdependencies among the separate political actions, each of which might be plausibly within political limits, must be evaluated.[4] Admittedly, those of us who share the constitutionalist-contractarian approach have been neglectful here. We have not done our homework well, and the research agenda facing us is large indeed.

Meanwhile, we can, as philosophical fellow travelers, welcome the arguments put forth by the libertarian anarchists in condemning the political suppressions of many individual liberties. We can go part of the way on genuine contractarian principles, and we can leave open many other cases that the anarchists can directly condemn. As I have noted elsewhere,[5] the limited-government ideals of the constitutionalist-contractarian may not excite the minds of modern man, and given the demonstrable overextension of political powers, the no-government ideals propounded by the libertarian anarchists may help to tilt the balance toward the individualistic and away from the nonindividualistic pole.

I have acknowledged above that the anarchist critique of existing political institutions is probably intellectually more satisfying than that which may be advanced by the contractarian. But where the anarchist critique falters, and where the contractarian paradigm is at its strongest, is at the bridge between negative criticism and constructive proposals for change. To the libertarian anarchist, all political action is unjustified. He cannot, therefore, proceed to advocate a politically orchestrated dismantling of existing structure. He has no test save his own values, and he has no means of introducing these values short of revolution. The contractarian, by contrast, has a continuing test which he applies to observed political structure. Do these basic laws and institutions reflect consensus of the citizenry? If they do not, and if his arguments to this effect are convincing, it becomes conceptually possible to secure agreement on modification. The rules of the game may be modified while the game continues to be played, so long as we all agree on the changes. But why not eliminate the game?

This returns us to the initial distinction made between the ideal society of the philosophical anarchist and that of the contractarian. To eliminate all rules and require that play in the social game take place within self-imposed and self-policed ethical standards places too much faith in human nature. Why do we observe rules in ordinary games, along with referees and umpires? Empirical examination of such voluntary games among persons offers us perhaps the most direct evidence for the central contractarian hypothesis that rules, laws, are generally necessary.

VI. DEFINITION OF INDIVIDUAL RIGHTS

I could end this paper here and remain within the limits of most discussion by economists. Traditionally, economists have been content to treat exchange and contract, in all possible complexities, on the assumption that individual participants are well-defined entities, capable of making choices among alternatives, and in mutual agreement concerning legal titles or rights to things that are subject to exchange. The distribution of basic endowments, human and nonhuman, among persons has been taken as a given for most economic analysis, both positive and normative. The libertarian anarchist has gone further; in order to develop his argument that any and all political structure is illegitimate, he finds it necessary to presume that there are definitive and well-understood "natural boundaries" to individuals' rights. These boundaries on rights are held sacrosanct, subject to no justifiable "crossings" without consent.[6]

The problem of defining individual boundaries, individual rights, or, indeed, defining "individuals" must arise in any discussion of social order that commences with individuals as the basic units. Who is a person? How are rights defined? What is the benchmark or starting point from which voluntary contractual arrangements may be made?

I stated earlier that the primary value premise of individualism is the moral equality of men as men, that no man counts for more than another. This remains, and must remain, the fundamental normative framework even when we recognize inequalities among persons in other respects. The libertarian anarchist accepts this framework, but in a much more restricted application than others who also fall within the individualistic set. The libertarian anarchist applies the moral equality norm in holding that each and every man is *equally* entitled to have the natural boundaries of his rights respected, regardless of the fact that, among persons, these boundaries may vary widely.[7] *If* such natural boundaries exist, the contractarian may also use the individual units defined by such limits as the starting point for the complex contractual arrangements that emerge finally in observed, or conceptually observed, political structures.[8] Within the presupposition that natural boundaries exist, the differences between the constitutionalist-contractarian and the libertarian anarchist reduce to the variant hypotheses concerning the interdependencies among persons, as defined, interdependencies that could be, as noted above, subjected to testing at a conjecturally empirical level.

But do such natural limits or boundaries exist? Once we move beyond the simple rights to persons in the strictly physical sense, what are the distinguishing characteristics of boundary lines? In all cases where separate individual claims may come into conflict, or potential conflict, what is the natural boundary? Robin Hood and Little John meet squarely in the center of the footbridge. Who has the right of first passage? [9]

Robert Nozick makes a bold attempt to answer such questions by referring to the process of acquisition. In his formulation, the legitimacy of the boundary limits among persons depends upon the process through which rights are acquired and not on the absolute or relative size of the bundle that may be in the possession or nominal ownership of a person or group. A person who has acquired assets by voluntary transfer holds the rights to these assets within admissible natural boundary limits. A person who holds assets that have been acquired, by him or by others in the past, by nonvoluntary methods has little claim to include these assets within the natural limits.

What is the ultimate test for the existence of natural boundaries? This must lie in the observed attitudes of individuals themselves. Do we observe persons to act as if there were natural boundaries on the rights of others, beyond those formally defined in legal restrictions? The evidence is not all on one side. In rejecting the extreme claims of the libertarian anarchists, we should not overlook the important fact that a great deal of social interaction does proceed without formalized rules. For large areas of human intercourse, anarchy prevails and it works. We need no rules for directing pedestrian traffic on busy city sidewalks; no rules for ordinary conversation in groups of up to, say, ten persons; no rules for behavior in elevators.

In the larger context, however, the evidence seems to indicate that persons do not mutually and simultaneously agree on dividing lines among separate rights. There is surely a contractual logic for at least some of the activity of the state in defining and enforcing the limits on the activities of persons. To accept this, however, does not imply that the legally defined rights of individuals, and the distribution of these rights, are arbitrarily determined by the political authorities. If we reject the empirical existence of natural boundaries, however, we return to the initial question. How do we define "individuals" for the purpose of deriving the contractual basis for political authority?

VII. THE HOBBESIAN SETTING

The only alternative seems to be found in the distribution of limits on individuals' spheres of action that would be found in the total absence of formalized rules, that is, in genuine Hobbesian anarchy. In this setting, some "equilibrium," some sustainable distribution of allowable activities would emerge. This distribution would depend on the relative strengths and abilities of persons to acquire and to maintain desirable goods and assets. The "law of the jungle" would be controlling, and no serious effort could be made to attribute moral legitimacy to the relative holdings of persons. But this construction does have the major advantage of allowing us to define, in a conjecturally positive sense, a starting point, an "original position" from which any contractual process might commence.[10] Individuals need not be "natural equals" in this Hobbesian equilibrium, but they would still find it mutually advantageous to enter into contractual agreements which impose limits on their own activities, which set up ideally neutral governmental units to enforce these limits.

The perspective changes dramatically when this, essentially Hobbesian, vision is substituted for the natural boundaries or Lockean vision, when the existence of natural boundaries to the rights of persons that would be generally agreed upon and respected is denied. In the Nozick variant of the Lockean vision, anarchy, the absence of formalized rules, the absence of law along with means of enforcement, offers a highly attractive prospect. By contrast, in the basic Hobbesian vision, or in any paradigm that is derivative from this, anarchy is not a state to be desired at all. Life for the individual in genuine anarchy is indeed predicted to be "poor, nasty, brutish, and short." The Hobbesian jungle is something to be avoided, and something that rational self-interested persons will seek to avoid through general agreement on law, along with requisite enforcement institutions, even if, in the extreme, the contract may be irreversible and Hobbes's Leviathan may threaten.[11]

VIII. CONCLUSIONS

We have here a paradox of sorts. The libertarian anarchist and the contractarian share the individualistic value premise. In addition, their diagnoses of current social malaise is likely to be similar in condemning overextended governmental authority. Further, the items on both agenda for policy reform may be identical over a rather wide range. In their descriptions of the "good society," however, these two sets of political philosophers are likely to differ widely. The constitutionalist-contractarian, who looks to his stage two set of ideals, and who adopts at least some variant of the Hobbesian assumption about human nature, views anarchy, as an institution, with horror. To remove all laws, all institutions of order, in a world peopled by Hobbesian men would produce chaos. The contractarian must hold fast to a normative vision that is not nearly so simplistic as that which is possible either for the libertarian anarchist or for the collectivist. The contractarian seeks "ordered anarchy," that is, a situation described as one that offers maximal freedom for individuals within a minimal set of formalized rules and constraints on behavior. He takes from classical economics the important idea that the independent actions of many persons can be spontaneously coordinated through marketlike institutions so as to produce mutually desirable outcomes without detailed and direct interferences of the state. But he insists, with Adam Smith, that this coordination can be effective only if individual actions are limited by laws that cannot themselves spontaneously emerge.

The contractarian position requires sophisticated discrimination between those areas of potential human activity where "law" is required and those areas that had best be left alone. The "efficient" dividing line must be based on empirical reality. Formal law may be severely limited in a society characterized by widespread agreement on the structure of rights and embodying agreed-on ethical standards of mutual respect. The scope for law becomes much more extensive in a society populated by hedonists who neither agree upon reciprocal rights nor upon desired standards of personal conduct. Between the libertarian anarchist, who sees no cause for any laws, and who trusts to individuals' own respect for each others' reciprocal natural boundaries, and the collectivist-socialist, who sees chaos as the result of any human activities that are not politically controlled, the constitutionalist-contractarian necessarily occupies the middle ground. Regardless of his empirical presuppositions, his ideal world falls "between anarchy and Leviathan," both of which are to be avoided.

NOTES

1. Murray Rothbard, *For a New Liberty* (New York: Macmillan, 1973). See also David Friedman, *The Machinery of Freedom* (New York: Harper and Row, 1973). I shall not discuss those putative anarchists who fail to see the internal contradiction between anarchy and socialism. The absurdity of such juxtaposition should be apparent without serious argument.
2. This is recognized by Plattner when he places John Rawls, an avowed contractarian, and Robert Nozick, almost a libertarian-anarchist, in

the same category "on the deepest level." Against both, Plattner advances the transcendentalist view of politics as supraindividualistic. See Marc F. Plattner, "The New Political Theory," *The Public Interest,* 40 (Summer 1975), 119-28, notably p. 127.

3. For an elaboration of the underlying theory, see James M. Buchanan and Gordon Tullock, *The Calculus of Consent* (Ann Arbor: University of Michigan Press, 1962).

4. For a general discussion of this sort of interdependence, see James M. Buchanan and Alberto di Pierro, "Pragmatic Reform and Constitutional Revolution," *Ethics,* 79 (January 1969), 95-104.

5. See my review of David Friedman's book, *The Machinery of Freedom,* in *Journal of Economic Literature,* XII (September 1974), 914-15.

6. One merit of Robert Nozick's analysis is his explicit discussion of the underlying presumptions of the "natural-boundaries" model. See Robert Nozick, *Anarchy, State, and Utopia* (New York: Basic Books, 1974).

7. For purposes of discussion here, I am including Robert Nozick as being among the libertarian anarchists. Although he defends the emergence of the minimal protective state from anarchy, and specifically refutes the strict anarchist model in this respect, he does provide the most sophisticated argument for the presumption of inherent natural boundaries on individuals' rights, which is the focus of my attention here. Cf. Robert Nozick, *Anarchy, State, and Utopia,* op. cit.

8. John Locke provides a good example.

9. I use this example in several places to discuss this set of problems in my recent book, *The Limits of Liberty: Between Anarchy and Leviathan* (Chicago: University of Chicago Press, 1975).

10. In his much-acclaimed book, *A Theory of Justice* (Cambridge: Harvard University Press, 1971), John Rawls attempts to derive principles of justice from conceptual contractual agreement among persons who place themselves in an "original position" behind a "veil of ignorance." Rawls does not, however, fully describe the characteristics of the "original position." I have interpreted this position in essentially Hobbesian terms, with interesting implications. See my "A Hobbesian Interpretation of the Rawlsian Difference Principle," Working Paper CE 75-2-3, Center for Study of Public Choice, Virginia Polytechnic Institute and State University, 1975.

11. The argument of the few preceding paragraphs is developed much more fully in my book, *The Limits of Liberty,* op. cit. Also see *Explorations in the Theory of Anarchy,* edited by Gordon Tullock (Blacksburg: Center for Study of Public Choice, 1972).

3

NOZICK'S ANARCHISM

ERIC MACK

Locke and his close followers in political philosophy have argued that from a moral starting point in which persons are ascribed Lockean state-of-nature rights the nightwatchman state can be shown to be a legitimate state. A nightwatchman state is one which restricts its activities to defending the Lockean rights of its citizens and punishing those who violate these rights. While granting that given this moral starting point the nightwatchman state is the only plausible candidate for legitimacy, I shall contend that not even the nightwatchman state can be justified from a Lockean state-of-nature perspective. My particular target will be the ingenious defense of the nightwatchman state recently elaborated in Part I of Robert Nozick's *Anarchy, State and Utopia*.[1] We shall see why the Lockean must turn to the type of strategy adopted by Nozick and why the employment of this strategy does not legitimate even the nightwatchman state. I should add that I take the anarchistic implications of the Lockean state-of-nature starting point to be, not a problem for this starting point, but rather a sign of its plausibility.

I

Central to any Lockean state-of-nature perspective is the view that individuals can and do possess various moral or human rights and that these rights are possessed independently of any state interest, independently of the utility or overall social value of these rights being respected, and independently of any agreements or compacts among persons. All these rights are genuinely independent of any calculus of social interests. For Locke, human rights rest on the natural moral equality and independence of persons or on the fact that no person is made for another's purposes. For each person, his own rights provide him with a sphere of moral immunity within which he may do what it is right for him to do, namely, preserve himself. As long as his self-preservation is not at stake, each person is obligated to respect a like sphere of immunity around others. This entire doctrine is contained in the passage,

> ... being all equal and independent, no one ought to harm another in his life, health, or possessions; ... being furnished with like faculties, sharing all in one community of nature, there cannot be supposed any such subordination among us that may authorize us to destroy another, as if we were made for one another's uses as the inferior ranks of creatures are for ours. Everyone, as he is bound to preserve himself and not quit his station wilfully, so by the like reason, when his preservation comes not in competition, ought he, as much as he can to preserve the rest of mankind and [this comes down to] may not, unless, it be to do justice to an offender, take away or impair the life, or what tends to the preservation of the life, the liberty, health, limb or goods of another.[2]

Each person possesses, then, a right to life and liberty, that is, a right to freedom from the coercion of his person or activity. Second, persons may acquire property rights to various external objects. Whatever the details of the processes by which specific property rights are acquired (cf. para. 27), these rights also do not require the sanction of the state. Nor are they defined in terms of, and therefore generally subject to being overridden by, considerations of utility or overall social welfare. Nor are they the products of agreements.[3] Third, each person possesses, independently of state confirmation and of considerations of utility and of agreement among persons, a right to defend what is his by right and to punish those who aggress against rights.

> . . . the execution of the law of nature is, in that state of nature, put into every man's hands, whereby everyone has a right to punish the transgressors of that law to such a degree as may hinder its violation. (para. 7)

According to Locke, certain "inconveniences" are apt to arise (para. 13) when individuals retain their original rights to defend and punish. As the familiar story goes, these inconveniences are traceable to persons' being the judges of their own cases and, in response to these inconveniences, we find people "putting themselves into society" (para. 21), creating a "common judge" (para. 20). The state is represented as being born as the universally authorized executor of persons' original rights to defend and to punish.[4] Due to its pedigree, this state can legitimately prohibit (what we can now call) "private" acts of defense and punishment. Its prohibition of these private acts is essential to its being a state. The problem, of course, for this line of argument, is that there has never been any free and genuine universal authorization, nor are the prospects for one particularly bright. Some persons always have exercised, and it is likely that some persons (of those within a given territory) always will exercise their rights to abstain from transferring to some one aspiring political institution their original rights to defend and to punish.[5] It seems that if the legitimacy of the prohibition of private defense and punishment requires the authorization of all who are subject to this prohibition, then no past or current state has acted legitimately, and no likely future state will act legitimately, in prohibiting the private execution of the law of nature. If universal authorization is required, it seems that there has never been nor is ever likely to be a legitimate state. Furthermore, it seems that the legitimacy of the prohibition of all private defense and punishment *does* require that everyone freely surrender these original rights. For neither private defensive nor private punitive activity is naturally prohibitable. To engage in these activities is merely to exercise one's original rights. To engage in such activities is merely to do what the Lockean authorization-justification of the state presumes everyone has a natural right to do.

What is the Lockean in search of a legitimate nightwatchman State to do? The prospects for successful tinkering with the notion of consent with the result that in some significant sense persons really have universally consented, or really are likely universally to consent, to a "common judge" are dim. The alternative is to argue that persons can be legitimately prohibited from engaging in the private execution of the law of nature even if they have not partaken of any social compact. This is the general alternative pursued by Nozick in Part I of *Anarchy, State and Utopia*. I shall argue that this pursuit cannot arrive at the legitimization of (even) the nightwatchman state. The problem for the Lockean pursuing this alternative can be characterized as follows.

A legitimate nightwatchman state must satisfy both the conditions necessary for being a morally legitimate organization and the conditions necessary for being a state. But there is a tension between the satisfaction of these two sets of conditions. Let us label any agent which provides individuals (in return for payment or without explicit charge) with the service of exercising their defensive and punitive rights a "protective agency." To be a state a protective agency must possess some type of monopoly or dominance, within a given territory, in the provision of defensive and punitive, that is, "protective," services. And it seems that to possess the requisite monopoly or dominance a protective agency must prohibit in part or in whole the operation of other protective agencies. If protective agency P_1 does not prohibit or limit the operation of other protective agencies, then P_1 would just be one among a number of such agencies and would not possess the type of monopoly or dominance in providing protective services that is a necessary condition of its being a state. (If P_1, as one among many protection agencies, qualified as a state then so might the others—hence, the prospect of a multiplicity of states within a given territory.) Yet to be a legitimate state P_1 must not violate Lockean rights. It must not include among its putatively protective activities the prohibition of any legitimate, non-rights-violating, actions. Since the performance of genuinely defensive and punitive actions is legitimate, it seems that to be a legitimate state P_1 would have to abstain from prohibiting other agencies from performing protective services. But if P_1 abstains from enforcing such prohibitions it does not qualify as a state.

Let us refer to the rights that an agency (or an individual) has to prohibit activities on the part of others as its (his) "prohibition rights." What the Lockean defender of the nightwatchman state must show is that an agency's prohibition rights may be powerful enough that, under their auspices, this agency can prohibit or limit the protective activities of other agencies in a way or to the extent that it will possess the type of monopoly or dominance necessary to its being a state. My contention, against Nozick, is that no agency's prohibition rights would be powerful enough for their exercise to provide that agency with the type of monopoly or dominance characteristic of Statehood. I shall sketch Nozick's defense of the Lockean state and indicate why, even if we accept a number of philosophically controversial moves, we cannot allow that the state has been legitimated.

Any protective agency, P_1, may prohibit any forceful and not genuinely protective act which is directed against any one of its clients. But P_1's having this prohibition right and exercising it is compatible with there being other protective agencies which have the right and exercise the right to offer genuinely protective services in competition with P_1. P_1 has the right to require that other agencies' actions be "in line with" its own only in the sense that it may prohibit activities which P_1 (reliably) deems to be morally impermissible, not in the sense that P_1 can require uniformity of offered services. Furthermore, in an important sense each genuinely protective agency is morally equal. Each has the same prohibition rights against other agencies as they have against it. No extension of the range of prohibitable acts, that is, no broadening of prohibition rights will undercut this moral symmetry. This symmetry among all agencies which do not engage in prohibitable acts is a powerful barrier to the legitimization of the state. We shall see how Nozick attempts to take account of, yet circumvent, this barrier by holding that the legitimate state is a protective agency that holds a *de facto,* but not a *de jure,* monopoly in the provision of protection.

The bulk of Nozick's argument, however, is not directed toward

introducing asymmetry in prohibitions rights, but rather in expanding the scope of acknowledged prohibition rights. The restriction of
legitimate prohibition to acts that as such violate rights poses a
general problem for state-of-nature theory. This is the problem of
risky actions, that is, actions that impose a significant risk of
eventuating in rights violation without being rights violating as
such. An example might be the use of machinery by A on his own
property which occasionally gives off sparks that might ignite
farmer B's haystack. Whether this does constitute an example of a
risky action depends on the details of the case and the exact criteria
involved in determining significant risk. The relevance of the
problem of risky actions to the anarchist-archist dispute is that
protective procedures too may fail to be rights violating as such
while still imposing a significant risk of eventuating in rights
violation. If P_1's prohibition rights extend only to acts that are
rights violating as such, then P_1 cannot legitimately prohibit risky
protective procedures that are employed by other protection
agencies against P_1's clients.[6]

Nozick argues for the view (the "Principle of Compensation")
that a risky act may legitimately be prohibited provided that those
who are forbidden to act are compensated for the disadvantages
which the prohibition causes them (54-87). For the purposes of this
paper, I shall accept the extension of prohibition rights involved in
the principle of compensation. Given this principle, the range of
actions by P_1's competitors which are immune from P_1's legitimate
prohibition is greatly narrowed.[7] P_1 may forbid any putatively
protective procedure that violates the rights of one of its clients or
poses a significant risk of eventuating in such a violation of rights.
Acceptance of the principle of compensation increases the acknowledged extent to which P_1 can legitimately require that the
procedures of other protective agencies be "in line with" its own.
They must be similarly nonrisky.

But the principle of compensation does nothing to alter the moral
symmetry among protective agencies. If risky acts are prohibitable,
then all agencies are obligated to abstain from them and each
agency has the right to require, in the name of its clients, that all
other agencies abstain from risky actions. Something other than the
principle of compensation is necessary to pave the way to P_1's

legitimate statehood. This additional factor is a matter of power. Suppose that P_1 has the power to require all others to abstain from any procedures (including risky ones) which P_1 deems it may prohibit, that P_1 makes its decisions about what procedures are prohibitable through goodwilled application of Lockean state-of-nature principles, and that P_1 exercises this power. Nozick's view, which I will not challenge here,[8] is that in the exercise of this power P_1 would be exercising a right that it has and which, symmetrically, each other protective agency has. P_1, however, in virtue of its power, is (at least after a period of struggle) the only protective agency which does exercise this right. Nozick is not arguing for a further extension of prohibition rights. Rather he is making a claim about the "logic" of the exercise of prohibition rights.[9] If goodwilled agency P_1 is sufficiently powerful and exercises this power, its decisions set the legitimate restrictions on the actions taken toward its clients, and hence on the protective activities offered against its clients and carried out against its clients, by any other protective agency. So the powerful P_1 can legitimately restrict the protective services of all other agencies insofar as those services are offered against P_1's clients. According to Nozick, under such conditions the powerful P_1 would be a *de facto* monopoly, that is, "a monopoly that is not *de jure* because it is not the result of some unique grant of exclusive right while others are excluded from exercising a similar privilege" (109). According to Nozick, this holder of a *de facto* monopoly will be a dominant agency qualifying as a legitimate state.

II

Against Nozick, I argue along the following lines. There are three senses in which, without doing violence to the spirit of Nozick's argument, one may conceive a legitimate protective agency as being dominant. (1) P_1 may be conceived as dominant in the sense of having the unique power (the power which at most one agency in a given territory can have) to require that all other agencies restrict their procedures against P_1's clients to procedures that P_1 deems permissible. I will argue that the possession of dominance in this first sense is not sufficient for being a state. (2) P_1 may be conceived as dominant in the sense of having a special competitive advantage in its search for clients in virtue of its unique power. This is the sense of "dominant" suggested by Nozick's remark that

> ... being the already dominant protective agency gives an agency a significant market advantage in the competition for clients. The dominant agency can offer its customers a guarantee that no other agencies can match: "Only those procedures *we* deem appropriate will be used on our customers." (109)

Here it is the agency's power (possessed, perhaps, because of its size) in virtue of which the agency can offer a guarantee which appears to be especially attractive. If there were an agency dominant in this second sense, it might qualify as a state. However, I will argue that while it is conceivable that a legitimate agency has a special competitive advantage in virtue of its unique power, there is no reason to suppose that unique power would confer such an advantage, and there are numerous reasons to suppose that it would not. Thus, there is no reason to believe in, and numerous reasons to disbelieve in, the emergence out of competition among legitimate protective agencies of an agency dominant in this second sense. (3) P_1 may be conceived as dominant in the sense of having and retaining a high percentage of the buyers of protective services as its clients. I will argue that possession of dominance in this third sense is not sufficient for being a state. I shall conclude, then, that each conceived dominant legitimate agency either falls short of being a state or is such that there is no reason to suppose that it would ever exist. Hence, there is no reason to believe that a dominant legitimate agency qualifying as a state would emerge out of a state-of-nature in which protective services were provided by a variety of legitimate protective agencies. Both the argument against the emergence of an agency dominant in second sense and the argument against construing an agency which is dominant in the third sense as a state are based on an informal survey of the potential for market competition among legitimate protective agencies. This potential, in turn, exists because prohibition rights, even informed by the principle of compensation, remain both symmetrical and too narrow for any protective agency to require anything like conformity to its own procedures in the services offered by its competitors.

Is P_1 a state if P_1 is dominant in the sense of having the unique power to require that all other agencies restrict their procedures against P_1's clients to procedures deemed permissible by P_1? An affirmative answer has odd implications. In the limiting case, if a single person acting as his own protective agency had the power—concentrated, perhaps, in his magic wand—to require that *in their dealings with him* everyone in the world eschew procedures which he deemed impermissible, this single person would be the world state. He would be the world state even if he had nothing to do with how any two other persons dealt with one another. It seems that the possession of dominance in the first sense will not suffice for being a state.

But what of a case in which a small but powerful group systematically ("legally") preys upon the remaining population within a given territory while not interesting themselves in the relationships among the members of the exploited group? Would not these powerful few constitute a state? Indeed they would. But, on the basis of state-of-nature principles, they would not constitute a legitimate organization, and hence, they would not constitute a legitimate state. Power exercised in this way will give dominance, but not dominance of a sort that is consistent with legitimacy. Such a powerful predatory group would achieve statehood by engaging in certain procedures against other groups and individuals which it (effectively) prohibits those groups and individuals from engaging in with respect to it. In contrast, a legitimate powerful agency would not prohibit the performance of any procedure against itself or its clients if it itself performed, or was prepared to perform, that procedure. Although the wielder of the magic wand might require that in their dealings with him everyone in the world follow procedures that he deems legitimate, if he is to constitute a legitimate (self)-protective agency he must disavow any procedures he prohibits others and must allow others to perform any procedure he is prepared to engage in.[10] This restriction on the exercise of his power stands as a barrier to his statehood. Of course, possession of unique power would confer unique opportunity to act on (and enforce) one's moral judgments (about, say, permissible procedures). But the existence of a powerful agent taking the opportunity to act on its judgment need not constitute the existence of a state. For these judgments may demand (and judgments that follow state-of-nature principles do demand) constraints on the use or monopolization of power such that if these demands are satisfied the powerful agency will not constitute a state. Unique power, legitimately exercised, does not as such confer statehood.

Would P_1 be a state if it were dominant in the sense of having a special competitive advantage in its search for clients because of its unique power? There is some plausibility to an affirmative answer. Here we imagine P_1 as having a high percentage of the populace as its clients and being in this position because of its enforcement power and not merely in virtue of the attractiveness of its services in terms of cost, variety, speed of delivery, etc.; that is, not merely in terms of the sort of features which contribute to mere market success. If P_1 is dominant in thise sense, its dominance is not a matter of ordinary business success and the difference is made by that feature associated with all common conceptions of statehood: enforcement power. Such a dominant P_1 would still be peculiarly nonpolitical. For instance, its revenue would be in the form of payments for services which persons would be free not to purchase and not in the form of taxes. Still, we might well classify it as a state. But I contend that there would be no special competitive advantage for an agency in being the uniquely powerful agency.

Following Nozick (103), let us imagine that the uniquely powerful P_1 publishes a list (however long this list would have to be) of the procedures which, in its goodwilled and Lockean-minded judgment, it deems to be permissible. And P_1 makes clear its intention to prohibit any other procedures. P_1 itself offers to provide customers with certain combinations of the procedures which it deems permissible. Now imagine a single competitor, P_2. P_2 could offer all sorts of combinations of the procedures judged permissible by P_1, including combinations not offered by P_1. It could also offer, in various combinations, those procedures deemed permissible by P_1 but not offered by P_1. And it could offer to apply these procedures to all persons, *including the clients of P_1*. Clients of P_1 have no immunity against protective activities which are judged permissible by P_1 and are performed by P_2 on behalf of P_2's constituents. For P_1, to be legitimate, must allow against its customers any procedure it has deemed permissible. P_2, then, can offer the same depth of service that P_1 offers. For while it is true that in describing its protective prohibitions P_2 could not give its clients the guarantee that "Only procedures *we* deem permissible will be used on our customers," it *can* guarantee that only procedures deemed permissible by the Lockean-minded and goodwilled P_1 will be used against them. And while in describing the punitive (retaliatory) procedures it offers it cannot give its clients the guarantee that "Retaliatory procedures among those which *we* deem permissible will be carried on at your behalf," it *can* guarantee its clients that punitive procedures among those judged permissible by P_1 will be carried out on their behalf. Nor would clients of P_2 be more subject to unexpected procedures than clients of P_1. For if P_1 were to carry out a procedure for one of its customers against some customer of P_2 which P_1 had previously held to be impermissible, then P_1 would be committed to allowing P_2 to carry out this procedure against P_1's customers. The moral symmetry of protective agencies blocks the uniquely powerful agency from offering its customers any special immunity. P_2 may compete successfully for customers because of its efficiency in production or delivery, or simply because it does not have the expense of compiling the list of permissible procedures.

What about multiple competitors with P_1? P_3 would deal with the existence of a uniquely powerful P_1 just as P_2 does. But for both P_2 and P_3 there has to be a concern about what guarantees it can give its own customers about the procedures it will employ against clients of the other nonpowerful agency and about the procedures that will be used on them by the other nonpowerful agency. Of course, each agency has a right to use any permissible procedure and this encompasses a right to defend against any impermissible procedures. But to attract customers, to be serious competitors of P_1, P_2 and P_3 must be able to offer guarantees. The natural solution would be for each to agree to restrict the procedures it will use against customers of the other to those on P_1's list and to allow against its own customers any procedure on the list. But many other solutions are possible and some of these might give these agencies a competitive edge on P_1. P_2 and P_3 might agree on their own common list of permissible actions. Or these agencies might mutually tailor the procedures which will be allowed to their customers and allowed against their customers in order to attract clients. For instance, P_2 might agree to allow procedure C, which would otherwise be impermissible, to be carried out against its clients by P_3 in return for P_3's agreeing that in the name of its clients P_2 could carry out procedure D, which otherwise would be impermissible, against clients of P_3. Patronizing P_2 would involve giving voluntary consent to being subject to P_3's doing C on behalf of one of its clients and patronizing P_3 would involve voluntary consent to being subject to P_2's performance of D on behalf of one of its clients. Persons with a relative high preference for being able to initiate C and a relative low distaste for being subject to D would be attracted to P_3. Persons with a relatively high preference for being able to initiate D and a relatively low distaste for being subject to C would be attracted to P_2. Protective agencies will promote such mini-social contracts to the extent that they anticipate that participation in such trade-offs will attract customers.[11] All such mini-social contracts leave individuals who do not wish to enter them free to patronize protective agencies, say P_1 or P_4, which are not vehicles for such contracts.

I shall not pursue further the respects in which protective agencies could function as brokers for mini-social contracts. However, it is important to explore other respects in which protective agencies could compete with the uniquely powerful P_1 within the limits defined by P_1's goodwilled reading of state-of-nature principles. Agencies may specialize in the protective procedures they carry out. Not everyone wants to pay for protection from, say, industrial espionage or the dumping of pollutants into some particular river system. Agencies may be entirely devoted to catering to such special interests, or they may offer policies including normal and specialized protection services. Individuals have varying preferences for the speed at which certain procedures are carried out. Presumably those less interested in rapid justice (if there were enough of them) could purchase lower-priced stand-by contracts. Protective agencies might compete for clients by offering various combination policies: protection and insurance, protection and loans, and so forth. Individuals may be willing to pay extra for protective procedures with "something extra," say judicial proceedings presided over by topless judges. There can be great variation in "style" between procedures that are similarly nonrisky and directed toward the same result. And different individuals will be attracted to different styles. For instance, the tribunals of one agency may be manned by certified sages, while the tribunals of another agency may be terminals of a carefully programmed computer. Of course, persons are free to induce others, perhaps by means of monetary payment, to agree to the style of proceedings which the buyers prefer. The purchase of such an agreement would constitute yet another mini-social contract. In these and many other respects protective agencies could compete for customers against a uniquely powerful agency while suffering no disadvantage because of that agency's power. P_1's being the uniquely powerful agency gives it no special competitive advantage. There is no reason, then, to expect the emergence of a legitimate dominant agency which is dominant in the sense of possessing a special competitive advantage in virtue of its special power.

There is a decentralizing factor of a somewhat different sort which merits comment here. Comment is merited partially because there is a certain irony about Nozick's invocation of this factor. Nozick points out that there is an assumption.

> . . . common to much utopian and anarchist theorizing, that there is some set of principles obvious enough to be accepted by all men of good will, precise enough to give unambiguous guidance in particular situations, clear enough so that all will realize its dictates, and complete enough to cover all problems that actually will arise. (141)

According to Nozick, (a) the individualist anarchist is wrong in thinking that he has available to him (in state-of-nature principles) a set of principles which gives unambiguous prescriptions for all particular cases; and (b) the unavailability of such a set of principles provides the base for an argument in defense of the state. It is odd that Nozick asserts (b) since, on his own view, no protective agency, not even a uniquely powerful one, has any more moral guidance than the individual anarchist. The underdetermination of particular cases by state-of-nature principles will lead to disagreements between the best willed and morally perceptive persons and agencies. But it is no solution to this moral problem that there be an agency which always has the power to enforce its will.

The significance of the underdetermination of particular cases for protective agencies is that, in the case of some goodwilled disagreements, neither party would be on morally solid ground in enforcing its own judgment. In general, then, each protective agency, even a uniquely powerful agency, would know or would be in position to know that sometimes its enforcement of its favored opinion would not be sanctioned by state-of-nature principles. Furthermore, there are numerous crucial judgments which quite clearly are not dictated by state-of-nature principles; for example, judgments about what degree of punishment is merited by a given crime, about what degree of risk renders an action (significantly) risky, and about what degree of riskiness is sufficient for an action being, as such, rights violating. Within clearly underdetermined areas, P's enforcement of any of its judgments against other agencies which, apparently in goodwill, read the state-of-nature principles differently is *prima facie* evidence (available to P) that P has engaged in unjustified enforcement. Hence, mutually recognizing goodwilled agencies which are cognizant of the underdetermination by state-of-nature principles will not seek to enforce, or will at least hesitate in their enforcement of, their idiosyncratic judgments.[12] Rather they will seek to negotiate their disagreements—at least those disagreements that lie within clearly underdetermined areas.

Negotiated agreement is the appropriate means of resolution. For on state-of-nature theory, whenever state-of-nature principles as such do not determine the legitimacy of a given act or practice, legitimacy can be determined only by an agreement among the concerned parties, either with regard to the legitimacy of that act or practice, or with regard to what decision mechanism will be accepted as authoritative.[13] Negotiations and, *a fortiori*, vehicles for negotiations are crucial for the determination of procedural rights. For, in the absence of any morally constraining agreement, any agency is at liberty to engage in any investigatory or judicial procedure that does not violate the accused's Lockean rights. Since, typically, there will be many different procedures which would not violate the accused's Lockean rights, in the absence of any agreement constraining the agency, the accused typically has no right to any *particular* procedure. Rights to particular procedures (and rights against procedures which, in the state of nature, would not violate Lockean rights) can appear only as the products of agreements.[14]

Moral underdetermination *is* pervasive in the Lockean state of nature. However, the solution is not the enforcement of one disputant's view, but rather an accommodation among the good-willed and Lockean-minded parties. Rather than showing the necessity for a state, or for a powerful protective agency ascending to statehood, the underdetermination by state-of-nature principles shows that a powerful agency universally judging "by its own lights" (109) just what actions are prohibitable and enforcing these judgments in the name of its clients would not be legitimate on state-of-nature grounds. The underdetermination also shows the importance of protective agencies as vehicles for the accommodations which, so to speak, fill in the gaps between the implications of state-of-nature principles.[15]

Finally, we turn to a consideration of the prospects for, and the significance of, a protective agency which is dominant in the weak sense of having and retaining over some significant time a high percentage of the buyers of protective services as its customers. What is the likelihood of there being an agency that is dominant in this sense? And would such a dominant agency be a state? The two questions are related because if such a dominant agency is just one possible, and even unlikely, result of the operation of a market for legitimate protective services, then it would not be plausible to classify such an agency, should it arise, as a state. Whether such dominance will occur depends upon the detailed characteristics of the complex and ever changing demand for protection and on the detailed economic, and even sociological and psychological, factors governing the capacity of agencies, actual or potential, to satisfy elements of this complex demand. One cannot predict that at no time would there arise a single supplier of protective procedures so relatively efficient over the whole range of protective services demanded that it would attract and retain for a substantial time a dominating percentage of the protection clientele. This is comparable to not being able to predict that no single shoe manufacturer (or single, close-knit, association of shoe manufacturers) will ever capture and retain for a significant time a dominating percentage of the shoe market. Still, in both the protection and the shoe industries, the variety of products it is permissible to offer and the diversity possible among the firms within each industry with respect to the specific products they may be best at producing, marketing, or delivering, combined with the divergent preferences among purchasers with regard to specialized type and style makes the appearance and survival over time of a single firm with a dominating percentage of the customers seem unlikely. At least it seems unlikely as long as one does not endorse the empirical historical thesis that unregulated industries by nature become progressively more concentrated. This is a thesis which anyone defending the nightwatchman state must reject and which Nozick explicitly rejects (182).[16]

But suppose there were to appear an agency which was dominant in this third sense? Would it be a state? There are many reasons against this classification. The dominant agency's decisions about what services to offer and how resources were to be allotted in the provision of these services would be economic-market (presumably, profit-maximizing) decisions, not political decisions. These decisions, while made with an eye to the market, would be made by the agency's owners or their agents. The agency's revenue would consist of payments for services and not of taxes. In no sense would such a dominant agency be politically sovereign. Indeed it seems that the existence of such a dominant agency is compatible with there being no political realm. This agency's dominance, while it lasted, would be a matter of ordinary business success. It would be in continual danger of losing its clientele and hence its dominance through changes in its capacity, relative to its competitors and potential competitors, to deliver the particular legitimate protective services which persons, with their everchanging preferences, would be demanding. The existence of a dominant agency in this third sense would be the realization of one possibility along a spectrum of possible market solutions to the demand for protective services. It would be the realization of the possible solution which, of all the possible solutions, appears most like a state—at least when viewed in isolation from the other possibilities along the solution spectrum. But when it is seen as merely one solution along this spectrum any statelike appearance is recognized as mere appearance.

If we begin with the Lockean premises that each man possesses a right to his life, liberty, and property; a right to protect these rights; and a right to appoint whomever he chooses to exercise this protective right for him; and if we recognize that all sorts of appointments are permissible, that is, are not such that others or their appointed agents have a right to defend against them, then we are morally committed to allowing a market in (genuinely) protective services. Whatever the details of the institutional structure called forth in this market, that structure will not qualify as a state.

NOTES

1. Robert Nozick, *Anarchy, State and Utopia* (New York: Basic Books, 1974).
2. John Locke, *Two Treatises on Government,* ed. Peter Laslett (London: Cambridge University Press, 1960), "The Second Treatise of Government" (para. 6).
3. According to Locke, the possibility of certain extensions of property holdings rests on an agreement among persons to use money. For, supposedly, this agreement circumvents the spoilage restriction on property holdings (paras. 46-50). I ignore this complication in Locke's development of Lockean property theory.
4. While Locke holds (cf. para. 88) that those who have not made themselves members of society but who do injury to some member of society are subject to society's punishment, he offers no doctrine about how the body politic may deal with those who remain outside the jurisdiction of the state, do not do injury to any member of society, but do defend themselves against or punish members of society. It seems that despite the suggestion that not everyone need participate in the formation of society (para. 87), Locke comes to presume that no one retains the executive power of the law of nature. Certainly it is the sense of paragraphs 112, 117, and 119-122 that, in virtue of tacit consent, there is no significant authorization which the state lacks.
5. How likely persons are, if not placed under duress, to abstain from such a universal authorization can be seen in the light of the subsequent discussion of the potential for market competition among private protection agencies.

6. Among the disturbing implications of P_1's prohibition rights extending only to rights-violating acts is that nonclients of P_1 would be able to elicit payments from the clients of P_1 (or from P_1) for merely agreeing to adopt nonrisky (to the clients of P_1) protective procedures.

7. The range of legitimate prohibitions is also narrowed in that risky prohibitions are now deemed prohibitable.

8. The natural charge against Nozick is that he runs together an agency's being subjectively justified in following its own best judgment about what is permissible and an agency's being objectively justified in its actions because they are the results of its own best judgment about what is permissible. For Nozick's discussion, see pp. 106-7.

9. P_1 might make more modest claims than other agencies with regard to what prohibitions are permissible. Of course, the correlative of this modesty is a relatively boldness with regard to what prohibitions of prohibitions are permissible.

10. Of course, for Nozick, the wand wielder is a legitimate (self)-protective agency only if, in addition, his judgments about what is permissible are rational and goodwilled applications of state-of-nature principles. Those who do not accept Nozick's claim that a goodwilled, Lockean-minded prohibition is a legitimate prohibition will demand, not that the wand wielder be goodwilled, but that he be right.

11. See David Friedman's *The Machinery of Freedom* (New York: Harper and Row, 1973), pp. 151-78, for a discussion of, among other things, the role of private protective agencies as vehicles for and brokers of mini-social contracts; or, as Friedman would put it, as producers of laws that most conform to the market demand for laws.

12. To be more precise, in the absence of agreement, no goodwilled agency will (readily) act more harshly (within areas that are clearly underdetermined) than other goodwilled agencies deem permissible. But also, if P_1 does act more harshly than P_2 deems permissible, P_2 may not (readily) enforce, in the form of punishment of P_1, its judgment of P_1's action. For P_2 may still judge P_1 to be a goodwilled agency, and if it does, then P_2's punishment would be more harsh than some other (apparently) goodwilled agency *(viz., P_1)* deems permissible. For a discussion of the prudential constraints on the enforcement of idiosyncratic judgments (goodwilled or not) see, Nozick, pp. 13-15; Friedman, pp. 157-58 and 173-78; and Murray Rothbard, *For a New Liberty* (New York: Macmillan, 1973), pp. 227-34. As Nozick notes (142), if people prefer peace to the (struggle for the) enforcement of their idiosyncratic views, they will patronize protection agencies which arrange not to do battle. Peace does not require the state.

13. Such agreements need not result in everyone being subject to the same

rules. Recall the relevantly similar case of the agreement between P_2 and P_3 with respect to procedures C and D.

14. While I have denied the existence of procedural rights in a state of nature by claiming that in the state of nature a person has rights against only those actions which violate his Lockean rights (hence, his rights are not essentially procedural but, rather, substantive), Nozick affirms the existence of procedural rights in the state of nature by holding that "many procedural rights stem not from the rights of the person acted upon, but rather from moral considerations about the person or persons doing the acting" (107). However, even if Nozick's argument for procedural rights was acceptable, it would not establish rights to *particular* procedures. And the argument itself dangerously relies on the moral consideration that persons should not employ unreliable procedures. The reason that this is dangerous for Nozick's purposes is that, if anything like the principle of compensation is accepted, then it seems that this moral consideration itself stems from the substantive state-of-nature right of persons not to have risks imposed upon them. That is, this consideration may reflect only "the rights of the person acted upon." Whether there remains some independent moral consideration capable of sustaining state-of-nature procedural rights depends upon in what sense (if any) something impermissible is done if unreliable procedures are used in reaching the conclusion that some individual is guilty when, in fact, he is guilty. See Nozick, pp. 101-8. Of course, to deny the existence of state-of-nature procedural rights (of the sort that do not stem from the state-of-nature rights of the persons acted upon) is not to deny that by means of certain procedures persons may acquire various rights (entitlements) to goods or services.

15. State-of-nature principles place moral constraints on negotiations. No legitimate party can "offer," in return for concessions from a second party, to respect the second party's rights. For this respect is not something which the first party may legitimately withhold. Such an "offer" would itself constitute a rights-violating threat.

16. Nozick's claims that what is distinctive about protection agencies (such that something like this empirical historical thesis is true of them) is that they (properly) use force in situations of conflict, and hence an agency is "not merely in competition with other agencies" (182). But we have emphasized the size of the realm within which protection agencies are proscribed from using force against other agencies. Within this significant realm, they are merely in competition with one another. In support of Nozick's (and the individualist anarchist's) rejection of the concentration thesis see, e.g., Gabriel Kolko, *The Triumph of*

Conservatism (Chicago: Quadrangle Books, 1967); Murray Rothbard, *Man, Economy, and State* (Los Angeles: Nash, 1970), Chapter 10, "Monopoly and Competition"; D. T. Armentano, *The Myths of Antitrust* (New Rochelle, New York: Arlington House, 1972); and Yale Brozen, ed., *The Competitive Economy,* (Morristown, New Jersey: General Learning Press, 1975).

4

ANARCHISM AND WORLD ORDER

RICHARD A. FALK

Mere anarchy is loosed upon the world.
—W. B. Yeats, "The Second Coming"

We do not fear anarchy, we invoke it.
Mikhail Bakunin, *The Program of the International Brotherhood*

I. AN INTRODUCTORY PERSPECTIVE

Anarchism has largely directed its thought and actions against the sovereign state, seeking primarily to bring about the radical reconstruction of economic, political, and social life within individual domestic arenas. In addition, however, like any radical movement that challenges fundamental organizing norms and structures, anarchism has wider implications. These wider implications extend the critique of the state as domestic institutional nexus to a critique of statism or the state system as a global framework for political organization. Nevertheless, surprisingly little attention has been given to anarchism as a perspective relevant to global reform.[1] This neglect is somewhat surprising because anarchists generally appreciate the extent to which their goals can be realized only by the transformation of the world scene as a whole.

This lack of attention can, however, be explained by several factors. First, it reflects the previously noted domestic focus of anarchism—indeed, of all modern revolutionary theory. Second, it probably reflects the popular association of anarchy with disorder, while by almost everyone's definition disorder is precisely the opposite of the primary desideratum of global reform, namely, a quantum leap in the capacities to maintain order. Even an antistatist, progressive thinker such as Doris Lessing seems to associate anarchist potentialities of our present civilization, and the declining capacities of governments to sustain elementary order and reliability even within national boundaries, with still further disintegration.[2] This identification of anarchism with disarray is juxtaposed against a generally accepted conviction that global reform will entail the globalization of governmental structures rather than the destructuring of national governments. The League of Nations and the United Nations are generally viewed as positive experiments to the extent that they have constituted tentative steps toward world government, as failures because they have represented too little by way of bureaucratic centralism.[3] Alternatively, an anarchist might hold that the League and the United Nations present suitable pretexts for partially dismantling bureaucratic structures at the state level *without* building up a superstate to compensate at the global level. In other words, it is the weakness of global institutions as bureaucratic presence that would appeal to anarchists. (Of course, in actuality, these global institutions, in both their mode of creation and their mode of operations, have proven to be elitist in the extreme and therefore antithetical to the anarchist ethos.) [4]

Third, there is a lingering tendency, given plausibility by the pervasiveness of nongovernmental terror in contemporary life, to dismiss anarchism on moral grounds as a more or less explicit avowal of terrorism, and on political grounds as an absurdly romantic gesture of nihilistic sentiment whose only consequence is to strengthen the case for governmental repression. The belief that anarchists glorify terror has historical roots in the nineteenth century, especially in Russia, and was given widespread currency in Dostoevski's great novel *The Devils* which re-created in fictional form the actual nihilism of Nechayev, an extremist follower of Bakunin.

Jean-Paul Sartre has for this reason, until very recently, avoided acknowledging his own anarchist affinity: "then, by way of philosophy, I discovered the anarchist being in me. But when I discovered it I did not call it that, because today's anarchy no longer has anything to do with the anarchy of 1890." [5]

True, one form of individual resistance to state power is the use of random violence by self-styled anarchist revolutionaries for the avowed purpose of exposing the vulnerability of individuals or of the community as a whole. It is no accident when antibureaucratic radicals identify with anarchism as a means of registering their dissent from the prevailing forms of state socialism; typical in this regard was the unfurling of black flags from Sorbonne buildings liberated during the student uprisings of May 1968.[6] However, terrorism bears no inherent relationship to anarchist thinking; many pacifists, including Tolstoy, Gandhi, and Paul Goodman, have been associated with anarchist traditions of thought.[7]

Conversely, the mere adoption of terrorist tactics does not necessarily imply a disavowal of statist goals, as witness the manifold examples of terrorism by contemporary "liberation groups." The Palestinian Liberation Organization, consumed by statist objectives, has embraced indiscriminate terror for apparently expediential reasons: to get a hearing for its grievances, and to give its claims a potency allegedly unattainable through less extreme forms of persuasion or even through conventional warfare. Terrorism is a desperate strategy of a powerless (or unimaginative) claimant, but it is not a necessary component of the anarchist perspective.[8]

In this essay I regard the anarchist position as characterized mainly by its opposition to bureaucratic centralism of all forms and by its advocacy of libertarian socialism. This attempt to delineate the anarchist position is less drastic than the dictionary definition of anarchism as entailing the absence of government. My understanding of anarchist thought, admittedly a personal interpretation, suggests that the basic anarchist impulse is toward something positive, namely, toward a minimalist governing structure in a setting that encourages the full realization of human potentialities for cooperation and happiness. As such, the quest is for humane

government, with a corresponding rejection of large-scale impersonal institutions that accord priority to efficiency and rely upon
force and intimidation rather than upon voluntary patterns of
cooperation to sustain order. This quest puts the anarchist into a
posture of opposition to the modern state, especially the most
successful and powerful states, but it is only the most extreme
examples of anarchist thought that devote their main energy to
negation rather than to their affirmative case for radical reform on
all levels of social, economic, and political organization.

On this basis, I believe that the anarchist tradition has something
important to contribute to the emergent dialogue on the tactics and
shape of global reform. This contribution must be predicated on a
response to each of the three issues just considered. In effect, (1) an
anarchist concept of global reform needs to be fully worked out; (2)
anarchist ideas on "security" and "organization" must be set forth;
(3) anarchist thinking on the relevance of violence must be clarified
in relation to its practical and moral consequences. This paper seeks
to take tentative constructive steps in these directions, after first
considering two additional preliminary issues:

· What kind of "a vision" do anarchists propose for the future?
· Why is anarchism an attractive antidote (or complement) to
mainstream thinking on global reform?

In a perceptive essay on the full sweep of anarchist thought,
Irving Louis Horowitz observed that "it scarcely requires any feats
of mind to show that modern industrial life is incompatible with the
anarchist demand for the liquidation of State authority. Anarchism
can be no more than a posture. It cannot be a viable political
position." [9] The validity of such an assertion depends on what is
meant by "modern industrial life" and by "the anarchist demand
for the liquidation of State authority." For example, representatives
from many and diverse disciplines now contend, independent of any
concern with statist organization, that the modern industrial ethos
as we have known it is not sustainable on ecological grounds.[10] The
revival of interest in "benign" or "gentle" technology, and of lifestyles outside the money economy, provide further evidence that the
momentum of industrial civilization may possibly be reversible.[11]

Indeed, one could reverse Horowitz's assertion and contend that
any political perspective that does not propose doing away with
modern industrial life is doomed to failure and futility, and is an

exercise in bad faith. Furthermore, the anarchist demand is not directed at eliminating all forms of authority in human existence, but at their destructive embodiment in exploitative institutions associated with the modern bureaucratic state. Contrary to general impressions, nothing in anarchist thought precludes a minimum institutional presence at all levels of social organization, provided only that this presence emanates from *populist* rather than *elitist* impulses, and that its structure is deliberately designed fully to protect the liberty of all participants, starting with and centering on the individual. Indeed Bakunin, with his admiration of American federalism of the nineteenth century [12] and his tentative advocacy of a universal confederation of peoples, lent anarchist support to the globalist approach to world order challenges. As Bakunin put it in 1866: "it is absolutely necessary for any country wishing to join the free federations of peoples to replace its centralized, bureaucratic, and military organizations by a federalist organization based on the absolute liberty and autonomy of regions, provinces, communes, associations, and individuals." [13] In essence, the anarchist proposes dismantling the bureaucratic state and reconstituting a world society from the bottom up (what Bakunin calls a "universal world federation" and "directed from the bottom up, from the circumference to the center"), with constant accountability to the bottom. Paul Goodman has expressed in a modern idiom this anarchist view of creative reordering: "My own bias is to decentralize and localize wherever it is feasible, because this makes for alternatives and more vivid and intimate life. . . . On this basis of weakening of the Powers, and of the substitution of function for power, it would be possible also to organize the world community, as by the functional agencies of the United Nations, UNICEF, WHO, somewhat UNESCO; and to provide *ad hoc* cooperation like the Geo-physical Year, exploring space, or feeding the Chinese." [14] Furthermore, anarchist thinking has a notable antiterritorial bias which tends to deride national frontiers as artificial and dangerously inconsistent with the wholeness of its humanist affirmations.[15]

But reverting to Horowitz's characterization once again, doesn't such an anarchist approach to global reform lie far beyond the horizon of attainability? And hence, how can anarchism reasonably be regarded as a viable possibility that could materialize in our lifetimes? One could answer these questions in several ways. To quote Bakunin once more, as he is discounting the failures of the revolutionary uprisings of 1848 in Europe, "Must we . . . doubt the future itself, and the present strength of socialism? Christianity, which had set as its goal the creation of the kingdom of justice in heaven, needed several centuries to triumph in Europe. Is there any cause for surprise if socialism, which has set for itself a more difficult problem, that of creating the kingdom of justice on earth, has not triumphed in a few years?" [16] In this view, the anarchist position is no less coherent or relevant merely because its prospects of realization are not proximate. Bureaucratic socialists, those who seek to seize state power rather than to decompose it, contemptuously dismiss anarchist or libertarian socialists as utopians, or worse, as reactionaries.[17] But the anarchist response is more credible than the challenge here presented. The anarchist quite properly contends that merely to seize power is to default upon the humanist content of socialism and to create a new form of despotism. The real revolution cannot be rushed, but neither can it be dispensed with. I think, in this regard, that Herbert Read is wrong when he says of anarchism that ". . . if the conception of society which it thus arrives at seems utopian and even chimerical, it does not matter, for what is established by right reasoning cannot be surrendered to expediency." [18] I think it does matter, and anarchists generally act as if it matters, both by their arguments about the cooperative capacities of human society (which, incidentally, Read strongly endorses) and by their belief in the revolutionary possibility lying dormant within mass consciousness. Of course, Read correctly stresses the principled character of anarchist thinking, its unwillingness to corrupt its values merely for the sake of power. This high-mindedness distinguishes anarchism from bureaucratic socialism in theory and vindicates its ethical purism in practice. The contrast seems particularly great in view of the consistent betrayal of socialist ideals at each new opportunity—not only in the Soviet Union but even in China and Cuba.[19] In this regard, the anarchist refuses both the facile radicalism of the conventional Marxist (who would merely replace one form of exploitation and repression with another) and the facile gradualism of the liberal (who would acquiesce in the structure of exploitation and repression, provided its cruelest manifestations can be gradually diminished).

A further anarchist response to the counsel of patience claims that the revolutionary possibility is hidden from view in the evolving currents of popular consciousness. According to Bakunin, revolutions "make themselves; they are produced by the force of circumstance, the movement of facts and events. They receive a long preparation of the masses, then they burst forth, often seemingly triggered by trivial causes." [20] Thus, the revolutionary moment may be closer than we think; it may be building toward eruption; and it may enter the field of history with unexpected haste and fury. The Paris Commune of 1871 is a favorite illustration of this possibility.[21] A time of crisis enhances revolutionary prospects; it creates receptivity to new ideas, however radical; it exposes existing injustice; and it generates a willingness to take risks. Naturally, however, there is no available calculus for determining the most propitious moment for actually instituting an anarchist program of destructuring the state and replacing international statism with global confederation.

Finally, the anarchist is not obliged to wait for the days of triumph. Although his concept of the future is visionary and vital to his position, it is not detached in time from present possibilities for actualization.[22] As Howard Zinn writes, "The anarchist sees revolutionary change as something immediate, something we must do now, where we are, where we live, where we work. It means starting this moment to do away with authoritarian, cruel relationships—between men and women, between children and parents, between one kind of worker and another kind. Such revolutionary action cannot be crushed like an armed uprising." [23] Paul Goodman vividly makes the same point through his characterization of a well-known peace activist: "Best of all, in principle, is the policy that Dave Dellinger espouses and tries to live by, to live communally and without authority, to work usefully and feel friendly, and so positively to replace an area of power with peaceful functioning." [24] By conducting his life in this way, the anarchist can initiate a process of change that is virtually invulnerable to external pressures, criticisms, and threats. The anarchist posture is thus deepened through experience and engenders credibility for the seriousness of its claims about the future. Unlike the utopian who tends to dichotomize present and future, regarding one mode as suitable given present practicalities and another as desirable given future wishes, the anarchist integrates his present behavior with his future hopes. The anarchist correctly perceives that the future is the eventual culmination of the present and that liberty is an existential condition enabling degrees of immediate realization.

The anarchist thus joins immediate action with his program for drastic societal reform. Herbert Read expresses this dual commitment as follows: "Our practical activity may be a gradual approximation towards the ideal, or it may be a sudden revolutionary realization of that ideal, but it must never be a compromise." [25]

Of course, despite this attempt at refutation, there is still a measure of common sense in Horowitz's observation. Surely, anarchism may serve as no more than a posture, and its immediate impact may consist primarily in leavening the more deeply rooted political traditions of Marxism and liberalism. However, even in this ancillary capacity, anarchism can perform the highly positive function of providing a corrective for the bureaucratic and repressive tendencies of Marxist politics, and for the apologetics and rationalizations of liberal politics.[26] Therefore, I would argue that anarchist thought, correctly understood, is both a position *and* a posture.

Let us consider now our second preliminary question: Why is anarchism an attractive antidote (or complement) to mainstream thinking on global reform? Most proposals for global reform have uncritically affirmed the ordering contributions of the state to domestic life and have, in one or another form, sought to make those contributions available to the world as a whole. Indeed, the argument for global reform, at least since World War I, has assumed the strident tones of necessity. Since Hiroshima these claims of necessity have been pitched on an apocalyptic level and have been extended to embrace biosocial survival in light of the allegedly deepening ecological crisis—the crowding, poisoning, and straining of planetary facilities. The unexamined premise in world-order thinking has been that *only* governmental solutions can organize planetary life, that only existing governmental structures and their leaders can command the authority required for this essential undertaking, and that only argument and persuasion can release the political energy needed to overcome the inertia that sustains the state system in the face of the most unmistakable writing on the wall. A major variant to this line of reformist thinking is that persuasion must be supplemented by tragedy before enough political energy is released to achieve a world-order solution.

Generally, such advocacy of bureaucratic centralism is coupled with confidence in the moderating capacities of law and institutionalism. The ideal world order would still consist of a realm of states, but with the venom drawn by substituting "law" for "force." Conflict would remain, but war would disappear. Peaceful methods of resolving conflicts would be accepted since all states would be unanimously committed to upholding the federalist edifice.

This kind of mainstream "idealism" often coexists with "realism." Until the existing world system is reconstructed according to the principles of legalist architecture, one is thrown back into the state system with its logic of power and its reliance on force to achieve "security" and to "manage" change. The world-order idealist of tomorrow can easily justify being Machiavellian today. Hence, the issue of "transition" emerges as critical, and it is a fascinating indictment of mainstream thinking that no sustained attention has been given to the central challenge of transition—namely, access to, and transformation of, state power.

The anarchist comes forward with a quite different set of ideas, easily adapted to the world-order debate: first of all, a skeptical regard for the state and an unwillingness to accept it as "a model" for achieving a just order on any level of social organization; second, a positive belief in the capacities of various other collectivities—communes, cities, provinces, regions, associations—to provide the creative impetus for reorganizing the human enterprise; third, a bias toward decentralization of wisdom, authority, and capability, coupled with an insistence upon the autonomy of smaller units and the absolute status of individual liberty; fourth, a structural critique of the present organization of power, wealth, and prestige coupled with a revolutionary set of demands that existing leaders of society would never voluntarily meet; fifth, a processive view of the future, based on embodying the vision of a new order in immediate personal and political activities; sixth, a substitution of "justice" for "order" as the primary test of the adequacy of a given arrangement of power in world society; seventh, a refusal to blueprint the future in a manner that precludes creativity within the eventual setting that will give rise to the revolutionary possibility itself.[27]

These seven elements of anarchist thinking can be positively adapted to movement for global reform. What is most impressive about anarchist thought, taken from a world-order perspective, is its blending of critique, vision, and transition strategy. In the words of George Woodstock, a close student of anarchism:

> Historically, anarchism is a doctrine which poses a criticism of existing society; a view of a desirable future society; and a means of passing from one to the other.[28]

Often, proposals for global reform have been sterile because they lacked one or more of these three essential elements (most typically, the transition strategy), or else presented one of them in unacceptable form (e.g., the vision as a blueprint). Despite this general attractiveness of anarchism as a world order perspective, the anarchist position also poses several difficulties that must be considered in the course of evaluating its possible relevance to a beneficial movement of global reform.[29]

II. THREE HARD QUESTIONS FOR ANARCHISTS

1. *Are not the preconditions for anarchist success insurmountable?* The great anarchist success stories have been episodic, short-lived (e.g., the Paris Commune of 1871, the anarchist collectives in parts of Spain during the 1930s, the May uprising in Paris in 1968). Nowhere have anarchists enjoyed a period of sustained success. Generally, anarchist success has generated an overpowering reaction of repression, as when the mercenary soldiery of Versailles crushed and massacred the Paris Communards in May 1871 only weeks after their extraordinary triumph. Anarchists view such failures as inevitable "first attempts"; Kropotkin calls "the Commune of Paris, the child of a period of transition . . . doomed to perish" but "the forerunner of social revolution."[30] Murry Bookchin and Daniel Guérin make a similar assessment of the Paris uprising of 1968, regarding its occurrence as proof of the anarchist critique, its collapse as evidence that "the molecular movement below that prepares the condition for revolution" had not yet carried far enough.[31]

On a deeper level, anarchists understand that the prerequisite for anarchist success *anywhere* is its success *everywhere*. It is this vital precondition that is at once so convincing and so formidable as to call into question whether the anarchist position can in fact be taken seriously as a progressive alternative to state socialism.

Bakunin expressed the anarchist demand and rationale with clarity: "A federalist in the internal affairs of the country, he desires an international confederation, first of all in the spirit of justice, and second because he is convinced that the economic and social revolution, transcending all the artificial and pernicious barriers between states, can only be brought about, in part at least, by the solidarity in action, if not of all, then at least of the majority of the nations constituting the civilized world today, so that sooner or later all nations must join together." [32] Or, as Daniel Guérin expressed it: "An isolated national revolution cannot succeed. The social revolution inevitably becomes a world revolution." [33]

In essence, not only is it difficult for anarchists to attain power, but once they manage to do so their "organic institutions" seem incapable of holding it. Their movements will be liquidated ruthlessly by statists of "the left" or "the right." [34] Given such vulnerability, it may even be a betrayal of one's followers to expose them to slaughter by mounting a challenge against the entrenched forces of statism in the absence of either the will or the capabilities to protect the challengers.[35]

There is a report of a fascinating conversation between Lenin and Kropotkin in May 1919 in which Lenin mounts such an argument in two ways. First, he makes his familiar point that "You can't make a revolution wearing white gloves. We know perfectly well that we have made and will make a great many mistakes. . . . But it is impossible not to make mistakes during a revolution. Not to make them means to renounce life entirely and do nothing at all. But we have preferred to make errors and thus to act. . . . We want to act and we will, despite all the mistakes, and will bring our socialist revolution to the final and inevitably victorious end." [36] Lenin here in effect acknowledges the errors that flow from using state power to secure the revolutionary victory from external and internal enemies, and he rebuffs the anarchist view that state power can be dissolved. Lenin's second rebuff of the anarchist position is his condescending view of its revolutionary power: "Do you really think that the capitalist world will submit to the path of the cooperative movement? . . . You will pardon me, but this is all nonsense! We need direct action of the masses, revolutionary action of the masses, that activity which seizes the capitalist world by the throat and brings it down." [37] Of anarchist concepts of "social revolution," Lenin says "these are children's playthings, idle chatter, having no realist soil underneath, no force, no means, and almost nothing approaching our socialist goals. . . . We don't need the struggle and violent acts of separate persons. It is high time that the anarchists understood this and stopped scattering their revolutionary energy on utterly useless affairs." [38] In sum, Lenin is arguing that the ends of anarchists must be pursued by mass violent revolution and secured through state power. The anarchist response is, of course, that the choice of such means perverts and dooms the ends. The antagonism of anarchists toward the Bolshevik Revolution has been vindicated many times over.[39] On the level of their discussion, it seems that both Lenin and Kropotkin are correct,[40]—Lenin in saying that there is no other way to succeed, the anarchists by contending that such success is as bad as, if not worse than, defeat.

But, in my view, the strongest case for the feasibility of the anarchist position still remains to be argued. It is implicit, perhaps, in Kropotkin's own work on the origins of the modern state and on its feudal antecedents in the European cities of the eleventh and twelfth centuries.[41] Kropotkin's argument rests on the historical claim that a vital society of communes and free cities created by brotherhoods, guilds, and individual initiative existed earlier: ". . . it is shown by an immense documentation from many sources, that never, either before or since, has mankind known a period of relative well-being for all as in the cities of the Middle Ages. The poverty, insecurity, and physical exploitation of labor that exist in our times were then unknown." [42] Drawing on non-Western experience as well, Kropotkin argues in effect that societal well-being and security based on anarchist conceptions of organic institutions (of a cooperative character) were immensely successful over a wide geographical and cultural expanse until crushed by the emergent states of the fifteenth and sixteenth centuries. Thus, there is a kind of *prima facie* case for plausibility of the anarchist model, although in a prestatal context.

But evidence of the anarchist potential for "success" does not end with medieval Europe. The direction of contemporary China, especially its antiparty, populist phase that culminated in the

Cultural Revolution, contains strong anarchist elements.[43] Indeed, it was precisely on these grounds of repudiating "organization" and "bureaucracy" as a basis for communist discipline that China made itself so offensive to communist ideologues in the Kremlin.[44] China is, of course, a mixed case. In its foreign policy it places great stress on statist prerogatives. Nevertheless, in its domestic patterns the Chinese example lends some credibility to Bakunin's and Kropotkin's claim that there are nonbureaucratic roads to socialism, and gives the anarchist orientation renewed plausibility as a serious political alternative.[45]

Such plausibility can, it seems to me, be extrapolated in a poststatal context. Here, my argument, sustained by sources as dissimilar as Saul Mendlovitz and Henry Kissinger, is that we are undergoing a profound historical transformation that is destroying the organizational matrix of a global system based on territorial states.[46] That is, we are entering a poststatal period, although its character remains highly conjectural. Whatever the outcome, however, the anarchist stress on nonterritorial associations and communal consciousness seems highly relevant because of its basic compatibility with the inevitable shift in the relation of forces.

In sum, the anarchist case for radical reform (i.e., for social revolution) was *chimerical within* the confines of the state system. However, the state system is now being superseded. In this context, one set of plausible possibilities is the globalization of societal life in a way that allows cooperative organizational forms to flourish. That is, the anarchist vision (as epitomized in Bakunin's writings) of a fusion between a universal confederation and organic societal forms of a communal character lies at the very center of the *only* hopeful prospect for the future of world order.[47] Needless to say, such a prospect has slim chances for success, but at least the possibility is no longer chimerical, given the change of objective circumstances. The state system is not an implacable foe, for many economic, political, technological, and sociological forces are everywhere undermining its bases of potency, if unevenly and at an uncertain rate. Therefore, although the political precondition of scale imposed by anarchism still remains formidable, it may yet prove historically surmountable. It may be surmountable because the preparatory processes going on throughout the world during this historical period are creating more favorable global conditions for the anarchist cause than have hitherto existed for several centuries. This assessment arises from several distinct developments. Perhaps the most significant is the growing disenchantment with the values, goals, and methods of industrial society. This sense of disenchantment is coming to be shared by increasing numbers of citizens, particularly in the developed nations of the West, and is finding various forms of expression that reflect revised notions of necessity based on "limits to growth," notions of well-being based on intermediate technology and small-scale institutions, and notions of personal transcendence based on a new spiritual energy that repudiates both conventional religion and secular humanism. In this setting, the quest for an appropriate politics coverges rather dramatically with the central tenets of anarchist belief. This modern sensibility realizes, at last, that the state is simultaneously *too large* to satisfy human needs and *too small* to cope with the requirements of guidance for an increasingly interdependent planet. This realization is temporarily offset by a rising tide of statism in many other parts of the world, where political independence is a forbidden fruit only recently tasted, but where the fruit will be poisoned, as everywhere else, by a world of nuclear weapons, ecological decay, and mass economic privation. The main *problematique* of our age is whether an appropriate politics of global reform, combining a centralized form of functional guidance with decentralized economic, social, and political structures, can be shaped by voluntary action, or whether it must be formed in a crucible of tragedy and catastrophe. Attentiveness to the anarchist tradition can be one part of an effort to achieve an appropriate politics *this* side of catastrophe. Obviously, the objective conditions which require such a reassessment of political forms are not by themselves sufficient to effect a transformation. Indeed, the very relevance of these ideas may lead their powerful opponents to regard them as even more dangerous now than in the past. Prudence and patience are essential in these circumstances. The crisis of the state system may yet require several decades to develop to the point where eruptions of spontaneous anarchistic energies would not unleash a variety of devastating backlashes.

2. *Given the urgency of global reform, isn't the anarchist prospect too remote in time?* Even accepting the optimistic assessment of the preceding section, namely, that the hour of anarchism may coincide with the

collapse of statism, restructuring of the world system would still appear to be developed for an unnecessarily and dangerously long period of several decades or more. Just as the emergence of the state system was a matter of centuries, so might the consolidation of a new system of political order require hundreds of years.[48] Two sets of questions call for judgment based on imponderables. First, how serious and pressing is the crisis? Is the fire close at hand, or still barely visible on a distant horizon? How can we know? Second, are any alternative means available through which the principal goals of global reform could be attained more reliably and rapidly than through anarchism? Do we have any responsible basis for selecting or rejecting these alternatives? In part, we are forced here to confront the most fundamental issues of politics, knowledge, and action. In the abstract, we do not know enough to choose or to act. Of course this same limitation bears on every school of political thought, including those that defend the status quo or incline toward gradualism. But it has even greater bearing on a political position that proposes radical tactics and goals, especially if large-scale violence is likely to ensue. On the other hand, this line of reasoning may be deceptive. In a moment of crisis, to do nothing may be the most risky of all postures toward the future. It is generally better to jump from a sinking ship than it is to stay on board, even if one knows nothing about the prospects of rescue from the waters below. The collective situation of human society cannot be cast in such deceptive simplicity. The veil of ignorance is thick indeed when it comes to assessing policy alternatives for the future of world society.

But the argument from ignorance cuts the other way as well. We have no real way to assess the degrees of progress along the transition path. Perhaps the collapse of statism is closer than we think. As Paul Goodman wrote:

> It will be said that there is no time. Yes, probably. But let me cite a remark of Tocqueville. In his last work, *L'Ancien Régime,* he notes "with terror," as he says, how throughout the eighteenth century writer after writer and expert after expert pointed out that this and that detail of the Old Regime was unviable and could not possibly survive; added up, they proved that the entire Old Regime was doomed and must soon

collapse; and yet *there was not a single man who foretold that there would be a mighty revolution.*[49]

In the face of such uncertainty, compounded by the many evidences of pressure on the state system, it makes political as well as moral sense to pursue a *principled set of conclusions* even if their realization cannot be immediately foreseen. In one sense Herbert Read is correct in saying that "the task of the anarchist philosopher is not to prove the imminence of a Golden Age, but to justify the value of believing in its possibility."[50]

Such a value depends on some degree of plausibility, but also on whether or not there are any preferable alternatives. Given the established bankruptcy of statist solutions on the right and left, given the vulnerability of the state system as a whole to catastrophic and, quite possibly, irreversible damage, and given the insufficiency of gradualist strategies of amelioration, the case for some variant of radical anarchism seems strong despite the inability of the anarchist to provide skeptics with a credible timetable.

In essence, the issue of urgency reinforces the anarchist case. The primary world order need is to find an alternative to statism. Anarchism, despite its limited political success during the statist era, provides the most coherent, widespread, and persistent tradition of antistatist thought. It is also a tradition that has generally been inclined toward world-order values: peace, economic equity, civil liberties, ecological defense. As such, it represents the most normatively acceptable sequel to the state system. Other sequels include imperial consolidation; world state; regional federation; intergovernmental functionalism.[51]

To affirm the relevance of the anarchist tradition is not to accept the adequacy of its current formulations but only of its general orientation. Advocates of an anarchist approach need to formulate the globalist implications of anarchism in a manner responsive to the current world-order crisis. As far as I know, this has not yet been done. Indeed, anarchism suffers from the tendency of other traditions of philosophical speculation generated during the statist era, namely, to concentrate upon the national question and to assume that the global question will disappear when all nations have correctly resolved their own domestic problems. As I have suggested, anarchists are more dependent than other reformers on supportive transnational developments; but their analysis of international events is usually identical to that of Marxists, on the level of critique, and highly impressionistic when it comes to making specific proposals. Thus, the claims of anarchism are not weakened by the urgency of the world crisis, but the need for a more historically sensitive interpretation and for a globally oriented formulation of anarchist response is essential.

3. *Does the receptivity of anarchism to violence undermine the moral basis of its claim to provide an ideology for global reform?* I am not discussing here the anarchist as "bomb-thrower," but neither do I identify anarchism with pacifist ethics. As a philosophical position anarchism adopts an equivocal view of violence as an agent of change. Although anarchists tend to rely on spontaneous militancy of a nonviolent character—most typically, the general strike or other forms of unarmed struggle and resistance—there is no prevailing anarchist view on the role of violence.

I think Howard Zinn has sympathetically, but reliably, presented the anarchist position on violence in this assessment:

> Some anarchists—like other revolutionaries throughout history ... have emphasized violent uprising. Some have advocated, and tried, assassination and terror.... What makes anarchists unique among revolutionaries, however, is that most of them see revolution as a cultural, ideological, creative process, in which violence would be as incidental as the outcries of mother and baby in childbirth. It might be unavoidable—given the natural resistance to change—but something to be kept at a minimum while more important things happen.[52]

The question is whether, given the technology of destruction and the ruthlessness of statist leadership, this view of violence is adequate. It can be attacked from either side, as underestimating the role of violence for any serious revolutionary position, or as too willing to accept the moral Trojan Horse of political violence.

Mainstream Marxists and neo-Marxists generally contend that revolution depends upon mass-based armed struggle. A recent formulation is "the political statement of the Weather Underground" released under the title *Prairie Fire:*

> It's an illusion that imperialism will decay peacefully. Imperialism has meant constant war. Imperialists defend their control

of the means of life with terrible force. There is no reason to believe they will become humane or relinquish power. . . . To not prepare the people for this struggle is to disarm them ideologically and physically and to perpetrate a cruel hoax.[53]

The cruel hoax is, of course, the illusion that revolution can occur without armed struggle, that a revolution can be made with white gloves. But as Kropotkin soon perceived, once the white gloves have been thrown away, it becomes all too easy to adopt terror and torture.[54] In my view, the abuse of state power by socialism has reversed the presumption that violence is a necessary concomitant of revolution. On the contrary, it now seems a cruel hoax to promise humane outcomes from any revolutionary process that embraces violence with anything other than the utmost reluctance. Any genuinely radical position that purports moral (as well as political) credibility must, above all else, reject a cult of violence, and justify the use of specific forms of violence in the most careful and conditional manner.

But what, then, of the revolutionary triumphs of China, Vietnam, and Cuba? Was not violence essential to their success, and did they not achieve a net gain by prevailing on the level of armed struggle? I would answer that first of all, in each of these domestic contexts there were no options other than extremist ones. Second, reliance on violent tactics may yet doom these revolutionary societies to Stalinist or other repressive patterns of governance. Third, the struggle for global reform should not be confused with the struggle for reform within an individual nation, although the two undertakings are closely related.

In other words, it is not enough to acknowledge that the imperialists are also violent, nor even that anarchists are prepared to accept violence only reluctantly and as incidental to their purposes. Something more considered, more explicit, is needed, even though specific choices cannot always be anticipated or determined in the abstract.

At the same time, an unequivocal renunciation of violence is probably "a cruel hoax," given the realities of power. There may be no way, in particular situations, to remain aloof from armed struggle without acquiescing, oneself, in violence of at least equal proportions.

If anarchism is to qualify as a morally suitable ideology for global reform, it requires a considered analysis of the role of violence, with emphasis on:

- Necessity of recourse, as an instrument of last resort (the futility of nonviolent militancy having already been demonstrated beyond reasonable doubt);
- Discrimination in application (with no intentional subjection of innocent people to foreseeable risks of harm);
- Limitation of the form and degree of application (absolute prohibition on torture and cruelty).

Such a middle position is no guarantee against revolutionary excess, but this doctrinal stance may at least exert some influence when it comes to choosing tactics, strategies, and policies. Also, it provides a defense against both Leninist and pacifist critiques. Finally, it acknowledges what has been so agonizingly confirmed in recent decades, namely, that revolutionaries must protect their own programs from their own propensities to embrace "evil."

Violence in the context of global reform is even more problematic. If national struggles are waged successfully in critical countries, then violence will not be necessary on a global level. On the other hand, if such struggles end inconclusively or are defeated, then no degree of global violence will help. Given both the preponderance of military power possessed by state institutions, and the objectives of global reform, it is possible to renounce violence for the exclusive purpose of reform but to retain militant nonviolence as a tactic. Indeed, in the years ahead it will be vital for the forces of global reform to confront statist institutions, in order that the latter be forced to expose their destructive patterns of behavior to a wider public.

III. SOME CONCLUSIONS

Several broad lines of conclusion emerge from the preceding discussion:

(1) There are no serious obstacles to the adoption of an anarchist perspective toward global reform; there are, to be sure, unacceptable variants of the anarchist position, but they do not invalidate

the main lines of anarchist thought as represented by Proudhon, Bakunin, and Kropotkin, and more recently exemplified by Guérin, Herbert Read, and Paul Goodman.

(2) Anarchism impressively links its goals for revolutionary change within national societies with a vision of a transformed global society; the linkage is integral and progressive in terms of world order values commonly affirmed; as a consequence, anarchism deals with entrenched power and avoids the political sterility associated with legalistic and moralistic blueprints of "a new world order," as well as the static images of the future characteristic of utopography.

(3) Anarchist thought is alive to the twin dangers of socialism and capitalism if pursued within the structure of statism; its espousal of populist strategies of change gains some historical credibility from its affinity with Mao Tse-tung's efforts to avoid the decay of revolutionary momentum in contemporary China.[55]

(4) Anarchist thought on organic institutions of cooperation is creatively freed from either territorial or statist constraints and draws inspiration from both prestatist (Kropotkin) and poststatist possibilities of moving dialectically toward decentralizing bureaucratic power while centralizing human function (Goodman); in this regard, images of global functionalism and political confederation of nations merge with the deconcentration of power and role of national governments; the state is understood to be both inhumanly large in its bureaucratic dimension, and inhumanly small in its territorial and exclusionary dimensions; this dualism implicit in anarchism is excellently adapted to the purposes of global reform.

(5) Anarchist thought, although often perceived as oscillating between extremes of terrorism and pacificism, is capable of evolving from within its framework of values an intermediate interpretation of violence. Such an interpretation would bias action in the direction of militant nonviolence, without depending on either the "white gloves" of utopians or the torture chambers of state socialists and cultist advocates of violence.

(6) As yet, there is no comprehensive and satisfactory formulation of an anarchist position on global reform, only fragments here and there; a well-integrated statement could help crystallize enthusiasm for global reform of a drastic, yet constructive kind in many parts of the world where the internal strains of an obsolescent and moribund

statism are being rapidly translated into repression, militarism, imperialism, and interventionary diplomacy; for weak states, even genuine national autonomy requires a radical program of global reform.

For those who view our era as one of transition between the state system and some globalist sequel, the anarchist perspective becomes increasingly relevant and attractive. Of course, it remains to be tested as an ideology for hope and action, as well as a basis for social, economic, and political reconstruction. Maoism, as embodied in the China of the 1960s and 1970s, is a peculiar mixture of statism and populism that should be generally, although not fully, encouraging. As Franz Schurmann notes: "... the very word 'Maoism' came to mean a kind of anarchist, ultraleft troublemaking-for-troublemaking's sake. And when the New Left began to clash with older communist parties, as in France, China was invoked as a new Marxist Rome sanctioning this path to revolution." [56]

NOTES

1. For one notable exception see Thomas G. Weiss, "The Tradition of Philosophic Anarchism and Future Directions in World Policy" (mimeographed); I have treated the anarchist briefly and analytically in *A Study of Future Worlds* (New York: Free Press, 1975), pp. 214-19.
2. "We believed we were living in a peculiarly anarchist community." Doris Lessing, *Memoirs of a Survivor* (New York: Knopf, 1975), p. 81.
3. See depiction of Franklin Roosevelt's vision of a new world order based on the primacy of the United Nations in Franz Schurmann, *The Logic of World Power* (New York: Pantheon, 1974), pp. 13-17, esp. 67-76.
4. Sir Herbert Read expresses the anarchist attitude toward order and efficiency in social relations as follows: "... anarchism implies a universal decentralization of authority, and a universal simplification of life. Inhuman entities like the modern city will disappear. But anarchism does not necessarily imply a reversion to handicraft and outdoor sanitation. There is no contradiction between anarchism and air transport, anarchism and the division of labour, anarchism and industrial efficiency." Sir Herbert Read, *Anarchy and Order* (Boston: Beacon, 1971), p. 134. In other words, anarchist images involve reconstituting order in the world rather than eliminating it.
5. "Sartre at Seventy: An Interview," *New York Review of Books,* August 7, 1975, pp. 10-17, at p. 14. Because anarchists are viewed as extremists there is a temptation to avoid the label. Consider, for instance, this

passage by E. M. Cioran: ". . . from the moment your actions and your thoughts serve a form of real or imagined city you are its idolators and its captives. The timidest employee and the wildest anarchist, if they take a different interest here, live as its function: they are both citizens internally though one prefers his slippers and the other his bomb." *A Short History of Decay* (New York: Viking, 1975), pp. 75-76.

6. See interpretation by French anarchist Daniel Guérin in *Anarchism: From Theory to Practice* (New York: Monthly Review Press, 1970), pp. 155-59.

7. For consideration of pacifist ethos in relation to an anarchist orientation see Karl Shapiro, "On the Revival of Anarchism," in Irving Louis Horowitz, ed., *The Anarchists* (New York: Dell, 1964), pp. 572-81; also Howard Zinn's Introductory essay in Read, note 4, pp. ix-xxii.

8. The PLO's adoption of terror as a tactic can also be condemned as a consequence of its failure to initiate a mass movement of nonviolent struggle. Such a movement would not necessarily succeed, but its failure is far from assured.

9. Introduction, Horowitz, ed., *The Anarchists,* pp. 15-64, at p. 26.

10. E.g., Barry Commoner, *The Closing Circle* (New York: Knopf, 1971); Edward Goldsmith and others, *Blueprint for Survival* (Boston: Houghton Mifflin, 1972); Donella Meadows and others, *The Limits to Growth* (Washington, D.C.: Potomac Associates, 1972); R. A. Falk, *This Endangered Planet: Prospects and Proposals for Human Survival* (New York: Random House), 1971.

11. Among those who have discerned and charted this new direction of human energy, perhaps Theodore Roszak is most notable. See *The Making of a Counter Culture* (New York: Anchor, 1969); *Where the Wasteland Ends* (New York: Anchor, 1973).

12. Sam Dolgoff, ed., *Bakunin on Anarchy* (New York: Knopf, 1972), p. 107: Bakunin characterized the American system as "the finest political organization that ever existed in history." [Hereafter cited as *Bakunin.*]

13. *Bakunin,* p. 98; see also p. 152.

14. Goodman, "The Ambiguities of Pacifist Politics," in Leonard I. Krimerman and Lewis Perry, eds., *Patterns of Anarchy* (New York: Anchor, 1966), pp. 125-36, at 127.

15. E.g., Bakunin's conceptions are based on federations of many different, overlapping units, including "regions, provinces, communes, associations, and individuals," p. 98.

16. *Bakunin,* pp. 121-22.

17. On dismissal see George Plekanov, "Anarchist Tactics: A Pageant of Futility, Obstruction, and Decadence?" in Krimerman and Perry, note 15, pp. 495-99; for an anarchist response to these kinds of allegations

see Guérin, *Anarchism,* pp. 41-69; Read, note 4, pp. 22-23 usefully distinguishes between positive and negative roles for utopian projections of the future.

18. Read, *Anarchy and Order,* p. 129.
19. In general see Nadezhda Mandelstam, *Hope Against Hope* (New York: Atheneum, 1970); also on repression at Kronstadt by Soviet government see Guérin, *Anarchism,* pp. 102-5; Alexander Berkman, "Kronstadt: The Final Act in Russian Anarchism," in Horowitz, *The Anarchists,* pp. 495-506.
20. *Bakunin,* p. 155.
21. See Kropotkin's essay "The Commune of Paris," in Martin A. Miller, ed., *Selected Writings on Anarchism and Revolution by P. A. Kropotkin* (Cambridge, Mass.: MIT Press, 1970), pp. 119-32 [hereafter cited as *Kropotkin*] for a comparable anarchist appreciation of the spontaneous character of the Paris risings of 1968 and their relationship to the experience of the Paris Commune a century earlier see Murray Bookchin, *Post-Scarcity Anarchism* (Berkeley, Calif.: Ramparts Press, 1971), pp. 249-70.
22. See Kropotkin's essay "Must We Occupy Ourselves with an Examination of the Ideal of a Future System?" in *Kropotkin,* pp. 47-116.
23. Howard Zinn, Introduction, Read, *Anarchy and Order,* p. xviii.
24. Goodman, "Ambiguities of Pacifist Politics," at p. 136.
25. Read, *Anarchy and Order,* p. 129.
26. Sartre ascribed a similar role to existentialism in relation to Marxism. Sartre, *Search for a Method,* tr. Hazel E. Barnes (New York: Vintage, 1968), pp. 3-34.
27. See Bookchin's discussion of spontaneous features of the Paris 1968 events, in Bookchin, *Post-Scarcity Anarchism,* pp. 250-52; Herbert Read, *Anarchy and Order,* p. 23, argues that blueprints of the future pervert the genuine utopian impulse to transcend present societal arrangements. Such blueprints are condemned as "an advance on the spontaneous sources of life itself. They presume to plan what can only germinate . . . such scientific utopias will certainly fail, for the sources of life when threatened are driven underground to emerge in some new wilderness."
28. George Woodstock, *Anarchism* (New York: World Publishing Co., 1962), p. 9.
29. By "beneficial" I mean a movement that realizes world-order values associated with peace, economic well-being, social and political justice, and ecological balance. For an elaboration of why these values have been preferred and of the interplay between them see Falk, *Future Worlds,* pp. 7-55.

30. *Kropotkin*, p. 127.
31. Bookchin, *Post-Scarcity Anarchism*, p. 258.
32. *Bukanin*, p. 118.
33. Guérin, *Anarchism*, p. 69.
34. See references in note 19; Woodstock, *Anarchism*, pp. 275-424.
35. Such allegations have been made with respect to Salvador Allende's efforts in the early 1970s to transform the societal base of Chile without dismantling the state apparatus with its strong links to the vested interests of the old order.
36. *Kropotkin*, p. 328.
37. *Kropotkin*, pp. 329-30.
38. *Kropotkin*, p. 330.
39. One of the earliest and most eloquent anarchist critics of the Soviet experience was Emma Goldmann. See her *My Disillusionment with Russia* (Garden City, New York: Doubleday, 1923).
40. Kropotkin's position can be extrapolated from his general anarchist writings; he did not state the anarchist case in his conversations with Lenin.
41. See Kropotkin's excellent essay, "The State: Its Historic Role," in *Kropotkin*, pp. 211-64.
42. *Kropotkin*, p. 231.
43. See perceptive discussion, in Schurmann, *Logic of World Power*, pp. 369-80.
44. Schurmann, *Logic of World Power*, p. 380.
45. For a skeptical interpretation of China's domestic experience see Donald Zagoria, "China by Daylight," *Dissent* (Spring 1975), pp. 135-47.
46. For opposing interpretations on the durability of the state and the state system see Saul H. Mendlovitz, Introduction, in Saul H. Mendlovitz, ed., *On the Creation of a Just World Order* (New York: Free Press, 1975), pp. vii-xvii, and Stanley Hoffmann, "Obstinate or Obsolete? The Fate of the Nation-State and the Case of Western Europe," *Daedalus* (Summer 1966), pp. 862-915.
47. A general interpretation can be found in Robert Heilbroner, *An Inquiry into the Human Prospect* (New York: Norton, 1974); see also Falk, *Future Worlds*, pp. 417-37; Richard A. Falk, "A New Paradigm for International Legal Studies: Prospects and Proposals," *Yale Law Journal* 84: 969-1021 (1975).
48. See Joseph R. Strayer, *On the Medieval Origins of the Modern State* (Princeton University Press, 1970).
49. Goodman, "Ambiguities of Pacifist Politics," p. 136; see also *Kropotkin*, pp. 121-24.

50. Read, *Anarchy and Order,* p. 14.
51. For consideration of world order option see Falk, *Future Worlds,* pp. 150-276; Falk, "A New Paradigm . . ." pp. 999-1017.
52. Zinn, Introduction, Read, *Anarchy and Order,* p. xvii.
53. *Prairie Fire,* Political Statement of the Weather Underground, 1974, p. 3.
54. See Kropotkin letter to Lenin date 21 December 1920, in *Kropotkin,* pp. 338-39.
55. See Schurmann, *Logic of World Power,* p. 369; generally, pp. 268-80.
56. Schurmann, *Logic of World Power,* p. 369.

AUTHORITY AND ANARCHISM

5

ANARCHISM AND AUTHORITY

RICHARD T. DE GEORGE

The various theories ranging from divine right to general will to social contract to consent are all attempts to formulate the reasoned ground justifying the acceptance of government and law. Each has its defects; some are still debated; and none forms the reason why ordinary citizens of a state accept or accede to the laws and government of that state. In default of finding sufficiently solid, rational, and articulated grounds, however, tradition tends to induce acceptance in the ordinary citizen—though not in the anarchist—of what has existed and has been accepted for a long time, despite the fact that what is so justified may be radically different from what was accepted and acceptable originally, or just a short while before.[1] The anarchist, by contrast, is a skeptic in the political arena. He insists on the complete justification for any political or legal system prior to accepting it.

I. THE ANARCHIST POSITION

Anarchism, a theory of society without a ruler, has come to refer to any theory about a society without a government; without a state; and hence without laws, courts, police, armies, politics, or bureaucracy. By extension it is often considered to be a theory about society without any established authority on any level, that is, not only without government, but also without established authority in business, industry, commerce, education, religion, and the family.[2] Some theories of anarchism are total in their views concerning the absence of established authority, ranging from the smallest units of society to the largest; others are more restrictive and piecemeal. Historically theories of anarchism range from the radical individualism of Max Stirner to the anarchist communism of Kropotkin, with the views of Proudhon, Bakunin, and the anarcho-syndicalists falling in between.[3] There is no single statement of anarchism to which all recognized or self-proclaimed anarchists would adhere, and they are more easily identifiable by what they are against than by what they are for. Yet despite their many differences, the skeleton of all these views is similar, though they are fleshed out differently. The basic argument underlying them all can be sketched as follows:

(1) Certain goods of man are absolute in the sense that they should be given up for no other kind of good. The chief of these is freedom. (Some anarchists conceive of freedom as moral autonomy; some also add justice as primary; still others emphasize the importance of maximizing human well-being, though this is not an absolute.) [4]

(2) Since freedom, justice, and maximized human well-being are incompatible with the state, government, and law, and in general with any form of organized authority, they should be done away with.

Though radically individualistic anarchists such as Max Stirner might stop here, constructive communitarian anarchists from Proudhon to Bakunin and Kropotkin argue that:

(3) Once the existing state and institutions are done away with, a new and better society will be possible and should be constructed.

In the remainder of this paper I shall examine the anarchist position outlined here, not to prove it wrong, though it has its defects, but rather to argue that it is not authority as such that the anarchist attacks, his words to the contrary notwithstanding. Rather he implicitly and rightly attacks authoritarianism, which anarchists have tended to equate with established authority.

II. THE ANARCHIST ATTACK ON THE STATUS QUO

The anarchist agrees with the traditional political theorist that if the state, government, and law can be justified, they must be justified in terms of promoting freedom, justice, or human well-being. But whereas the traditional political theorist starts out accepting the state, government, and law and sees his task as articulating their justification, the anarchist sees clearly existing injustices and restraints on freedom and denies that the present social order is the best possible under the circumstances. For he envisages something better, and he feels that the sources of many of the social evils are imbedded in the structure of the state, its laws, and its government, and that merely to tinker with them is insufficient.

The anarchist argues first that no satisfactory external [5] justification of the state, law, and government has ever been given (hence they have not been justified), and secondly that they cannot be justified and so are unjustifiable.

The first argument proceeds by challenging those who defend established authority to produce a valid external justification of the state, law, or government. The anarchist examines and shows the deficiencies of such theories as divine right, social contract, and consent, and confidently awaits any other suggested justificatory theory. He of course has a great deal of assistance in this task, and he willingly adopts the utilitarian critique of contract theories and the contract theorists' critique of utilitarianism. That no justification which is generally accepted by philosophers and political and legal theorists has been developed cannot be denied. It does not prove that there can be no such justification. But for the anarchist it does raise the question as to why people, who have no such explicit justification for doing so, submit to demands and commands of governments. Moreover, to the extent that various justifications have in the past been accepted for a time, only to be cast aside later as flawed, the anarchist is reinforced in his belief that all such attempts at justification are deliberate or unconscious ideological rationalizations of the status quo.

Convinced that no adequate justification for them has been given, the anarchist then uses either of two types of argument to show that the state, government, and law are unjustifiable. Each of the arguments depends on his definitions, though he claims that his definitions are appropriate to the facts of the case. In the first type he defines the state as the instrument of oppression of one class by another; he defines law as a tool used by the ruling class to protect itself and its property and to foster its aims; and he defines government, together with its army and police force, as the handmaiden of this ruling class and the means whereby it dominates the ruled and enforces its will.[6] Now if the state, law, and government are defined in this way, then it is of course impossible to justify them, since they have injustice built into them. Hence they are unjustifiable. The traditionalist's reply is that these definitions do not accurately capture existing institutions. Laws, he claims, are the means whereby justice is achieved; government is the servant of the people and the means whereby they achieve their joint projects; the state is the unity of a people in a certain territory, and it is through the state that they carry on intercourse with other large groupings of people. But the anarchist's counter, and one with which many nonanarchists would tend to agree, is that this view does not accurately describe the actual conditions in which men live, though it may state some ideal.

The division between the anarchist and the defender of the established order at this point is not one of theory but one of fact. Is more justice achieved by the existing laws than harm done through the protection of the interests of the affluent at the expense of the masses? Is more freedom developed by the existing state and government than would otherwise be the case, or do they in fact unduly restrict freedom? Is there more crime and violence in a society with police than there is or would be in one without? The anarchist here points to governmental abuse, to unjust imprisonment, to war between states, to police brutality, to domination of the poor by the rich, and so on. And he then claims that because of the evil they do, government, law, police, and other oppressive instruments of the state are unjustifiable.[7] There is no doubt that some of the facts to which anarchists point, if taken in isolation, would tend to support their claims. But the critics of anarchism assert that the anarchists are selective and do not weigh all the appropriate facts, that no society without law and some formal authority—for instance the Wild West in the United States—has had more justice, freedom, or well-being before law arrived than after, and that though claims are made for how a society without authority should or will work, these are only unsubstantiated claims with no data or experience to support them.

In the second type of argument, instead of defining the state as an instrument of oppression and so by its very nature unjust, some anarchists first define freedom (or autonomy) and then define authority in such a way as to make them incompatible. This for instance is the main line of attack used by Robert Paul Wolff [8] in his well-known book *In Defense of Anarchism*.[9] It is possible to refuse to accept these definitions as appropriate (because they do not apply to actual societies); but more importantly it is possible to deny the claims made by them. Thus Taylor denies the absolute status Wolff imputes to moral autonomy,[10] Perkins claims the two concepts are not only incompatible but that autonomy requires authority;[11] Martin argues that Wolff really describes the incompatibility of moral autonomy with moral obligation to obey laws or with the government's right through legislation to decree what is or is not moral.[12]

At best, therefore, what the anarchist actually proves is not that political and legal arrangements, no matter how described, cannot be justified, but that the state, law, and government as he describes them cannot be justified; and though he may show that moral autonomy and political obligation as he defines them are incompatible, he does not show that alternative defensible definitions are not valid. In fact, the development of his argument requires, as I shall show, that various forms of authority which come fairly close to what other political theorists mean by "state," "law," and "government," are justifiable under certain conditions.

The anarchist moves quickly and without much argument from the claimed unjustifiability of state, government, and law to the assertion that they should be done away with. It is not necessarily the case that whatever cannot be justified should be eliminated. But the anarchist argues that the existing structures are in large part the cause of injustice, restraint of freedom, and exploitation, and that they can be done away with because (he believes) there are viable alternatives. And surely it is not unreasonable to claim that the sources of injustice should be removed, providing this can be done without causing even more harm.

The means by which the state, government, and law should be

eliminated and the speed with which this should take place are matters not only of disagreement among anarchists, but they are areas of special theoretical weakness in anarchistic writings. The anarchists usually see the workers as the movers of change in opposition to the established order; but how these masses are to be motivated to do something about their situation is problematic. Education is one method, though a slow process, especially since the schools are controlled by those in the status quo. Anarchist communists fall back on a Marxian type of analysis, though their views are repudiated by Marxists just as they were repudiated by Marx and Engels.[13] And those who resort to terror and bombings have not only shown that such actions are usually counterproductive, but they also act in violation of the claimed freedom, autonomy, and valued well-being of others. Hence a more gradual approach, with the workers taking over control of their factories and businesses either through unions or on their own, and working from there to demolish the instruments of the state and government, is the most plausible alternative. In recent times anarchists such as Daniel Guérin emphasize workers' self-management on the Yugoslav model,[14] and Paul Goodman called for reform and change in education and in neighborhoods and civic groups which he thought could seize the initiative from government.[15]

III. THE ANARCHIST PROGRAM

Defending the final step of the skeletal argument by detailing how the new society is to function after the revolution is both a matter of dispute and in general another weakness of the anarchist position. The anarchist can hardly spell out what society after the revolution will be like if he maintains that those who live in the society must enjoy the freedom to do what they wish. The most he can do is rule out the existence of the state, law, and government as previously defined; affirm certain very general conditions which will prevail; and answer certain objections proposed by his critics.[16]

It is crucial to note that though the anarchist insists on extremely high standards of justification for the state, law, and government, he does not insist on such high standards for all forms of social organization. For he must leave open the possibility of justifying alternative modes of social organization if the third part of his argument is to stand.

The anarchist principle of freedom does not preclude but clearly allows social organizations, freely entered into. Since some of the things a person wishes to achieve cannot be attained on his own, he may join with others to achieve common ends. Individuals, therefore, will be free to establish the groups they need to achieve their goals. Groups will enjoy freedom comparable to that enjoyed by individuals and will suffer comparable restrictions. Just as individuals join groups to attain their ends, so groups may also affiliate or join with other groups to achieve the goals they cannot attain in isolation.

The syndicalists spoke of trade unions and organizations of labor managing the affairs of a people; Bakunin envisaged small groups organizing themselves and carrying on their affairs; the anarchist communists described the stateless society in which each would give according to his ability and receive according to his needs, fully aware that production and distribution would continue in such a society. Such present-day anarchists as Guérin do not seek a return to an earlier, simpler form of agriculture or industry. They seek a form of social communitarianism. But unlike the Marxist-Leninists for whom the withering away of the state is a far-off event, they deny the necessity of centralism in society, of statism, of the dictatorship of the proletariat or of the leadership and domination of a party—communist or other.[17]

Since these communitarian anarchists are obviously not opposed to social organization, they must accept the conditions necessary for the existence of any society. These include the moral norms common to all societies as well as the public conditions necessary for people to meet and act together. Furthermore they cannot consistently be opposed to those forms or structures of authority necessary for organization. But if authority is to operate in these groups and organizations, the anarchist insists on the principle of authority from below. This asserts that the only justifiable form of authority comes ultimately from below, not from above. The autonomy of each individual and of each lower group should be respected by each higher group. The higher groups are formed to achieve the will of the lower groups and remain responsible to them and responsive to their will. In general, anything which can be done by the lower groups is to be done by them and not taken over by the higher groups. The function of higher groups is simply to achieve those ends which the lower groups desire but cannot achieve on their own.

Neither the existence of groups or organizations nor the principle of authority from below either justifies or necessitates present forms of state, government, and law. The anarchist correctly maintains they can be eliminated from society. A model of society without them is neither unthinkable nor inconsistent. But just as the overthrow of the state, law, and government does not preclude organizations or associations, neither does it preclude rules or leaders of a certain type. To the extent that these in turn all imply some kind of authority, what the anarchist actually attacks is not authority as such, but a particular form of authority, namely authoritarianism, or the imposition of authority from above.

Authoritarianism starts at the top and directs those below for the benefit of those above. If authority is to be compatible with anarchism it must start from below, be constantly responsive to its source, and be used for the benefit of the people subject to it. The root problem is to provide organization without authoritarianism.

Both the anarchist and many of his critics consider authority as the right to command with the concomitant obligation on the part of those subject to authority to obey.[18] But there are various ways of construing this right. Since the essential part of the anarchist's argument involves alternative types of social organization, and since all organizations involve some kind of authority (though it may be called by other names), the anarchist is not faced with the alternative either of accepting all kinds of authority or of eliminating all kinds of authority. Rather he should explain which kinds of authority he finds acceptable, and within what limits they are to be exercised. That he typically fails to do so in no way affects the fact that the internal logic of his position requires it.

IV. TYPES OF AUTHORITY

In the broadest terms authority is a relation between a bearer (X) and a subject (Y) with respect to some field (Z), when Y reacts in an appropriate manner as a result of X's enunciating some sort of communication (p). The characterization of the appropriate reaction differentiates different kinds of authority. Thus if X is an epistemic authority for Y, Y's appropriate reaction is belief in what X says.[19]

If X is an executive authority for Y, then Y should do what X says he is to do in *p* (or commands him to do), simply because X says so (or commands it). Now obviously there are many conditions we would wish to add if authority is to be justifiable; and the anarchist is correct in asserting that at least some uses of authority are unjustifiable, and that some, perhaps many, presently existing institutions are either unjustifiable or have not been satisfactorily justified. Which kinds of authority are justifiable and how are they justified?

We should initially distinguish some kinds of authority especially pertinent for anarchism: epistemic, parental, operative, and political. Each of them may be either *de facto* or *de jure* (internally justified), illegitimate or legitimate (according to some external criteria), effective or ineffective; and for each of them we can speak of its extent (number of subjects), intensity (degree of acceptance), scope (range of fields), ground, and source.

Epistemic authority is authority based on knowledge. The justification for Y's believing *p* is both that he has good reason to believe X when he says *p* and that it is a way Y gains knowledge. No one knows everything, and we all learn a great deal from other people, from reference books others have written, from maps others have drawn, and so on. If we each had to learn everything first hand mankind would scarcely have moved out of the Stone Age. It would be absurd for an anarchist to deny epistemic authority, or to deny that some people knew things which others could learn from them not by demonstration of the truth of what they said but simply from belief. But the anarchist (such as Bakunin) [20] while admitting the legitimacy of epistemic authority rightly emphasizes both that ultimately the reason for accepting *p* is the belief that what *p* asserts is the case independently of X's saying so, and that epistemic authority by itself implies no right to command. Y is free to accept or reject what X says, and X has no right to force his assent. Nor, simply by virtue of his knowledge, does X have any right to command Y in any way.

Epistemic authority is related to authority grounded on competence. It would be a mistake to think that an anarchist is forced by consistency to deny that some people are more competent than others, or that when he required brain surgery he would, because of his principles, be as willing to let just anyone operate on him as letting a brain surgeon do the job. There is no reason to think that in a society without government someone would not bring his car to a mechanic to be fixed, and his shoes to a shoemaker to be repaired. Authority based on competence will exist no matter how society is organized. But the anarchist insists that though brain surgery, car repairing, and shoemaking require special skills and knowledge, this is not obviously the case in running a government—where the talent most necessary has been to get elected or to be born into the right family. Part of what government does is set the ends which a society will pursue; and it is not the case that any special group knows better than the people themselves what the people want. The people should decide for themselves how they will spend their money, how much they want to be taxed, when and if they will go to war.

The authority of competence, therefore, remains in an anarchist society; but it does not extend to the governing of people. In industry as well as in areas of self-government presently presided over by state power there will be need for information, for facts, for knowledge; and so there will be the need for epistemic authorities in a great many areas. But they should not have any special right to decide what should be done; they should simply convey pertinent knowledge.

In ordinary practice the doctor is an example of an epistemic authority who also prescribes and whose prescription based on competence carries authority with it. But when a doctor says "Take two of these pills a day," he is not ordering his patient to do what the patient does not want to do. Presumably the patient goes to the doctor to improve his health. Both the doctor and the patient want the same thing: the health of the patient. The doctor's orders are therefore hypothetical: if you want to get better, then take two of these pills a day.

In both the case of epistemic authority and of authority based on competence, the benefit that the subject hopes to derive supplies the rationale under appropriate conditions for his acknowledgement or acceptance of the bearer of authority as an authority. The case is similar with parental authority. The basis and justification is the good of the child, with consent reasonably assumed. Parental authority arises from the fact that young children are not competent to care for themselves. Parents therefore have the authority to act for their children, and by their guidance to help them achieve a state of maturity. They do not make acts right or wrong, but they may well instruct the child in what is right and wrong by their commanding right actions for the child to do and wrong ones for him to avoid. The command to a young child not to play in the street is a means to keep him from getting run over and a way to teach him that certain actions will endanger him, even if no explanation is given together with the command. But parental authority diminishes as the child grows in competence and becomes able to act and think more and more for himself.

Some governments justify their actions on the model of parental authority. They claim that the ordinary member of the state is not competent to take care of himself or to know what is best for him; he must be constantly taught and cared for. And this is the job of a benevolent, paternalistic government. The anarchist need not deny the justifiability of parental authority with respect to children, but he does deny the validity of the claim that government can be justified in paternalistic terms. Grown men and women may vary in their intelligence, education, strength, and in a great many other ways. But each—unless he is seriously impaired mentally or physically—is free, should take responsibility for his actions, and knows his wants and needs better than some supposedly benevolent parent figure.

Operative authority is the type of authority that exists in any kind of freely established organization that claims to achieve the ends of its members. Such organizations range from an informal group or club to a business, or industry, and from the smallest scale to the largest. Organizational rules and the existence of officers in no way violate any of the principles of anarchism, so long as the organization is one in which the members are free to belong or not, the rules are made by the members, and the authority of the officers is given to them by the members in order that they may carry out the will of the members. Those with authority have it delegated to them by those subject to it, who hold them accountable and subject to review and removal. This stands in direct opposition to imposed authority, or authoritarianism, which since it is initiated from above is not revokable by those subject to it.

Operative authority may be substitutional in that the authorities act for those whom they represent; or it may be substantive either in the sense that the members of a group agree that those placed in authority may make decisions for them or in the sense that those in authority have the right to command them in matters relating to their common end. The very nature of an enterprise often demands this, as an orchestra needs a conductor and a ship a captain. But this does not mean that either the conductor or the captain can issue commands arbitrarily or that he is not to be held accountable or that he cannot be summarily removed. Removal need not constitute mutiny.

The claim that anarchism is the negation of all authority is therefore not true. Nor need the operation of a group involve unanimous agreement on what is decided for or by the group. Within the limits circumscribed by justice and morality continued membership in the group merely implies that the member finds that he achieves more of what he wants by belonging than he could otherwise.

There is one kind of operative group, however, which deserves particular mention since it poses particular problems and illustrates another facet of the relation of anarchism and authority. This is the entrepreneurial group. Such a group is established to achieve some end and then hires or otherwise gets others to work toward that end. The organizers of this group aggregate the authority for running their enterprise to themselves, and others who join or belong come into an organization which they did not form, but one with which they affiliate for reasons of their own. We can distinguish within this group the service organization from the production organization. In the first the entrepreneurs organize and specify the conditions and advantages of membership; those who join have no control and no authority to make changes. But the authority the organizer exercises, which is given him by the members through joining, is to act for them; it is not any right to command them, though he may make hypothetical demands on them such as if they wish some *a* they must do some *b* (e.g., pay a fee). If the organization is truly a free one, there is no reason why it could not exist in an anarchistic society. But if it is not truly free, if for instance, one could receive electricity, which is a necessity of modern life, only by becoming a member of the electrical association, then different principles (particularly that of justice) apply, and the bearer of authority is not free to set any conditions he chooses.

The production type of entrepreneurial authority involves the bearer of authority in hiring others to help him produce certain goods. He sets the conditions of employment and retains the authority, which he exercises and which does not come from those whom he hires. Moreover, his authority is not representative, but imperative, in that he commands those whom he hires to do certain tasks in return for which he pays them. Now if this type organization were truly free, then the anarchist would have no legitimate complaint. But he argues that in a society in which all work is organized in this way, men become forced laborers even though they are not forced to work at any particular job. The system as a whole is a forced one, and hence the conditions of work cannot be set only by the bearer of authority. Secondly, those who adopt the labor theory of value argue that the entrepreneur makes a profit by paying the worker less than the value he produces through his labor, which is intrinsically immoral. Thirdly, many anarchists argue that private ownership of capital also brings with it an emphasis on property, goods, wealth, and conspicuous consumption and so should be done away with in a good society for reasons other than those having to do with authority and its justifiable limits. Authority is to be circumscribed by justice and morality.

None of this should be taken to preclude the possibility of some people exercising leadership, providing the authority given the leader is justifiable in some of the ways indicated here or in some similar ways.

These form some of the positive features of authority. If we now turn to political authority, it might be argued that this is simply another type of operational authority; but instead of speaking about a club or an industry, we are speaking about a state; and instead of speaking about rules, we are speaking about laws; and instead of speaking about officers we speak about officials or leaders or members of the government. The ploy is a plausible one; and with the proper substitution of terms, if it could be shown to be comparable to the model of operative authority described above, it might even satisfy the anarchist. It might do so if its officials were easily recallable when they failed to perform as the people wanted; if they acted as the representatives of the people and for their good as the latter saw it; if the rules were adopted for their good and achieved their purposes; and if it were possible for the society to be freely joined and freely left.

V. ANARCHIST SUBSTITUTES FOR POLITICAL AUTHORITY

Conditions of universal direct democracy are not strict requirements for most anarchists. For whenever one joins smaller groups
and abides by decisions of the group with which he disagrees, he
may well remain a member if he feels that he has more to gain by
sometimes being outvoted than by leaving, that is, if he gets what he
wants more often than he otherwise could, even though he does not
always get what he wants. If he were always outvoted and never
achieved any good from his association, then the achievement of his
own ends would not be a reason for remaining a member, and he
could not be legitimately forced to remain one.

Traditionally, political authority is considered a special type of
authority, in part because the state is not a free association; its rules
apply to all members of the state, and they cover a very broad field.
For the anarchist such authority, since unjustifiable, should be
replaced by various kinds of operative authority, which should be
justified in terms of the good (freedom, justice, well-being) of its
members and the possibility of their achieving their individual,
freely chosen aims.

If laws are the instrument by which rulers of a state dominate the
others, there will be no law in this sense in an anarchist society. But
there will be certain rules of society, publicly stated and considered
binding.

For the communitarian anarchist, freedom is not equivalent to
license. The principle of freedom which he accepts establishes the
right of each person to act as he wishes insofar as this is consistent
with the right of every other person to do likewise. An individual's
moral autonomy is completely compatible with his being subject to
the moral law. The laws which an individual gives himself should
be rational and universally applicable. Hence if respect for human
life is morally right and murder morally wrong, they cannot be
made otherwise by someone deciding to legislate differently for
himself. The moral law therefore is the same for all rational
creatures. To be subject to the moral law is to be free, and all men
to the extent that they are rational beings are free together when
subject to it. Autonomy and moral law are in this view not only

mutually compatible, but autonomy requires the moral law. Thus, if the rules governing a society are moral rules, they in no way impinge on the freedom of any individual.

The basic rules of society turn out to be the basic moral rules common to almost all societies, which outlaw such things as murder and violence against another member of the society, dishonesty, and injustice, and which promote respect for the freedom of each member of society and respect for him as an end in himself.[21] Since freedom and autonomy are to be tempered by justice—equality of treatment and opportunity—and concern for the welfare of all individuals, exploitation is precluded.[22] What in general is outlawed by both the moral law and present-day criminal law would continue to be outlawed. Those aspects of civil law which specify and facilitate certain kinds of activities will also be continued.[23]

If the state is an instrument of oppression, there will be no state in this sense in anarchist society. But this does not preclude organizations, administration, or delegated authority. Nation-states will be replaced by a variety of self-governing units. As organizations develop they may eventually approach the scope of present-day national or international levels. Size does not bother the anarchist. What he objects to is the state's claimed right to interfere with the autonomy of individuals or of groups, to impose its will on them, or to usurp their functions. But this does not preclude an internal arrangement among groups in a society such that there are recognized rules specifying the limits of their autonomous actions and governing them in accordance with the principles of justice and in a manner analogous to the regulation of the conduct of responsible, morally autonomous individuals.

There may be a variety of functions which a large territorial group may perform which smaller units cannot. But there is no reason to assume that the same units must carry out all the functions on that level. With the rise of worldwide trade and commerce many regions of the world are increasingly interdependent. Multinational corporations already operate beyond national boundaries and form natural groupings. Without national boundaries the fear of invasion by a foreign nation will no longer be a problem, since there will be no other nations.[24] The fear of violence and the need for some sort of security force—voluntary or other—

may be necessary; but it should be controlled by those below and serve their interests, and not be controlled by any particular group or state.

In the economic realm private ownership would be discarded, and industry would be run on the self-management principle, according to which those involved make the decisions and operate the industry, not for the benefit of stockholders, but jointly for the benefit of themselves and of society. Competition would be allowed where it enhances productivity, and spontaneously discarded where it does not. Since there would be no state, state ownership is precluded, as well as private ownership of capital. The very notion of ownership would be superseded for land as well as for everything beyond personal possessions, and these would be kept within reasonable limits, since prestige would not be based on what one had.

There may of course be conflicts between justice, freedom, and well-being, which will have to be resolved. Some persons will be inclined to disrupt social harmony. But protection from them does not require state apparatus. To insure justice certain recognized unabridgeable and inalienable rights must be recognized and there must be effective procedures to protect the innocent and settle disputes. But minor offenses can well be handled locally by neighborhood groups, which could sit as informal courts and dispense reasonable sanctions which they could enforce—be it a fine or suspension of privilege for a certain period, or some extra work, or schooling (e.g., for traffic abuses). More serious crimes could be handled differently, though such cases too should be heard quickly and need not involve penal institutions of the sort most states presently have.

The highest social organs that enforce the general rules governing society so as to provide protection of individual rights and the fair adjudication of disputes and breaches of the rules need not be large; their charge should be as narrow as possible, and their members recallable. Society without a state thus means that the various organs necessary for running society will not be centrally controlled and a variety of different groups of varying sizes will operate at any number of levels to replace the monolithic organization of modern states.

Finally, if anarchist principles provide the basis for something like government, it is the basis for a minimal government, closely controlled from below and responsive to those below; it is anti-bureaucratic, and dedicated to lower autonomous units doing as much as possible before any task is taken on by units above.

This broad brush sketch leaves many of the details to be filled in. But it is typical of most anarchists to refrain from filling in all the details as to how society should be organized. It suffices to point out the defects of the present systems and the basis of the future system, and then in the spirit of freedom let people evolve their own kinds of organizations necessary to fulfill their own purposes.

The anarchist has frequently overstated his theses, which have as frequently been dismissed without an adequate hearing. His threshold of acceptance of political authority is exceedingly high; his faith in the rationality and morality of the ordinary person has little in common with what many people experience in their dealings with their fellow men; and his scheme for bringing about his desired anarchist society is distressingly vague. He leaves many practical questions unanswered. Hence he is an idealistic utopian and not a political realist. Nonetheless his model of the good society is not as absurd or chaotic as frequently imagined. In particular I have argued that a consistent, rational anarchism is perfectly compatible with many forms of authority. In a time when the dangers of unlimited power, the need for rethinking the structure of government, and the necessity of developing new social models have been made perfectly clear, anarchism forces us to reconsider and defend those forms of authority we consider legitimate. It also helps us discover those forms which are illegitimate, and it challenges us to refuse to submit to them. In these respects anarchism is not an outdated nineteenth-century doctrine, but a timely antidote to political and moral complacency.

NOTES

1. Thus the United States government is vastly larger, more complex, more bureaucratic, possibly more secretive, and more authoritarian than at the time of its inception. To claim that "it was good enough for Washington, so it's good enough for me," fails to take into account how "it" has changed.

   Carl J. Friedrich suggests that political authority involves a "capacity for reasoned elaboration" *(Tradition and Autohrity* [London: Macmillan, 1972], p. 52). Acceptance of such authority, if he is correct, implies the *belief* that there is such a capacity. But such belief does not imply that a valid, reasoned elaboration can actually be produced.

2. Whether this is what anarchists actually wish to achieve is questionable. Max Nomad, for instance, in reviewing James Joll's *The Anarchists (Saturday Review,* 24 April 1966) shrewdly remarks that in fact Proudhon sought to establish a decentralized democracy. Bakunin mentions in an unpublished letter the need for an "invisible dictatorship," and the anarcho-syndicalists wished to give all power to the union leaders or to municipal governments. See also Nomad's *The Anarchist Tradition and Other Essays* (New York, 1967) (available at the Hoover Institution on War, Revolution, and Peace).

3. There are anarchists of the right such as Murray Rothbard *(For a New Liberty* [New York: Macmillan, 1973]) who defend private property and free enterprise. Since Professor Rothbard is presenting his own paper in this volume, I shall not attempt to speak for him or for other "anarchists of the right."

4. The list would vary slightly depending on the individual anarchists included. For Max Stirner self-ownership is absolute; for Leo Tolstoy, obedience to divine law; for William Godwin (at least at times), peace. The argument, however, remains substantially the same in all these cases.

5. Broadly speaking, a law may be internally justified (in the sense of being formally valid) by showing that it has been passed by the appropriate bodies, in the specified way, and that it conforms to the constitution of the state. Justifying law in general within a state might be considered internally as similar to justifying rules for a game: they are to some extent constitutive of it. The state, the government, and the law are all internally related in that they form a system and their definitions form a conceptual network. Similarly, political obligation and political freedom make sense only within such a political framework. The anarchist does not deny that such rationales can be given either for law, the state, or government in general or for particular instances of them, or for political obligation or limited political freedom. What he denies is that any justification in a strong sense, that is, any external justification—for instance, on moral grounds—can be provided for political systems as such. And without such justification he sees no reason for accepting any political system and claims that he cannot rightfully be forced to belong to one.

6. The definitions, held for instance by Bakunin *(Bakunin on Anarchy,* ed. Sam Dolgoff [New York: Vintage Books, 1972], *passim)* and other anarchists, were also held by Marx and his followers.

7. For example, see William Godwin's *Enquiry Concerning Political Justice,* Benjamin Tucker's *Instead of a Book,* Max Stirner's *The Ego and His Own,* and Emma Goldman's *Anarchism and Other Essays.* Two readily available anthologies containing extracts from the anarchists are Leonard I. Krimerman and Lewis Perry, eds., *Patterns of Anarchy* (New York: Anchor Books, 1966), and Marshall Shatz, ed., *The Essential Works of Anarchism* (New York: Bantam, 1971).

8. Robert Paul Wolff, *In Defense of Anarchism* (New York: Harper Torchbook, 1970).

9. For a reply to this book see Jeffrey H. Reiman, *In Defense of Political Philosophy* (New York: Harper Torchbook, 1972).

10. Richard Taylor, *Freedom, Anarchy and the Law* (Englewood Cliffs, N.J.: Prentice-Hall, 1973), pp. 46-54.

11. Lisa H. Perkins, "On Reconciling Autonomy and Authority," *Ethics,* LXXXII (1972), 114-23.

12. Rex Martin, "Wolff's Defense of Philosophical Anarchism," *The Philosophical Quarterly,* XXIV (1974), pp. 140-49.

13. The relevant texts of Marx, Engels, and Lenin on anarchism have been collected in *Anarchism and Anarcho-Syndicalism* (New York: International Publishers, 1972).

14. Daniel Guérin, *Anarchism* (New York: Monthly Review Press, 1970).

15. For samples of his views see *Patterns of Anarchy,* pp. 449-72.

16. For instance, in reply to the charge that a society without a government and without an army would be easy prey to the armed forces of another country, the anarchist replies first, that he expects anarchism to spread so that there will be no nation states; and secondly, even if anarchism were to succeed initially in only one country, no foreign power would gain much by the use of its arms with respect to it. For without a centralized government to take over, any invader would find no seat of authority to capture and replace. It would find a multitude of independent overlapping organizations, together with a people who individually would not readily submit to losing their freedom. Under these conditions no army could keep a whole large population in subjugation, nor could any foreign power manipulate such people through the ordinary means of manipulation— law, police, government—since these will have been done away with and could not easily be restored.

17. Bakunin's critique of Marxism with respect to the dictatorship of the proletariat has been vindicated by history. The descriptions in Solzhenitsyn's *Gulag Archipelago* go far beyond Bakunin's worse fears.

18. Wolff, *In Defense of Anarchism,* p. 4; D. D. Raphael, *Problems of Political Philosophy* (New York: Praeger Publishers, 1970), p. 67.

19. For a fuller analysis of epistemic authority, see my paper, "The

Function and Limits of Epistemic Authority," *The Southern Journal of Philosophy,* VIII (1970), pp. 199-204.

20. *Bakunin on Anarchy,* pp. 229-33.

21. The anarchist could adopt much, though not all, of Rawls's theory of justice. He could adopt in any event the "veil of ignorance" in order to argue for some specific principles of justice and freedom.

22. The close relation of freedom and justice is clear, for instance in the "Revolutionary Catechism" partially reprinted in *Bakunin on Anarchy,* pp. 76-97.

23. The remaining cases, namely, those in which laws do not command what is immoral, do not simply repeat the moral law, and are not indirectly moral, may be troublesome, since it is frequently difficult to determine what their relation to morality is. An example would be tax laws. There is certainly a legal obligation to pay one's taxes. But whether there is also a moral obligation to do so depends on more than legislation: e.g., are the taxes just and justly imposed?

24. It is noteworthy that many of those who defend the state and its sovereignty against anarchists promote anarchy in its negative sense on the international level by refusing to give up any sovereignty.

6

COMMENTS ON "ANARCHISM AND AUTHORITY"

RICHARD WASSERSTROM

Two of the most important questions that anyone can ask about anarchism are: (1) What is anarchism and how is it different from other views or theories with which it might be confused? and (2) Is anarchism a plausible or correct doctrine? Are its arguments sound and its premises true?

Professor De George holds, I take it, that the anarchist is committed to the view that the state is an unjustifiable entity. De George also thinks that nothing about anarchism is incompatible with the exercise of authority over individuals by many social institutions. The anarchist sometimes talks about the unjustifiability of all exercises of authority but does not, if I understand De George correctly, really mean it.

One of De George's chief theses is that what the anarchist opposes is not authority but authoritarianism. The anarchists, he says, ". . . refused to submit their will to an alien will. They refused to be dominated and ordered and used for the good of the rulers. But though such domination is a type of authority, it is not the only type." And, again, "What the anarchist actually attacks is not authority as such but authoritarianism which starts at the top and directs those below for the benefit of those above. If authority is to be compatible with anarchism it must start from below, be constantly responsive to its sources, and be used for the benefit of the people subject to it." (Page 98 in modified form.)

As I understand De George's argument, the crucial point is this: the anarchists call for the abolition of the state, not the abolition of society. They specifically envision that humans will always live and interact in various social organizations. But any form of social organization requires that authority will be exercised over the members of that social organization. Therefore, the anarchist is not opposed to all impositions of authority. Anarchism does not, that is, hold that all authority is wrong. The problem instead is to see what kinds of exercises of authority are compatible with anarchism and which are not.

The difficulty I have with this is twofold. First, I do not find De George's account of nonauthoritarian exercises of authority sufficiently clear to be effectively assessed and understood. Secondly, I do not think that the various kinds of authority De George would allow are consistent with the anarchist's chief concern.

I think that the anarchist qua anarchist is worried primarily about all cases in which one person compels or requires another to act in a certain way. For anyone (or group) to compel or require another is to do something that is intrinsically wrong. Because compulsion is the essence of the nation-state, the nation-state is manifestly unjustifiable. And so is any other social institution which makes people do things. It may be that all forms of authority are not unjustifiable, according to the anarchist, but all forms of coercive authority are.

I think that De George has not distinguished two cases sufficiently, for when we talk about whether someone is justified in exercising authority over or in respect to another, there are, I think, two different things that we might have in mind. In both cases the individual tells the other what he or she is to do. In one case, however, that is as far as it goes; the individual who has been told what he or she is to do is then wholly free to decide whether to do it. If the individual elects not to do it, that may be stupid, unwise, or foolish, but it is not in any other sense wrong to ignore what the authority has said is to be done. And it would, of course, be wrong for the authority to in any way force or require the individual to do what the authority says is to be done. This is the case, also talked about by De George, of the doctor and the patient. The anarchist can, I think, live quite comfortably with this case.

In the other case, telling the other what he or she is to do is not the end of the matter. If the individual elects not to do it, the individual has acted wrongly (in some nonprudential sense) and the authority can appropriately require the individual to behave in the specified way. This is, I believe, the sense in which officials in organizations (as well as games) exercise authority over individuals, and it is also the sense in which rules and laws exercise authority over the persons subject to them.

Now it seems to me that it is the latter case that the anarchist is worried about. The anarchist is opposed to any exercise of authority which carries with it the right to require individuals to do what they do not choose to do. It appears to me, although I am not certain, that De George regards some instances of this latter sort as consistent with anarchism.

Usually, he talks about justifiable authority in terms of its place of origin, that is, from above or below, in terms of who is benefitted—the bearer or the subject of authority—and who is responsive to him. One fairly complete statement is this: "The general principle is that these kinds of authority are justifiable if the exercise of authority is in the interest of both the proximate and ultimate good of the subject; they are also justifiable if it is in the ultimate but not the proximate good of the subject, providing the subject, if a competent adult, obeys the authority willingly. They are not justifiable if compliance is coerced or if the exercise of authority is not in the interest of the subject, but only in the interest of the bearer of authority." [1]

There are things in this passage which suggest both that requiring someone to do something is sometimes a justifiable part of the exercise of authority and that it never is. It seems to me very important that this question be resolved. Obviously, much will turn upon what does and does not count as a case of *willing* obedience.

Although this and other passages are ambiguous in this regard, the concluding passages of De George's paper appear to be relatively unequivocal. For example, when he talks more specifically about authority and social organizations (and if I am right this clearly is the kind of authority the anarchist is most interested in and worried about), De George asserts, "Organizational rules and the existence of officers in no way violate any of the principles of anarchism, so long as the organization is one in which the members are free to belong or not, the rules are made by the members, and the authority of the officers is given to them by the members in order that they may carry out the will of the members . . ." (p. 101). In addition, ". . . the operation of the group [need not] involve unanimous agreement on what is decided for or by the group. Within the limits circumscribed by justice and morality, continued membership in the group merely implies that the member finds that he achieves more of what he wants by belonging than he could otherwise" (p. 102).

I understand these passages to assert that a social institution can justifiably have rules which require the members to do things and which permit the officials of the group to exercise authority over the members. I understand them to assert, too, that the rules need not receive the assent of all of the members of the group. It is sufficient that a member has not seen fit to withdraw.

If all of this is consistent with the principles of anarchism, then I think De George is surely right when he says that anarchism is compatible with many forms of authority and when he imagines an anarchistic society which will have even small social institutions which ". . . enforce the general rules governing society so as to provide protection of individual rights and the fair adjudication of disputes and breaches of the rules . . ." (p. 106). But I am now unconvinced that De George has preserved intact either the spirit or the substance of the anarchist point of view.

NOTE

1. This quotation appeared in De George's original paper, but for reasons of space was omitted or altered in form in his revised paper.

7

ANARCHISM AND SKEPTICISM

REX MARTIN

In his interesting paper "Anarchism and Authority," Richard De George develops an account of theoretical anarchism which has, I think, some unusual twists and turnings. Starting from the familiar claim that the anarchist theoretician denies that there is adequate justification for government or law or organized authority as such (see De George, p. 93), he goes on to provide a substantially different version of philosophical anarchism.[1] In this latter version, the philosophical anarchist is conceived as being in basic agreement with the doctrines of standard political philosophy, as sharing in a rather traditional moral consensus, as accepting many forms of authority (including *political* authority), and as being in principle an advocate, not of "no government," but of "minimal government" (see De George, pp. 104ff, esp. 106-107). These conclusions are, of course, controversial; and they provoked the most heated challenges, at the meeting at which his paper was read, to De George's rendering of the tradition of philosophical anarchism.

In my own discussion here I want to show that De George's account of philosophical anarchism is, in its controversial conclusions, fundamentally sound. I will attempt to do this, moreover, by showing that a connection can be traced between his unexceptionable initial characterization of the anarchist and the conclusions he draws. I think the principal point of linkage is provided by a suggested analogy between the anarchist and the skeptic, an analogy which is alluded to but not developed in De George's paper.

I. THE ANALOGY WITH SKEPTICISM

Now, it should be clear that the anarchist, when he denies that there is a justification for governmental authority, is not saying that governments never claim to have "legitimate" power; he is not saying that subjects never concede this power. Rather, he is concerned to show that such claims can never be established. The anarchist wants to show that one is in error when he says that there could be a government which has a "right to command" and whose subjects are supposed to follow those commands, indeed "whose subjects have a binding obligation to obey." [2] Or, alternatively, to show that one is in error when he says that it could be granted to governments, as a matter of this same right, to back up their laws with force and to employ this force against lawbreakers.

The philosophical anarchist, then, is one who doubts and is prepared to deny any assertion of rightful or "legitimate" authority on behalf of a government. So conceived, might not the philosophical anarchist have much in common with the philosophical skeptic?

I have already indicated that De George suggests such an analogy in his paper (see p. 91). There are several hints that help us see the nature of the analogy he has in mind. Basically it is this: like the Cartesian skeptic who begins with the conviction that he "should abstain from belief in things which are not entirely certain and indubitable" and who follows the maxim that he should "put aside every belief in which [he] could imagine the least doubt, just as though [he] knew that it was absolutely false," De George's anarchist-skeptic treats anything less than an absolute justification as absolutely unjustified.[3] The anarchist-skeptic insists on "complete justification" (p. 91; see also note 5, p. 108) because he operates, De George tells us, with "extremely high standards" (p. 8). "And without such justification he sees no reason for accepting any political system and claims that he cannot rightfully be forced to belong to one" (De George, note 5, p. 108).

In searching through the recent philosophical literature on anarchism, I have found only one other philosopher who has made use of an explicit analogy between skepticism and anarchism. Robert Ladenson remarks, in what amounts to an aside, that an appropriate analogy to draw respecting the anarchist "would be between his doubts about the existence of morally legitimate political authority and the radical doubts about the existence of an external world. . . ." Ladenson continues,

> The parallel with radical scepticism in the realm of epistemology is almost exact. According to this kind of scepticism, even after we have checked all the considerations which, even in the widest sense, count as evidence for empirical knowledge, it still does not follow that the existence claims one makes about physical objects, presumably on the basis of this evidence, are well founded.[4]

Nonetheless, the analogy between anarchism and skepticism, despite its obviousness, has received very little attention. This is somewhat surprising; for there does appear to be, in the logic of the arguments, a significant similarity between the two. It might prove a connection worth exploring. Accordingly, I want to work out this suggested analogy further and to indicate its principal implications for anarchist theory.

The skeptic often expresses himself by saying that he has examined a variety of different grounds to claims of knowledge and found all of them wanting. By the same token, the anarchist could say what Robert Paul Wolff says in the preface to his *Defense of Anarchism:* "My failure to find any theoretical justification for the authority of the state had convinced me that there was no justification. In short," Wolff tells us, "I had become a philosophical anarchist."[5]

Such statements fall short of genuine philosophical skepticism, or anarchism, in a significant way. We might call them, then, preliminary positions. Let me make this point clearer by showing why I would say that Wolff's formula represents at best a preliminary stage on the road to genuine philosophical anarchism.

When the anarchist says that all the claims which favor governmental authority, or appear to justify it, are false, his generalization covers only claims that are actually made. It is these which are believed to be false or can be shown to be false. But his generalization would not license a belief that *no* claim favorable to the authority of government could ever be true. The anarchist might *want* to believe this but he has no conclusive rational ground for the belief.

By the same token, the *critic* of the anarchist-skeptic cannot rest content with the assumption that *some* of the claims to authority actually made are, presumptively, sound. If preliminary anarchism is philosophically inconclusive, the refutation of it which merely takes for granted what the anarchist calls into doubt is equally inconclusive. Thus, Ladenson's short way with the anarchist won't do. He says,

> Now the beliefs which the radical skeptic about the external world seeks to undermine are so basic that they cannot be rejected. Accordingly, the fact that a given epistemological theory leads to radical scepticism about the external world is sufficient reason for rejecting it. The same is true of Wolff's account of legitimate political authority. The fact that it leads to the kind of scepticism that it does shows his account to be unacceptable. ("Legitimate Authority," p. 337.)

But this is equivalent to Dr. Johnson's "refutation" of Bishop Berkeley: he kicked the stone, something obviously solid, and thought that made an end of the matter. And Ladenson, assuming the fact of authority to be equally solid and equally basic, merely points to the accepted *belief* in authority and says that Wolff's skeptical doubts about authority must therefore be unacceptable. Surely, though, the dispute between the philosophical anarchist as skeptic and the defender of claims to authority can be pitched at a more profound level than the preliminary one we have discerned. The dispute is not over whether a certain belief is accepted, or even accepted as basic, but over whether such beliefs *can* be justified or not. Preliminary anarchism is very like its skeptical analogue and very like the preliminary refutations it has launched; each one is always dogged by the limitations of its own case.

What the genuine skeptic has to show is the *impossibility* of any knowledge of matter of fact insofar as it is based on sense experience. Likewise, the philosophical anarchist has to show the *impossibility* of establishing any claim to the effect that any group of men can have a title of right to issue commands to other men with any presumption of obligatory compliance or that force can be rightfully threatened, and even used, to back up these commands. Hence, De George is quite right to divide the issue so as to assert: "The anarchist argues first that no satisfactory external justification [for instance, on moral grounds] of the state, law, and government has ever been given (hence they have not been justified), and secondly *that they cannot be justified and so are unjustifiable*" (p. 93, italics added; at the word "external" De George's paper refers us to note 5 [on p. 108]).

The skeptic's strategy is to take any knowledge claim and to say, this claim being what it is, it is impossible that it could be established. The skeptic takes any particular factual claim, like "This table is brown," or the whole class of such claims, and says it is not possible that it can be established as true or false, by experience or by any other means. But to make his point, he must allow the *meaning* of the statement to remain invariant between the case of its being true and the case of its being false. Otherwise, its truth or falsity would be an internal mark of the statement itself and we could decide its truth value for it. So the skeptic never disturbs the surface of language in any particular. Statements can be perfectly understood, and just so long as there is meaning invariance between true and false statements he is in a position to say that it is impossible to establish a statement's being true. Of course, the skeptic must play out his strategy through a series of moves, and will require that "experience" itself be treated in exactly the same way as the statements just discussed.

Here experience is, so to speak, pried loose from the world and treated as a sort of "semantical vehicle" whose content is invariant between the case of its being veridical and the case of its not being so.

The skeptic rather must be committed to the view that we have no way of telling whether our experience is or is not illusory— and this would be compatible with there being in fact *no* illusions *whatever*. He has to insist that even if there are in fact none *we* cannot tell that this is so. Skepticism, accordingly, is not an hypothesis which rests upon evidence, that is, evidence that men have been taken in by illusions in the past; for the position undercuts *entirely* all such evidence. . . .

We may experience things just as they are. Or we may not. Things may be radically different from what our experience would lead us to suppose. But then we cannot fill in the blank in the ratio with terms which have application to experience. Since it is experience itself which he calls in question, and calls in question in an absolute and total way. . . .

[T]he skeptic need but insist that whatever pertains to the surface can be incorporated into the surface, the test for whether one is dreaming can always be dreamt itself, and so forth. Against this strategy there is no recourse.[6]

The strategy is, however, in the end self-defeating. For to assert the *meaning* of any statement is to assert the conditions under which it *could* be true or, as the case might be, false. And if we have the criteria which, if satisfied, would make the statement true, we cannot say that it is philosophically impossible for the statement ever to be true.

The philosophical anarchist is in a situation similar to that of the philosophical skeptic. The anarchist wants to say that it is impossible in principle to establish any claim to rightful authority by a government, or on behalf of a government.

The anarchist's assertion is made, not against so-called *de facto* authority, but against *de jure* or rightful authority. The drawing of this particular distinction appears to be crucial to the argument of the philosophical anarchist, as we have already noted. For it is important to the anarchist to be able to distinguish between the situation in which a state is *believed* by its subjects to be legitimate and the situation in which it *really* has the authority claimed for it (see Wolff, DA 10). *De jure* and *de facto* authority differ, then, simply in that the one names a situation in which the authority belief is true and the other a situation in which it is *merely* believed but is not known to be true. But the *content* of the authority belief here must be invariant between the two cases; otherwise the anarchist and the believer in state authority are talking about two different things and the anarchist's critique would prove to be beside the point. What the anarchist wants to do, then, is to block any possible move to establish the authority belief: he wants to say of that belief that we *cannot* in principle ever establish what the belief asserts, as really being so. This much at least is surely involved in portraying the anarchist as a skeptic.

But merely to draw the *de jure-de facto* distinction requires that the notion of rightful authority be a meaningful one. It follows from this that the philosophical anarchist, inasmuch as he does use the notion of *de jure* authority, stands committed to the meaningfulness of statements about rightful authority. And clearly, the *de facto-de jure* distinction is deeply embedded conceptually in the anarchist's argument: if there were no belief in authority, there would be no grasping point for the anarchist's critique and he would lose his grip on what was at issue in the dispute; but if there were no *content* to authority beliefs, there would be no point and no basis to his assertion that such beliefs are not justifiable. If there were no normative notion of *de jure* authority (i.e., no sense of what it would take for there really to be rightful political authority), he would have nothing to measure these beliefs against.

Hence, the philosophical anarchist requires the coherence of the concept of a government's "legitimate" authority in order even to assert, characteristically, that no true claim favoring the holding of such authority is possible. But the consequences of this for philosophical anarchism are profound. For, of course, to allow meaning to statements about the rightful authority of government is, in effect, to assert that there are conditions under which such statements could be true.

Accordingly, the philosophical anarchist could not say that statements claiming rightful authority for governments can never possibly be true. Since this is the very proposition that the philosophical anarchist needs to assert, it would appear that his position breaks down internally.

Insofar as there is an analogy with philosophical skepticism, this is where it leads: to a dead end. In analogy with skepticism, the position of the philosophical anarchist must, in order to be stated at all, turn out to be self-contradictory. We should abandon the analogy suggested by De George and Ladenson then.

II. A DIFFERENT CLAIM ABOUT IMPOSSIBILITY

Let us allow, however, that the anarchist might be taken as asserting something else. Instead of saying that statements affirming the rightful authority of governments could never *possibly* be true, he could be saying that none of them can *in fact* be true. This way of putting it upholds certain criteria as the ultimate standard and says, by reference to the facts that "answer to" these criteria, that no government measures up in deed.

Specifically, I would want to claim that the philosophical anarchist should be taken as saying that "rightful political authority" (i.e., political authority which has been morally legitimated) is a *coherent* notion and that there are criteria available to help us decide the question of the instantiation of such authority. These criteria are basic moral notions, like freedom, justice, well-being (the ones De George mentions, e.g., on p. 92). It's simply that it's factually impossible, or at least extremely difficult and unlikely, for any government to stand close enough to fulfilling these conditions for attributing rightful (or *de jure*) authority for us to call it a "legitimate" government. The anarchist's point, then, is that *instances* of rightful political authority are, for all practical purposes, impossible as a matter of fact.

In other words, let us take it that the philosophical anarchist has translated his claim of impossibility from the level of skeptical doubt to the level of facts. The anarchist is here willing to concede that rightful political authority is *logically* eligible: it *could* exist and it could be established that it exists. The problem, though, is that he can discern in the world of facts no possibility of exemplification of the *de jure* state at all. What he now claims is not the conceptual or the epistemological impossibility of a government's having rightful authority but rather the factual impossibility of it, for reasons physical or, perhaps, psychological. This provides, I think, the point to De George's remark (though it would require his withdrawing the suggested analogy with skepticism) that what the anarchist "denies is that any justification in a strong sense, that is, any external justification—for instance, on moral grounds—can be provided for political systems as such" (note 5, p. 108).

This then would become the position of philosophical anarchism: governments having rightful authority are impossible as a matter of fact. Whatever a government's title to rightful authority is said to be, it can't be met. The criteria are clear enough, but no government can ever actually live up to them.

Taking this line might appear to offer philosophical anarchism the opportunity of a really decisive blow against political authority. But the appearance would, I think, prove deceptive.

The anarchist, historically considered, has tended to base his case against government on "evidence" of a sort. We find him pointing out that governments do many evil things, like fighting wars or oppressing people; we are told that governments cow people through the threat of coercion, maintain social inequalities, penalize lawbreakers. Governments, even at their best, instill habits of subservience and have proven, every one of them, to be altogether inimical to individual liberty and dignity. The anarchist is usually not prepared to reverse Hobbes by asserting that any form of having no government at all is better than having any government. But the anarchist would probably believe that some situations without government are better than any that could be provided with, or by, governments. (See De George, p. 93.)

But the value to anarchism of all these assertions has suddenly become very problematic. When the anarchist puts himself in the position of saying that no government can have authority, due to certain matters of fact, then the catalogue of abuses and crimes with which he belabors government in no way tells against *de jure* authority itself. For the governments which he castigates, perhaps with justice, one and all do not have, by his own proclamation, any sort of rightful authority. Here anarchism can have, whatever its case against governments, no brief against authority.

Another point is, I think, worth making. The anarchist is often thought to be saying that governments pretend to have rightful authority, but none of them really does. This is usually taken, and presumably is intended, as an indictment. But could it really be an indictment if governments could not possibly, for reasons factual, have such authority?

The anarchist could, of course, score governments for *pretending* to have authority. And he could excoriate the man on the street for believing such foolishness (just as the man of science could scoff at the faith-healer and deplore the gullibility of people for believing such stuff). But he couldn't condemn governments for failing, really, to have authority (any more than the man of science could hold it against the faith healer for not being able, really, to cure the lame and the sick). Where the alleged failure is due to some physical incapacity, to some unalterable fact of nature, perhaps of a psychological sort, then there is no *moral* fault and the question of blame is out of place.

The matter of the alleged factual impossibility of *de jure* authority is perhaps more restrictive of the repertory of anarchist arguments than at first it appeared. It seems that the claim of factual impossibility and the moral argumentation of anarchism are at cross-purposes. To make his historic moral case against governmental authority the anarchist would require that *de jure* authority at least be factually possible. The moralist case must rest on the undesirability of *de jure* authority, on its being wrong rather than on its being impossible.

Perhaps the essential thrust of the traditional anarchist moralist argument can be found along some such lines as this. The anarchist could be taken as arguing that the having of *de jure* authority is possible, although he might believe that governments never, or rarely ever, actually have it. (In saying this he would not be significantly distinguished from a rigorous legitimist like Rousseau.) The anarchist's moral critique of government, then, would embrace two points. First, existing governments don't have what they all claim to have—rightful authority; indeed, honoring the pretense contributes to the iniquity. The anarchist might believe, second, that even governments having *de jure* authority are still governments and that the essential evils of government do attend *any* government. (See De George, p. 94.)

Now there is no point in prejudging the issue here. I do believe it is possible to show that the exercise even of *de jure* authority can be immoral, perhaps in general and certainly on some occasions. It would, I think, be more difficult to show that situations of no government tend to have better results, morally, than situations in which governments have *de jure* authority. If the anarchist rejects Hobbes's unflattering portrait of anarchism in his account of the "state of nature" as not adequately grounded in the facts, then much the same could be said of the anarchist utopias against which existing governments are measured. (See De George, p. 94.)

I do not, in saying all this, want to rest much weight on the traditional moralist case of anarchism. I am unable to attach much significance, philosophically, to its arguments. For one thing is never made entirely clear: whether a government's actually having *de jure* authority would be a good thing or a bad thing, that is, relative to its *not* having such authority.

The important thing here, for my purposes, is simply to note that these traditional moral arguments of anarchism are really inappropriate given the proposition that a government's having rightful authority is factually impossible. But if this proposition is dropped, then philosophical anarchism moves much nearer to traditional theories of the state. It becomes not so much a critique of such theories as an alternative theory of political legitimacy, with the curious twist that it tends to downgrade the moral adequacy of such legitimacy.

On the other hand, the philosophical anarchist may decide to retain the proposition asserting the factual impossibility of *de jure* authority. Philosophical anarchism then becomes a very austere doctrine, for it is reduced to that solitary proposition and the traditional moral arguments are jettisoned as beside the point. Not only this. Philosophical anarchism, so conceived, will not have to differ from the statist view on what authority is *in concept;* indeed, in this austere version of philosophical anarchism, the anarchist and the statist could even agree that it would be a morally good thing for there to be *de jure* legitimate governments. They need differ *only* about the facts of the world, as to whether authority can be exemplified or not.

Somehow this austere version goes against our intuitions: the philosophical anarchist does seem to be saying something different from this. We see, though, that there is a kind of "tension" in anarchist theory, which the austere doctrine serves to bring out, between the anarchist claim that there cannot be such a thing as legitimate authority and the historic anarchist moral argumentation against authority. Instinctively, we want to hold up these moral strictures as the essential core of anarchist theory, but to do so we must relax our grip on the countervailing thesis that rightful governmental authority cannot exist.

III. A TENSION IN THE ANARCHIST ARGUMENT

I am not sure where all this leaves philosophical anarchism. It does seem clear that the crucial proposition respecting the impossibility of *de jure* authority is either self-contradictory, when construed as skeptic's impossibility, or radically austere, when construed as factual impossibility. The only recourse for the anarchist here would seem to be to desert this proposition and to take up arguments asserting the moral undesirability of a government's having *de jure* authority.

The single most interesting conclusion which we can draw from our brief survey of the relationship of anarchism to skepticism, then, is that a deep fault line runs between two main theses of historic anarchism. There is a kind of "tension" between the thesis that claims to rightful political authority *cannot* be established, which is the thesis that gave rise to De George's suggestion that the anarchist is the skeptic of politics, and the thesis that governmental authority is morally bad. This tension has to be managed conceptually, in some way. And, more to the point, a kind of *logical* profile of philosophical anarchism can be developed by attending to the various eligible ways in which this tension can be conceptually controlled.

Moreover, we find in this metaphor of a "tension" which gives definition to philosophical anarchism the reason why the anarchist-skeptic position developed as it did. The anarchist has, by and large, been unwilling to avail himself of the *entire* range of possible skeptical positions. We do not, for example, find him asserting that rightful governmental authority cannot be established *because* moral standards and moral principles are themselves a kind of nonsense (or "non-sense," as Ayer would have it). Nor do we find him asserting that such authority cannot be established *because* the notion of rightful governmental authority is itself inherently unintelligible (in the way that Berkeley said the notion of material substance was).[7] In each case, the reason is the same: to take the standpoint of either the positivist skeptic, who denies the moral standards, or the Berkeleian skeptic, who denies the essential coherence of the whole notion of rightful authority, would be to resolve the basic "tension" by deserting the moral argumentation of historic anarchism in favor of an all-out version of the thesis that it is impossible to establish the *de jure* legitimate authority of government.

Unlike these two versions of skepticism, only the Cartesian or epistemological version held out any prospect of reconciling the tension by allowing the anarchist-skeptic to hold *both* that it was impossible to establish authority and that governmental authority was morally undesirable. As I have tried to show, however, the Cartesian version of anarchism-skepticism fails, not because it forces the anarchist to give up his moral brief against authority, but because it is self-contradictory. Hence, the Cartesian anarchist-skeptic cannot provide an eligible solution to the problem I have identified.

It seems clear, indeed, that there are only two eligible solutions and each involves giving up one of the main theses of historic philosophical anarchism. The anarchist can resolve the tension by cutting free the traditional moral argumentation from its entanglement with the thesis about the impossibility of rightful political authority and letting the latter drop. Or he can do the opposite.

In De George's account of anarchism it is the thesis about the impossibility of authority that is let go. This is readily explained by the emphasis he puts on the anarchist's detailed moral critique of governmental and other social institutions. This emphasis is evident from the very beginning of his paper; we can take it that De George had decided that the traditional moral argumentation is anarchism's paramount feature. In doing this I believe he has discerned correctly the nature of theoretical anarchism, historically conceived.

Nonetheless his principal conclusions have proven to be controversial. Accordingly, I have tried to show in this paper that a studied elaboration of the relationship between anarchism and skepticism opens up a tension in the anarchist argument which forces that argument to the conclusions De George has sketched. In short, I think that, if one takes the moral argumentation as basic, conclusions of the sort De George draws are unavoidable. And anarchism has to be viewed as an alternative theory of political legitimacy, one among several, rather than as the critique and denial of all such theories.[8]

The only real alternative to this is to take the austere route of affirming that rightful political authority *cannot* be established and letting the detail of the moral argument go. I think the peculiar interest of Robert Paul Wolff's advocacy of philosophical anarchism lies, precisely, in his having taken this very path.

Three points about Wolff's theory, then, are worth noting briefly. (1) His principal contention is that the notion of rightful political authority, though a coherent one and hence logically eligible for exemplification, cannot (i.e., *cannot in point of fact*) be instantiated (see Wolff, esp. DA 23, 38, 69).[9] (2) Accordingly, he is not particularly concerned, as an attentive reading of his work would attest, to bring a list of charges of moral wrong against governmental authority, since this would be, by and large, beside the point. (3) In taking this tack he is unusual among anarchist theoreticians. Indeed, I would regard him as standing outside the main tradition of philosophical anarchism, the moralistic one which De George has emphasized. He is breaking new ground. This, of course, is his importance and the reason we should attend his work with care.

For I think the single greatest achievement of anarchism may well be that it forces yet a radical reconstruction on traditional political philosophy.

NOTES

1. My comments refer to the paper by Richard De George published in this volume. An earlier version of his paper was read at the meeting of the American Society for Political and Legal Philosophy, December 29, 1974, in Washington, D.C.

2. "On the basis of a lengthy reflection upon the concept of *de jure* legitimate authority, I have come to the conclusion that philosophical anarchism is true. That is to say, I believe that there is not, and there could not be, a state that has a right to command and whose subjects have a binding obligation to obey" (R. P. Wolff, "On Violence," *The Journal of Philosophy,* LXVI, 19 [2 October 1969], 607).

3. The passages quoted from Descartes are from, respectively, the First and the Second of his *Meditations.*

4. Robert F. Ladenson, "Legitimate Authority," *American Philosophical Quarterly,* IX, 4 (October 1972), 337. The skeptic is mentioned, briefly, also in G. Dworkin, "Reasons and Authority" (abstract), *Journal of Philosophy,* LXIX, 20 (9 November 1972), 717, and in Robert Nozick, *Anarchy, State, and Utopia* (New York: Basic Books, 1974), p. 4. Interestingly, the analogy with skepticism does not figure at all in Ladenson's other paper on Wolff: Ladenson, "Wolff on Legitimate Authority," *Philosophical Studies,* XXXIII, 6 (December 1972), 376-84.

5. R. P. Wolff, *In Defense of Anarchism* (New York: Harper Torchbook, 1970), p. viii. (Hereafter: Wolff, DA viii.)

6. I am indebted for the notion of a "semantical vehicle" and in my treatment of skepticism throughout to the work of Arthur C. Danto.

See, in particular, his *Analytical Philosophy of Knowledge* (Cambridge: Cambridge University Press, 1968), pp. 186-89, 194, 201, and his *What Philosophy Is* (New York: Harper and Row, 1968), pp. 80-82, 84. See *What Philosophy Is,* pp. 81-82, for the first two and *Analytical Philosophy of Knowledge,* p. 187, for the last of the three passages quoted.

7. It is sometimes thought that Wolff's position is that the notion of rightful political authority is *inherently unintelligible.* This judgment does not altogether lack foundation in what Wolff has written (see, for example, "On Violence," esp. pp. 602, 612; DA 19, 71). Nonetheless this suggestion of a *logical* incoherence in the concept of authority simply won't do in the context of his book. It contradicts express remarks of Wolff to the effect that we do have a concept of *de jure* political authority (see DA 10-11) and that this primitive conception can be combined with a notion of moral autonomy to give us a coherent conception of morally justified rightful authority, that is, in the conception of a unanimous direct democracy (see DA 20-23, 27, 58). Moreover, if the notion of authority really were conceived by him as self-contradictory, then we could make no sense of Wolff's contention that the conception is inadequately exemplified by existing states.

8. For another argument along the same lines as De George's and for a lucid and helpful discussion of the theoretical complexity of anarchism, of important points of difference that divide anarchists, and of the many affinities anarchism has with traditional political philosophy, see April Carter's *The Political Theory of Anarchism* (New York: Harper Torchbook, 1971).

9. I have discussed Wolff's principal contention more fully elsewhere: see "Wolff's Defence of Philosophical Anarchism," *Philosophical Quarterly,* XXIV (April 1974), 140-49. I have elaborated upon the logical relationship that holds between anarchism and the justifying of authority in "Two Models for Justifying Authority," *Ethics,* LXXXVI, 1 (October 1975), 70-75, and in "On the Justification of Political Authority." in R. Baine Harris, ed., *Authority: A Philosophical Analysis* (University: University of Alabama Press, 1976), pp. 54-75.

8

THE ANARCHIST JUSTIFICATION OF AUTHORITY

ALAN RITTER

We are in debt to Professor De George for his conclusive demonstration that anarchists endorse authority, despite what they say. Proof of this contention is long overdue, for anyone who reads the anarchists will note the conflict stressed by De George between their explicit denunciations of authority and their tacit use of it to help make their ideal society cohere. Since I agree with Professor De George that anarchists support authority, my comments will not bear on his claim's general validity. What I will question is its concrete application, for I shall argue that Professor De George has misdescribed the tests employed in anarchist theory to distinguish legitimate from illegitimate authority.

Before presenting this argument, I must indicate how far it will extend. Professor De George's investigation of authority in an anarchy is comprehensive. He asks how anarchists justify authority over belief as well as conduct, and in the private realm of groups and families, as well as in the public, social realm of life. My remarks will bear on Professor De George's findings only so far as they apply to public conduct. More precisely, I will limit myself to showing that he misreads how anarchists justify authority over the actions of individuals in their capacity as members of an ideal social order. Focusing on this narrow issue brings out what is distinctive about the anarchists' justification of authority, for their argument is not markedly original, so far as it applies to private action or belief. It is their way of justifying authority over public conduct that is unique.[1]

I

Authority, as applied to conduct, is a way to secure compliance with a directive, distinguished by the ground on which the directive is obeyed. You exercise authority over my conduct, if you issue me a directive, and I follow it because I believe that something about you, not the directive, makes compliance the proper course. This something about you that elicits my compliance is something I attribute either to your *position* or to your *character*. I may submit to your authority because I think your position (say as president) makes you an appropriate issuer of directives, or because I think you are personally equipped (perhaps by advanced training) to direct my acts with special competence.[2] Anarchists never regard the personal character of an authority as entitling him to obedience; what gives him this title, in their view, are attributes of his position. Hence the answer to the question how anarchists justify authority depends on the specification of these attributes.

According to De George, anarchists make restrictions placed on the position of an authority by its subjects the mark of its legitimacy. If an authority's subjects put him in a position to direct their conduct, if they limit his directive power with rules, and if they can revoke it, then, says De George, anarchists consider the authority legitimate. Yet what the seminal nineteenth-century anarchists—Godwin, Proudhon, Bakunin, and Kropotkin—say about authority shows, I think, that they do not decide on its legitimacy in this way.

I can find no statements in their writings that the ways of limiting authority mentioned by De George are conditions for its legitimacy. Furthermore, these anarchists denounce even direct democracy as coercive and demeaning, though it limits authority as De George whose position is limited "from below" does not depend on their describes. But De George's thesis that anarchists endorse authority expressly saying so for its validity. For he backs his thesis with an *a priori* argument, which concludes from premises about the requisites for social order and about what anarchists mean by freedom that they must support authority, if its subjects limit it enough. Even if anarchists never state this conclusion, even if they deny it, De George could still be right to ascribe it to them, for they might have failed to reach it, though it is implicit in their thought. Hence the validity of his thesis about the character of authority under anarchy depends on the implications for authority of the fundamental premises of anarchism.

Of these premises, the one most crucial for the anarchists' justification of authority is their commitment to the overriding value of rational deliberation, understood as choosing and acting on the basis of evidence and arguments that one has systematically evaluated for oneself. Godwin regards "the conviction of man's individual understanding" as "the only legitimate principle imposing on him the duty of adopting any species of conduct." Bakunin insists that all man's actions be determined "by his own will and by his own convictions." The other anarchists resoundingly agree.[3]

Now authority, however limited, *must* interfere with rational deliberation so conceived. Whenever an authority issues a directive to a subject who concludes from his own assessment of arguments and evidence that the act the authority prescribes for him is wrong, the authority interferes with his deliberations by causing him to renounce them as his guide. For a subject cannot obey an authority and also follow his own deliberations when the courses prescribed by the authority and his deliberations conflict. It is of course possible to limit authority so that it interferes very little with deliberation. One effective way of doing this, identified by De George, is to give its subjects so much control over its power to issue directives that it prescribes the same conduct for them as they prescribe for themselves. But no matter how responsive to his subjects an authority may be, he must sometimes direct some of them to do what they think wrong, for otherwise, not receiving obedience because of *who* he is, he would not be an authority. Anarchists are usually thinking of unlimited authority when they denounce it for enslaving minds and brutalizing character.[4] But their denunciation also applies to authority which has limits. For even the most limited authority impedes deliberation, thus damaging what anarchists most cherish as a source of human worth.[5]

II

Two arguments can be found in De George's paper to refute the finding that authority impedes deliberation. The first argument claims that if an authority responds enough to the wants of a subject so that he thinks obeying it is generally advantageous, he can do what it requires, without impeding his deliberations, even when (for whatever reasons he finds conclusive) he objects to an act the authority prescribes. For when he performs this objectionable act, he follows his deliberations, which lead him to conclude that since the act, though wrong, is prescribed by an authority meriting general obedience, it should be done. What this argument overlooks is that deliberation about general obedience to authority (over public conduct, at any rate) is viewed by anarchists as inadequate. Adequate deliberation involves making and following judgments about the merit of each of an authority's *particular* prescribed acts. Hence subjects who obey an authority on any general ground, such as general advantage, hinder their deliberations, because in giving him obedience they renounce their own conclusions about the specific merit of the act they carry out.

By requiring deliberation about the merit of particular acts, the anarchists also defeat the second of the arguments suggested by De George for viewing deliberation and authority as compatible. This (Kantian) argument claims that I deliberate freely, though subject to an authority, if I obey him because his directive can be universally applied. Deliberation is only unobstructed, in this view, when its upshot is a course of action everyone can take. Since I am sure to perform such an action when I obey a universally applicable directive, obedience to an authority because he issues one guarantees that my deliberation is free.

Whatever the force of this argument, it is unacceptable to anarchists, for whom free deliberation depends, not on verifying the universal applicability of an authority's directive, but on approving of the action it prescribes. Even Proudhon, most sympathetic of the anarchists to Kantian universalizability, asks, "what difference does that abstraction make to me?"[6] As already noted, I deliberate freely, for the anarchists, only if I obey an authority on the ground that the specific merit of his prescribed act makes it right. Since I cannot obey an authority for this reason while also obeying him because his directives are universalizable (except when I believe that he deserves obedience on both grounds), obedience to an authority's universalizable directives must sometimes make my deliberations incomplete.

The anarchists' commitment to rational deliberation seems to prevent them not only from backing the limited authority De George says they favor but from backing authority of any kind. For any authority, however limited, sometimes keeps its subjects from following their own deliberations about the merit of the action it prescribes. If anarchists really do oppose all kinds of authority, they make the task of maintaining peace in their ideal society extremely difficult, because authority is an effective and reliable method of behavioral control. Physical coercion is obviously unacceptable to anarchists as a way to control behavior. If authority too is inadmissible, there remains one recourse for preventing harmful acts: reasoned argument to convince the potential wrongdoer that his contemplated conduct is incorrect.[7] Reasoned argument of this type is the only way to control behavior that unquestionably leaves deliberation free. For someone who convinces me with reasons to change my conduct, far from interfering with my deliberation, actually supports it, by supplying arguments and evidence which help me reach and follow my own conclusion concerning how to act. But though reasoned argument is much relied on by anarchists as a method of control, and though it can protect society to some extent from harm, it is a hazardous guarantee of security, even in an anarchy, where the temptation to misbehave would be much weaker than in the world we know. Because anarchists fear the danger of relying on nothing but reasoned argument to control behavior, they admit that under anarchy some authority is legitimate. Because they want anarchy to protect rational deliberation fully, they seek an authority that interferes with it the least. It is thus the conflict in the anarchists' perspective between their desire to protect rational deliberation and their mistrust of reasoned argument as a behavioral control that shapes their test for legitimate authority. An authority, to be legitimate for anarchists, must allow as much rational deliberation as possible, while also successfully protecting peace.

III

The authority that anarchists think satisfies these conditions is like the authority from below that De George claims they favor in being wielded from a position hemmed in by restraints. But whereas De George defines these restraints by who applies them, anarchists define them by what they say. What makes an authority legitimate for anarchists are restraints on his position, which, owing to their content, and regardless of their origin, compel him to direct conduct in ways which, without causing disorder, leave deliberation most free. One of the restraints which anarchists think does this determines who fills positions of authority; another regulates its exercise; a third prescribes its sanctions. In the search to clarify how anarchists justify authority, identifying these restraints is the crucial step.

Authority is usually conceived as attached to specially designated positions, which individuals must occupy to have their directives obeyed. Anarchists reject authority conferred by designated positions. "The only great and all powerful authority ... we can respect," writes Bakunin, is "the collective and public spirit." [8] Legitimate authority, for Godwin, is "exercised by every individual over the actions of another." [9] Proudhon would "eliminate the last shadow of authority from judges" and "submit decisions to the scrutiny and sanction of opinion." [10] And Kropotkin welcomes authority "when we see anti-social acts committed," so long as it is exercized by saying "aloud in anyone's presence what we think of such acts." [11] What anarchists are here stating is the distinctive proposition that justified authority must be shared by all. Specialized positions, however widespread and numerous, confer no right to obedience. All members of society must exercise authority before its directives can deserve support.

To defend the legitimacy of authority exercised by all, anarchists show how it serves deliberation. Wielders of authority who hold specially designated positions, being few in number, and so unable to know the details of their subjects' situations, must treat them as an undifferentiated group. Such treatment must often seem mistaken to the subjects, who, more familiar with their situations, are apt to conclude that circumstances unknown to the authorities make it wrong to act as they direct. But if everybody has authority, it can obstruct deliberation less, because its wielders, intermingled with its subjects, can intimately know the circumstances to which its directives apply. Equipped with this knowledge, they can bring these directives and the deliberations of their subjects into closer accord.[12]

Besides requiring that legitimate authority be exercised by all, anarchists insist that its directives be concrete. Rather than being bound by or embodied in general rules, they must be flexible and specific, formed, "not according to maxims previously written, but according to the circumstances of each particular cause."[13] The anarchists' argument for thus restraining authority appeals again to effects on deliberation. Authority which issues general directives impedes deliberation, no matter how numerous its wielders are, because general directives, applying to broad classes of action, and hence unable to adjust much to specific circumstances, are often opposed by subjects for failing to take these circumstances into account. An authority whose directives are particular, being more able to consider individual situations, can better avoid contradicting the deliberations of its subjects about the merit of its prescribed acts.

The third restraint imposed by anarchists on legitimate authority requires it to enforce directives with public rebuke. That anarchists make rebuke the sanction for authority is evident from passages already cited, in which Proudhon and Bakunin mention "opinion" and "public spirit" as methods to enforce authority's decrees. Godwin is more specific about how anarchist rebuke works. Most participants in anarchy "readily yield to the expostulations of authority," being convinced that its position entitles it to respect. But sometimes an authority's title to obedience is challenged. If the challengers disobey the authority's directive, they are made to comply with it by being openly rebuked. So "uneasy" are they "under the unequivocal disapprobation and observant eye of public judgment" that they are "inevitably obliged . . . either to reform or to emigrate."[14]

In arguing for authority sanctioned by rebuke, the anarchists' first consideration is social peace. Authority needs a sanction, even under anarchy, where its title to obedience receives unusually strong support. For an anarchist authority, though perhaps less than any other, confronts subjects who refuse to do what it directs. Unless it can use sanctions to exact obedience from these recalcitrants, they will break domestic peace. Thus, regard for social order leads anarchists to acknowledge that even their authority needs a sanction of some sort.

If concern for order convinces anarchists to legitimize some sanction, regard for deliberation leads them to legitimize the specific sanction of rebuke. All sanctions impede deliberation by overpowering it with fear. But rebuke differs from other sanctions in a way which anarchists think makes it impede deliberation less. Rebuke, being a psychological sanction, is readily internalized; it is easily incorporated into minds. Now anarchists believe that internalized sanctions, far from blocking deliberation, are one of its essential parts. They "are not imposed by an external legislator; . . . but are immanent in us, inherent, they constitute the very basis of our being." [15] When a subject who has internalized a sanction acts as the authority who imposes it directs, he reaches and follows his own conclusion. He issues "a sort of secret commandment from himself to himself" with which the authority's directive coincides.[16] Thus anarchists, persuaded that rebuke, compared to other sanctions, is benign, naturally choose it for their authority to invoke.

IV

The main evaluative issue raised by the foregoing analysis is whether anarchists are right to endorse the authority they favor, rather than endorsing authority from below. It is easy to show, if we accept their theory as valid, that their preference for their authority is correct. Anarchist theory directs us to evaluate authorities by choosing the one which (among those that protect order) hinders deliberation least; and it tells us what attributes of the authorities we are comparing are relevant for the making of this choice. Now the authority from below envisaged by De George carries none of the attributes favorable to deliberation which anarchist theory recommends. It is neither conferred on everyone, nor concretely wielded, nor sanctioned solely by rebuke. Rather, special officials exercise it, by issuing general directives, whose ultimate sanction is physical force.[17] Lacking the restraints that anarchist theory says protect deliberation, and burdened by others that it counts as impediments, authority from below is hardly of a type that one who accepts this theory can endorse.

It is true that authority limited from below impedes deliberation less than most. For its subjects, being able to restrain its power, can make it prescribe actions they deem right. But the subjects of an anarchist authority, being the same persons who wield it, can also make it prescribe what they approve. Hence the responsiveness to its subjects of authority from below gives it no advantage, so far as anarchist theory is concerned. Assessed from that standpoint, its general directives and physical sanctions make it less conducive to deliberation, and less legitimate, than the authority anarchists in fact support.

Even though the anarchists are warranted by their theory to endorse their authority rather than authority from below, perhaps their theory is incorrect. In that case, though their justification of authority would be internally consistent, as a convincing argument it would fail. Among the more dubious of their theory's elements that would need to be vindicated before their case for authority could carry weight are its claims that rational deliberation has overriding value, that internalized sanctions leave deliberation free and that the authority they favor, despite its mildness, is strong enough to safeguard peace.

Though I cannot here give these claims the scrutiny that a definitive appraisal of the anarchists' argument for authority needs, I can at least point to a startling conclusion entailed by acceptance of their case. If anarchists are right to say that rational deliberation is better served by their authority than by any other kind, they overturn the commonplace that deliberation proceeds most rationally under the rule of law. The essential marks of law, such as the official source of its directives, their general form, and their external sanction, are ordinarily said to aid deliberation by allowing subjects, within known, fixed limits, to choose and act as they see fit. Now, anarchist authority, being intimate, particular and internal, cannot issue directives of a legal sort. In fact, it must reject them, and for the very reason they are usually praised. For the official, general, and external attributes of legal regulation, which are the ordinary grounds for calling it an aid to rationality, are precisely what make anarchists denounce it as a threat. If anarchists are right in how they justify authority, the traditional alliance between law and rationality rests on a mistake.

NOTES

1. Proudhon, for instance, takes a patriarchal stand reminiscent of Filmer on the issue of domestic authority, while Godwin and Bakunin follow Plato in defending the authority of experts over private action and belief. William Godwin, *Political Justice* (Toronto: University of Toronto Press, 1946), I, 236; Pierre-Joseph Proudhon, *De la Justice dans la Révolution et dans l'Eglise* (Paris: Rivière, 1930-35), IV, 322; Michael Bakunin, *Oeuvres* (Paris: Stock, 1895-1913), III, 55.

2. The anarchists, De George, and most recent writers on authority all define it in about this way. For some anarchist analyses see Godwin, *Political Justice,* I, 121; Proudhon, *De la Justice,* II, 312; Peter Kropotkin, *Revolutionary Pamphlets* (New York: Benjamin Blom, 1968), p. 217. Two especially helpful contemporary essays are Richard Friedman, "On the Concept of Authority in Political Philosophy," in *Concepts in Social and Political Philosophy,* ed., Richard Flathman (New York: Macmillan, 1973), pp. 121-45, and Kurt Baier, "The Justification of Governmental Authority," *Journal of Philosophy* (Fall 1972), pp. 200-216.

3. *Political Justice,* I, 181; *Oeuvres,* V, 313; cf. Proudhon, *De la Justice,* I, 326, IV, 350; Kropotkin, *Pamphlets,* pp. 167, 285.

4. Eg. Godwin, *Political Justice,* I, 237; Proudhon, *De la Justice,* II, 312; Proudhon, *Idée générale de la Révolution au dix-neuvième siècle* (Paris: Rivière, 1924), p. 207, Bakunin, *Oeuvres,* III, 52; Kropotkin, *Pamphlets,* p. 284.

5. Carl Friedrich has defined a type of authority which may seem to escape the anarchists' charge that *all* authority hinders deliberation. According to Friedrich, what makes an issuer of directives an authority is his capacity to argue for his directives with reasons. "Authority, Reason and Discretion," reprinted in Flathman, *Concepts,* p. 179; *Man and His Government* (New York, Macmillan, 1963), p. 223. Why must someone who give reasons for his directives hinder the deliberations of the persons he directs? The answer to this question becomes clear once one sees that even for Friedrich the obedience of an authority's subjects is not conditional on their own assessment of its prescribed acts. All I need to be an authority in Friedrich's sense is the *capacity* to defend my directives with *plausible* reasons. I need not exercize this capacity; nor

need I convince my subjects that my arguments are right. Hence the same conflict, unacceptable to anarchists, between an authority's directives and the deliberations of his subjects arises even with authority limited as Friedrich suggests.

6. *De la Justice,* I, 430, cf. Kropotkin, *Ethics* (New York: The Dial Press, 1924), pp. 216-17.

7. It is perhaps because De George ignores coercive and rationale controls that he thinks "all organization involves some kind of authority" (p. 98). Organizations held together by reasoned argument, by coercion, or by some combination of these (as in the state ruled by Hume's sultan and mamelukes) are at least possible.

8. *Oeuvres,* III, 69n.

9. *Political Justice,* II, 496.

10. *De la Justice,* II, 218.

11. *Pamphlets,* p. 143.

12. Godwin, *Political Justice,* II, 352-53.

13. Godwin, *Political Justice,* II, 294, 399-400; Bakunin, *Oeuvres,* IV, 261.

14. *Political Justice,* II, 211, 340. It might seem that anarchists, by giving a sanction to issuers of directives, deprive them of authority. For an authority receives obedience not by imposing sanctions, but out of respect for who he is. Yet anarchists are on firm logical ground in giving authority a sanction. An issuer of directives who imposes sanctions still has authority, so long as some of his subjects sometimes obey him because of who he is. Since issuers of directives in an anarchist society usually receive obedience on this ground, despite their use of sanctions, they are still authorities.

15. Bakunin, *Oeuvres,* IV, 249.

16. Proudhon, *De la Justice,* I, 325.

17. Cf. p. 104 on specialized officials and on general rules; pp. 105-06 on sanctions. Though De George is vague about how authority from below enforces its directives, he implies that it sometimes resorts to physical force.

ANARCHISM AND THE RULE
OF LAW

9

DISRESPECT FOR LAW

LESTER J. MAZOR

Respect for law is the cornerstone on which the framework of the legal order and the political structure of the modern nation-state have been erected.[1] The argument for the rule of law asserts both the possibility and the benefit of a government by means of a widely accepted rational administration of norms. Absent the reciprocal relation of the rule of law by government on the one hand and respect for law by the citizenry on the other, the state would owe its continued existence only to brute force, and this is seen to be both perilous and costly. Not least of these costs is loss of liberty. And since liberty is both the guarantor of the separation between the public realm and the inviolable private sphere of activity and the protector of the opportunity to better one's life position by competition in the economic market, both personal privacy and free enterprise are threatened by the development of a situation in which respect for law is in jeopardy.[2]

To a generation that thought it had survived World War II, the vital function of respect for law as a bulwark against totalitarianism seemed evident. The personal rule of a malevolent dictator had wrought havoc, killed millions, and magnified suspicion that the veneer of Western civilization might not be strong enough to contain the beast within us. As the age-old debate between the doctors of the natural law and the priests of legal positivism resumed in the 1950s, the volleys of Hart and Fuller took as their starting point the need to give an account of law that would most strongly sustain its capacity to entail obligation, its ability to foster fidelity to law.[3] Ignoring evidence of the part that the Weimar judiciary had played in the rise of Hitler,[4] those who spoke for a strengthening of the rule of law claimed that it would serve as primary insurance against a repetition of the Holocaust. Indeed, the more ambitious saw the war itself as but an instance of the lack of an adequate international legal order. With world peace through law as its slogan, the creation of new arenas of world public order as its technique, and the extension of multinational corporativism as its material base, a system of global security for the atomic age was propounded.

In this context, attention turned to the necessity of creating respect for law in the newly emerging underdeveloped nations and to extending and deepening the degree of that respect in the free-world countries who would be called upon to serve as models for their younger brethren. The theory of economic stage development recognized the importance of the legal foundations of economic growth. Domestic legal thinking in the United States shouldered the tasks of purifying the American legal order, bringing retarded sectors up to an appropriate national standard, removing the last remnants of feudalism from an otherwise thoroughly modern legal system, and assuring that its benefits were made available to all. Realism taught that concern had to be given not merely to the content of legal rules on paper but also to the workings of legal processes in the field. Thus was initiated a new round of the empiricist work which had begun early in the century and which had been broken off by the depression and war. Since procedure already was known to be the real substance of law and the quest for justice quixotic if not Machiavellian, discussion centered on considerations of fairness and the process that was due, a focus that seemed entirely justified by the one occurrence which seemed to cloud the otherwise bright legal skies, the McCarthyist interlude. Of course there remained a portion of the world that was well understood to abjure the ideal of rule based on respect for law.[5] Yet even that cold and unfree world put some stock in a socialist form of legality, and though most doubted that this was anything more than window dressing, some argued that history indicated that men could come to believe in even their most extreme hypocrisies and that the reign of terror might someday be suppressed by the effort to clothe it in the garb of legitimacy. In the meantime the free world, at least, could differentiate itself by its secure monopoly of that most precious social resource, an uncoerced respect for law.

The comfort of this prospect and the sense of unimpeded forward motion were shattered at home by the appearance of the phenomenon of civil disobedience, abroad by the failure to reproduce the American model in sufficient quantity. Yet both of these developments, though troubling, were momentarily absorbed by the prevailing confidence. Despite those angry but unlearned souls who saw all civil disobedience if not all acts of protest as fundamentally disrespectful to law and country,[6] theory demonstrated that disobedience, if truly civil, paid even more regard to the need to maintain an overarching aura of respect for law than did mere mindless daily conformity. The critical issue seemed to be one of contagion, or, in the archaic vocabulary of Aquinas, prudence. So long as disobedient protest could be contained within the conditions that it be public, open, moral, accepting of sanction, and especially, dignified, restrained, narrow in its target and not too frequent, law might live with it.[7] We were left to differ only over the precise location of the point where that limit might be reached; perhaps the groups engaging in the activity might even be induced to relieve us of the burden and accept themselves the task of agreeing to manage the level of protest so that it would remain in bounds.[8] They would take turns.

Likewise an explanation began to emerge for the fact that respect for law was so slow in establishing itself in the new nations. Once again our American optimism and naiveté had betrayed us. The barriers of culture were deeper than we had thought in the flush of victory. It was not enough to write constitutions, create law schools, indoctrinate the leadership in the ideals which had created our standard of living and our way of life. We had forgotten how many generations it had taken to build respect for law in our own culture, how imperfect that achievement had proved to be in lands not so dissimilar to our own, how much the entire enterprise was dependent on a set of attitudes which could be expected to become widespread only as the material culture of these primitive people was brought into the twentieth century. How can you expect people to talk of freedom when they do not even have a Coke?

There were elements that refused to be fully absorbed, however, whatever the potency of the drink. Civil disobedience could also be construed as a renewal of the assertion of the priority of conscience over the claims of authority, of the primacy of group solidarity over the commands of legitimated power, of the preference for direct and immediate action rather than the incrementalism of intrasystemic reform. The course of antidevelopment in the uncolonies could be interpreted as a choice for liberation ahead of productivity, decentralization instead of neocolonization, polyculturalism rather than submission to the hegemony of a standardized Americanism. A generation that had known few heroes and almost forgotten the meaning of martyrdom awoke to discover that its precursors were dead, in prison, under attack, on trial: the Berrigans, the Black Panthers, the little people of Southeast Asia. Revolution, political and economic; social, cultural and countercultural, reappeared in our vocabulary. And among those who took to the streets in Watts and Paris, who liberated Morningside Heights and levitated the Pentagon, who above all kept the Hermetic decalogue,[9] names long forgotten began to be uttered: Proudhon and St. Simon, Bakunin and Kropotkin, Emma Goldman, Haymarket. At last the dread word itself: "anarchy."

What is anarchy, and what does it entail? The question is made difficult because the concept had been obscured in the pervasive neglect that it has received in the forum of political theory. Until yesterday we could expect it to be mentioned only as one of the bogey persons that might appear if law and order were allowed to fail. Thus it has been defined almost entirely by its otherness. Though it opposes war, it is accused of espousing violence. Though it opposes tyranny of all kinds, it is supposed to accept the tyranny of complete disorder. For if there is a single word with which it is most often identified, it is chaos.[10] And since chaos is a point before Genesis, beyond good and evil, beneath both form and substance, by this identification it can be made the enemy not only of all things human but also of all earthly existence.[11] Such are the characteristics awarded to heresy.

Against this chorus, the small voice of its advocates has barely been heard. Its literature is rarely accessible, where it has not been burned. Its history is largely unwritten, and dies a little each day in the villages of the Pyrenees, the fields of the Ukraine, the alleys of Paris. What should we make, then, of the fact that interest in its position should have emerged with new vitality in the last decade? Suddenly a spate of new books, compendia, anthologies, translations, summaries, even a few attempts to pick up the argument, to extend and expand it.[12] Has anarchy become so tame that a group of academic philosophers, social scientists, and *(mirabile dictu)* lawyers would dare to make it a topic of their annual debate, refined of course? No. Anarchism has been studied. Its essential works have been compiled. It has even been defended. Anarchism, yes. But anarchy—the idea of people living together without government, without law—no. Liberty, authority, responsibility, equality—each has taken its turn under the microscope of philosophic examination, but anarchy remains too fearful a subject to be looked so straight in the eye. Anarchism must stand in its stead. Is the power of anarchy so overwhelming that it must be approached only in this oblique manner? Certainly a portion of this power is generated by the critique which anarchy makes of law. Our object is to examine that critique, to suggest the justification that may be offered for a lack of respect for law, and finally to explore the consequences of admitting that the ultimate result of lack of respect for law is anarchy.

We begin by knowing that anarchy opposes law. Law claims to be the necessary instrument of that degree of order and justice which society can expect to achieve. Law, in the words of its adherents, is the glue that holds society together, the language of human interaction, the expression of social solidarity, the objectification of social relations. Yet those who embrace anarchy say that law cannot lead to justice, cannot establish order. Law, in their experience, only denies freedom, represses individuality, and maintains that greatest of all thieveries—property. Law cannot create; at best it can clear a path for creativity. Yet each obstacle it removes appears on closer examination to be but something that law itself had placed in the way, and somehow the work of removal, arduous as it is, only serves to establish a new set of legal barriers. "No cure for law but more law." [13] Law may win a battle, but the ultimate victory of justice and order is always over the hill.

If by law we mean nothing more pretentious than what the

officials of a given state will do, then the test of these propositions resides in the character of the people who exercise state power, the process that selects them, and the forces that impinge upon them in the discharge of their duties. We must consider judges, of course, but we have been warned not to allow their hierarchical prominence to divert us from an examination of the ubiquitous administrators, clerks, and anonymous petty officials who exercise legal discretion, much less to ignore the lawyers and the police, who do much of the daily drudgery on the front lines of the legal system. From the standpoint of those who prefer anarchy, it has seemed that those who exercise state power will use it above all to maintain their own position in society, that of the institutions to which they owe their title, and that of the class whose control of the state they are sworn to uphold.[14] The case once rested on direct, specific, and largely undocumented experience. Thanks to the wonders of social science, it has become possible to provide a more complete account.

The judges, it is now possible to determine, include only a few handfuls of women, though they are a majority of the populace, and apparently no children at all, although the possibility of the total exclusion of children seems so bizarre that we may want to attribute it to some failure of research design or error of statistical analysis. If we consider only the salaries of the judges, they are indeed an elite. Substantially more than 90 percent of American families have annual incomes less than theirs. Strangely, almost all the judges are lawyers by training and profession, although fewer than one-fourth of one percent of Americans have been admitted to this aristocracy of merit. They are answerable to the people, of course, through the politics of their selection, although life tenure in the case of some and the mysterious character of judicial elections in the circumstances of the others has assured a large measure of independence. Though they may be rather removed from the daily experience of life of most of us, at least they have frequent reminders, in the form of social engagements and professional meetings, of their close attachments to the inner circle of leadership of business, politics, and the organized bar.

Given these identifying marks, one might think that the judges would be concerned lest the authenticity of their great power in this most democratic of countries be drawn into question. Legal theory often has been a pillar of their support, insofar as it has served to demonstrate that they are but oracles of the law, above the controversies of those who litigate before them, a voice through which the will of society is heard. True that realism disclosed that they were also men, whose personal histories could be recounted and whose decisions could be quantified as instances of judicial behavior. This line of inquiry had been played out, however, as it became clear that is might lead too strongly in the direction of the conclusion that there was not enough to separate judges from other human beings to guarantee the moral authority of their decisions. The cure for an overdose of realism was recognition of the overriding strength of role expectation, that modern version of the *noblesse de la robe,* and emphasis upon the capacities of adult socialization, what once had been captured in the maxim that "taught law is tough law." Judges might be almost exclusively male, white, affluent, and either politically or professionally elite; yet the wand of theory could make them impartial, unbiased, disinterested, and reasonable. In America, there are no political trials. Yet if theory proved to be inadequate protection, there was always the obligation of the bar to defend the defenseless judiciary;[15] the doctrine of judicial immunity; and, when push came to shove, the contempt power. For those who somehow managed to pierce the shield of judicial neutrality and incapacity, to raise the question why the promises of liberty and fair procedure were not fulfilled, let alone those of equality and democracy, there was always the ultimate weaponry of the need to maintain judicial authority. For after all, "To distrust the judiciary marks the beginning of the end of society."[16]

The situation of lesser officialdom is different. These little rulers must face the resentment of the supplicant without an elevated bench behind which to hide, in quarters lacking the trappings of majesty, and wanting not only the magnificent titles of the magistracy but also most of the emoluments and the independent status that go with them. At the higher ranks, no doubt, the status differentials between administration and judiciary are slight. What is lost in oracular paraphernalia is compensated by the size of the organization that they head. As one descends through the layers of government, however, it becomes clearer that the only real protection of the degree of autonomy that administrators are able to preserve, the power over others they are allowed, and the station in life that these permit them to afford is the blizzard of paper that beclouds so much of their activity. Science has found it difficult to dispel the fog sufficiently to inform us of many of the mechanical details of the process by which social welfare programs that superficially appear to be designed to benefit the poor instead provide their principal advantage to those who are employed in distributing the benefits. The technique by which one agency evades responsibility by suggesting that a matter belongs in the jurisdiction of another, which when approached repeats the maneuver, would need the kind of extended analysis usually reserved for Supreme Court decisions or consumer preferences in cereal-package design were it to cease to be merely an art. If Nader's Raiders have managed to confirm that the ICC has not given us the finest railroad system in the world, that some of our medicines are poisonous, despite the close scrutiny of FDA and careful testing on prison volunteers; that competitive markets a la Friedman have not arrived, notwithstanding the indefatigable enforcement of the antitrust laws and the close monitoring by the regulatory agencies; that the air we breathe is hazardous to our health, the tireless efforts of the Environmental Protection Agency notwithstanding; we can take solace in the fact that a commodious nursing home awaits us in our old age, where we can draw a pension that a lifetime of toil has earned, comforted by the ready availability of medical care and the sure knowledge of an inexpensive burial—all these with the constant help and assistance of law and its minions.

Whatever we lack in knowledge of other officers of low visibility, the police, fortunately, have been much more thoroughly studied by people working in a variety of disciplinary traditions and funded lavishly by foundations; special government commissions; and most recently, by an agency of the federal government devoted entirely to spending its annual millions on assistance to law enforcement. To the Cleveland Crime Study and the Wickersham Report we have added, in just a few short years, the Report of the President's Commission on Crime, the Walker Report, the Report of the Eisenhower Commission on the Causes of Violence, and the Knapp Commission Report, to mention only a few of the most prominent and extensive studies. We have had a sociologist portray our vaunted system of justice without trial, a political scientist categorize the varieties of police behavior, an ethnomethodologist describe in submicroscopic detail the workings of the city police.[17] All this has helped greatly to explain the respect in which the police are held by the citizenry, manifested in the proportion of prime time allocated to their exploits. That they have managed to solve the crime problem of our society, even though engaged largely not in law enforcement but in order maintenance and social service, is one of the wonders of the modern world. Pity that in the moments of greatest stress that the police of Watts, Newark, Detroit, Chicago, of college campuses like Kent and Jackson State have had to call for military support, even though they had expended vast effort in community relations over the years. At least our society has not degenerated to that low estate where the police would have to carry guns. But then, we are a nation that has respect for law.

The legal profession shares with the police a large measure of the responsibility for the growth of disrespect for law. Lawyers have sought and obtained an elevated place in society, close to the centers of power. Most of their work is done on behalf of the corporations or those who have a substantial interest in them. The bar wrings its hands at the evidence that middle-income families, much less the great majority below that level, find the assistance of lawyers to be a luxury, and not a very enjoyable one at that. The legal profession has not yet managed, though undoubtedly it will, to establish a scheme comparable to its brother medicine's plan to insure that it is paid well and on time by secreting its fees within a payroll deduction.[18] Meanwhile, the spectacle of lawyers participating at the highest levels of abuse of power on behalf of the rulers of multinational corporations or the executives of government has sufficed to reinforce the image of the lawyer as the lackey of the wealthy and the powerful. What little the installation of legal services and cognate maneuvers did to suggest a larger public interest role for lawyers was swiftly undone as it became clear that the main contribution of these programs was to the employment of young lawyers and that when these modest reforms threatened in the least the power relations of agribusiness or the symbols of government their funding would be restricted and their authority eviscerated.

If we turn from consideration of the legal system as a set of personnel to examine law as a process of authoritative decision-making, the basis of growing disrespect for law may be seen to lie in the limited efficacy of this process to deal in a just, scientific, and expeditious manner with the variety, volume, and nature of issues calling for social resolution. The legal process is deeply rooted in the assumption that the disposition of a limited number of cases and controversies will influence behavior in enough situations to maintain domestic tranquillity. This is possible only on the view that the great mass of daily actions will occur within the limits set by law and that the consequences of particular actions will accrue in a significant way only to the immediate parties. The underlying notion is of the existence of separate and distinct private and public realms, which touch at points without ever becoming wholly congruent. Human interdependence is barely perceived by such an atomized and fragmented version of civil society, though it is both the dominant fact of human experience and the predicate of global survival. Boundary notions fundamental to law such as jurisdiction and justiciability can only be perceived as artificial and archaic under contemporary circumstances, and the conditions of the next century or two will make them appear even more so.

The legal process is loaded with devices that cause it to operate primarily to the benefit of those who approach it from a position of superiority. Although law has been depicted as a great equalizer, more often it serves as the means of multiplying advantage. Those who use the legal process most often have the greatest opportunity to structure its content in a way that will render it most welcome to their interests when next they draw on its resources. These repeat players also are those most likely to be able to muster the most powerful and numerous array of specialized lawyer talent, to best withstand the pressure of lengthy and costly negotiation or litigation, to define situations in advance in such a way as to put themselves in a favorable position, and to have nine points of the law in hand when conflict arises.[19] Although these points of criticism have been directed most often to the adjudicative process, their underlying thrust is no less applicable to the administrative and legislative processes. Indeed, the legislature, once conceived as the most highly democratic and versatile agency in the entire governmental structure, has become inaccessible to all but the most highly concentrated forces in society, almost totally incapable of innovation and unable to move at a pace remotely comparable to the velocity of events.

The causes of legislative immobilization are more than a temporary condition in our politics or an aberration of our historical
situation. They can be located in the representative character of
legislative bodies, doomed to choosing institutional objectives over
personal truth, to finding a vector of interests instead of a course of
action, to preserving the careers of the membership at the expense of
the lives of the constituents.[20] More fundamentally, legislative
ineptitude can be traced to the limits of rules as a means of
accomplishing change and as an expression of the character of social
relations. The task of the lawgiver, be it judge, legislator or
constitution maker, is not just a difficult one, it is impossible. For to
state a law for human affairs is either to rise to a level of generality
that invites escape, evasion, and manipulation or to descend to a
degree of specificity which leaves innumerable critical matters
unresolved and indeterminate.[21]

Law viewed as a system of norms, of directions or ought-
propositions is no more capable of procuring respect than in any of
its other incarnations. While philosophers have been searching for
the minimum content of natural law, other people have been
seeking for the way to give quality to life, to establish relationships
on a basis of equality, to have an end to domination and
exploitation of each other and of the universe. In the content of the
books of law, by contrast, can be found the elaboration of the
structure of inequality, the regime of repression, the scaffold of state
supremacy. We encounter the law of inheritance, increasingly
secreted in the interstices of the Internal Revenue Code, designed as
always to preserve dynastic continuity. But the advantage of
inheritance is also protected by the array of legal provisions that
purport to guarantee consideration of individual attainment and
merit, which function as a vehicle for maintaining and extending
the privilege that flows from birth into a family that has status and
position, a race that has control and hegemony, a sex that has
dominance and authority. Legal equality stops short of full
equality. Equality before the law cannot transcend the consequences of classification. Equality of opportunity is not enough to
overcome centuries of subordination. Affirmative action, however,
runs quickly aground on the shoals of equal protection, while
suburban racism sits back and lets white and black ghettos scramble
for the crumbs it leaves for public education.[22]

Restraints on alienation of property are even more extensive in the domain of corporate perpetuity. The bulk of legal activity surrounds the machinations of these immortal creatures, whose very personality is only a legal fiction. Those who have warned us not to think of the law exclusively as a negative force but to keep its facilitative aspect firmly in mind must have been thinking of the modern corporation and its increasingly etherealized forms of property. Labor too is a subject of legislation and adjudication, but only as a commodity. Within the framework of worker alienation, a limited right to bargain over the price of subservience has been recognized, though even that was long restricted to unions whose leadership could swear to political purity. Management prerogative remains the great untouched area of private power, with the lockout and the merger as its final recourse.

Commerce has been first friend to law since the beginning of legal memory, so it is not surprising that a substantial body of law's normative content is designed to foster and to regulate commercial practice. In matters within the mercantile community, the law has always been governed largely by custom. Contract is the commercial institution of strangers who bargain at arm's length. If rumors of its death are greatly exaggerated, the regulation under which contract has come for the protection of the consumer has done little more than give us one last wave before we sign on the dotted line. The illusion of voluntarism in contract has long been dissolved in the cynical acidity of the structure of the marketplace. Criminal law, small corner that it is, remains as the last vestige of the older version of the exchange relation. There at least the price list is on the menu and bargaining is in full force.[23]

Yet if we approach the subject not through law's hoary rubrics but from the angle of the problems the world faces, we confront not just ancient monuments and makeshift solutions but the abyss of extinction or the desert of tyranny. For others have been taking the temperature of the human prospect and coming to the conclusion that these legal mechanisms are incapable of escaping the narrowness of territoriality, of adopting a time horizon long enough to avoid leaving a legacy of death, of achieving a distribution of the world's goods and life's necessities equitable enough to forestall a disastrous collision. The call for an abandonment of law's limitations has come not so much from those who advocate anarchy as it has from those who would rather enforce tyranny than surrender their prerogative and mastery.

Against mounting evidence of law's inability to command respect and the ample grounds for loss of its capacity to do so, what arguments are offered for its continuation in authority? Those based on divine authorship and sacred tradition carry little weight in a secularized world of sharply differing religious and cultural heritages. The prevailing myth structure offered in support of the legal order posits some hypothetical original position from which is derived a social contract that adopts law as a means to obtain order and justice.[24] The more this story has been told, and its assumptions clarified in the telling, the more peculiar its premises appear.[25] To assent to its account one must seemingly accept on faith the plausibility of the restrictions set on those in the original position or bow to its wisdom because the unfolding of its logic coincides with one man's considered judgments, which remarkably happen to coincide with the principal features of the modern welfare state. No wonder, then, when we discover that the underlying objective of the enterprise is to provide an explanation, however circumlocutory, of the reasons why those least advantaged by these social arrangements should accept the justness of the superior benefits conferred on others.[26]

A more cautious argument is bottomed in fear. Fearful of human capacity for evil, of greed and the will to power, it posits the need for a sovereign legal order to constrain our dangerous propensities. As a reflection of the tragedy of a notion of society that reduces human beings to possessive individuals, the argument is a vivid social commentary. Yet how can it persuade those who see that there is more to be feared from a malefactor armed with law, a court, a police force, or an army than from the same person limited to the use of bare hands? The fear of loss that sets the tone of the argument is the trepidation of one who has something to lose, that is, one who stands in a position of dominance over others. The abstraction of the argument as it is usually stated conceals its unarticulated foundation. Law must be sovereign because without its rule there is only direct coercion to maintain the supremacy of the state. The state is the only secure foundation of the institutions of private property. Property is the necessary support for the maintenance of private life, the sphere of the household, the family

in which men dominate over women and children.[27] As Aeschylus
depicted in the Oresteia, the traditional order of convention must
surrender to a structured legal justice for the sake of male
supremacy, the archetype of all relations of domination.

If we must choose a starting point for our social existence, why
choose that which assumes the inevitability of domination? History
and anthropology are as susceptible to an interpretation that shows
the will to revolt as the will to dominate. But we are under no
injunction to abstract ourselves from our specificity, to imagine
some fanciful human nature or to dream of some utopia of
liberalism. If we reject the inevitability of domination, we can deny
the necessity of law. Without a world conceived exclusively in terms
of mine and thine, what is law but an officious intermeddler
suspended between universals and individuals in a manner that
allows neither the full virtue of universality nor the concrete
character of individuality to be realized? Our lack of respect for law
begins in an understanding that it is at best a substitute for a justice
that fully accepts our equality, our individuality, and our unity
with nature; that it is no more than a feeble replacement for an
order that emerges from community and consensus.[28] In an
antagonistically based society, the necessity of law is clear enough.
Better then to abandon the antagonistic basis of civil society.
Against the possibility of the sharing of the world's resources in
pursuit of a more joyful existence, the dark myth that justifies
authority and dominance has little appeal.

This is the burning attraction of anarchy. In raising this prospect,
it shows itself to be the enemy of the central tenet on which is
predicated our allegiance to the modern state and its legal
superstructure. We can conceive of anarchy as analogous to
religious toleration in its rejection of an established orthodoxy in
favor of a plurality of belief. As respect for law is waning we can
submit to tyranny, or we can struggle to create a world in which
persons are free to develop their own structure of order, a plurality
of social relations, subject only to the principles that no one shall be
habitually obeyed or recognized as entitled to be dominant. This
requires the rediscovery and reassertion of our political being and
the building of a space within which it can be exercised. In the
pursuit of liberation, the rejection of all forms of rule, and the
acceptance of eternal change as the only constant in experience lies

the oft-hidden promise of anarchy and the source of disrespect for law.

NOTES

1. "Books of history, of political science, of social economy, are stuffed with this respect for law. . . . The same work is done by newspapers. They have not an article which does not preach respect for law, even where the third page proves every day the imbecility of that law, and shows how it is dragged through every variety of mud and filth by those charged with its administration. Servility before the law has become a virtue, and I doubt if there was ever even a revolutionist who did not begin in his youth as the defender of law against what are generally called 'abuses,' although these last are inevitable consequences of the law itself." P. Kropotkin, *Law and Authority,* in Kropotkin's Revolutionary Pamphlets (Baldwin ed., 1927), pp. 197-98.

2. The function of the concept of the rule of law in the prevailing ideology is elaborated in R. Unger, *Knowledge and Politics* (1975), pp. 63-103.

3. See J. Shklar, *Legalism* (1964), pp. 107-9.

4. O. Kirchheimer, *Political Justice* (1961), pp. 211-14.

5. Beginning in 1950, the American Bar Association has had a series of special committees and, more recently, a standing committee, on the subject. For several years the committee's formal title was "On Education about Communism and its Contrast with Liberty under Law."

6. E.g., L. Waldman, *Civil Rights—Yes; Civil Disobedience—No,* 37 N.Y. St. B.J. 331 (1965).

7. See M. Keeton, *The Morality of Civil Disobedience,* 43 Texas L. Rev. 507 (1965).

8. J. Rawls, *A Theory of Justice* (1971), pp. 373-75.

9. W. H. Auden, "Under Which Lyre," in *Collected Shorter Poems 1927-1957* (1966), pp. 221-25.

10. Bakunin, for his part, located the source of social chaos in the assumption of individual self-sufficiency. See G. Maximoff, ed., *The Political Philosophy of Bakunin* (1953), p. 102.

11. "I have always been a doer and a builder, it was in my blood and the blood of my tribe, as it is born in the blood of beavers. When I meet a man who is a loafer and a destroyer, I know he is alien to me. I fear him and all his breed. The beaver is a builder and the rat is a destroyer; yet they both belong to the rodent race. The beaver harvests his food in the summer; he builds a house and stores that food for the

winter. The rat sneaks to the food stores of others; he eats what he wants and ruins the rest and then runs and hides in his hole. He lives in the builder's house, but he is not a builder. He undermines that house; he is a rat.

"Some men are by nature beavers, and some are rats; yet they all belong to the human race. The people that came to this country in the early days were of the beaver type and they built up America because it was in their nature to build. Then the rat-people began coming here, to house under the roof that others built. And they try to undermine and ruin it because it is in their nature to destroy. They call themselves anarchists." J. David, *The Iron Puddler* (1922), pp. 60-61.

12. L. Krimmerman and L. Perry, *Patterns of Anarchy* (1966); E. Goldman, *Anarchism and Other Essays* (1969); D. Guérin, *Anarchism* (M. Klopper, tr., 1970); I. Horowitz, *The Anarchists* (1970); R. Wolff, *In Defense of Anarchism* (1970); A. Carter, *The Political Theory of Anarchism* (1971); M. Shatz, ed., *The Essential Works of Anarchism* (1971); G. Runkle, *Anarchism* (1972).

13. K. Llewellyn, *The Bramble Bush* (1951), p. 106. "One result of the institution of law, is, that the institution, once begun, can never be brought to a close. Edict is heaped upon edict, and volume upon volume." W. Godwin, *Enquiry Concerning Political Justice* (K. Carter, ed., 1971), p. 273.

14. "To term the proceedings during this trial justice, would be a sneer. Justice has not been done, more than this, could not be done. If one class is arrayed against the other, it is idle and hypocritical to think about justice. Anarchy was on trial, as the state's attorney put it in his closing speech. A doctrine, an opinion hostile to brute force, hostile to our present murderous system of production and distribution. I am condemned to die for writing magazine articles and making speeches." Address of Michael Schwab to the court before sentence was pronounced, in A. Parsons, *Anarchism* (1887).

15. "Adjudicatory officials, not being wholly free to defend themselves, are entitled to receive the support of the bar against unjust criticism." American Bar Association, Code of Professional Responsibility, EC 8-6.

16. Balzac, as translated and quoted by O. Kirchheimer, *Political Justice,* p. 175.

17. J. Skolnick, *Justice Without Trial* (1966); J. Wilson, *Varieties of Police Behavior* (1972); J. Rubinstein, *City Police* (1973).

18. The situation is canvassed in J. Frank, "Legal Services for Citizens of Moderate Income," in *Law and the American Future* (M. Schwartz, ed., 1976), pp. 116-30.

19. See M. Galanter, *Why the "Haves" Come out Ahead: Speculations on the Limits of Legal Change,* 9 Law & Soc. Rev. 95 (1974).

20. "They see a race of law-makers legislating without knowing what their laws are about; today voting a law on the sanitation of towns, without the faintest notion of hygiene, tomorrow making regulations for the armament of troops, without so much as understanding a gun; making laws about teaching and education without ever having given a lesson of any sort, or even an honest education to their own children; legislating at random in all directions, but never forgetting the penalties to be meted out to ragamuffins, the prison and the galleys, which are to be the portion of men a thousand times less immoral than these legislators themselves." P. Kropotkin, *loc. cit.,* p. 201.

21. "The law is stationary, fixed, mechanical, 'a chariot wheel' which grinds all alike without regard to time, place and condition, without ever taking into account cause and effect, without ever going into the complexity of the human soul." Emma Goldman, "Address to the Jury," in *Red Emma Speaks* (A. Shulman, ed., 1972), p. 323.

22. See Max Weber on law in *Economy and Society* (M. Rheinstein, ed., 1954), pp. 355-56.

23. See E. Pashukanis, "General Theory of Law and Marxism," in *Soviet Legal Philosophy* (J. Hazard, ed., 1951), pp. 205-25; A. Rosett and D. Cressey, *Justice by Consent* (1976).

24. J. Rawls, *A Theory of Justice.*

25. See G. Maximoff, *The Political Philosophy of Bakunin,* pp. 208-9.

26. J. Rawls, *A Theory of Justice,* p. 15.

27. This is the classical argument for sovereignty offered by Bodin. See J. Allen, *Political Thought in the Sixteenth Century* (1928), pp. 46-47.

28. See S. Diamond, "The Rule of Law Versus the Order of Custom," in *The Rule of Law* (R. Wolff, ed., 1971), pp. 117-39.

10

THE PROFOUNDEST RESPECT FOR LAW: MAZOR'S ANARCHY AND THE POLITICAL ASSOCIATION

LISA NEWTON

Professor Mazor has given us a magnificent summation for a conference on the philosophy of law and politics. His paper is well argued, thorough, and contagious in its conviction; I cannot say I have any real objection or criticism. But he has yielded one crucial point to his enemy: he has allowed his adversary the right of definition, and consequently, requires himself throughout to argue the very reverse of his own thesis. Grant to him, or to the apparent course of his argument, the right to define the crucial terms, and his paper becomes an excellent polemic *against* anarchy, drawn by an Aristotelian vision of the functioning political association and motivated by the profoundest *respect* for law. I shall attempt, in these comments, first: to *reread* Mazor's paper, not criticize it, showing in a more coherent terminology the actual course of the argument; and second; to suggest, very briefly, one way in which the insights of the anarchist tradition may inform the argument's conclusion.

I. THE NATURE OF LAW

In a different context, Robert Paul Wolff once pointed out that the greatest task and triumph of a dominant doctrine (in that case, utilitarianism) is to convince us that its point of view—its method, its goal—is the only one *possible*.[1] Should it accomplish this task, we are forced to argue within the framework it lays down. We find it difficult, for example, to argue in favor of any meaningful conception of "community" if we have already granted that the only possible "happiness" is apart from community, in individually pleasurable states of consciousness; we would be compelled to argue in favor of unhappiness. Under those circumstances, we may be willing to argue for unhappiness. Such is the case in Mazor's argument: his paper is a ringing denunciation of lawlessness, a plea for justice; but having granted to the criminals the title to the word "law," acknowledging their will as the only *possible* "law," he finds himself arguing for anarchy.

For what *is* law, or rule of law? The formulation to which we always return is from Euripides: "you have known/ *A good Greek state, and the long still grasp of law, not changing with the strong man's pleasure.*"[2] That "long still grasp of law," *opposed* to the whims and financial interests of the strong men who wield power, is the unchanging touchstone of lawful government. (Be it noted well: in its original context, as in *most* later contexts, that beautiful formula is uttered by a powerful man who has just committed a terrible injustice; that circumstance was, and still is, irrelevant to its value, as the sincerity of the utterer is irrelevant to the truth of any but an autobiographical psychological statement.) Rule of law is always *opposed* to "the interest of the stronger party"; and it seems that Mazor's denunciatory catalogue of sins is directed only at the latter. For, if we examine some of the items in the catalogue, we discover that the major complaint is that "those who exercise state power will use it above all to maintain their own position in society" (p. 148), although that is not what the Constitution requires them to do; that to achieve this end the membership of the judiciary is almost exclusively restricted to "male, white, affluent" citizens (p. 149), although the law does not permit discrimination on grounds of sex, race, or personal assets; further, as corollaries, we find that social welfare programs benefit primarily "those who are employed in disttributing the benefits" (p. 150) although they were designed to help the poor; that federal agencies cannot or will not enforce the law in the areas entrusted to them (p. 150); that our municipal police cannot or will not enforce the law in our cities (p. 151), that lawyers use their expertise to help the rich evade the law (p. 151). Surely none of this complaint is directed *against* law; quite the contrary. It can be read only as a rejection of the essentially wrongheaded conception of law as "what powerful people (the officials of a given state) will do;" but such rejection is unnecessary, for the opposition between "law" and the preferred and predictable actions of the strong is built into the notion of law. And much the same commentary could be made on Mazor's next proposed understanding of "law," as "a process of authoritative decision-making" (p. 151); the argument turns immediately on the actual workings of that process as administered by decision-making authorities, who turn out to be less than fully committed to enforcing the law when it works to their disadvantage and to ensuring the full participation of the poor in the benefits of the law. Again he presents us with a plea for law and justice against the self-interested finagling of the rich and powerful. He comes no closer to articulating this plea even when he proposes to consider law as a "system of norms" (p. 153)—the "norms" turn out to be details of statute and the common law, totally removed from that long still grasp of law; they are, as he points out, mere legitimations of the strong man's pleasure. Objections could be raised to his character-ization of the workings of the legal system in this country at this time, but I have no intention of raising them; as I said at the beginning, I have no objection or criticism to level against his argument. I object only to his initial concessions: Mazor has allowed the rich and powerful to have *title* to the law; he has allowed Thrasymachus to define justice and George Wallace to define "law and order." He should never have done this: he not only deprives himself of a normative base for his criticisms, but he leaves himself without a name for his ultimate objective. This objective, suggested only in his final paragraph, is the creation of the political association.

One of the most frustrating features of this paper is its end. It stops precisely where chaos and tyranny end and law begins. The situation given us in the last paragraph is precisely that sketched by Aristotle in the fifth book of the *Nichomachean Ethics* and elaborated in the *Politics:* it is the condition of the simultaneous establishment of the institution of the *polis,* of the rule of law which constitutes its essential feature, of justice, its essential condition or virtue, and above all, of the new status of "citizenship," a status defined by equality among its members: equality in participation in making the law, equality before the law as subject to it, equality in ruling and being ruled.[3] This collective action, taken by the citizens, effectively constituting the political association and themselves as its citizenry, is the essential expression of (in Mazor's terminology) the discovery and assertion of their political being, the rational completion of their social being; the political association they create is the space in which it is exercised, the "public space" (Hannah Arendt's terminology) in which the political dialogue is carried on.[4] The conditions for this dialogue are, very simply, liberty and law: "liberty" summarizes the conditions of full (and informed) individual participation, and from it may be derived our traditional "liberties" of speech, press, and assembly; "law" summarizes the conditions necessary to protect those liberties, primarily the condition of equality in this political space. Be it noted: the establishment of *this* equality will not bring in its wake the inevitable equalization of all else among the citizens. They remain, for all we know, as unequal in strength, beauty, wealth, and intellect *after* constitution of the *polis* as they were before. Once constituted, they are free to take, as a body, any constitutional collective action they like. (Conceptual considerations lead us to rule out action which effectively abolishes the political association by negating one or more necessary conditions for it; such action, described as "unconstitutional," cannot be accommodated within the space created.) Well within the scope of permitted collective action is legislation enhancing equality in domains other than the political, and nothing forbids the enactment of measures of *social* justice, measures designed to bring about a more equitable distribution of the goods and services available to the community. Once enacted, such measures deserve strict enforcement; but the justification of the enforcement lies in the citizenry's *respect for law,* not in some free-floating moral principle demanding pity for the poor among us. Such social legislation is not ever *required* of the citizenry; logically, there is no connection between political and economic equality. But the very existence of the public space and its citizenry, the very existence of the open and ongoing dialogue in which all citizens participate, is the best possible condition to motivate social legislation: it exposes to public view the contrasts in economic condition existing in the society; it prompts the question, whether a citizen who must struggle to survive can participate in the dialogue with full effectiveness; and if Aristotle's own solution (exclude the poor from politics) is ruled out, it demands the institution of a program of economic aid sufficient to ensure leisure for political activity for everyone. Above all, it creates a moral climate in which earnest consideration can be given to a program of full economic equalization by insisting on that equality of moral agency and human dignity required for dialogue.[5] The fashionable "radicalism" which professes to scorn "bourgeois" political equality because it has not yet produced economic equality, and would abolish "bourgeois" liberty and political justice in the name of welfare and social justice, is therefore, from the point of view of its own ends, the height of folly. It is only in the political space that we can see the inequities that radicalism denounces; the destruction of that space would render them, and all further inequities the destroyer chose to impose, invisible and therefore irremediable.[6] Liberty and law are the conditions Mazor is seeking in his last hopeful appeal to what he is trapped into calling "anarchy"; it is the renewal of that collective action establishing rule of law that he advocates. Only his unnecessary initial grant of the concept of law, bestowed as a free gift upon the debased company of Watergate, has him apparently arguing for anarchy.

II. ANARCHY'S COMMENT ON THE RULE OF LAW

No elaborate research is needed to establish that the Anarchist tradition is not self-consistent. Practically every point of view other than support of the existing nation-state can be found somewhere within it. We should not be surprised to find anarchists wholly supportive of tyranny, as Stirner is; and we should not be surprised to find an interesting strain of anarchist theory, perhaps best represented by Proudhon (and the utopian socialists who preceded him), able to support and complete the Aristotelian model of political association.[7] I find this communitarian thread of the anarchist tradition more sympathetic than some of the others, if only because it spends less time indulging in fantasies. Like Aristotle, it recognizes the simple fact that human beings do not live in good-hearted playful association, devoid of rule, structure, or order of dominance. Otters, perhaps, may enjoy such a playground existence, although I could not vouch for it; but human beings turn out to be the sort of social animal that always establishes an order of dominance in association. The only question is, what kind of order? Aristotle spoke to an immediate past of tribal order: monarchy, hereditary hierarchy, rule by unquestioned tradition, and he found it wanting because it did not fulfill the rational (hence autonomous) nature of man. The anarchist (of the Proudhonian, or communitarian variety) speaks to a monstrous empire, the modern nation-state, which crushes and absorbs into its imperial self all natural communities within its reach, and he finds it wanting for the same reason. Neither the tribe nor the nation-state can find room for the public space: the tribe because it is too small for the diversity required for dialogue, the nation-state because it preempts for itself the powers of decision which should belong to the citizenry in smaller associations. I cannot deny that this failure is a matter of degree; a military dictatorship clearly allows less political participation at any level than the representative government and earnest attempt at federalism found in the United States. The fact remains: the very size of the United States removes the possibility that the ordinary working civilian will participate fully and directly and with full information in the decisions that crucially affect his life. The anarchist is opposed to the nation-state and works for its dissolution, for only in a society fully decentralized will man's political being be rediscovered and reasserted. But of course, Aristotle also insisted that the *polis* had to be small: for the same reason. The anarchist (at least the realistic anarchist who does not indulge in useless fantasies of otterdom) has far more in common with the conservative tradition than he would ever want to admit.

It must seem odd to conclude any argument on political philosophy with sentences that begin, "As Aristotle and the anarchists agree ... etc." But this agreement is not in the least paradoxical. The anarchists and communards in our own time have only reminded us of Aristotle's simply discovery: man is a political animal, a being whose natural association is governed by the laws he himself has created and to which he has subjected himself. He cannot complete his own nature in any other setting, and it is his nature and his duty to transcend and to resist any power that preempts his autonomy. Against tradition or against the arrogant will of the strong man and the lawless official this autonomy is perennially rediscovered and reasserted, providing political philosophy with its most fundamental ongoing dialogue and "anarchy" with its perennial appeal.

NOTES

1. Robert Paul Wolff, *The Poverty of Liberalism* (Boston: Beacon Press, 1968), pp. 164-67, 193-94.
2. Euripides, *Medea*. G. H. Murray, trans. and ed.
3. Aristotle, *Nicomachean Ethics, V,* vi: 1134a. *Politics* I, ii: 1252b-1253a; III, i-iv; 1274b-1277a.
4. Hannah Arendt, *On Revolution* (New York: Viking Press, 1963).
5. Again, see Wolff, *loc. cit.*
6. The "radical" is discontent because "the rules" do not seem to *equalize the strength* of strong and weak, but they were never meant to do that. All they can do is restrain the strong from *using* their strength to render the weak permanently incapable of action, and that service alone merits their establishment and support. (Consider: if a sadistic judge sentenced you to go three rounds with Muhammad Ali, would you prefer to fight according to the Marquis of Queensberry rules or without any rules at all? Rules will restrict you, but they restrict Ali much more, and there is *no* set of arrangements we can make for the fight that will allow you to emerge the victor. By the rules, you stand a good chance of emerging *alive.*)
7. Useful summaries of anarchist views can be found in George Woodcock's *Anarchism* (New York: World Publishing Co., 1962); James Joll's *The Anarchists* (New York: Grosset and Dunlap, 1964); Irving L. Horowitz's *The Anarchists* (New York: Dell Publishing Co., 1964); and Leonard Krimerman and Lewis Perry's *Patterns of Anarchy* (Garden City, New York: Doubleday & Co., 1966). And Martin Buber's magnificent *Paths in Utopia,* recently reprinted (Boston: Beacon Press, 1970), should not be overlooked. For Proudhon, see Joll, *The Anarchists,* pp. 76 ff.

11

DISRESPECT FOR LAW AND THE CASE FOR ANARCHY

ALAN WERTHEIMER

When the irony and rhetorical flourish of Professor Mazor's article are stripped away, it appears that he has set himself four tasks: to state the critique that anarchy makes of law; to examine the evidence for that critique; to consider two arguments (in the face of this weighty evidence) in defense of respect for law; and finally, to explore the consequences of accepting the anarchist critique. The anarchists assert that the law cannot establish justice and cannot provide social order. Our knowledge of legal systems suggests that there is no reason to think that it could provide either justice or order. If the law is "what the officials of a given state will do," given what we know about the way in which state officials are recruited, to whom they respond, and the procedures by which they operate, there is no reason to expect anyone to pay even a modicum of respect to the law.[1] No state of nature theory, Rawlsian or Hobbesian, can adequately shore up the law under the anarchist attack. Consequently, disrespect for law is a widespread, growing, and (most important) an appropriate response to the inherent inadequacies and cruelties of law. While others have defended a *(prima facie)* obligation to obey the law by rejecting the alternative of universalizing the maxim of disobedience, for Mazor the prospect of a universalized disrespect for law is among the most attractive features of the anarchist position. Unlike Wolff, who arrives at the truth of anarchism through an *a priori* argument, Mazor reaches the promised land by traveling through the evidence of social science. And unlike Wolff, who cautiously suggests that "we have survived the death of God, and we may yet survive the death of the state," for Mazor the death of the state is a precondition of our survival.[2] While Wolff anguishes over the consequence of discovering that the emperor is wearing no legitimate clothes, Mazor is prepared to lead us to the joy of the nudist colony. Not only is anarchy both possible and desirable, but, like Tolstoy, Mazor is convinced that "no anarchical disorder could be worse than the position to which governments have already led their peoples, and to which they are leading them."[3]

Just as psychiatrists generally recoil from the claim that "mental illness is a myth," there is a natural resistance among political scientists and political philosophers to the anarchist challenge to the institutions and concepts upon which their noble professions inevitably rest. That Mazor's case for anarchy is not rooted in the cautious, sober, and analytic style to which academics have become accustomed makes it even more tempting to dismiss the argument out of hand. But Mazor has rightly reminded us that the modern state and its legal superstructure have not eradicated human misery, may justly be held accountable for history's most extensive cases of human cruelty, and may be irrelevant to a crisis which is global. I propose to continue the dialogue, to take a few steps back and examine the assumptions and arguments that Mazor employs in making his case for anarchy, and to offer some speculations as to whether or not anarchy is the course which others should be encouraged to follow.

One is told that "anarchy opposes law" because law "cannot lead to justice, cannot establish order."[4] It is important to remember that the rule of law requires a widespread respect for law, a respect which is "uncoerced"[5] and that the rule of law must therefore be distinguished from the rule of "brute force."[6] A society may be characterized by disrespect for law when the social order becomes unglued or when it is held together only by the use of force. That the police carry guns in the United States suffices to show that it is a nation in which disrespect for law is rampant. Basic to the anarchist critique is that the "law's inability to command respect" stems from the "ample grounds for loss of its capacity to do so ..." [7] Thus having claimed that the law does not, in fact, receive respect, Mazor embarks on the most extensive part of his analysis—to show that the law does not deserve respect. The anarchist believes that "those who exercise state power will use [the law] above all to maintain their own position in society, that of the institutions to which they owe their title, and that of the class whose control of the state they are sworn to uphold." [8] Because the law cannot provide justice, it does not deserve respect. Because the law does not deserve respect, it does not receive respect.

The anarchist critique of law makes three distinct claims: (1) the law does not receive respect; (2) the law does not deserve respect; (3) the law does not receive respect *because* the law does not deserve respect. Even if the second claim were true, it is entirely possible that the first claim might be false. A legal system thoroughly underserving of respect might nevertheless receive a considerable degree of respect and provide a high degree of order. Even if the first and second claims were true in a given society, the third claim might be false. The causes of disrespect may be located in varying social, economic, and cultural sources. If the law does not receive respect, this may be true for reasons entirely unconnected to the law's undeservingness of respect.

In order to examine this critique, it is first necessary to take a closer look at the concept "disrespect for law." What is entailed by respect for law? Given the opportunity to engage in illegal gambling, my behavior (viewed externally) might conform with the law for at least three different reasons. First, I might simply think it unwise (on either prudential or moral grounds) for me to gamble, and refrain for that reason alone. Secondly, knowing that I might be punished for engaging in an illegal activity, I might decide that the risk of incurring the punishment outweighs my expected benefit (psychic or monetary) from gambling. Thirdly, I might refrain from gambling simply because gambling is illegal and because I believe I am under a *(prima facie)* obligation to obey the laws of the state. Mazor would be compelled to argue that only in the third case is it proper to say that I am demonstrating "respect for law." Respect for law is not an external matter, turning solely on the behavioral fact of compliance, but an internal matter, turning on the reasons for compliance. In the first case, that gambling is illegal is irrelevant to my behavior. In the second case, I obey the law because I feel "obliged" to obey, not because I feel "obligated" to obey. As Hart points out, one may feel "obliged" to hand over one's money to a gunman without feeling "obligated" to do so.[9] In that case, compliance stems from "brute force" which Mazor wishes to contrast with an "uncoerced" respect for law.

Compliance with the law is not identical with respect for law. It is also true that noncompliance with the law is not identical with disrespect for law. If, as Mazor suggests, an act of civil disobedience may signify a great respect for the rule of law as such, to what does he refer when he claims that there is a widespread and growing disrespect for law?[10] Most persons would point to crime. Thieves, muggers, rapists, murderers, dope peddlers, embezzlers, Watergate burglars—it is they who do not respect the law. Yet if I can feel "obliged" to obey the law without feeling "obligated" to do so, I can also feel "obligated" to obey the law without feeling "obliged" to do so. To disobey a law is not necessarily to assert the illegitimacy of the particular law or the legal system as such. To disobey a law is not even to claim that one thinks it is right to disobey. Most of us will, on occasion, place considerations of our *interest* or *desires* over considerations of our obligations or duties, although people may vary in their tendency to do so. I suspect that a considerable proportion of disobedience stems simply from a calculation that disobedience serves one's interests or desires more effectively than obedience, that is, the probable gains of disobedience outweigh the probable costs. Thieves do not, by their actions, necessarily signify their belief that the laws which uphold the institution of private property are unjust. They may simply wish to evade the law because they believe they stand to gain by doing so.

If "respect for law" means "to accept the law as legitimate," just as one can obey the law while not respecting the law, one can disobey the law while continuing to respect the law. It might be argued, however, that respect for law must entail more than mere acceptance of the law as legitimate, and that noncompliance (except in the case of civil disobedience, in which one is not attempting to *evade* the law) does signify disrespect for the law. It could be argued that one who claims to accept the legitimacy of the law and an obligation to obey it, but disobeys the law for reasons of personal interests is not respecting the law, because to "respect the law" means to "voluntarily abide by the law."

Let us assume that this latter account of "respect for law" is more plausible. "Respect for law" requires voluntary or "uncoerced" obedience. There is, however, a crucial difficulty with the notion of "voluntary obedience" or "uncoerced respect." Hart points out that all legal systems exhibit a tension between "those who . . . accept and voluntarily co-operate in maintaining the rules . . . and those . . . reject the rules and attend to them only from the external point of view as a sign of possible punishment." [11] Not only is there a tension between those who obey the law from different perspectives, there is an inherent tension between the perspectives. I wish to argue that it is difficult to sustain a sharp distinction between "voluntary obedience" and "uncoerced respect" on the one hand and obedience secured by the threat of punishment or "brute force" on the other. Respect for *law* can never be purely voluntary—it will always require an amount of "brute force."

The law requires that I drive no faster than fifty-five miles per hour on interstate highways. While I would prefer to drive faster, I accept the legitimacy of the laws (in general) and I think the purpose of this particular law (to reduce gasoline consumption) is quite sound. I respect the law and I am willing to abide by it. Hart has reminded us that when one obeys the law one is not paying homage to some mystical deity, but rather is "cooperating" with one's fellow citizens by making some sacrifice (paying taxes, joining the army, driving at fifty-five miles per hour) in order that some good be provided or some harm be avoided. My continued voluntary obedience to the law is sustained by my belief that I am, in fact, "cooperating" with my fellow citizens. Let us say that I begin by driving along at fifty-five miles per hour, but find that most of my fellow drivers are unwilling to do likewise. I am annoyed at those drivers who pass me, because they are unwilling to make the sacrifice I have made, and my annoyance is increased by my realization that the tension supposedly inherent in any legal system appears to be absent: they receive no penalty for their disobedience.

When disobedience to the law becomes sufficiently widespread and the law is unenforced, it becomes literally impossible for me voluntarily to "cooperate" with my fellow citizens by obeying the law, for "cooperation," by definition, requires that a sufficient number of them do likewise. Obedience to the law is no longer an act of voluntary cooperation, but an act of philanthropy, in which one makes sacrifices for one's fellow citizens that they are unwilling and are not forced to make for you. As Schelling puts it, the law involves an "enforceable social contract. I'll cooperate if you and everybody else will; I'm better off if we all cooperate than if we all go our separate ways." [12] The person who is willing to cooperate and obey the law, but is not willing to do so if others are not (externally) doing so, is not being inconsistent. "He's *not* interested in doing minute favors for a multitude of individuals, most of whom he doesn't know...." [13] I suggest, then that the ability and willingness of the state to penalize those who violate the laws, to use "brute force," is a precondition for sustaining an "uncoerced" respect for law. It is respect for *law* that is at stake, and law is, by definition, a system that stipulates that disobedience will normally be met with coercion. The tension between the two perspectives is complex. Some "brute force" may be necessary to ensure that a sufficient number of citizens obey the law. Only when enough citizens (externally) obey the law (for whatever internal reason) is it possible for one to "voluntarily cooperate" by obeying the law.

At the conceptual level, it appears that there are two major difficulties with Mazor's analysis of disrespect for law. First, noncompliance with the law does not require that one have moral objection to the law. One can, without contradiction, accept the legitimacy of the law and disobey the law. One can even believe that it is "right" that one be punsihed if caught disobeying, while simultaneously attempting to evade getting caught. There is no necessary connection between disrespect for law viewed externally as disobedience, and disrespect for law viewed internally as disobedience stemming from a rejection of one's obligation to obey the law. Secondly, it is wrong to draw a sharp distinction between voluntary or "uncoerced" respect for the law, and obedience to the law which stems from the fear of punishment. There is no incompatibility between strict enforcement of the laws (the willingness to use "brute force") and respect for the law. If respect for law is consistent with enforcement of the law, those charged with that responsibility will have to perform their duties in a manner which is responsive to the characteristics of the society. If, for historical, ideological, and economic reasons, the ownership of guns is widespread in the Unites States, it is unreasonable to expect the police not to carry guns.[14] Thus, the fact that the police carry guns in the United States does not entail that the United States is a society characterized by widespread disrespect for law. The police also carry guns in Tokyo, a city in which respect for law is reputed to be quite high.[15]

At the empirical level, there are still further difficulties with Mazor's analysis. If, as defenders of anarchy are prone to argue, a sound defense of the need for law cannot be rooted in generalizations about human behavior based on observations of particular societies, as adequate defense of anarchy must avoid ethnocentrism. Yet one of the most striking characteristics of Mazor's argument is its extraordinary emphasis on American phenomena. If we look elsewhere we find that it is just not true that the legal systems of modern nation-states are incapable of providing order. Even if the law's undeservingness of respect is a moral universal, the fact is that there are societies in which compliance with and respect for the law is the norm. In Tokyo, it is said that "cars left unlocked are not rifled. Money left in hotel rooms is there when you get back. Almost no one counts the change received in shops." [16] In 1973, Tokyo experienced 361 reported robberies, compared with 72,750 in New York City.[17] There are even societies *(mirabile dictu)* in which the police do not carry guns. If, when the police carry guns we have disrespect for law, can we conclude that when the police do not carry guns we have respect for law? If "those who exercise state power will use it above all to maintain their own position in society" in all legally organized societies, it may be true that the law "cannot lead to justice" and therefore does not deserve respect in any legally organized society. Unfortunately, for the anarchist, it is not universally true that the law is unable to "command respect." Although God is dead, some people continue to believe that he lives. And while law is dead, some people continue to believe in the illusion that it is alive—and they even behave accordingly.

Not only is it untrue that the law is incapable of providing order, there is reason to believe that the best explanations of the varying levels of disobedience are external to the law, that is, not an inevitable systemic consequence of having laws. In accounting for the varying crime rates among different groups in a society or in explaining the varying crime rates among various societies, it is a commonplace to stress social, economic, and cultural variables; for example, the degree of social homogeneity, economic inequality, cultural and subcultural norms, and the opportunity to disobey the law. If crime is more prevalent among males, are we to conclude that men tend to appreciate the force of the anarchist critique of law to a greater degree than females? Is the increase in shoplifting more plausibly attributable to a growing rejection of the institution of private property, or to the fact that an increasing percentage of merchandise is "out there" to be taken, rather than behind counters and handled by salespersons?

Disrespect for law, of course, may take many different forms. The United States has experienced, not only a rise in crimes of violence and attacks on property, but the exposure of multiple crimes in the highest political offices of the land. That those charged with enforcing the laws have seen fit to break the law when they believe doing so serves their interests is often put forth as a justification and explanation of the increase in crime among those of less wealth and power. As a *justification,* there is some plausibility to this line of argument. But it would be a wonderfully illustrative case of what Robert Nozick calls "normative sociology" ("the study of what the causes of problems *ought to be*") to tie the one to the other empirically.[18] As Wolff puts it, "disrespect for law is not a contagious disease which spreads through a society by contact . . . no one would be so foolish as to look for correlations between muggings and conscientious objection." [19] I suggest, then, that there is little evidence to support the anarchist claim that law does not receive respect *because* the law does not deserve respect. When people demonstrate disrespect for law they often do so for reasons that are not particularly supportive of the anarchist case.

Nothing that I have said about the nature and causes of disrespect for law negates Mazor's claim that the laws are incapable of providing justice and therefore do not deserve respect. It is the demonstration of the moral basis for disrespect for law that constitutes the bulk of Mazor's argument and to which I now turn. Mazor does not, however, serve his argument well by defining the law as "what the officials of a given state will do." First, this definition makes it difficult to sustain the anarchist claim that the law cannot provide order. There are and have been societies in which the officials of given states have (through whatever means) established a rather high degree of order. If law is defined as what the officials of a given state will do, then it is trivially true that law can provide order, if that order is attributable to the actions of the officials of the state. Secondly, this definition gives up any claim to the idea of "law" as a standard by which to evaluate the behavior of the officials of a given state. When Thrasymachus says that " 'just' or 'right' means nothing but what is to the interest of the stronger party," he precludes the use of "justice" or "right" as standards by which to criticize and evaluate the actions of the stronger party. Similarly, Mazor cannot say that the officials of a state have acted illegally, because what they do is (by definition) law, nor can they be criticized for failing to live up to the idea of law which they are supposed to uphold.

I am not, however, primarily concerned with what Mazor's definition of law allows him to *say*, although it does not allow him (without contradiction) to say enough. I am more concerned with what I take to be an underlying fundamental commitment to the idea and rule of law. Ronald Dworkin points out that many of those who oppose the law (understood in a positivist sense) are, in fact, quite committed to the idea of law: "They are committed to the idea that government should be regulated by principle, and that those who have social power should extend to everyone the rights that they have consciously or habitually claimed for themselves. . . ." [20] When Mazor examines the realities of the legal system, he finds that system wanting because the realities do not square with "the fundamental principles of social obligation" upon which the system rests, that is, the law does not promote "justice." [21] Mazor's argument for anarchy rests on the claim that the reality of the legal system does not live up to the society's own understanding of what the idea of law entails. In this sense, Mazor is quite committed to the idea of law as something distinct from "what the officials of a given state will do."

Regardless of any definitional problems in his argument, Mazor is right in arguing that a defense of law must attend to the functional realities of legal systems. Unfortunately, because he focuses exclusively on the United States, there is no evidence that what he finds there is either also true of all modern nation-states or an inevitable systemic consequence of having a legal system. In any

case, what does he find? The judges are not representative of the
society; they are an adult, male, legally trained, wealthy elite, who
do not and cannot be expected to set aside their class interests when
acting in their professional capacity. Those who make law by
administration in the multiple bureaucracies do not and cannot
achieve the institutional goals which justify their existence. HEW
provides neither health, education, nor welfare. The bureaucracies
not only fail, their very existence lulls the citizen into falsely
believing that his interests are being protected. While poisonous
drugs slip through the careful screening of the FDA, in that agency's
absence we would all act on the maxim *caveat emptor,* and the law of
supply and demand would prevent those drugs from appearing on
the shelves of the local pharmacy.[22] The police can neither solve
crime nor prevent it. Lawyers are largely corporate or (what
amounts to the same thing) corrupt. Legal equality, when not a
mere fiction, only reinforces social inequalities. Most important, the
law is not merely unjust, it is irrelevant. To assume that "the
disposition of a limited number of cases and controversies will
influence behavior in enough situations to maintain domestic
tranquility"[23] is an archaic notion in a crisis which is "apocalyptic
... global ... ecological ... technological ... psychological ...
evolutionary...."[24] Thus, while legislation cannot provide the
needed domestic social changes, Mazor finds that the entire nation-
state basis of the legal structure is inappropriate to a world which
must escape the "narrowness of territoriality" if it is to avoid
disaster.[25]

Our nation and the world are in bad shape. Material scarcity has
not been eliminated and may even be growing. Even where a degree
of affluence has been achieved, people encounter a "whole new set
of human problems, centering in the realm of the interpersonal"
with which to contend and from which they suffer.[26] One can
quarrel here and there with Mazor's analysis, and it is even
occasionally difficult to determine if he is serious. Yet the thrust of
the analysis cannot be ignored. The legal system does not live up to
its own standards, much less a more rigorous set of norms. Rather
than quarrel with the critique, let us accept the claim that the
operational reality of the legal system is that it does not provide
justice. Still, we must ask, does the acceptance of that claim entail
anarchy?

In the face of all this evidence, one might wonder why any reasonable person could continue to think that mankind is better off with law than without it. Thus, before stating his case for anarchy, Mazor pauses to consider two lines of justification for respecting law. The more optimistic line, exemplified by Rawls, suggests that men in an original position, placed under a "veil of ignorance" about their own characteristics and the characteristics of their society, would choose to establish a set of rules and practices that would permit considerable inequalities if these inequalities work out to everyone's advantage. Suspecting any line of argument which could support the claim that the inequalities exhibited by the modern nation-state could conceivably be just, and rejecting the "peculiar" premises that Rawls's conception of the original position involves, Mazor quickly dismisses this argument and moves on to consider the Hobbesian defense of law.[27]

This line of argument claims that the purpose of law is to protect men from their own "dangerous propensities," to avoid the *summum malum* inherent in the contradiction between the characteristics of the human condition. If stripped of its Hobbesian flavor, this argument may be somewhat stronger than Mazor allows. First, the argument does not require the malevolent assumptions which Mazor attributes to it. The argument need not assume that human behavior is characterized by "evil" or "greed," as Mazor puts it; or, in Hobbes's words, a "perpetual and restless desire of power after power, that ceaseth only in death."[28] The argument need only reject the anarchist claim that we would be better off if individuals were always permitted to act according to their own moral judgments and to settle their accounts directly with those with whom they may have differences. The argument need only claim that "some areas of human behavior are too risky to be left to individual moral judgment" and that it is preferable to have a third party resolve some disputes than to permit individuals to settle all their own disputes.[29] I am not making this argument here, but do wish to suggest that it cannot be dismissed by attributing to it assumptions which it does not need.

Secondly, according to Mazor, the Hobbesian argument should appeal only to one "who has something to lose, that is, one who stands in a position of dominance over others" and whose interests in maintaining that dominance are protected by the state and its

legal superstructure.[30] It is, however, wrong to equate those in a
position of "dominance" with those who have "something to lose."
The latter set is much larger than the former. In fact, it is those who
are in a position of weakness, not dominance, who stand to lose the
most in marginal terms. The less one has, the less one can afford to
lose. While blacks have suffered from discrimination and brutality
at the hand of the law, they have also suffered from the laissez-faire
(anarchic?) view the law has taken towards injuries which blacks
inflict on blacks. While those with very little may well fear the state
and its laws, they may be more concerned about their high level of
vulnerability to attack from their fellow citizens. It is not generally
blacks who wave the black flag.

Thirdly, let us recall that Hobbes prefers law to anarchy, not only
to avoid the "continual fear, and danger of violent death," but
because in the absence of the state "there is no place for industry . . .
no culture of the earth . . . no commodious building. . . ."[31] The
Hobbesian argument can be understood as claiming not only that
the law is needed to reduce interpersonal injuries, but in order to
provide certain goods and services without which life would be less
pleasant. A society may require or wish to provide certain "public
goods," that is, those goods which, if they are provided at all, cannot
be feasibly withheld from any member of the community. Similarly,
a society may need or wish to remove certain public harms, those
unwanted effects of too many individuals doing what they do; for
example, burning garbage, using phosphate detergent, watering
lawns during a water shortage. There are goods which it is
necessary, most feasible, or most efficient to provide as public goods
if they are provided at all, and there are harms the avoidance or
reduction of which will necessarily benefit all if they benefit anyone.
The "logic of collective action" claims that because one will receive
the good or avoid the harm regardless of one's contribution or
sacrifice, the rational man will attempt to free-ride, he will attempt
to enjoy the good without incurring the cost. Olson says, "unless the
number of individuals in a group is quite small, or unless there is
coercion or some other special device to make individuals act in
their common interest, rational, self-interested individuals will not
act to achieve their common or group interests."[32] Without
coercion or some other incentive, rational individuals will not do
their part in providing a public good, and thus it will not be

provided. In order to ensure that it be provided, the state employs coercion, thereby forcing us to do what we want to do, but would not do unless we were forced to do it. This version of the Hobbesian argument, then, suggests that the state and its laws are necessary, not only for life, but for the good life.

I believe it is this argument which presents the greatest difficulty for the defender of anarchy. The anarchist can, however, offer three lines of objection in an attempt to avoid its conclusion. First, it is no doubt true that as the level of economic development and complexity of a society increases, the need to provide public goods and respond to public harms also increases. The anarchist can accept the claim that public goods require coercion but state that he is unwilling to pay the cost for these material benefits, that he is willing to sacrifice the productivity of a modern society for the liberation and autonomy that a "less developed" society can offer. Thus, it becomes perfectly understandable that anarchism has traditionally been compatible "only with a less complex and therefore more primitive, economic, political, and social structure of society." [33] Secondly, the "logic of collective action" states that size is inversely related to the ability to provide public goods without coercion. The anarchist can argue that if the community is sufficiently small it will be possible to provide public goods without coercion. The two objections just considered, of course, assume that a large-scale modern society can and should be replaced by a different form of social organization, a problem which I will consider below.

The two objections just considered focus on the nature of an anarchist *society,* a third line of objection focuses on the *individual.* The "logic of collective action" assumes that in the absence of coercion (or other incentives), men will attempt to promote their self-interest and will (at least, too often) be unwilling freely to contribute to the provision of public goods. This argument can be defeated by simply claiming that it is wrong about men. The anarchist can argue that under the appropriate conditions men will be willing to contribute their share, that they can act morally in the Kantian sense. They can act "on the maxim through which you can at the same time will that it should become a universal law." This Wolff argues, "When rational men, in full knowledge of the proximate and distant consequences of their actions, determine to set private interest aside and pursue the general good, it *must* be possible for them to create a form of association which accomplishes that end without depriving some of them of their moral autonomy." [34] This argument assumes that it can be "rational" to "set private interest aside and pursue the general good." I will return to this problem below.

In the face of the defense of law, the anarchist argues that there is no reason to assume the "inevitability of domination." As Wolff suggests, under the appropriate conditions it must be "possible" for men to live both socially and freely. And as Mazor puts it, "Against the *possibility* of the sharing of the world's resources in pursuit of a joyous existence, the dark myth which justifies authority and dominance has little appeal." [35] Even if Mazor and Wolff are correct, even if anarchy is possible, even if the existence of legal systems does not inevitably flow from characteristics of the human personality, the defense of law does not automatically collapse. It does not collapse because what distinguishes (at least some) defenses of law from (at least some) defenses of anarchy is not a disagreement as to what is *possible,* but their respective understandings of how men should go about making choices in an uncertain world.

To grasp this distinction, let us consider the defenses of law which Mazor examines. Although their ultimate conceptions of the legitimate state are quite different, both Hobbes and Rawls rest their arguments on the notions of a "state of nature" and a "social contract." More important, for present purposes, is that they accept a certain understanding of how rational men should go about making choices. According to Hobbes and Rawls, one should act as if the world is out to get you. Under conditions of uncertainty, rational men make choices by using a maximin strategy, that is, that strategy which minimizes one's losses or maximizes one's worst possible position. Rather than assume that "somebody up there loves me," he acts as if "his enemy were to assign him his place." [36] A maximin strategy can be contrasted with a maximax strategy, that is, that strategy which maximizes one's gains, although it might leave one worse off than a maximin strategy. Regardless of the probability of rain tomorrow, a maximin strategy would dictate that I take my raincoat, because not having a raincoat when it does rain (and one can never be certain that it will not) is the worst position. It is worse than having a raincoat along if it does not rain, although that may be a nuisance.[37] A maximax strategy would dictate that I leave my raincoat home, since only by not taking my raincoat can I achieve the best possible situation—that it not rain and that I not have my raincoat.

It is clearly wrong to assume that a maximin strategy is always most rational. Depending on the amount of the respective losses and gains and the probability of losing or gaining, there are certainly conditions in which it makes sense to trade the possibility of a lesser position for the possibility of a better position, particularly when the probability of the lesser position is sufficiently low and the probability of the better position is sufficiently high. Even a rather cautious person might well leave his raincoat home if the weather bureau states there is a 10 percent probability of rain, although doing so makes possible the worst case—getting caught in the rain without a raincoat. One simply cannot say, *a priori*, that any strategy is always the most rational. One needs, as Barry says, "some sort of system for playing the percentages." [38] In making choices, political or nonpolitical, one must consider the percentages. No serious argument for anarchy as a political strategy, calling on us to "struggle to create a world in which persons are free to develop their own structure of order" and to begin the "building of a space within which it can be exercised," can avoid this problem.[39] A serious case for anarchy must assume that the "possibility" of the "joyous existence" is sufficiently high and sufficiently proximate (given that gains to be received in the distant future are discounted at a higher rate than gains to be received sooner) to justify forsaking whatever improvement over the "worst possible case" the state and its legal superstructure do or could provide. Given that the "decline in respect for established authority is . . . a threat to those reformers who seek to correct social injustice from the top down," one must consider whether or not it makes sense to encourage such disrespect.[40] Does anarchy represent a good bet, or, as with another decaying institution, should we stick with the law for "better or worse"?

Let us agree with Barrington Moore that "anarchist communities as such are within the range of general social possibilities, given the appropriate conditions." [41] As Mazor suggests, anthropologists have demonstrated that human behavior is quite plastic and that aggressive and acquisitive personalities are not universal phenomena. It is also true, that unlike those in Rawls's original position, we do not operate behind a "veil of ignorance." We know something about our history. We know the horrors that have occurred in and have been perpetrated by legally organized modern societies. No anarchist society could have produced the Holocaust. No anarchist society could produce or accumulate weapons which threaten to destroy the very existence of mankind.[42] But if we are not in the original position, and if we do not operate behind a "veil of ignorance," we must also lack the luxury of choosing "a starting point for our social existence." [43] We must start from where we are. Thus, even if anarchy is possible, the anarchist strategy may be wrong for several reasons: (1) the conditions which make anarchy possible do not exist and cannot be achieved; (2) even if those conditions could be achieved, they might not be desirable; (3) the amount and certainty of human suffering that the realization of those conditions would require outweigh the gains to be realized by an anarchist strategy. A defense of law, then, does not assume the impossibility of anarchy. It assumes that the pursuit of anarchy amounts to playing a maximax strategy under unfavorable conditions.

If we must start from where we are, where are we? Without regard to one's model of the desirable society, and without regard to the role that modern nations may have played in causing certain problems, there are facts about the contemporary world which must be considered. First, the population of the earth is (perhaps) too large, but increasing at a rapid rate with no immediate prospect for a serious reduction. Secondly, in much of the world, basic human needs are not being satisfied. If, as Wieck suggests, "it is the purpose of anarchism to look beyond survival," we must remember that many in the world are not even surviving.[44] Thirdly, the world's natural and human resources are not evenly distributed across the globe. Fourthly, the present level of subsistence is based on a high level of social and economic interdependence among various regions of the world and also within the regions themselves. How do these facts touch on the argument for anarchy?

The increasing world population touches on the argument for anarchy in several ways. First, it seems reasonable to assume that the more densely populated an area, the more difficult it becomes to do without law—"an increase in numbers multiplies the frequency of situations in which it becomes necessary to have rules and regulations to govern human activities." [45] Secondly, if individuals are to be encouraged or compelled to restrict their offspring, it may be impossible to do so without the intervention of the state. Thirdly, one function of the state has traditionally been its responsibility in protecting its members from external threats. It seems reasonable to assume that anarchy can best survive when the prospects of external threats are minimized, But, as Moore points out, "Given the size of the world's population there is no serious prospect that human beings can organize themselves into small autonomous groups largely isolated from each other." [46]

Regardless of the problems for anarchy which stem from the size of the world's population, that popoulation is not surviving at its present level of productivity. While anarchy may claim to minimize domination by other persons, it may not speak to those who feel most dominated by the needs of their bodies and their inability to control the natural world. A response to this problem will certainly require an increase in agricultural productivity in the "third world," a goal not likely to be achieved under conditions favorable to anarchy. The food shortage will not be solved by family or community organic gardens. In addition, if people demonstrate a desire for a level of comfort beyond mere survival, a greater level of productivity and industrialization in the Third World and continued productivity in the industrial nations may be required. If anarchy implies a "polyculturalism" in which individuals are free to choose their own values, it is possible that many persons will choose to value the goods which only industrialization makes possible.

The natural and human resources of the world are not evenly distributed. As Mazor argues, we must achieve "a distribution of the world's goods and life's necessities equitable enough to forestall a disastrous collision." [47] If a distribution is to be *achieved*, as Mazor says, it is absurd to think that it will occur spontaneously. If modern legal systems cannot escape the "narrowness of territoriality," I see no reason to think that small, decentralized anarchic communities will be less narrow. Moore poses an important question: "What may happen due to the fact that some anarchist communities will be much wealthier than others and have control of resources that others require?" [48] While modern nations may have reinforced or exacerbated the world's natural inequalities, it does not follow that those inequalities can be reduced without political institutions. A redistribution of the world's resources may necessitate a worldwide authority, but it does not require anarchy.

If a high level of interdependence among the regions of the world did not already exist, it would have to be invented. The fact is that it does exist and its very existence makes the anarchist strategy extraordinarily risky. Given the ways in which the people of the earth depend upon each other for the exchange of goods and services, "any substantial failure of the existing technical apparatus, including the failure to staff it adequately, could, if it happened suddenly produce as many deaths as a major war, even a nuclear war if the failure were complete and prolonged." [49] And within the various regions of the world, the very existence of modern cities depends upon political systems capable of effecting transfers between the city and the countryside. Cities may be inappropriate places for genuine anarchist communities. Perhaps cities are not desirable places for human life, although (once again) a genuine polyculturalism might want to allow citizens to choose the experiences which only urban life makes possible. Nevertheless, cities do exist, and "unless one is willing to exterminate the inhabitants of the city" there may well be a need for states and laws capable of providing for their internal and external needs.[50]

I have argued that the defense of anarchy which rests on a rejection of modern society faces severe difficulties which it must surmount. The defense of anarchy which claims that rational men can put aside their self-interest and act for the common good runs into its own difficulties. Human suffering cannot always be attributed to states and their legal superstructures. Some human suffering is a function of natural events, and some of the world's most severe problems result from the unintended consequences of a large set of individual choices made under relatively anarchic conditions. As Schelling puts it, "some severe problems result not from the evil of people but from their helplessness as individuals." [51] The starving poor of the world are trapped in a massive "prisoner's dilemma" problem. While we preach birth control, the Indian peasant continues to propagate children in order that he have help in working his fields and in order to ensure that someone will survive to take care of him when he is too old and infirm to care for himself. The peasant may even appreciate the force of the Kantian argument and realize that the public good would be served if he restricted his offspring. But can we or should we expect him voluntarily to sacrifice his very means of existence? Can he be morally blamed for wanting to live?

A similar problem is created by the need to defend one's community against external threats. Defense is a public good. If I remain within my community's borders, and it is (somehow) defended, I cannot be deprived of that benefit even if I have not contributed to its provision, either monetarily or bodily. Wolff suggests that "a society of anarchists . . . would be perfectly capable of choosing freely whether to defend the nation. . . ." [52] If the society were not capable of providing for its defense on a voluntary basis, this is reason to believe that the society should not continue to exist: "Why should a nation continue to exist if its populace does not wish to defend it?" [53] Wolff suggests we contrast the "Israeli soldiers, on the one hand, and the American forces in Vietnam on the other" to grasp the point he is making.[54] While this contrast is illuminating, it does not support his argument. There is no incompatibility (even for an Israeli) between "not wishing to defend" one's nation and also wishing that it "be defended." If Israel is a nation in which a rather significant segment of the population wishes that it be defended, it is also true that Israel does not rely on a voluntary defense force but employs a universal conscription system. Even for the noblest of purposes, even praiseworthy and public-spirited men cannot always be expected to act according to Kantian maxims.

I have argued that the objections a defender of anarchy may want to make to the defense of law run into their own difficulties when squared with the social and individual realities of the human situation. I have argued that while anarchy may indeed be possible, it does not follow that the anarchist strategy is wise. While the anarchist may be right in arguing that the state and its laws have indeed been responsible for much human suffering, it does not follow that we would, at this point, be better off without the law. Peter Berger has issued a warning which any social theory would do well to heed:

> No realistic actor . . . has any reason to suppose that his projects will be realized in the way he originally imagined them. Social reality is hard, obstreperous, resistant to our wishes. Any

situation of policy making should embrace as clear an awareness as possible of the likely limits this reality will set to the intended projects . . . it will be advisable to defend these limits narrowly rather than broadly, thus possibly reducing the probability of failure. In other words, since we know so little it is wiser to act toward goals that are relatively proximate and therefore relatively calculable, than toward goals that are so broad and remote that all calculations break down. It is easier to save a village than to save the world. . . .[55]

NOTES

1. Lester Mazor, *Disrespect for Law*, pp. 147-48.
2. Robert Paul Wolff, "Afterword," in Robert Paul Wolff, ed., *The Rule of Law* (New York: Simon and Schuster, 1971), p. 248.
3. Leo Tolstoy, "Patriotism and Government," in *Kingdom of God and Peace Essays,* trans. Louise and Aylmer Maude (London: Oxford University Press, 1935), reprinted in Robert Hoffman, ed., *Anarchism* (New York: Atherton Press, 1970), p. 83.
4. Mazor, p. 147.
5. Mazor, p. 145.
6. Mazor, p. 143.
7. Mazor, p. 155.
8. Mazor, p. 148.
9. H. L. A. Hart, *The Concept of Law* (Oxford: Oxford University Press, 1961), p. 80.
10. Mazor, p. 145.
11. Hart, *The Concept of Law,* p. 88.
12. Thomas Schelling, "On the Ecology of Micromotives," Discussion Paper No. 2. *The Public Interest* No. 24 (Fall 1971). Quotation taken from Lee Rainwater, ed., *Inequality and Justice* (Chicago: Aldine, 1974), p. 407.
13. Schelling, p. 407.
14. Robert Sherrill argues that the most plausible explanation of this nation's resistance to gun-control legislation is economic, not ideological. See *The Saturday Night Special* (New York: Charterhouse, 1973).
15. See the article on Crime in Toyko in *New York Times,* April 17, 1974.
16. *New York Times,* April 17, 1974.
17. *New York Times,* April 17, 1974. There is reason to believe that the actual difference in crime is greater than is reflected in these statistics, because there is less underreporting of crime in Tokyo than in New York.

18. Robert Nozick, *Anarchy, State, and Utopia* (New York: Basic Books, 1974), p. 247.

19. Robert Paul Wolff, "In Defense of Anarchism," in Eugene V. Rostow, ed., *Is Law Dead?* (New York: Simon and Schuster, 1971), p. 116.

20. Ronald Dworkin, "Philosophy and the Critique of Law," in Wolff, ed., *The Rule of Law,* pp. 164-165.

21. Dworkin, "Philosophy and the Critique of Law," p. 168.

22. While the claim that the FDA does let poisonous drugs through its screening process appears on page 150, the claim that *fewer* poisonous drugs would appear without the FDA was made in the discussion following the delivery of the paper at the 1974 Meeting of the American Society of Political and Legal Philosophy. One might argue that having to make decisions on all those items to be consumed is, itself, an infringement of our liberty. As Moore argues, "A very precious part of human freedom is that *not* to make decisions. . ." In Barrington Moore, *Reflections on the Causes of Human Misery* (Boston: Beacon Press, 1970), pp. 68-69.

23. Mazor, p. 152.

24. Lester Mazor, "The Crisis of Liberal Legalism," *Yale Law Journal* 81 [1972], p. 1050.

25. Mazor, p. 154.

26. Mazor, "The Crisis of Liberal Legalism," p. 1033.

27. Mazor, p. 155.

28. Thomas Hobbes, *Leviathan,* Chapter 11.

29. Jeffrey H. Reiman, *In Defense of Political Philosophy* (New York: Harper and Row, 1972), p. 42.

30. Mazor, p. 155.

31. Hobbes, *Leviathan,* Chapter 13.

32. Mancur Olson, Jr., *The Logic of Collective Action* (New York: Schocken Books, 1968), p. 2.

33. Derry Novak, "The Place of Anarchism in the History of Political Thought," *Review of Politics* (July 1968), reprinted in Hoffman, ed., *Anarchism,* p. 32.

34. Robert Paul Wolff, *In Defense of Anarchism* (New York: Harper and Row, 1970), p. 78.

35. Mazor, p. 156.

36. John Rawls, "Justice as Fairness," in Richard Flathman, ed., *Concepts in Social and Political Philosophy* (New York: Macmillan, 1973), p. 409. Rawls's article originally appeared in the *Philosophical Review,* 1958.

37. I have borrowed the raincoat example from Brian Barry's "On Social Justice," reprinted in Flathman, ed., *Concepts in Social and Political Philosophy,* pp. 422-33. The article originally appeared in *Oxford Review* (1967), pp. 29-43.

38. Barry, "On Social Justice," p. 429.

39. Mazor, p. 156.

40. Wolff, Afterword, in Wolff, ed., *The Rule of Law,* p. 252.

41. Moore, *Reflections* . . . , p. 73.

42. Mazor quite correctly argued that we are not under a "veil of ignorance" with respect to the past in his response to my comments on his paper at the 1974 Meeting of the American Society for Political and Legal Philosophy. But if we are not under a "veil of ignorance" with respect to the past, we may nevertheless be quite ignorant with regard to the future.

43. Mazor, p. 156.

44. David Wieck, "Essentials of Anarchism" in Hoffman, ed., *Anarchism,* p. 88. This article orignally appeared in *Resistance,* XI (1953) pp. 4-7, 18.

45. Moore, *Reflections* . . . , p. 44.

46. Moore, *Reflections* . . . , pp. 19-20.

47. Mazor, p. 154.

48. Moore, *Reflections* . . . , p. 75.

49. Moore, *Reflections* . . . , p. 47.

50. Moore, *Reflections* . . . , p. 75.

51. Schelling, "On the Ecology of Micromotives," p. 416.

52. Wolff, *In Defense of Anarchism,* p. 80.

53. Wolff, *In Defense of Anarchism,* p. 80.

54. Wolff, *In Defense of Anarchism,* p. 80.

55. Peter Berger, *Pyramids of Sacrifice* (New York: Basic Books, 1974), p. 130.

ANARCHIST THEORIES OF
JUSTICE

12

SOCIETY WITHOUT A STATE

MURRAY N. ROTHBARD

In attempting to outline how a "society without a State"—that is, an anarchist society—might function successfully, I would first like to defuse two common but mistaken criticisms of this approach. First, is the argument that in providing for such defense or protection services as courts, police, or even law itself, I am simply smuggling the state back into society in another form, and that therefore the system I am both analyzing and advocating is not "really" anarchism. This sort of criticism can only involve us in an endless and arid dispute over semantics. Let me say from the beginning that I define the state as that institution which possesses one or both (almost always both) of the following properties: (1) it acquires its income by the physical coercion known as "taxation"; and (2) it asserts and usually obtains a coerced monopoly of the provision of defense service (police and courts) over a given territorial area. Any institution not possessing either of these properties is not and cannot be, in accordance with my definition, a State. On the other hand, I define anarchist society as one where there is no legal possibility for coercive aggression against the person or property of any individual. Anarchists oppose the state because it has its very being in such aggression, namely, the expropriation of private property through taxation, the coercive exclusion of other providers of defense service from its territory, and all of the other depredations and coercions that are built upon these twin foci of invasions of individual rights.

Nor is our definition of the state arbitrary, for these two characteristics have been possessed by what is generally acknowledged to be states throughout recorded history. The state, by its use of physical coercion, has arrogated to itself a compulsory monopoly of defense services over its territorial jurisdiction. But it is certainly conceptually possible for such services to be supplied by private, nonstate institutions, and indeed such services have historically been supplied by other organizations than the state. To be opposed to the state is then not necessarily to be opposed to services that have often been linked with it; to be opposed to the state does not necessarily imply that we must be opposed to police protection, courts, arbitration, the minting of money, postal service, or roads and highways. *Some* anarchists have indeed been opposed to police and to all physical coercion *in defense of* person and property, but this is not inherent in and is fundamentally irrelevant to the anarchist position, which is precisely marked by opposition to all physical coercion invasive of, or aggressing against, person and property.

The crucial role of taxation may be seen in the fact that the state is the only institution or organization in society which regularly and systematically acquires its income through the use of physical coercion. All other individuals or organizations acquire their income voluntarily, either (1) through the voluntary sale of goods and services to consumers on the market, or (2) through voluntary gifts or donations by members or other donors. If I cease or refrain from purchasing Wheaties on the market, the Wheaties producers do not come after me with a gun or the threat of imprisonment to force me to purchase; if I fail to join the American Philosophical Association, the association may not force me to join or prevent me from giving up my membership. Only the state can do so; only the state can confiscate my property or put me in jail if I do not pay its tax tribute. Therefore, only the state regularly exists and has its very being by means of coercive depredations on private property.

Neither is it legitimate to challenge this sort of analysis by claiming that in some other sense, the purchase of Wheaties or membership in the APA is in some way "coercive"; there again, we can only be trapped in an endless semantic dispute. Apart from other rebuttals which cannot be considered here, I would simply say that anarchists are interested in the abolition of this type of action: for example, aggressive physical violence against person and property, and that this is how we define "coercion." Anyone who is still unhappy with this use of the term "coercion" can simply eliminate the word from this discussion and substitute for it "physical violence or the threat thereof," with the only loss being in literary style rather than in the substance of the argument. What anarchism proposes to do, then, is to abolish the state, that is to abolish the regularized institution of aggressive coercion.

It need hardly be added that the state habitually builds upon its coercive source of income by adding a host of other aggressions upon society, ranging from economic controls to the prohibition of pornography to the compelling of religious observance to the mass murder of civilians in organized warfare. In short, the state, in the words of Albert Jay Nock, "claims and exercises a monopoly of crime" over its territorial area.

The second criticism I would like to defuse before beginning the main body of the paper is the common charge that anarchists "assume that all people are good" and that without the state no crime would be committed. In short, that anarchism assumes that with the abolition of the state a New Anarchist Man will emerge, cooperative, humane, and benevolent, so that no problem of crime will then plague the society. I confess that I do not understand the basis for this charge. Whatever other schools of anarchism profess—and I do not believe that they are open to this charge—I certainly do not adopt this view. I assume with most observers that mankind is a mixture of good and evil, of cooperative and criminal tendencies. In my view, the anarchist society is one which maximizes the tendencies for the good and the cooperative, while it minimizes both the opportunity and the moral legitimacy of the evil and the criminal. If the anarchist view is correct and the state is indeed the great legalized and socially legitimated channel for all manner of antisocial crime—theft, oppression, mass murder—on a massive scale, then surely the abolition of such an engine of crime can do nothing but favor the good in man and discourage the bad.

A further point: in a profound sense, *no* social system, whether anarchist or statist, can work at all unless most people are "good" in the sense that they are not all hell-bent upon assaulting and robbing their neighbors. If everyone were so disposed, no amount of protection, whether state or private, could succeed in staving off chaos. Furthermore, the more that people are disposed to be peaceful and not aggress against their neighbors, the more successfully *any* social system will work, and the fewer resources will need to be devoted to police protection. The anarchist view holds that, given the "nature of man," given the degree of goodness or badness at any point of time, anarchism will maximize the opportunities for the good and minimize the channels for the bad. The rest depends on the values held by the individual members of society. The only further point that need be made is that by eliminating the living example and the social legitimacy of the massive legalized crime of the state, anarchism will to a large extent promote peaceful values in the minds of the public.

We cannot of course deal here with the numerous arguments in favor of anarchism or against the state, moral, political, and economic. Nor can we take up the various goods and services now provided by the state and show how private individuals and groups will be able to supply them far more efficiently on the free market. Here we can only deal with perhaps the most difficult area, the area where it is almost universally assumed that the state must exist and act, even if it is only a "necessary evil" instead of a positive good: the vital realm of defense or protection of person and property against agggression. Surely, it is universally asserted, the state is at least vitally necessary to provide police protection, the judicial resolution of disputes and enforcement of contracts, and the creation of the law itself that is to be enforced. My contention is that all of these admittedly necessary services of protection can be satisfactorily and efficiently supplied by private persons and institutions on the free market.

One important caveat before we begin the body of this paper: new proposals such as anarchism are almost always gauged against the implicit assumption that the present, or statist, system works to perfection. Any laucunae or difficulties with the picture of the anarchist society are considered net liabilities, and enough to dismiss anarchism out of hand. It is, in short, implicitly assumed that the state is doing its self-assumed job of protecting person and property to perfection. We cannot here go into the reasons why the state is bound to suffer inherently from grave flaws and inefficiencies in such a task. All we need do now is to point to the black and unprecedented record of the state through history: no combination of private marauders can possibly begin to match the state's unremitting record of theft, confiscation, oppression, and mass murder. No collection of Mafia or private bank robbers can begin to compare with all the Hiroshimas, Dresdens, and Lidices and their analogues through the history of mankind.

This point can be made more philosophically: it is illegitimate to compare the merits of anarchism and statism by starting with the present system as the implicit given and then critically examining only the anarchist alternative. What we must do is to begin at the zero point and then critically examine *both* suggested alternatives. Suppose, for example, that we were all suddenly dropped down on the earth *de novo* and that we were all then confronted with the question of what societal arrangements to adopt. And suppose then that someone suggested: "We are all bound to suffer from those of us who wish to aggress against their fellow men. Let us then solve this problem of crime by handing all of our weapons to the Jones family, over there, by giving all of our ultimate power to settle disputes to that family. In that way, with their monopoly of coercion and of ultimate decision making, the Jones family will be able to protect each of us from each other." I submit that this proposal would get very short shrift, except perhaps from the Jones family themselves. And yet this is precisely the common argument for the existence of the state. When we start from zero point, as in the case of the Jones family, the question of "who will guard the guardians?" becomes not simply an abiding lacuna in the theory of the state but an overwhelming barrier to its existence.

A final caveat: the anarchist is always at a disadvantage in attempting to forecast the shape of the future anarchist society. For it is impossible for observers to predict voluntary social arrangements, including the provision of goods and services, on the free market. Suppose, for example, that this were the year 1874 and that someone predicted that eventually there would be a radio-manufacturing industry. To be able to make such a forecast successfully, does he have to be challenged to state immediately how many radio manufacturers there would be a century hence, how big they would be, where they would be located, what technology and marketing techniques they would use, and so on? Obviously, such a challenge would make no sense, and in a profound sense the same is true of those who demand a precise portrayal of the pattern of protection activities on the market. Anarchism advocates the dissolution of the state into social and market arrangements, and these arrangements are far more flexible and less predictable than political institutions. The most that we can do, then, is to offer broad guidelines and perspectives on the shape of a projected anarchist society.

One important point to make here is that the advance of modern technology makes anarchistic arrangements increasingly feasible. Take, for example, the case of lighthouses, where it is often charged that it is unfeasible for private lighthouse operators to row out to each ship to charge it for use of the light. Apart from the fact that this argument ignores the successful existence of private lighthouses in earlier days, as in England in the eighteenth century, another vital consideration is that modern electronic technology makes charging each ship for the light far more feasible. Thus, the ship would have to have paid for an electronically controlled beam which could then be automatically turned on for those ships which had paid for the service.

II

Let us turn now to the problem of how disputes—in particular disputes over alleged violations of person and property—would be resolved in an anarchist society. First, it should be noted that all disputes involve two parties: the plaintiff, the alleged victim of the crime or tort; and the defendant, the alleged aggressor. In many cases of broken contract, of course, each of the two parties alleging that the other is the culprit is at the same time a plaintiff and a defendant.

An important point to remember is that *any* society, be it statist or anarchist, has to have *some* way of resolving disputes that will gain a majority consensus in society. There would be no need for courts or arbitrators if everyone were omniscient and knew instantaneously *which* persons were guilty of any given crime or violation of contract. Since none of us is omniscient, there has to be some method of deciding who is the criminal or lawbreaker which will gain legitimacy; in short, whose decision will be accepted by the great majority of the public.

In the first place, a dispute may be resolved voluntarily between the two parties themselves, either unaided or with the help of a third mediator. This poses no problem, and will automatically be accepted by society at large. It is so accepted even now, much less in a society imbued with the anarchistic values of peaceful cooperation and agreement. Secondly and similarly, the two parties, unable to reach agreement, may decide to submit voluntarily to the decision of an arbitrator. This agreement may arise either after a dispute has arisen, or be provided for in advance in the original contract. Again, there is no problem in such an arrangement gaining legitimacy. Even in the present statist era. the notorious inefficiency and coercive and cumbersome procedures of the politically run government courts has lead increasing numbers of citizens to turn to voluntary and expert arbitration for a speedy and harmonious settling of disputes.

Thus, William C. Wooldridge has written that

arbitration has grown to proportions that make the courts a secondary recourse in many areas and completely superfluous in others. The ancient fear of the courts that arbitration would 'oust' them of their jurisdiction has been fulfilled with a vengeance the common-law judges probably never anticipated. Insurance companies adjust over fifty thousand claims a year among themselves through arbitration, and the American Arbitration Association (AAA), with headquarters in New York and twenty-five regional offices across the country, last year conducted over twenty-two thousand arbitrations. Its twenty-three thousand associates available to serve as arbitrators may outnumber the total number of judicial personnel . . . in the United States. . . . Add to this the unknown number of individuals who arbitrate disputes within particular industries or in particular localities, without formal AAA affiliation, and the quantitatively secondary role of official courts begins to be apparent.[1]

Wooldridge adds the important point that, in addition to the speed of arbitration procedures vis-à-vis the courts, the arbitrators can proceed as experts in disregard of the official government law; in a profound sense, then, they serve to create a voluntary body of private law. "In other words," states Wooldridge, "the system of extralegal, voluntary courts has progressed hand in hand with a body of private law; the rules of the state are circumvented by the same process that circumvents the forums established for the settlement of disputes over those rules. . . . In short, a private agreement between two people, a bilateral 'law,' has supplanted the official law. The write of the sovereign has ceased to run, and for it is substituted a rule tacitly or explicitly agreed to by the parties." Wooldridge concludes that "if an arbitrator can choose to ignore a penal damage rule or the statute of limitations applicable to the claim before him (and it is generally conceded that he has that power), arbitration can be viewed as a practically revolutionary instrument for self-liberation from the law. . . " [2]

It may be objected that arbitration only works successfully because the courts enforce the award of the arbitrator. Wooldridge points out, however, that arbitration was unenforceable in the American courts before 1920, but that this did not prevent voluntary arbitration from being successful and expanding in the United States and in England. He points, furthermore, to the successful operations of merchant courts since the Middle Ages, those courts which successfully developed the entire body of the law merchant. None of those courts possessed the power of enforcement. He might have added the private courts of shippers which developed the body of admiralty law in a similar way.

How then did these private, "anarchistic," and voluntary courts ensure the acceptance of their decisions? By the method of social ostracism, and by the refusal to deal any further with the offending merchant. This method of voluntary "enforcement," indeed, proved highly successful. Wooldridge writes that "the merchants' courts were voluntary, and if a man ignored their judgment, he could not be sent to jail. . . . Nevertheless, it is apparent that . . .[their] decisions were generally respected even by the losers; otherwise people would never have used them in the first place. . . . Merchants made their courts work simply by agreeing to abide by the results. The merchant who broke the understanding would not be sent to jail, to be sure, but neither would he long continue to be a merchant, for the compliance exacted by his fellows . . . proved if

anything more effective than physical coercion."[3] Nor did this
voluntary method fail to work in modern times. Wooldridge writes
that it was precisely in the years before 1920, when arbitration
awards could not be enforced in the courts,

> that arbitration caught on and developed a following in the
> American mercantile community. Its popularity, gained at a
> time when abiding by an agreement to arbitrate had to be as
> voluntary as the agreement itself, casts doubt on whether legal
> coercion was an essential adjunct to the settlement of most
> disputes. Cases of refusal to abide by an arbitrator's award
> were rare; one founder of the American Arbitration Association
> could not recall a single example. Like their medieval forerun-
> ners, merchants in the Americas did not have to rely on any
> sanctions other than those they could collectively impose on
> each other. One who refused to pay up might find access to his
> association's tribunal cut off in the future, or his name released
> to the membership of his trade association; these penalties were
> far more fearsome than the cost of the award with which he
> disagreed. Voluntary and private adjudications were volun-
> tarily and privately adhered to, if not out of honor, out of the
> self-interest of businessmen who knew that the arbitral mode of
> dispute settlement would cease to be available to them very
> quickly if they ignored an award.[4]

It should also be pointed out that modern technology makes even
more feasible the collection and dissemination of information about
people's credit ratings and records of keeping or violating their
contracts or arbitration agreements. Presumably, an anarchist
society would see the expansion of this sort of dissemination of data
and thereby facilitate the ostracism or boycotting of contract and
arbitration violators.

How would arbitrators be selected in an anarchist society? In the
same way as they are chosen now, and as they were chosen in the
days of strictly voluntary arbitration: the arbitrators with the best
reputation for efficiency and probity would be chosen by the various
parties on the market. As in other processes of the market, the
arbitrators with the best record in settling disputes will come to gain
an increasing amount of business, and those with poor records will

no longer enjoy clients and will have to shift to another line of endeavor. Here it must be emphasized that parties in dispute will seek out those arbitrators with the best reputation for both expertise and impartiality and that inefficient or biased arbitrators will rapidly have to find another occupation.

Thus, the Tannehills emphasize:

> the advocates of government see initiated force (the legal force of government) as the only solution to social disputes. According to them, if everyone in society were not forced to use the same court system . . . disputes would be insoluble. Apparently it doesn't occur to them that disputing parties are capable of freely choosing their own arbiters. . . . They have not realized that disputants would, in fact, be far better off if they could choose among competing arbitration agencies so that they could reap the benefits of competition and specialization. It should be obvious that a court systen which has a monopoly guaranteed by the force of statutory law will not give as good quality service as will free-market arbitration agencies which must compete for their customers. . . .
>
> Perhaps the least tenable argument for government arbitration of disputes is the one which holds that governmental judges are more impartial because they operate outside the market and so have no vested interests. . . . Owing political allegiance to government is certainly no guarantee of impartiality! A governmental judge is always impelled to be partial— in favor of the government, from whom he gets his pay and his power! On the other hand, an arbiter who sells his services in a free market knows that he must be as scrupulously honest, fair, and impartial as possible or no pair of disputants will buy his services to arbitrate their dispute. A free-market arbiter depends for his livelihood on his skill and fairness at settling disputes. A governmental judge depends on political pull.[5]

If desired, furthermore, the contracting parties could provide in advance for a series of arbitrators:

> It would be more economical and in most cases quite sufficient to have only one arbitration agency to hear the case. But if the

parties felt that a further appeal might be necessary and were willing to risk the extra expense, they could provide for a succession of two or even more arbitration agencies. The names of these agencies would be written into the contract in order from the "first court of appeal" to the "last court of appeal." It would be neither necessary nor desirable to have one single, final court of appeal for every person in the society, as we have today in the United States Supreme Court.[6]

Arbitration, then, poses little difficulty for a portrayal of the free society. But what of torts or crimes of aggression where there has been no contract? Or suppose that the breaker of a contract defies the arbitration award? Is ostracism enough? In short, how can courts develop in the free-market, anarchist society which will have the power to enforce judgments against criminals or contract breakers?

In the wide sense, defense service consists of guards or police who use force in defending person and property against attack, and judges or courts whose role is to use socially accepted procedures to determine *who* the criminals or tortfeasors are, as well as to enforce judicial awards, such as damages or the keeping of contracts. On the free market, many scenarios are possible on the relationship between the private courts and the police; they may be "vertically integrated," for example, or their services may be supplied by separate firms. Furthermore, it seems likely that police service will be supplied by insurance companies who will provide crime insurance to their clients. In that case, insurance companies will pay off the victims of crime or the breaking of contracts or arbitration awards and then pursue the aggressors in court to recoup their losses. There is a natural market connection between insurance companies and defense service, since they need pay out less benefits in proportion as they are able to keep down the rate of crime.

Courts might either charge fees for their services, with the losers of cases obliged to pay court costs, or else they may subsist on monthly or yearly premiums by their clients, who may be either individuals or the police or insurance agencies. Suppose, for example, that Smith is an aggrieved party, either because he has been assaulted or robbed, or because an arbitration award in his favor has not been honored. Smith believes that Jones is the party guilty of the crime. Smith then goes to a court, Court A, of which he is a client, and brings charges against Jones as a defendant. In my view, the hallmark of an anarchist society is one where no man may legally compel someone who is not a convicted criminal to do anything, since that would be aggression against an innocent man's person or property. Therefore, Court A can only invite rather than subpoena Jones to attend his trial. Of course, if Jones refused to appear or send a representative, his side of the case will not be heard. The trial of Jones proceeds. Suppose that Court A finds Jones innocent. In my view, part of the generally accepted law code of the anarchist society (on which see further below) is that this must end the matter unless Smith can prove charges of gross incompetence or bias on the part of the court.

Suppose, next, that Court A finds Jones guilty. Jones might accept the verdict, because he too is a client of the same court, because he knows he is guilty, or for some other reason. In that case, Court A proceeds to exercise judgment against Jones. Neither of these instances pose very difficult problems for our picture of the anarchist society. But suppose, instead, that Jones contests the decision; he, then, goes to his court, Court B, and the case is retried there. Suppose that Court B, too, finds Jones guilty. Again, it seems to me that the accepted law code of the anarchist society will assert that this ends the matter; both parties have had their say in courts which each has selected, and the decision for guilt is unanimous.

Suppose, however, the most difficult case: that Court B finds Jones innocent. The two courts, each subscribed to by one of the two parties, have split their verdicts. In that case, the two courts will submit the case to an appeals court, or arbitrator, which the two courts agree upon. There seems to be no real difficulty about the concept of an appeals court. As in the case of arbitration contracts, it seems very likely that the various private courts in the society will have prior agreements to submit their disputes to a particular appeals court. How will the appeals judges be chosen? Again, as in the case of arbitrators or of the first judges on the free market, they will be chosen for their expertise and their reputation for efficiency, honesty, and integrity. Obviously, appeals judges who are inefficient or biased will scarcely be chosen by courts who will have a dispute. The point here is that there is no need for a legally established or institutionalized single, monopoly appeals court system, as states now provide. There is no reason why there cannot arise a multitude of efficient and honest appeals judges who will be selected by the disputant courts, just as there are numerous private arbitrators on the market today. The appeals court renders its decision, and the courts proceed to enforce it if, in our example, Jones is considered guilty—unless, of course, Jones can prove bias in some other court proceedings.

No society can have unlimited judicial appeals, for in that case there would be no point to having judges or courts at all. Therefore, every society, whether statist or anarchist, will have to have some socially accepted cutoff point for trials and appeals. My suggestion is the rule that the agreement *of any two courts* be decisive. "Two" is not an arbitrary figure, for it reflects the fact that there are two parties, the plaintiff and the defendant, to any alleged crime or contract dispute.

If the courts are to be empowered to enforce decisions against guilty parties, does this not bring back the state in another form and thereby negate anarchism? No, for at the beginning of this paper I explicitly defined anarchism in such a way as not to rule out the use of defensive force—force in defense of person and property—by privately supported agencies. In the same way, it is not bringing back the state to allow persons to use force to defend themselves against aggression, or to hire guards or police agencies to defend them.

It should be noted, however, that in the anarchist society there will be no "district attorney" to press charges on behalf of "society." Only the victims will press charges as the plaintiffs. If, then, these victims should happen to be absolute pacifists who are opposed even to defensive force, then they will simply not press charges in the courts or otherwise retaliate against those who have aggressed against them. In a free society that would be their right. If the victim should suffer from murder, then his heir would have the right to press the charges.

What of the Hatfield-and-McCoy problem? Suppose that a Hatfield kills a McCoy, and that McCoy's heir does not belong to a private insurance, police agency, or court, and decides to retaliate himself? Since under anarchism there can be no coercion of the noncriminal, McCoy would have the perfect right to do so. No one may be compelled to bring his case to a court. Indeed, since the right to hire police or courts flows from the right of self-defense against aggression, it would be inconsistent and in contradiction to the very basis of the free society to institute such compulsion. Suppose, then, that the surviving McCoy finds what he believes to be the guilty Hatfield and kills him in turn? What then? This is fine, except that McCoy may have to worry about charges being brought against him by a surviving Hatfield. Here it must be emphasized that in the law of the anarchist society based on defense against aggression, the courts would not be able to proceed against McCoy if in fact he killed the right Hatfield. His problem would arise if the courts should find that he made a grievous mistake and killed the wrong man; in that case, he in turn would be found guilty of murder. Surely, in most instances, individuals will wish to obviate such problems by taking their case to a court and thereby gain social acceptability for their defensive retaliation—not for the *act* of retaliation but for the correctness of deciding who the criminal in any given case might be. The purpose of the judicial process, indeed, is to find a way of general agreement on who might be the criminal or contract breaker in any given case. The judicial process is not a good in itself; thus, in the case of an assassination, such as Jack Ruby's murder of Lee Harvey Oswald, on public television, there is no need for a complex judicial process, since the name of the murderer is evident to all.

Will not the possibility exist of a private court that may turn venal and dishonest, or of a private police force that turns criminal and extorts money by coercion? Of course such an event may occur, given the propensities of human nature. Anarchism is not a moral cure-all. But the important point is that market forces exist to place severe checks on such possibilities, especially in contrast to a society where a state exists. For, in the first place, judges, like arbitrators, will prosper on the market in proportion to their reputation for efficiency and impartiality. Secondly, on the free market important checks and balances exist against venal courts or criminal police forces. Namely, that there are competing courts and police agencies to whom the victims may turn for redress. If the "Prudential Police Agency" should turn outlaw and extract revenue from victims by coercion, the latter would have the option of turning to the "Mutual" or "Equitable" Police Agency for defense and for pressing charges against Prudential. These are the *genuine* "checks and balances" of the free market, genuine in contrast to the phony checks and balances of a state system, where all the alleged "balancing" agencies are in the hands of one monopoly government. Indeed, given the monopoly "protection service" of a state, what is there to prevent a state from using its monopoly channels of coercion to extort money from the public? What are the checks and limits of the state? None, except for the extremely difficult course of revolution against a power with all of the guns in its hands. In fact, the state provides an easy, legitimated channel for crime and aggression, since it has its very being in the crime of tax theft, and the coerced monopoly of "protection." It is the state, indeed, that functions as a mighty "protection racket" on a giant and massive scale. It is the state that says: "Pay us for your 'protection' or else." In the light of the massive and inherent activities of the state, the danger of a "protection racket" emerging from one or more private police agencies is relatively small indeed.

Moreover, it must be emphasized that a crucial element in the power of the state is its legitimacy in the eyes of the majority of the public, the fact that after centuries of propaganda, the depredations of the state are looked upon rather as benevolent services. Taxation is generally not seen as theft, nor war as mass murder, nor conscription as slavery. Should a private police agency turn outlaw, should "Prudential" become a protection racket, it would then lack the social legitimacy which the state has managed to accrue to itself over the centuries. "Prudential" would be seen by all as bandits, rather than as legitimate or divinely appointed "sovereigns" bent on promoting the "common good" or the "general welfare." And lacking such legitimacy, "Prudential" would have to face the wrath of the public and the defense and retaliation of the other private defense agencies, the police and courts, on the free market. Given these inherent checks and limits, a successful transformation from a free society to bandit rule becomes most unlikely. Indeed, historically, it has been very difficult for a state to arise to supplant a stateless society; usually, it has come about through external conquest rather than by evolution from within a society.

Within the anarchist camp, there has been much dispute on whether the private courts would have to be bound by a basic, common law code. Ingenious attempts have been made to work out a system where the laws or standards of decision-making by the courts would differ completely from one to another.[7] But in my view all would have to abide by the basic law code, in particular, prohibition of aggression against person and property, in order to fulfill our definition of anarchism as a system which provides no legal sanction for such aggression. Suppose, for example, that one group of people in society holds that all redheads are demons who deserve to be shot on sight. Suppose that Jones, one of this group, shoots Smith, a redhead. Suppose that Smith or his heir presses charges in a court, but that Jones's court, in philosophic agreement with Jones, finds him innocent therefore. It seems to me that in order to be considered legitimate, any court would have to follow the basic libertarian law code of the inviolate right of person and property. For otherwise, courts might legally subscribe to a code which sanctions such aggression in various cases, and which to that extent would violate the definition of anarchism and introduce, if not the state, then a strong element of statishness or legalized aggression into the society.

But again I see no insuperable difficulties here. For in that case, anarchists, in agitating for their creed, will simply include in their agitation the idea of a general libertarian law code as part and parcel of the anarchist creed of abolition of legalized aggression against person or property in the society.

In contrast to the general law code, other aspects of court decisions could legitimately vary in accordance with the market or the wishes of the clients; for example, the language the cases will be conducted in, the number of judges to be involved, and so on.

There are other problems of the basic law code which there is no time to go into here: for example, the definition of just property titles or the question of legitimate punishment of convicted offenders—though the latter problem of course exists in statist legal systems as well.[8] The basic point, however, is that the state is not needed to arrive at legal principles or their elaboration: indeed, much of the common law, the law merchant, admiralty law, and private law in general, grew up apart form the state, by judges not making the law but finding it on the basis·of agreed-upon principles derived either from custom or reason.[9] The idea that the state is needed to *make* law is as much a myth as that the state is needed to supply postal or police services.

Enough has been said here, I believe, to indicate that an anarchist system for settling disputes would be both viable and self-subsistent: that once adopted, it could work and continue indefinitely. *How to arrive* at that system is of course a very different problem, but certainly at the very least it will not likely come about unless people are convinced of its workability, are convinced, in short, that the state is not a *necessary* evil.

NOTES

1. William C. Wooldridge, *Uncle Sam, the Monopoly Man* (New Rochelle, New York: Arlington House, 1970), p. 101.
2. Ibid., pp. 103-104.
3. Ibid., pp. 95-96.
4. Ibid., pp. 100-101.
5. Morris and Linda Tannehill, *The Market for Liberty* (Lansing, Michigan: privately printed, 1970), pp. 65-67.
6. Ibid, p. 68.
7. E.g., David Friedman, *The Machinery of Freedom* (New York: Harper and Row, 1973).
8. For an elaboration of these points, see Murray N. Rothbard, *For a New Liberty* (New York: Macmillan, 1973).
9. Thus, see Bruno Leoni, *Freedom and the Law* (Princeton, New Jersey: D. Van Nostrand Co., 1961).

13

SOME REFLECTIONS ON ARBITRATING OUR WAY TO ANARCHY

CHRISTOPHER D. STONE

Could arbitration make anarchy workable? There is a consider-able amount to be said for Murray Rothbard's answer, even after we have thanked him for raising the question. To begin with, Rothbard operates upon an assumption about social order that distinguishes him from, and marks him, to my mind, far more sophisticated than, most anarchist critics. What Rothbard appreci-ates is that coordinated social arrangements have not merely a negative and binding aspect. Viewed from another perspective, some number of dependable, formal arrangements are a prerequi-site to satisfying our desires. To give a rather homely example, my freedom to travel from Los Angeles to Washington increases in proportion as I can rely upon the coordinated activities of taxi companies, airlines, baggage handlers, and what other unseen operatives, I do not know.

Because he has the good sense to worry about such things, Rothbard cannot give too short a shrift to the fundamental dilemma of anarchy: When power has been stripped from the state, how will we prevent some of the most basic elements of the social order from collapse? Rothbard, fortunately, is not about to assure us that, if only the state were slain, innate, indomitable human goodness would arise to the task. His answer, instead, is that various forms of private services will expand and adapt, filling the void more satisfactorily than before.

I feel it fairly safe to call this Rothbard's position, even though in this particular paper he focuses on only one of the many functions the modern state fulfills: the providing of what he calls "defense services," as distinct, for example, from the government's leasing of mineral rights, running the social security system, or regulating gas rates. His own justification for this particular emphasis is not, to me, wholly convincing, namely, that by definition the state "has arrogated to itself a compulsory monopoly of defense services over its territorial jurisdiction." It is not quite so: unlike some of the private letter-carrying companies that have found themselves in trouble for crowding the state's postal monopoly, the many private police services that compete with the government, such as Pinkerton's, have drawn, so far as I know, no heat. Indeed, the very success of these private policing ventures, however uncomfortably it sits with Rothbard's definition of the state, would seem to constitute a strong point in favor of the larger theses for which he is contending.

But even if Rothbard's principal justification for focusing on the defense-service function are a bit overstated, the instinct is surely right. Even people who will agree to winnow away some state functions—to abolish the Interstate Commerce Commission, for example, or to deregulate natural gas prices—are still likely to deem it "simply unthinkable" that the state give up the power to police us, to save us from our "nasty and brutish" selves. Thus if Rothbard can show us that state control over defense functions is not irreplaceable—nor, on balance, wise—the rest should follow, if not *a fortiori*, at least that much easier.

With this in mind, let us look a little more deeply at Rothbard's proposal. Most of us can see the possibility of transferring the postal service to private ownership; but can the same be done with defense services? Rothbard's optimism on this score is based largely on the success and potential of arbitration. And he is right that, historically, arbitration preceded organized and institutionalized judicial settlement, at least in the commercial area; just as it is true that in the past few decades arbitration has been resorted to increasingly as a means of dispute resolution. But if we are to consider replacing the state's police and courts with a private arbitration system, there are several limitations that ought to be kept in mind. First, much (though not all) of arbitrations's success rests upon the arbitrator's award having, typically, the power of the state in ultimate reserve. Equally important, the types of cases that have most readily lent themselves to arbitration historically are distinguishable in several important features from many matters Rothbard would want to wrest from state control.

Arbitration is at its most successful where there is some prior negotiating interface; union contracts typically provide arbitration provisions, but the procedure is fostered because there exists between union and management continuous interchanges that enable them to anticipate and provide for the contingencies that will arise. Management and labor also have between them, whatever their differences, a set of shared interests and common peers; this is what contributes to the success of arbitration-type courts in neighborhood and religious matters. When we turn, by way of contrast, to a sudden mass murder (I think of the elimination of the Clutter family as described by Truman Capote in *In Cold Blood*), half the parties, roused from their beds in nightshirts, have had no prior opportunity to delineate the standards they want the arbitrator to invoke.

The next problem is closely related to the first. Arbitration seems all the more attractive to Rothbard, on the view, encouraged by the legal system's designating a plaintiff and a defendant, that there are but two parties to every social disruption. If so, their troubles are "none of our business" and we might as well let the two of them dispose of their differences as they will. But society has long supposed that certain serious acts threaten "the community" (or disrupt, as earlier jurisprudence would have put it, "the King's peace"). Not that I want to beg Rothbard's question of which system is better. Through much of history, many wrongs that we punish today through the community were regarded as personal grievances only, and I would not deny the virtue of turning back the clock in some instances. For example, Rothbard would have widespread support for stripping the district attorney of power to prosecute such "victimless crimes" as pornography and homosexual acts. But from there on, his case gets stickier. In another class of cases, for example, espionage and subversion, where the victim is the state apparatus itself, Rothbard is probably committed to letting prosecution go by the boards, if only to avoid paradox. But I expect his good practical judgment gives him pause. And then, of course, there is the case of the mass murderer once more: it is not at all clear that the general society would, or should, be prepared to live with whatever settlement the heirs and/or their insurance companies cum police force agree to. *Their* assessment of the risk the killers pose (discounted by a compensatory payoff *they* receive) is not *ours*. Besides, the law has an important educative function, and if murder goes unpunished or underpunished, the lesson is a bad one.

It is worth questioning, too, how adequately an arbitration system can handle the class of problems in which the harm someone causes is large in the aggregate, but is diffused among many victims. Pollution by a steel mill is a classic example. One million persons may each suffer $100 in damages a year, leaving it not worth anyone's while to press suit. This is a situation that the state helps ameliorate at present, either by allowing the government to maintain the action for all, or by having its unified court system administer the appropriate class-action remedies. It ought to be noted that in doing so the government fulfills a useful role, not only for its soiled citizens, but for the mill as well: in a private market arbitration system such as Rothbard describes, I am not sure how the mill would protect itself against one million separate suits, should everyone who is injured, or thinks he is, be so inclined.

These are only a few of the procedural difficulties which might prove manageable in Rothbard's system, as remedies evolved; but presently they stump me. How does the arbitrator back up his subpoenas under this system? How does he enforce his awards? At one point Rothbard suggests (relying on early commercial experience) that acceptance of the system would be insured "by the method of social ostracism, and the refusal to deal any further." This may have carried weight among the merchants of Venice, but is a rape victim to be satisfied in the knowledge that she (and other women) can refuse to deal any further with the contumacious offender? That leaves them where they began. Elsewhere Rothbard seems to hint, without spelling it out in detail, that courts might be empowered to enforce decisions against guilty parties (which he suggests would be an exercise of "defensive force" consistent with anarchism). But his analysis (which is necessarily fragmentary in a seminal piece of this size) leaves too many questions unanswered, and still others answered unsatisfactorily. How and by whom would they be enforced without multiplying our problems geometrically? Whatever the defects of the present system, it does not pit our insurance companies in kidnap and tong warfare.

Rothbard also finds his future simpler than I do because he attaches little weight to a number of judicial functions that, in my view, are nearly as significant to a society as putting particular disputes to rest. At their best, courts set an example of how urgently felt needs should and could be compromised with the claims of principle; they set a stage on which we dramatize and act out changes that are taking place in moral political consciousness; they are forums for affirming and questioning authority, and for establishing what "facts" the society is going to live by. Thus, while Rothbard is confident that "Jack Ruby's murder of Oswald on public television" (which I did not see) needs no "complex judicial process," I am not so sure. Looking back, a public, authoritative, and, yes, complex trial of Oswald would have accomplished much that Jack Ruby did not. Could the arbitrators in Rothbard's scheme of things, pressed by a bereaved Marina Oswald, have fulfilled these functions? Rothbard might think so, in part because he is optimistic about the capacities and character of the judge-arbitrators that the free market will bring to the fore: they "will prosper on the market in proportion to their reputation for efficiency and impartiality"—not the stuff of which quick killings are made.

Finally there will exist a whole host of problems connected not with the selection of the arbitrator-judges, but with determining the laws which they will administer. One of the useful functions of the state, which Rothbard's system would in some manner have to supplant, is to create and declare valid laws. As I have already observed, in the classic arbitration arrangement, the parties contract their terms, so far as possible, in advance. Where "strangers" are involved, how will they know, in organizing their affairs, what code some arbitrator will ultimately consult in calling them to account? Rothbard gives the matter short shrift, apparently out of satisfaction that justice can be reduced to some biblical tooth-and-eye trading. If the surviving McCoy kills a Hatfield, it would be "fine" so long as he killed "the right Hatfield." I'm not so sure. And what does the anarchist society's basic rule of "defense against aggression" tell us to do with mitigating circumstances, the insanity defense, unknowing possession, vicarious liability, and, good God, all the other sources of fine and overly fine distinctions that thicken the treatises and make the system more or less run?

But finally, in spite of all my misgivings as to where, and how far, Rothbard's ideas would ultimately lead us, I must confess that I think the idea of offering arbitration as a substitute for present criminal law enforcement ought to be explored further. The reason is not merely that, in the abstract, the powers of the state over our lives is expanding too far too fast. Arbitration, so far as it can substitute, promises many virtues of a good society that anarchists have rightly championed. As an alternative to the national authoritarianism we are now moving toward, arbitration, particularly at local levels, offers to return some of lawmaking to the individual, to the enlargement of his self-esteem and voluntary citizenship. Studies have also shown it to be less costly—not only in terms of the expense of processing a case through a system, but in terms of the human capital it consumes as well. I myself have always been intrigued by the apparent successes of arbitration-type dispositions of criminal matters in Africa (as among the Tiv) and in rabbinical courts. But I was surprised, sometime after hearing Rothbard's paper, to learn that several cities, including Columbus, Ohio, and Tucson, Arizona, have recently begun diverting some minor and/or first-offense felonies into an arbitration-type system. In Columbus, where law students have served as facilitators, only 4 percent of the referred cases have had to be turned back into the ordinary criminal prosecution channels; in the other cases, victim and wrongdoers were able to agree on repayment, compensations, or cessation of the behavior complained of.

Looking back over these experiments, John M. Greacen, deputy director of the National Institute of Law Enforcement and Criminal Justice, has turned into something of an advocate for the cause. He observes that, under the present system, "in an ironic way, the offender often comes to see himself as the victim," emerging self-righteous, bitter—and unreformed. By way of contrast, Greacen points to some anecdotes out of the Tucson experience with arbitration:

A young man stole a color television set. At the diversion hearing he found that his victim was an invalid old woman, to whom the television set was life's central attraction. He was able to grasp the full consequences of his act—he had not just ripped off a TV, he had materially hurt the quality of the old woman's life. In the end, he agreed to paint her house, mow her lawn, and drive her to the doctor for her weekly checkup (in addition to returning the television set).

In another case the victim ultimately provided the offender with a $10,000 scholarship to attend medical school. Many of the victims have entered into the process reluctantly, only to find themselves later offering to serve as volunteer probation officers for other cases taken by the unit.

It is, I think, food for thought—practical as well as theoretical.

14

ANARCHIST JUSTICE

DAVID WIECK

No matter how valuable law may be to protect
your property, even to keep soul and body together, if it do not keep you and humanity
together.

—Henry Thoreau

Such terms as "socialism," "democracy," and "anarchism" have
been appropriated for diverse and conflicting uses. Professor Rothbard's association of anarchism with capitalism—a conjunction
usually called anarcho-capitalism—results in a conception that is
entirely outside the mainstream of anarchist theoretical writings or
social movements. To some of us who regard ourselves as anarchists,
this conjunction is a self-contradiction. Rothbard's definition of
"anarchist society" as a society in which there is "no legal possibility
for coercive aggression against the person or property of any
individual" may by its minimalism avoid formal contradiction. After
a preliminary discussion of this point, brief and inconclusive as it
must be, I shall proceed to analysis of his theory of "defense systems"
in a society without a state. Finally, since this is a symposium on

anarchism and not on a single variant of it, I shall feel free to discuss certain views of justice that derive from the main traditions of anarchism.

I admit to not being sure what "no legal possibility" for coercive aggression means. We are not to suppose, if I understand the latter part of Rothbard's paper, that there will be no laws and hence (vacuously) no legal possibility, for Rothbard proposes a "law code" that would prohibit coercive aggression and that would no doubt specify, among other things, what would count as acts of aggression and as appropriate punishments. He does not seek to eliminate law and judicial procedures but to eliminate aggressions that he believes are built into existing law codes and political constitutions, namely taxation and the arrogation of "defense services" by a monopolistic political authority. I think I am on safe ground in saying that he seeks to save law from the state.

The nature of a law code that is not integrated with a coercive political authority is not, however, easy to conceive. I take it that it must be more than a moral code; I doubt that Rothbard would accept the translation of "legally impossible" as "morally impossible" or "ethically impossible," both because it would be hard to make sense of the latter terms and because he consistently avoids moral terminology. Given that he allows every individual to act, at his or her own risk, as policeman, judge, and executioner, and perhaps jailer too, I think he means that *everyone* is a legal authority but that all "would have to" (p. 205) conform to the same legal code. The most favorable meaning I can give to "would have to" is as stipulating a necessary condition that would be guaranteed by the forceful action of adherents to the code against those who flout it. In that sense I shall construe him as attempting to articulate the principles of a "libertarian law code." But the basic question remains doubtful: Can there be the rule of law and yet no state, even on Professor Rothbard's minimal definition of the latter?

We are not given nearly enough material to allow pursuit of this question to the end; I have already had to supply propositions to which Professor Rothbard might not assent. It does *seem*, however, that in his system *there would stand over against every individual the legal authority of all the others.* An individual who did not recognize private property as legitimate would surely perceive this as a tyranny of law, a tyranny of the majority or of the most powerful—in short, a hydra-headed state. If the law code is itself unitary, then this multiple state might be said to have properly a single head—the law. The system would differ from the existing American system in that it would lack taxation, the economy would be unregulated by government (although property rights would be enforced), the present partial decentralization of legal authority under a rule of law would be maximized, and the enforcement of personal morality would be outlawed as aggression. But it looks as though one might still call this "a state," under Rothbard's definition, by its satisfying *de facto* one of his pair of sufficient conditions: "It asserts and usually obtains a coerced monopoly of the provision of defense service (police and courts) over a given territorial area" (p. 191, definition of "the state"). Hobbes's individual sovereign would seem to have become many sovereigns—with but one law, however, and in truth, therefore, a single sovereign in Hobbes's more important sense of the latter term. One might better, and less confusingly, call this a libertarian state than an anarchy.

Against such criticism Rothbard's "anarchism" might be defended on the ground that the "defensive" enforcement of a principle of individual liberty cannot fairly be classified as an infringement on individual liberty, and that such enforcement, dispersed as it would be and directed merely at preserving the integrity of the society, would not constitute a state in any serious sense. A further difficulty, however, results from the attachment of a principle of private property, and of unrestricted accumulation of wealth, to the principle of individual liberty. This increases sharply the possibility that many reasonable people who respect their fellow men and women will find themselves outside the law because of dissent from a property interpretation of liberty. There is, furthermore, broad ground for reasonable disagreement, even among those who would regard *some* form of property as a basic right, as to what should count as legitimate property and what modes of acquisition of property should be recognized. An obvious example is the right to bestow inheritance, to which Rothbard holds but which might be contested as an unreasonable extension of legitimate property rights; other examples of disputed conceptions of property rights abound in the lawbooks of our society. One can imagine, in addition, that those who lose out badly in the free competition of Rothbard's economic system, perhaps a considerable number, might regard the legal authority as an alien power, a state for them, based on violence, and might be quite unmoved by the fact that, just as under nineteenth-century capitalism, a principle of liberty was the justification for it all.

Most conceptions of anarchism that are not outright communist in economics minimize the possibility of great accumulations of private wealth, or of great disparities in economic well-being, by a concept of social property and social wealth that sets limits to private accumulation. It is of course just the absence of this category of *the social* that is crucial to Rothbard's system. Further consequences of this absence will appear in the more specific discussion below. At this point it seems fair to assert that Rothbard's inclusion of property in his definition of the individual and of liberty is likely to introduce heavy stresses into his system of justice, and that the compatibility of his system with anarchy, in other than a sheerly formal sense of the latter, is far from clear.

I. THE TWO PARTY MODEL

Whether Professor Rothbard's system is an anarchism is of course pertinent to the present symposium. But it is not the only pertinent question, because the society envisaged, however it should be called, would still have just those merits and failings that it has. The burden of my comment, as I develop it in this section and the two following, will be negative, because I believe that the shortcomings are truly serious.

Consistent with his antagonism to the social, Professor Rothbard adheres to a model for analysis and resolution of disputes and of more serious aggressions that I shall refer to as "the two-party model." "All disputes," he says, "involve two parties: the plaintiff, the alleged victim of the crime or tort, and the defendant, the alleged aggressor" (p. 196). If I understand Rothbard correctly, he *could* conceive of plaintiff or defendant, alleged victim or alleged aggressor, as (either or both) plural in number, and he *could* conceive also of cases where each alleges that the other is the offender. (If I am mistaken, it will not affect my discussion.) But it is clear that Rothbard recognizes no *third-party,* or what more extendedly might be called *social,* interests as legally and judicially relevant to an allegation of aggression. His severe individualism requires a two-party model, and the consequences are considerable.

The two-party model turns up first with respect to disputes, mainly economic, where negotiation and voluntary binding arbitration have failed to achieve a mutually acceptable settlement. With respect to disputes that are for practical purposes bilateral, Rothbard's emphasis upon arbitration is useful. It is not a specifically anarchist device, but I know of no reason why an anarchist would object to its utilization at many junctures in an anarchist society. But disputes are not, even for practical purposes, always bilateral.

Assuming the present family structure for context, a dispute over "custody" of a child, between the parents, affects very much a third party, namely the child, whose interests do not necessarily coincide with the interests of either parent—not necessarily, at any rate, with what they perceive their interests to be. (Even if the child is drawn into an arbitration process as an active party—contrary to the basic model—it is not very likely that a young child will be in a position to give informed consent to the procedures and proceedings.) A dispute between a landlord and a plumber may affect the tenants considerably. Far more importantly, it is not clear how, in a society that is defined as consisting of individuals and private enterprises, a matter such as the pollution of air and waterways by a papermill can be dealt with adequately. (Those affected by such disputes may not be nameable even in principle, because persons not yet born, whose parents may not even have been born, may be among them.) The interests of such affected individuals are not necessarily represented either by the disputants or by arbitrators they select. Such interests are commonly referred to as *social* interests, that is, interests that cannot be specified adequately as a set of individual interests. Conceivably, every person in the world, and every "possible" descendant, might be affected by a property owner's decision to construct a nuclear-energy installation of a certain design. Such "disputes" may not be the source of major overt social conflict (i.e., violence) in our society, but they have come to be recognized, although slowly, as affecting us in large numbers and vitally.

What Professor Rothbard has done, it seems to me, is to propose that complex human problems be dealt with by a model suited to disputes between two neighbors over a property line. This is just the kind of anarchism that Marxists have succeeded in discrediting because it seems to show so little awareness of the last hundred and fifty years of technological evolution. There are anarchists who meet the problem of technological socialization of the economy, and of life, by proposing return to preindustrial technology, even to an agricultural economy; but I am sure that Rothbard would reject this.

The consequences of the two-party model become more dramatic, if no more problematic, when Professor Rothbard discusses violent aggression against persons. Once more there is only "alleged victim" and "alleged criminal," and all proceedings are defined as those of the first against the second. The victim is held to be free to exact his or her own justice or vengeance, subject to legitimate reprisal only if found to have misidentified the criminal: "The courts would not be able to proceed against McCoy if in fact he killed the right Hatfield" (p. 204). A very strange saying indeed.

By now we have learned, I would have thought, that violence and other antisocial behavior arises out of some context of human relations within which responsibility is not only difficult to pinpoint but often so vague that the concept is useless if not noxious. The very Hatfield/McCoy example illustrates this. Does anyone know who is responsible for initiating a series of acts of vengeance? Does anyone know who committed acts of initial provocation, and is there any way of saying that some individual or either family can be held uniquely responsible? How can we differentiate between the "surviving McCoy" who finds "what he believes to be the guilty Hatfield" and the Hatfield who probably believed that he was fully justified in killing a McCoy? Aggression is not a simple observable fact; the aggressor is, notoriously, always someone other than oneself. We know in fact that a very high percentage of homicides and assaults occur within families and among friends, and the violent climax has usually arisen out of a long history of strife; the problem is not merely that it is hard to say which person is responsible but that it often makes no sense to say that *one individual or the other* must be, for it is as though their mutual hostility has made them into Siamese twins. If Professor Rothbard were to offer, in verdicts of responsibility and of punishment, to make allowance for such complexities, as does the present judicial system in fact, this would not meet my point; he would be taking a bad model as fundamental and doing patchwork upon it. A contemporary view of justice, I would expect, would seek out a model that took our psychological understanding, and the social psychology of aggression, into better account.

Professor Rothbard does not trouble himself either about the fact that acts of violence of the more anonymous sort, the "crime in the streets" that is a recent preoccupation, often if not almost invariably say more about the pathologies of a human community than about the pathologies of the individuals who commit them. There is of course a sense of "responsibility" by which one wants persons to accept responsibility for all their actions, and this is a powerful if not indispensable ethical principle. But the imputation of responsibility to others as justification for reprisal is a different matter entirely. Individuals do not create the social patterns and the community beliefs in terms of which they learn to make their choices. On the more personal level the social context intervenes in evident ways, as (for example) in a community where the concept of honor, or the disgrace of cuckoldry, attains a certain influence and force. On the more public level, we have had abundant experience of the influence of racial and religious bigotry, and of racial and religious and economic degradation. These are pathologies of society. A simplistic notion of responsibility, conjoined with legitimation of private acts of retaliation, would seem, among its consequences, to be invitational to blindly irrational acts of vengeance that worsen the injustice that exists.

An equally important limitation of Professor Rothbard's two-party model is that it excludes me (for example) as a "party" when an act of violence in my community does not involve me quite directly. But I do not know how I can fail to be affected and concerned by an act of violence in the community in which I live. In part, doubtless, I feel this because I think of people as living in communities, a concept rather alien to Professor Rothbard's way of thinking, and one reason I am an anarchist is that I would like to live in a world where there would be more genuine communities than exist now. But quite apart from that, I cannot but think that something is gravely amiss, that concerns me in numerous ways, when assault or rape or the like occurs in my community. Not only is my sense of human solidarity, and of concern for an injured person, evoked, not only do I feel a responsibility to the injured person, but I am also and especially concerned that what is done to rectify the injury, and to avert its repetition, be done well. I do not want to intervene in any and every case, but I want my concern to find effective expression, in the mode of rectification above all.

In certain cases one's concern as neighbor has special justification.

If a parent abuses or kills his or her infant child, the burden is surely not upon the victim or its "heirs" to seek redress. But any act of violence is a rent in the texture of a human community, and this, it seems to me, is something to which the community must respond. The fact that it is not practical that all of us intervene individually is perhaps the major justification for socialization of the justice process. One need not approve, as I do not, of the existing court system with its bail system, patronage judges, adversary court proceedings, and the rest. I am saying merely that the impulse to socialize justice, to transpose it from the purely private to the social realm, corresponds to the sense of most of us, shared by our ancestors for thousands of years at least, that justice is a social concern that must be dealt with socially. If we recognize the social character of justice, our problem will be to find a socialization of it that is different than our existing system and other than the institutionalization of private vengeance, as Rothbard's system threatens to be. We will not abandon the socialization of justice merely because its present socialization is rotten with injustices.

I have been stressing, in addition to "third party" and social responsibilities to those who suffer harm, a responsibility to seek the welfare of our community, of our social existence. It is perhaps implicit in the latter that we should think of ourselves as having a responsibility also toward those who have committed acts of aggression—but I should like to develop the point explicitly.

If we see violence as expressing a rent in the texture of community, we will be careful to avoid making neat and self-satisfying dichotomies of criminals and noncriminals, guilty and innocent, law-abiding and law-violating, aggressive and nonaggressive, and we will not be content with a justice of "Who did it?" Certainly we will not suppose that "the one who did it" (suppose it *was* Lee Oswald) has lost all claims of respect for life and person and is fair game for private vengeance, by one's own hand or by the hand of a hired assassin. We will not scapegoat so-called aggressors and thereby reassure ourselves of our utter blamelessness, and we may feel impelled to meditate upon the saying that "We are all murderers."

Thus, when I learn that someone who has committed a long series of major and minor acts of violence against persons was himself the victim, throughout childhood and adolescence, of abuse and contempt and denial of love, I cannot but feel that we have a responsibility toward that person. Nothing follows simply and logically about how that responsibility is to be fulfilled—but the difficulty of meeting a responsibility does not relieve one of it. What will be wrong will be to abstract from the fact that that person is a human being and to regard that person only as "the killer," "the rapist," "the aggressor," etc., an abstraction that runs systematically through Professor Rothbard's paper.

This misleading abstraction, and the other shortcomings that I have tried to indicate in this section, stem directly, I believe, from Rothbard's two-party model. The two-party model in turn stems directly from his severely individualistic conception of human being—a conception that is not characteristic of the anarchist traditions generally, even though, in one sense, all anarchisms are a kind of individualism. Underlying his two-party model of disputes is a unit model of man, and a unit of the thinnest sort, whose only predicates seem to be "has property," "is an aggressor," "defends himself," "kills so and so," and the like. I admit that this world with its curious population makes me uncomfortable.

II. JUSTICE BY PRIVATE ENTERPRISE

An equally misleading abstraction, still more damaging to Professor Rothbard's "society without a State," concerns the relation of his juridical system to the society of which it would be a part.

Each person is entitled to act as judge and policeman, and so on, but just as most of us do not make our own shoes Professor Rothbard imagines that there will be police agencies, primary courts, and courts to which such courts may appeal, all organized on a free-enterprise basis and available for hire. He wants to show that there can be machinery of adjudication and enforcement that obviates all need for a tax-based government.

If we are worried about the possible corruption and venality of "private" courts and police forces, we are assured that free-market competition among them will "place severe checks on such possibilities" (p. 204-05). But we should, I think, be worried about another problem than that of private courts "that may turn venal and dishonest" or a private police force that "turns criminal and extorts money by coercion." There is something more serious than the "Mafia danger," and this other problem concerns the role of such "defense" institutions in a given social and economic context.

Rothbard's context, we remember, is one of a free-market economy with no restraints upon accumulation of property. Now, we had an American experience, roughly from the end of the Civil War to the 1930s, in what were in effect private courts, private police, indeed private governments. We had the experience of the (private) Pinkerton police which, by its spies, by its *agents provocateurs,* and by methods that included violence and kidnapping, was one of the most powerful tools of large corporations and an instrument of the oppression of working people. We had the experience as well of the police forces established to the same end, within the corporations, by numerous companies, including the Colorado Fuel and Iron police of Vice President Rockefeller's ancestors and the private police of the Ford Motor Company. (The automobile companies drew upon additional covert instruments of a private nature, usually termed vigilante, such as the Black Legion.) These were in effect, and as such they were sometimes described, private armies. The territories owned by coal companies, which frequently included entire towns and their environs, the stores the miners were obliged by economic coercion to patronize, the houses they lived in, were commonly policed by the private police of the United States Steel Corporation or whatever company owned the properties. The chief practical function of these police was, of course, to prevent labor organization and preserve a certain balance of "bargaining."

On Rothbard's definition of "the state," such economic, judicial, and police complexes might not qualify for the designation "state" or "mini-state." They did not collect taxes—although this would have been absurd in many cases, since the miners were often paid in "scrip" rather than United States currency and their normal condition was indebtedness. These complexes were economically rather than territorially based and did not deny the territorial authority or tax-collecting authority of the government. But these complexes were a law unto themselves, powerful enough to ignore, when they did not purchase, the governments of various jurisdictions of the American federal system. This industrial system was, at the time, often characterized as feudalism. One may be a critic of the system of strong federal government that has emerged in America, and still recognize that one reason for its development was the demand of working people that the federal government protect them against, and put an end to, a system of industrial feudalism.

When private wealth is uncontrolled, then a police-judicial complex enjoying a clientele of wealthy corporations whose motto is self-interest is hardly an innocuous social force controllable by the possibility of forming or affiliating with competing "companies."

My point is not a merely empirical one, resulting from an effort to imagine how Professor Rothbard's system might work out. My conceptual point is that any judicial system is going to exist in the context of economic institutions. If there are gross inequalities of power in the economic and social domains, one has to imagine society as strangely compartmentalized in order to believe that those inequalities will fail to reflect themselves in the judicial and legal domain, and that the economically powerful will be unable to manipulate the legal and judicial system to their advantage. To abstract from such influences of context, and then to consider the merits of an abstract judicial system, as I believe Professor Rothbard does, is to follow a method that is not likely to take us far. This, by the way, is a criticism that applies not only to Professor Rothbard's but to any theory that relies on a rule of law to override the tendencies inherent in a given social and economic system.

III. THE MEANING OF DEFENSE

When one is talking about violence of person against person, about the destruction of human life even, one is, I do not wish to stop feeling, talking about human tragedies, human suffering, in short, pain. My sense of what anarchism is, is that it does not repudiate the great moral concerns—that, if anything, it seeks to enlarge them. But Professor Rothbard finds it possible to write, quite coolly, "This is fine," when in his example the surviving McCoy kills the "guilty" Hatfield. This wants some attention.

Hatfields and McCoys are of course by now legendary figures rather than real persons. To talk about them is in a way like talking about cartoon-comedy figures—these are one-dimensional beings, and one does not think of them as flesh-and-blood mortal fellow beings. I am pretty sure that Professor Rothbard would not talk so coolly if he were talking about some Wieck or some Rothbard. Yet I have before me the fact that he conducts his discourse about human justice in a way that abstracts not only from socioeconomic context, not only from the life and community context of social problems, but also from human feeling about life and death.

For Professor Rothbard, as I read his essay, there are no moral issues to be considered; merely self-defense and whatever it seems to justify. I cannot think of a harder problem, a harder moral problem, facing an anarchist society, or any society that would claim an ethical basis, than that of what to do when one human being has killed another, above all when that act has no reasonable claim of immediate self-defense. (It is not alleged that the McCoy who kills the Hatfield is himself in danger, nor is it in any way implied that he must justify his act by such claim.) I do not understand how it can be written about in Rothbard's manner, without a word that betrays a shadow of anguish. Of course, Rothbard may not be interested in morality or ethics; but in that case it is not clear what interest his society, as an object of intellectual contemplation, is going to have for me.

If I set aside such feelings, and pursue the meaning of Professor Rothbard's example and the discussion surrounding it, I find a philosophical move that on its own account is very serious. The right of self-defense has been offered as axiomatic. If we must have a Hobbesian axiom, I would prefer one that directs us to seek peace, perhaps while making some allowance for the occasional necessity of militant self-defense. But I will allow Rothbard his axiom. What I cannot allow is his move, without any argument, from self-defense to what he calls "retaliation" as a right legitimated by the defense axiom. As far as I can make out, Rothbard's "retaliation" would be equivalent to "retribution," "reprisal," "revenge."

I do not wish to argue here the merits of a retributivist theory of justice. (In my view, an "anarchist theory of punishment" would work out to a self-contradiction.) Important at the moment is the fact that Professor Rothbard introduces retribution under color of self-defense and does not seem to be aware that the matter requires discussion. (Again, "The courts would not be able to proceed against McCoy if in fact he killed the right Hatfield.") Since he is not overtly presenting a theory of punishment, it is difficult to pursue the relation between defense and retribution. But defense is always present and future-oriented, retaliation and retribution are predominantly past-oriented. Although I can imagine lines of argument that seek to bring them together, I have no idea what brings them together for Professor Rothbard. I think therefore that I have every reason to worry about what I would be assenting to if I assented to his defense axiom. Philosophically the problem could be expressed in this way: taken very strictly and literally, self-defense does not give us much in the way of a system of justice, and an attempt to enlarge it so as to produce a full-bodied theory of justice must, it seems, appeal to other axiomatic propositions. One would want to know if for Professor Rothbard the right of revenge is such a suppressed premise.

IV. ANARCHISM

What I have taxed Professor Rothbard (or his theory) with in my review is this. In attempting to say what a society without a state would be like he has offered principles and procedures by which "defense services" could be provided. The very term "defense" should have set us on guard, for already here the aggressor-victim model can be anticipated. Wrongs and injuries are defined as "crimes," a term which itself presupposes law that defines what is criminal. Rothbard's criminology is unfortunately rather like the commonsense criminology of the good citizen who thinks of criminals as *others*, as alien menaces, not conceivably himself. Not surprisingly, Rothbard provides us with a model for wrongs and injuries that seems to be useless either for understanding the events or for considering means of rectification, that is, for bringing the given story to the most desirable end. He reasons in terms of unit entities whose relations with each other are legal and economic but not in any specific way human. He not only disregards but rules out the socialization of justice. Most generally, he writes of society as though some part of it (government) can be extracted and replaced by another arrangement while other things go on as before, and he constructs a system of police and judicial power without any consideration of the influence of historical and economic context. Out of the history of anarchist thought and action Rothbard has pulled forth a single thread, the thread of individualism, and defines that individualism in a way alien even to the spirit of a Max Stirner or a Benjamin Tucker, whose heritage I presume he would claim—to say nothing of how alien is his way to the spirit of Godwin, Proudhon, Bakunin, Kropotkin, Malatesta, and the historically anonymous persons who through their thought and action have tried to give anarchism a living meaning. Out of this thread Rothbard manufactures one more bourgeois ideology.

In characterizing Professor Rothbard's theory as ideological, I am using the term in the sense of a system of ideas justificatory, by means of *a priori* principles, of a certain way of life, and of the privileges of certain classes or social strata. I do not think that we fully understand the meaning and limitations of various social theories unless we understand their perspective. The problems of human being and society will have a certain shape in the perspective of the middle classes, another shape in the perspective of a bureaucracy, another shape in the perspective of a feudal aristocracy, another shape in the perspective of a military caste; and it will not be just the *problems* of human being that have a particular shape, it will be, also, society and human being themselves that will have a particular shape, a particular definition, that pertains to the given perspective.

If we want to transcend such limited truths and partial conceptions, it will be important to reveal the bias inherent in them in order to attain a truth more adequate to humankind (perhaps even to more than humankind). It seems clear to me that Professor Rothbard articulates the values and concerns of members of a middle class, specifically their concern with property and taxation, their resentment at being taxed to relieve the economic distress of the poorer classes, their sense that government is protective of the monopoly position of large corporations against any efforts of middle-class persons to increase their wealth and become significant proprietors, their feeling of vulnerability to depredations against their limited and not easily replaceable property, and their awareness of the possibility, realized in communist nations, that the state may become the sole proprietor and therewith eliminate their social role. These concerns reflect social reality in considerable degree; they do not relate to phantoms. They are exactly the foci of Professor Rothbard's discussion. What are not the foci, what one will look for in vain, are the specific concerns of the poor, of wage workers, of socially and economically subordinated ethnic or racial groups, of the impoverished peoples of that American empire which, rather than the legally defined nation, should be understood as constituting our economic society. Nor of course does one find any reflection in Rothbard's paper of the concerns of those who find myriad shortcomings in middle-class values and ideas. The very definition of human being as an individual who possesses property is closely linked, it hardly needs saying, with those values and ideals.

The points made above have special relevance because the main traditions of anarchism are different entirely. These traditions, and the theoretical writings associated with them, express the perspective and the aspirations, and also, sometimes, the rage, of the oppressed people in human society: not only those economically oppressed, although the major anarchist movements have been mainly movements of workers and peasants, but also of those oppressed by power in all those social dimensions that have become (recently) themes of "liberation" movements, and in many other dimensions as well, including of course that of political power expressed in the state.

The strength of anarchism as a source of social idealism, and as expression of such idealism, lies partly in the fact that, unlike Marxian socialism, it is not wedded to a perspective of economic oppression solely. (At the same time it has not been affected, as has Marxian socialism, by the development of ideological political parties engaged in conquest of power; nor has it like recent Marxism been immixed with nationalism. Anarchist critique of such new forces of oppression or potential oppression, self-justified by their ideal aims, has been directed not only at Marxist movements but also, traditionally, as self-criticism, at similar potentialities within anarchist movements.) The "freedom" and "antiauthoritarianism" of anarchism did derive in large measure from the pluralistic socialism of the First International but the historical development of anarchism has been one in which these and related concepts have been generalized and universalized and so interpreted as to transcend any particular perspective of social oppression.

Thus, although one finds the concept of a working class in many anarchist writings, one finds that, generally, appeal is made to *people,* or to *the people,* in behalf of what are thought to be the true interests of *all* persons. In the enlarging and universalizing of such ideas as freedom, anarchism may have sacrificed "practicality"; rightly put, that question becomes complex and I cannot discuss it here. But however that may be, anarchism represents, as I understand it, a kind of intransigent effort to conceive of and to seek means to realize a *human* liberation from every power structure, every form of domination and hierarchy. Correlative with this negation is the positive faith that through the breakdown of mutually supportive institutions of power, possibilities can arise for noncoercive social cooperation, social unity, specifically a social unity in which individuality is fully realizable and in which freedom is defined not by rights and liberties but by the functioning of society as a network of voluntary cooperation. It is in this sense that anarchisms are a kind of individualism, contrasting sharply to the collectivism and centralism of Marxian theory but also contraasting sharply to the individualism associated with capitalist traditions.

Elsewhere I have tried to show that what is said above is, indeed, what anarchism "is about." [1] Here I will sketch, a little too hastily, some of the broad features of a general view of justice that I believe are implicit in this interpretation of anarchism.

The presumption underlying the negation of the various forms of power and of all those relations that can be characterized by the metaphor "slavery" is that social structures ordered by power prevent, and render people functionally incapable of, the exercise of capacities for free agreement and voluntary cooperation. Correlatively, they provide opportunity and temptation for the exertion of tendencies to which human being has demonstrated its proneness: tendencies to magnify oneself to a point that others are only means to one's ends, tendencies to magnify oneself by enslaving others, tendencies to self-deception and other-deception, tendencies to cower before the power of others, tendencies to herd against the anomalous individual, tendencies to avoid responsibility for decisions, and so on: for anarchism is as much a distrust as a faith. Anarchists insist upon a careful distinction between society and state in order to indicate that in seeking the abolition of the latter, which stands at the center of a network of power structures to which it provides legitimation and defense, they do not seek the breakup of human society but rather an order constituted freely through manifold agreements, contracts, negotiations that can avert the actualization of those personally and socially destructive tendencies that situations of power (generically: *political* relations) trigger. A different order entirely, and nonanarchist, will be an order attained through or rationalized as a single societal contract or through imposition of a central authority by any procedure whatever.

A *society* will be just, then, insofar as it is free, in the sense of the metaphor, of "enslaving" social or political institutions (military, familial, governmental, educational, sexual, ethnic-hierarchical, caste-stratificational, ecclesiastical, etc.); but it will not be a society at all unless patterns of cooperation capable of sustaining human communities and vital personal existence are achieved. (To be anarchist and just, a society need not be perfectly or even approximatively egalitarian in an economic sense, unless such a principle arises from mutual agreement; unjust would be such systematic discrepancies of wealth as would constitute *de facto* economic classes, where the inferior class or classes would be chronically blocked off from full participation in the life of the society.) It is generally assumed by anarchist writers that in an anarchic society the incidence of "antisocial," "delinquent" behavior would be negligible because its source in poverty, social degradations, and humiliations, and the alienation of person from person and person from community would have been eliminated. The existence of societies, and regions within some other societies, where homicide and lesser violence against persons is rare and where theft and vandalism are not ways of life gives reason to believe that such minimalization is not an absurd goal. But of course the causes of alienation and violence may be more complex than we understand them to be—we do not understand very well the ways in which the newborn becomes a human being. Conceivably, the freedom envisaged in an anarchist society might create serious tensions, although it would not be a freedom of constant opting among infinite alternatives but a freedom of social continuity in which persons make commitments and agreements and are involved in numerous patterns of ongoing cooperation.

Recognition of the *presence* of injustice would not, I think, be a problem of the magnitude it attains in our society. One assumes a generally shared will to realize and preserve the principles of voluntary agreement, of nonabuse of others, of noninvasive mutual aid, not as abstract ideas but as expressions of the life lived. Living in societies in which these are so very far from being the norm, we wonder how it is possible to decide what is just. If one grants that such norms have become realized, as the life that is lived, we have what I would call a "spirit of justice," and I do not see how recognition that the basic norms have been violated or disrupted would involve a tortuous decision. Rape, assault, homicide, "rip-off," fraud, and the like are in clear contradiction to the principle of voluntary cooperation and peace. More generally, the abuse of persons, and anything that tends toward creation of patterns of "enslavement" or that hinders the realization and continuity of free cooperation, is a wrong in such a society.

But if it would seem not so hard to define "injury," either personal or social, the labeling of an action as unjust, or the determination that some person or persons are *responsible* for an injury, raises deeper questions. I have suggested earlier that these are terms more appropriate in the context of moral education than in the context of dealing with injustice and injuries. For the latter purpose, they are appropriate perhaps for a society that believes that it must take reprisal upon wrongdoers, for their own good as well as for its own sake and also in order to deter others. Our long historical experience with many types of reprisals seems to indicate, almost beyond doubt, that they surely do not benefit the "criminal;" that reprisal may, in a society based in good part on fear, deter certain kinds of antisocial behavior, but that the price is enormous when the price is reckoned to include all the "disutilities" associated with (for example) imprisonment; and as to reprisal for its own sake ("vengeance"), this is hard to make sense of at all outside certain religious contexts. But on the other hand an ethical society cannot ignore, cannot let pass, the occurrence of injuries, abuses, and the like, or the threat of conflicts that promise to eventuate in serious harm.

We are premising a society in which people have stopped living in fear of one another, in which gross violence, hatred, and contempt for life have become uncommon, in which alienation of person from person seldom reaches the malignant extremes to which we are accustomed. We are premising a society in which the absence of economic monopolies, and of many other familiar incentives for seeking advantage at the expense of others, should allow social decisions to be made more easily on a rational basis, that is, through discovery of a resolution in which there are no losers. This is an essentially humanized society, not without friction, not without suffering, not without anguish and pain; but it is not pervaded with the radical evil of power, of systematized manipulation, deceit, indifference. (If this were not the case, then I do not see how "the abolition of the state" could be other than a fiction that masked the reintroduction, or even the continuance, of political institutions called [now] by euphonious libertarian names.) One could not know, from where we stand, what specific procedures would be followed in dealing with real conflict, obdurate people, madness, violence, unwillingness to keep the peace. Nor could one know the "philosophy" in terms of which these problems would be resolved. My way of thinking of it is this:

We can imagine that in this society people would try, together, to confront and deal with failures of their community, and break-downs of human peace and normal cooperation, with all the sympathy, love, and wisdom that they possessed. I imagine that they would take one problem at a time—if the "docket" were crowded, that would have to be taken as a sign that the society was in danger. They would try to find out how, in terms of what they value most deeply, they could restore the wholeness of social existence, a project that bears no relation to the project of "dealing with the criminal." I have no definite idea, and do not know how one could have, of what would be done, case by case; for a "case" is some distinct individual person, and some other individual person, and the next and the next, involved in some mess, some plight, some folly, some self-destruction, some misunderstanding. I imagine people having to face up, not often but sometimes, to hard and even terrible alternatives. To take the hardest possible case, and the hardest possible solution, I can even imagine that, *in extremis,* the persons in such a society might decide that someone had to die, a solution that at the very best is a lesser evil: done not as "punishment" but from despair that no way could be found of living at peace with this person. But if they did not somehow atone for that act and that choice, if they did not suffer for it and suffer terribly, I would fear for them.

If one asks whether there could be, in an anarchist society, either prison or other detention, or punitive deprivations, or denial of social and economic privileges, or banishment, the answer would be in these terms: insofar as the society were unable to respond to wrongs in a mode of nonretaliation, of nonviolence on a Gandhian or similar model, with willingness to make sacrifices in order to

restore a healthy peace, with unqualified respect for the humanity
of offenders, that society would fall short of the moral ideal of
anarchism, and if the people of the society were not concerned with
moving as near as practical to that ideal, the society would be
lacking in commitment to an anarchist morality. On this view,
anarchism represents, finally, not a specific social design but a moral
commitment. (Rothbard's anarchism I take to be diametrically
opposite.) Stated as an abstract ideal, anarchism would exclude all
forms of coercion; societies which could be properly described as
anarchist would not necessarily actualize that ideal but they would
seek to actualize it. In such societies it is hard to imagine the
existence of prisons, for these, as we know them, are instances of
what I have called slavery. One would imagine an emphasis upon
reparation, where reparation would not always be exclusively a
demand made upon a "guilty" person but a task for the community
concurrently. One would imagine that the withholding of social
privileges from persons who obstruct and are uncooperative or
irresponsible need not be dehumanizing. One would imagine that
something like older common law or tribal custom might have a
role. But in saying "one would imagine" I mean to say that one
could state only very tentatively what might be useful and within
the anarchist moral spectrum.

In lieu of further discussion of the character that anarchist justice
might in practice assume, I will try to suggest what might be its
core. In writing above that "they would take one problem at a
time" and "try to find out how . . . they could restore the wholeness
of social existence," I was consciously adopting the problem-solving
conception that was central in John Dewey's ethics. In societies of
power, of castes and classes, of collectivities that are noncom-
munitarian, Dewey's method degenerates into a technocracy of
social-scientific experts. There is no common "we," for example, in
terms of which to solve the problems of an American city, and no
common "we" in terms of which to consider the problems of a youth
lost in the slums of a city. But if an anarchist society is one in which
people have, by and large, a sense of living and working in
circumstances of mutual aid and voluntary agreement, then it does
not make sense (it seems to me) to ask what is abstractly right or
what is to the interest of the greatest number, or to proceed
individualistically to solve a problem affecting many. It makes sense

to ask "What can we do about this problem we have here?" Acts of imagination are called for, then, to rectify injustice, to resolve conflict, just as acts of imagination are called for in the "normal" creation of ongoing life.

It may seem ironical to take Dewey, the conscious theorist of democracy, so negative toward "utopian" thinking, as a kind of prophet of the ethics of an anarchist society. The truth, I believe, is that Dewey was, until late in life, exceedingly unrealistic and idealizing, in the manner of nineteenth-century evolutionary optimism, about the immediate potentialities of American society and about the ongoing force of older New England traditions; even in his later pessimism he did not take cognizance nearly adequately of the realities of economic and racial oppression—that is, of the fractured character of American society. As a liberal he expected conciliation of conflicts, as if there could be common ground for conciliation so long as the various relations of caste, class, and power remained in place. The values that Dewey hoped to be realized in a democracy, I suggest, are realizable only in something approaching anarchy, and the method he proposed for dealing with social problems would have its proper context only in such a society.

I can imagine that my remarks in this section might be taken as nothing other than the liberties of thought when one asks oneself fancifully; What might the best of societies, most pleasing to imagination, be like? Particularly might one expect this response because I make various assumptions about achieved social habits of cooperation, about recognition of the personhood of others, and so on, that represent a condition far removed from the existing. Professor Rothbard, by comparison, can appeal to self-interest of the sort with which we are familiar, and he is no more "utopian" than to suggest extending to the political realm the principles of the economic realm. Unfortunately, I do not see much justice in this latter society. As concerns the more usual anarchist vision of a free society, this is redeemed from the realm of fanciful speculation to the extent that there is strength in the thesis that what stands between us and some approximation of a free society is the prevalence of relations and institutions of power, dominance, hierarchy, "slavery," many of which—for example, the patterns of male-female relations, of parent-child relations, of teacher-student relations—have only recently and partially come to recognition as crucially supportive aspects of the networks of power to which every generation, in each of its members, is obliged to adapt. The anarchists' radical analysis of the state has hardly been given serious consideration by many even of those who count themselves as radical. If the anarchist analysis of power is fundamentally sound, it will tell, at the least, what would have to be resolved before a free society, in the strong anarchist sense of the term, could be achieved; and it might also tell something about the way.

NOTE

1. "The Negativity of Anarchism," in *Interrogations: Revue Internationale de Recherche Anarchiste,* Paris, France, No. 5 (December 1975). But this is not yet a complete formulation of my view of anarchism as a historical idea embodied in social movements.

THE MORAL PSYCHOLOGY OF ANARCHISM

15

THE DIMENSIONS OF ANARCHY

DONALD McINTOSH

I. INTRODUCTORY

This essay is a critical, multidimensional analysis of anarchism.[1] It seeks to ascertain on what grounds anarchism can be advanced as a point of view which is coherent, internally consistent, and does not run blatantly against the facts, and to show the relationship of this point of view to individualism and to social and political authority. It is neither a defense of anarchy nor an attack on it, but rather an examination of what it is to be an anarchist who thinks straight.

By "anarchism" I mean the movement of thought and practice which runs (I think) from the Anabaptists in the sixteenth century down to some of the contemporary counterculture communes, and some of the student movements in Europe. The picture drawn here will be "ideal typical": a description which attempts to be, in Weber's phrase, "adequate at the level of meaning," and which actual anarchistic movements and theories resemble to a greater or lesser degree.

The approach will be interdisciplinary, attempting to utilize and integrate philosophical, psychological, sociological, and political perspectives in a rounded treatment. As such, it rests on the general theories which I have developed at length elsewhere.[2]

Since the line of argument is long and complex, a one paragraph summary may help orient the reader. Definitionally, anarchy is not, as some have thought, lack of government, but a special form of government, resting on the principle of unanimity. (It is thus not to be identified with the "state of nature.") Anarchy takes its place alongside the traditional three of monarchy, aristocracy, and democracy, as a fourth basic form. Philosophically, one may distinguish between libertarianism (belief in subjective freedom) and individualism (primacy of the private will). Anarchism is not, as Hegel and others have supposed, a logical result of extreme libertarianism, for reasons which were already clear to Hobbes. An attempt to examine the relationship of individualism to anarchism, via a treatment of Hobbes, Rousseau, and Stirner, fails because the concept of individualism employed has been inadequate. A psychological investigation is needed. On the psychological level there are two types of authority: peer authority and parental authority. Individualism is the assertion of the independence of the "personal" (as against "private") will from both types. This area of independence is inherently limited, because freedom from all authority would destroy the basis on which individualism comes into being. Hence anarchism cannot successfully be argued on individualistic grounds, as freedom from all authority, as some have attempted. Rather, on the psychological level anarchism represents another polar type: acceptance of complete peer authority, coupled with rejection of all parental authority. On the sociological level the two types emerge as social authority (Durkheim's "collective conscience"), and political authority (Weber's *"legitime Herrschaft"*). Anarchism rejects all political authority. As a result, successful social organization requires an intense collectivistic equalitarianism (Durkheim's "mechanical solidarity"). Politically, anarchism is not opposed to the state itself, if the state is understood as a community of equals which possesses the authority to govern, but stands against political authority, political power, and any vestige of a state apparatus. Anarchy can thus be defined as "government without politics."

II. DEFINITIONAL

A. The Need for Government

The term "anarchy" is often taken to mean "lack of government," but this is a mistake. Almost all anarchists believe and have believed in government, and for good reason. The need for government seems incontrovertible, and indeed the very starting point of political theory.

If humans are to have any better than an animal existence, living in caves and eating roots and berries, they must live in communities in which activity is organized and coordinated by both general rules and specific directives. Humanity itself requires cooperative social activity, and this in turn requires government. Just as atoms, solar systems, and galaxies have "laws" which govern their behavior, so must human communities. Otherwise they could not exist. Lack of government is not anarchy but chaos.

B. Nondeliberate Government

By "government" is here meant primarily the deliberate or conscious regulation of social action: the formation of a decision by a person or persons as to how people are to behave, which is communicated and obeyed. However, in a more extended sense it is possible to speak of the nondeliberate "government" of social action. There are two types.

First, social groups are typically and characteristically "governed" by a set of informal social norms, which are not the product of deliberate decisions but instead arise spontaneously out of the interactions of the group members. These informal norms organize and regulate a great deal of the life of every social grouping, from the simplest tribe or street-corner gang to the most elaborate formal organization. The effectiveness of these rules depends first on their internalization—their inner acceptance by the group members—and second on the apparently universal tendency of the group members to enforce the rules on each other spontaneously, via various forms of coercion. I have elsewhere called this form of regulation "social control." [3]

In the second form of nondeliberate regulation, which can be called "automatic government," the regulation occurs as an unplanned aggregate result of the unilateral decisions of the actors. Classical economic theory envisions such a process. Each actor acts from personal motives (e.g., economic self-interest) without thought of the relation of the action to the overall pattern of the interaction. Given certain kinds of motives (e.g., a prudent desire to maximise profit) and a certain setting (e.g., a free market) the net resultant will be the regulation of economic interaction by certain "laws" (e.g., which set prices, allocate production and distribution, etc.).[4]

Many anarchists have been uneasy about any kind of deliberate government, and sought to rely as much as possible on some variation of the two nondeliberate forms. Almost without exception, however, they are forced to recognize that deliberate government cannot altogether be dispensed with. Even the most close-knit system of social control, as a small traditionally oriented tribe, where all social behavior is regulated by an elaborate normative system, finds itself faced from time to time with the need for deliberate governmental decisions, and, as I shall argue later, automatic government can exist only, if at all, within a framework of deliberate government.

C. Anarchy and the State of Nature

Nozick has used "anarchy" as synonomous with the "state of nature," as the idea was understood by a number of seventeenth- and eighteenth-century thinkers, especially Locke.[5] Locke defines the state of nature as "Men living together, according to reason, without a common superior on earth with authority to judge between them." [6] It is true that a good deal of government occurs in Locke's state of nature. The law of nature "governs" human behavior, not in a deliberate way, but through the force with which it operates within the minds of people. From the "self-evidence" of this law of nature, its divine origin, its universal acceptance, and the general willingness to enforce it spontaneously, a sociologist would likely conclude that Locke's law of nature is a set of social norms. Operating through its acceptance, this normative system (or *jus gentium*) governs the state of nature, but, Locke feels, not very well. It needs to be reinforced by deliberate government.

There are two stages in Locke's theory of the establishment of such a government. First the members of society agree unanimously to form an association which has the authority to execute the law of nature. Second this association, by majority vote, establishes a system of government.[7] In these terms, anarchy lies, not in the state of nature, but precisely between these two stages.

An anarchic society is a group of people who have, by unanimous agreement, formed together into an authoritative body, but who have not established and do not intend to establish any "common superior on earth to judge between them." Instead, all governmental action must, like the original formative decision, be the outcome of the unanimous agreement of the undifferentiated whole.

D. A Definition of Government

In political theory, the term "government" usually refers to the deliberate kind, and that sense will henceforward be used here, unless otherwise qualified. A strict definition of "government" can be obtained by generalising the following special case: Let A and B be two actors, each with two options, a_1 and a_2, and b_1 and b_2, respectively. This generates a field of interaction containing four possible states: a_1b_1, a_1b_2, a_2b_1, and a_2b_2. If the interaction is ungoverned, the interaction occurs in one stage. A and B each choose unilaterally one of their options, and the result is one of the four possible interactions. If the interaction is governed, however, it occurs in two stages, and involves two levels of choice. First, someone chooses not an option but a state of the field (an option pair), thus prescribing an option for each actor. For example, someone chooses a_1b_2: a_1 for A and b_2 for B. This someone can be A, or B, or A and B jointly (by agreement), or a third party, C. Second, after this governmental decision A and B individually (unilaterally) choose the option prescribed by the governmental decision. If they do not so choose, the government is not "effective" (does not occur).

E. A Definition of "Anarchy"

In terms of the formulation above, anarchy can be defined by two characteristics: first, the governmental decision is the product of a

unanimous joint agreement among all the governed; second, the
choice of the governed, whether to comply or not to comply with
this governmental decision, is not compelled or even influenced by
any political authority. The meaning of the second proviso, and its
relation to the first, will emerge in the course of the discussion.

Anarchy thus takes its place alongside the traditional three forms
of government: monarchy, aristocracy (or oligarchy), and democracy. If the nondeliberate forms are included, we have a sixfold
typology of government, as follows:

	Form of government	*Who governs*
nondeliberate	Automatic Government	nobody[8]
	Social Control	social norms[9]
	Monarchy	one
deliberate	Aristocracy	a few
	Democracy	a majority
	Anarchy	everyone

In practice, anarchic government is by no means unknown. Many
small informal groups make decisions via a rule of unanimity, and
at the other extreme an alliance between two states fulfills the
definition exactly, for the signatory parties unanimously decide how
their relations are to be regulated, and then proceed individually
and without compulsion from any common political authority to
put (or not to put) the provisions of the treaty into effect. (This
assumes that international law is not backed by any political
authority.)

Anarchy is nevertheless a very difficult form to make work,
especially if the regulation involved is at all extensive. Decisions are
extremely hard to arrive at, and compliance is uncertain, precisely
because of its two defining features. Where anarchy is most effective,
in small informal groups (e.g., communes), is where it is most likely
to be transmuted into less than unanimous and politically authoritative government. The question arises: What principles could
possibly justify an attempt to adopt such a difficult, ineffective, and
unstable form of government?

III. PHILOSOPHICAL

A. Anarchy and Libertarianism

Anarchism has been interpreted by some as a particularly pure and uncompromising expression of the ideal of "subjective freedom," to use Hegel's term. This ideal, most closely associated with classical liberalism and utilitarianism, holds that freedom consists of lack of restraint, or the ability to do what we want. The belief that subjective freedom is the highest social and political value can be termed "libertarianism." An examination of the issue, however, will reveal that anarchism is not the logical or natural outcome of libertarianism.

The case that libertarianism leads to anarchism was made with great clarity by Hegel, and I will begin by summarizing his argument.[10]

Subjective freedom is lack of effective restraint or prohibition against whatever the individual wishes to do. "From this principle follows as a matter of course that no law is valid except by agreement of all." But in practice it is impossible to apply the principle of unanimity. Even in the unlikely event that everyone could agree to a set of rules, to put them into effect would require an administrative apparatus whose posts were occupied by a special group of people, who directed activity in accordance with these rules. "Thus the distinction between commanding and obeying seems necessary for the very function of the state. . . . Hence one recommends—as a matter of purely external necessity, which is in opposition to the nature of freedom in its abstract aspect—that the constitution should at least be so framed that the citizens have to obey as little as possible and the authorities are allowed to command as little as possible."

On this interpretation, anarchy is the radical left of classical liberalism. What is best is the principle of unanimity and the absence of any state apparatus which possesses political authority. But in practice this is impossible. Hence one advocates liberal republicanism: a government of the most limited possible powers and functions. The anarchists are those who share these principles but refuse to make any compromise, and who argue that given the proper conditions it is possible to establish a sufficient and effective government on purely anarchic principles.

Most anarchists, however, have not based their case on the principle of subjective freedom, but on different principles, and I think rightly so. A closer look at the principle of subjective freedom will show its inadequacy as a ground for anarchism.

Let us look at the matter from the standpoint of the doctrine of unanimous consent or agreement. It might be supposed that in consenting to something a person is acting freely (in the subjective sense), but such a supposition ignores the network of coercion in which all human action is embedded. To say that freedom is "doing what we wish" is too abstract to have any clear meaning. If most people could do as they wished, they would be immortal, be able to move instantly from one place to another, to become invisible at will, and so on—that is, they would immediately divest themselves of and transcend their human and mortal condition. But in practice those restrictions imposed by nature which are beyond one's control must perforce be accepted as given, and choice restricted to the alternatives actually open within this framework of necessity.

This point also holds true for the imperatives of the social environment, which presents us with a structure of opportunities and limitations (restrictions) only within which are we free to act as we wish. Hence a stipulation that governmental decisions must be unanimous would not at all guarantee "freedom from restraint" to the parties involved in the governmental process, even in the complete absence of any coercive state apparatus.

This point, that the principle of unanimity need not promote subjective freedom, is evident at a glance in international relations, for example. As I have pointed out, an alliance is an anarchic form of government. Yet a strong nation can use force or threat of force to compel a weak one to sign and respect an agreement with which it is very unhappy. The unanimity has been produced by coercion.

The doctrine of consent thus has at best limited bearing on the question of subjective freedom. This is Hobbes's point when he is discussing the difference between government by institution (established by the consent of all) and government by conquest (established by force of arms). It might seem that the first is the freer form of government. Not so, says Hobbes. The "free" consent of all the citizens in establishing their own government, and the "coerced" consent produced by the point of the sword when a conqueror sets up a government, are at bottom the same. Both rest on fear, the difference being that in the first case it is fear of each other, and in the second fear of the conqueror that drives a people into obedience.[11]

Hegel is thus in error when he sees anarchism as the most logical (but an impractical) expression of the libertarian ideology, for Hobbes's solution is equally logical. Hobbes's point is that people have more to fear from each other in the absence of government than they have to fear from their rulers in the presence of government. They are freer with compulsory government than without it, and the firmer the rule the freer they are.

The consent wrung by the many from the few under anarchy may be just as unfree as the consent wrung from the many by the sword of the state. The point that "compulsory" government need not restrict subjective freedom any more than "voluntary" government, holds even if we confine ourselves to the question of violent coercion, for the subjects of Hobbes's sovereign have nothing to fear from him on this score as long as they do what he says. Hence it makes no sense to oppose compulsory government per se simply on the basis of the principle of subjective freedom.

Faced with these considerations, the principle of subjective freedom assumes its most logical and coherent form when it adopts the idea of a government which is compulsory but limited, capable of acting strongly, but only within a circumscribed area, thus minimizing both the restraints which people can exercise on each other, and the restraints which government can exercise on them all. This in fact was the conclusion drawn by modern liberalism. Within this tradition we can distinguish political liberalism, which primarily fears the restrictions on freedom imposed by government and hence seeks to limit it, and social liberalism, which primarily fears limitations on freedom imposed by people on each other and seeks to use government to prevent this.

Anarchists have differed in their attitudes toward the various forms of restrictions on subjective freedom. Some have opposed any form of violence, while others have glorified it. None has been so utopian as to seek to eliminate all forms of coercion from human relations. What is anathema to all is not compulsion itself, but any

form of compulsion which proceeds from a position of supremacy—
from a superior to a subordinate. In fact, the relation of superior to
subordinate is opposed just as vehemently if no compulsion
whatsoever is involved. Among the various kinds of government
only anarchism does not involve the imposition of the will of the
higher on the will of the lower. It is the passion for equality, not
freedom, that lies behind the anarchistic temper of mind.

B. Anarchism and Individualism

While the idea of freedom as the absence of restraint or possibility
of doing what one wishes turns out not to be central to anarchism,
there is another sense of the term whose bearing merits examination: freedom as individuality. Pending the analysis in the next
section, I will here follow Kant and others in holding that the core
of individualism is the moral autonomy of the individual. What is
at issue is not the freedom from external restraints, but rather
freedom to act as a responsible individual, on the basis of one's own
standards. The central value of individualism, on this account, is
the primacy of the private will of the individual. As with the case of
libertarianism, I will first make the case that individualism leads
logically to anarchism,[12] and then show why this view is in error.

As Max Weber put it, successful government by the state
typically rests on a combination of external and internal means.
The external means include various forms of coercion and also
various services and benefits—that is, both sticks and carrots—which
combine to induce compliance. The internal means is the sense of
legitimacy: the belief on the part of the governed that what the state
commands is rightful and hence should be obeyed. Among these
legitimate rights, at least for the modern state, is the exclusive right
to use force within its territory.[13] While the libertarian focuses on
the external instrumentalities of state authority, the individualist is
concerned with the internal instrumentalities.

To say that the command of the state is legitimate is to say that
this command takes recognized precedence over the private will of
the subject. The citizens believe that a command to do A ought to
be obeyed, even if they wanted to do B, or had thought that B was
right. Once the command has been issued, then A is right and B is
not. It is the will of the state that determines whether A or B is right.

A legitimate command automatically takes precedence over the private will of the individual. For the individualist, to accept such a command is to violate the integrity and autonomy of the self. It is individualism, not libertarianism, which I think is mainly behind the intense, even passionate, distaste that the liberal temper of mind has always felt toward government authority.

It is not coercion itself, or even the coercive power of the state that is at issue, but rather the claim of the state to supersede the will of the individual in the individual's own mind. Unpleasant though it may, it is no disgrace to bow to superior power, whether of the state, another member of society, or simply the nexus of circumstance in which everyone is imbedded. What is ignoble and demeaning is to submit freely without external compulsion to a will and a judgment other than one's own. "Better to reign in Hell than serve in Heaven," asserts Milton's Satan, thereby defining himself as a true modern, and an authentic individual. While mortals cannot reign in hell, they can still maintain their integrity, and say, with Max Stirner, "Every moment the fetters of reality cut the sharpest welts in my flesh, but *my own* I remain." [14]

Civil disobedience is individualistic in meaning. Instead of complying voluntarily and hence acquiescing, one disobeys, which forces the state to bring its coercive apparatus into play. Faced with the bald threat or exercise of force, the individual can then comply without loss of integrity.

It is the value of individualism that explains the preoccupation of classical liberal thought with the ideas of consent and contract, and why the attacks on these ideas, successful as they may be, always seem to throw the baby out with the bathwater. Thus Hume's argument that it is not consent or contract, but whether or not political authority is useful to the individual that matters, logical though it is (as always with Hume), misses the point: useful according to whose judgment? [15] Individuality, as defined so far, consists in forming judgments about what is useful, or right, or moral, or expedient, or "my own," and then acting according to these judgments. Obedience cannot be justified (and hence rightly enforced) by establishing an "objective" standard of utility, to which the state can be shown to conform. Even God in heaven, according to Milton, does not enforce obedience to His law, because such obedience would be worthless. From the religious point of view, God's will is done when the individual denies his or her own will and accepts God's. The true individualist, like Satan, cannot accept even God's will this way, much less that of the state.

Thus the real problem posed to political theory by modern individualism is not "freedom versus order," but whether the individual can accept political authority without violating his or her integrity and autonomy, and, if so, how and under what circumstances. It is instructive to examine two answers proposed to this question, by Hobbes and Rousseau.

For Hobbes, sovereign power is never "legitimate" in the sense used here, for he did not admit of any moral or ethical principle not reducible to utility or interest. The subjects obey only when they think it to be to their interest to do so, not from a sense of duty that is independent of considerations of interest. Hence the private will always takes precedence. People should consent and obey only when it is to their rational interest to do so. It is almost always to their interest to obey an effectively enforced political power, and if none exists they should set one up by mutual agreement, but, for example, they may rightly (rationally) resist the sovereign when their lives are at stake.[16]

To put the matter another way, radical individualism can find nothing inherently wrong with an absolute state ruled by purely external means (coercion and utility), as long as the citizen is presented with the *choice* between obedience and punishment. It must, however, object when the state punishes people not for what they do but for what they are, as with Nazi Germany. As long as the coercive power of the state is a threat that the individual can avoid by obedience, radical individualism has no grounds to object to the most absolute form of government, as long as such a government does not claim legitimacy. Hence individualism does not necessarily lead to anarchism.

A second attempted reconciliation of compulsory governmental power with the values of radical individualism is that of Rousseau. His solution appears to be straightforward and logical. If everyone wills the same thing, then authority is reconciled with individualism. If what rules is a truly general will, then its acceptance does not give precedence to anything over and above one's own will. With the establishment of such a general will, power and coercion disappear, for where there is no conflict there is no power, and coercion is not needed to compel what one has already willed.

Among political thinkers of the very first rank, Rousseau comes closest to anarchism, and his influence on anarchist thinkers, for example Proudhon, was very great. He passes the first test in favoring a rule of unanimity, at least in a sense, but fails the second in holding, somewhat regretfully it is true, that the general will should be executed and enforced by political authority.

Hobbes and Rousseau illustrate two ways in which radical individualism and effective government can be reconciled. The first is to establish a nonlegitimate government, whose effectiveness rests entirely on the external compulsions of force and utility, without using the integrity-violating inner compulsions of legitimacy. The second is to establish a rule of unanimity.

While both solutions are perfectly logical, they fail in practice. Taking Hobbes first, effective government almost always requires its acceptance as legitimate (in the sense used here) by at least a significant part of society, including especially those who do the enforcing. This holds even for the "rule by force" of a single individual. It is always a police or army which wields this force, and this armed group in turn must be bound to their leader by strong ties of loyalty over and above the external advantages of their position. The tyrant whose minions do not regard his rule as legitimate (as well as useful) will not stay in power for long.

Turning to Rousseau, the formation of a general will does not harmonize the particular wills of the members of society; it destroys them. Rousseau understood this perfectly. In joining the unanimity of the social contract, the individual merges his or her self into a cohesive social collectivity, in which total legitimacy now rests, and leaves entirely behind the private self, the private will, and its private rights. Any remnants of this private world, Rousseau felt, might legitimately be crushed. I will return to this question later.

In sum, the attempt to justify an effective government on the grounds of individualism (as defined so far) poses a dilemma, nicely pointed by Hobbes and Rousseau, which anarchism cannot resolve, and from which there is in fact no escape. Individualism is caught between the absolutism of Hobbes and the collectivism of Rousseau.

Individualism, defined as the precedence of the private will, assumed its most adequate political and social expression in Max Stirner's *The Ego and His Own,* first published in 1845.[17] The unique force of Stirner's work springs from his uncompromising acceptance of two facts that most individualists have had difficulty swallowing:

first that effective government requires internalized social controls, and second that true individualists (as defined) cannot achieve more than fleeting and partial unanimity.

Stirner has a clear grasp of the internalized controls on which much of the political power of the modern state rests. "Every Prussian," he said, "carries his gendarme in his breast." [18] "The master is a thing made by the servant. If submissiveness ceased, it would be all over with lordship." [19] The authority of the state is internalized and experienced by the citizen as a sense of duty. It is not only the motive of obedience to political authority, but the whole complex of morality , piety, civility, and self-restraint instilled by society within the individual as a conscience which forms the basis both of political power and of organized society itself. Hence the assertion of one's individuality pits one not only against the state but also against society and therefore against all rules of morality and civility, including those prohibiting murder and incest.[20] Anything that suits one's individuality should be done, provided only that it is possible to get away with it. The individualist opposes all established authority, not by revolution, for a revolution requires a movement and the subservience of the individual will to this movement, but by rebellion and evasion, legal and illegal. "A self possessive man cannot desist from being a criminal, for crime is his life." [21]

If everyone were an individualist, not only government but also society as we know it would not exist. The only organizing elements would be loose and shifting alliances and coalitions, based on mutual advantage, and existing only while all parties thought them to their interest, which, Stirner felt, would not usually be long. For the most part there would be unremitting conflict and struggle for supremacy.[22]

Stirner's society, a loose grouping of such "association(s) of egoists" strongly resembles Hobbes's state of nature, even to the use of the phrase, "the war of all against all," and indeed this is what Hobbes's theory leaves us with if we accept his individualistic premises but deny the possibility that stable government can be based on force and fear alone.

Although Stirner is usually considered to be an anarchist, the appellation has been challenged, and I think rightly so, for his views differ profoundly from those of any reasonable list of "major anarchist thinkers." R. W. K. Patterson has argued that Stirner is not an anarchist but a nihilist, and this seems to me a very appropriate term.[23] In Stirner's own words, "I have founded what is my own on nothing." [24]

Stirner wished to do away with all social ties and allegiances, all identifications with persons or groups outside the self, in order to unearth the true inner private self. When this is done, however—when we have peeled off all the layers of the self that derive from its participation in society—we will find at the center: nothing at all. To deny one's social nature is thus nihilistic in the most literal sense: it does away not only with society but with the individual as well, of whom nothing is left but the abstract possibility of becoming a human—that is to say a social—being.

The case of Stirner reveals the inadequacy of treating the private will as something external to society. Such a view not only leads to the rejection of all social and political authority, it destroys individuality itself. It is necessary to redefine individualism and reexamine its bearing to authority before the relation of the two to anarchism can be understood.

IV. PSYCHOLOGICAL

We are here following the usual definition of authority as legitimate power: regulation whose effectiveness rests at least partly on its acceptance as rightful. Such acceptance of regulation as morally binding logically presupposes that the psyche is divided into two parts: that which binds and that which is bound. There is the part of the mind that accepts the authority and applies it on and even against the rest of the mind—the feelings, desires, interests, and so on, which would govern behavior in the absence of the authoritative principle, and which still may prevail despite the presence of that principle within the mind. This necessity of assuming that the psyche is structurally and dynamically differentiated was already evident to Plato, and forms the starting point of his psychological analysis.[25]

The argument cannot proceed without using a psychological theory, and the one employed here will be the Freudian—in my view, the most adequate. In Freudian terms the two selves involved in the operation of authority are ego and superego. Authority operates through the regulation of behavior by superego values which arise via identification with an external authority figure.

However, it will not do to regard the superego as social and the ego as private, as many have done. The ego itself is formed in a process to which social relations are integral. For example, the idea of the self as male or female resides in the ego. What it means to the self to be masculine or feminine arises out of a complex set of identifications, and the cultural influence on this conception of self is evident from the fact that masculinity and femininity mean different things in different societies.

There are two phases or aspects of identification, projection and introjection.[26] In projection the other person is seen as an extension or externalization of the self. In introjection the other person—or more accurately the image of the other person—is incorporated as part of the self. These two phases explain the duality which is the essence of authority. On the one hand, via projection, the will of another person is taken as authoritative: one submits to the will of another. On the other hand, via introjection, the values and standards of the authority figure are incorporated within the self. The submission is only to one's own will, one's own standards of right and wrong. This duality solves Rousseau's problem: how to submit to the will of another, yet remain as free as before.

Authority falls into two broad types, depending on the dominant underlying identification. First there is authority as a hierarchical principle—the command of a superior to a subordinate. It is precisely this position of superiority which renders the command binding. The prototypical case is the authority of parent over child, and all other instances are displacements from the underlying identification of son or daughter with mother or father; hence I will use the term "parental authority."

Secondly, there is authority that proceeds laterally, from a group of peers. Here what is authoritative is the standards of the group as a collective whole. The group does not define the standards; rather the standards define the group. Sociologically, we are dealing here with the authority of social norms, as they are transmitted by tradition or arise spontaneously out of group interaction. The relationship is one of equality; the norms apply equally to each, are accepted by each, and enforced by each on all. The underlying psychological formation is the mutual identifications among siblings—brothers and sisters with a common identity and a common code. Hence the term "peer authority."

Actual authority is regularly an admixture of these two types. The utility of the distinction will become clear in later sections of this essay. For the time being they will be lumped together as "authority."

In psychological terms, individualism arises as a further stage in the development of authority (whether parental or peer). After the authority identifications have formed, the projective aspect is broken off, at least consciously, and the superego code becomes detached from its original link with the external authority figure, which still remains within the psyche, but only in its internalized, introjective aspect. Here we have "moral autonomy": the force of a superego code which is autonomous with respect to existing parental and peer authority, and asserts itself independently of them. This moral autonomy, and its claim to be respected, are the defining characteristics of individualism. What seeks primacy is not a private will as against a social will, but what might be called a "personal will," born of the will of another or others, but with the umbilical cord of projective identification cut.

Individualism thus has a dual relationship to authority. On the one hand it is the product of authority and cannot come into being without it. On the other hand, it asserts itself against this authority and denies the legitimacy of its governance. If individualism were carried through to the denial of all authority of one person over another, then the only legitimate form of government would be an individualistic anarchy: a rule of unanimity based, not on conformity, but on a harmonious agreement among personal wills. But this is impossible. Individualism first derives from then reacts against existing authority. If there were no such authority, individualism could not come into being. To carry individualism to the point of denying all authority is self-defeating.

The principle of individuality emerges from these considerations as a moral precept that does not stand against authority itself, but instead states what authority ought to be like, namely that it should define and protect an area of autonomy within which behavior is not authoritatively regulated. It stands for the self-limitation, not the abolition, of authority. Its inherent tnedency is thus not anarchic but liberal. I will support this point further in the next section.

V. SOCIOLOGICAL

In the main, anarchistic thought has been collectivistic in its thrust. This is appropriate, for while anarchism cannot successfully be maintained on individualistic grounds, it fits in well with a collectivistic orientation. In his survey of anarchistic thought, Woodstock regretfully admits that there is, in Orwell's words, a

> totalitarian tendency . . . implicit in the anarchist or pacifist vision of society. In a society where there is no law, and in theory no compulsion, the only arbiter of behavior is public opinion. But public opinion, because of the tremendous urge to conformity in gregarious animals, is less tolerant than any system of law. When human beings are governed by "thou shalt not," the individual can practice a certain amount of eccentricity; when they are supposedly governed by "love" and "reason," he is under continuous pressure to make him behave and think exactly the same way as everyone else does.[27]

Thus Godwin, whose anarchism is usually thought to be individualistic, advocates a community in which,

> opinion would be all sufficient; the inspection of every man over the conduct of his neighbors, when unstained by caprice, would constitute a censorship of the most irresistible nature. But the force of this censorship would depend upon its freedom, not following the positive dictates of law, but the spontaneous decisions of the understanding.[28]

Proudhon, also usually placed in the individualistic wing, thought that in an anarchic society everyone should engage in productive labor. If anyone refuses, he says, "We owe it to ourselves to give him nothing, but, since he must live, to put him under supervision and compel him to labor." His point (and Godwin's) is that the "we" exercising supervision and compulsion should be the community as an undifferentiated whole, not any specially constituted authority.[29]

The underlying collectivism of most of the individualistic wing of anarchism puts them much closer to the communalists, such as Tolstoy, Kropotkin, and Bakunin, than is usually thought. Only some of the American anarchists, such as Josiah Warren and Benjamin Tucker, seem to me truly individualistic in orientation. Nozick has been influenced by this tradition, but argues, as I do here on different grounds, that if individualism is thought through it arrives not at anarchy but at limited political authority.

In this section I will inquire into the nature of collectivism and how it fits into anarchism. Just as in the previous section it was necessary to understand the psychological meaning of individualism before its relation to anarchism could be found, so here the relation of anarchism to collectivism will emerge only after a sociological analysis of the latter term has been undertaken.

A. Social and Political Authority

On the sociological level one can distinguish two polar types of authority which have as their psychological basis the two types distinguished in the previous section. I will call these "social authority," which has peer authority as its psychological content, and "political authority," which has parental authority as its psychological content. By this I do not mean that social and political authority are simply peer and parental authority writ large. Such a reductionism seems to me untenable. Rather, social action always has a psychological meaning or content for the actors, and the psychological content of social and political authority are peer and parental authority, respectively.

By "social authority" I mean something very close to what Durkheim called the "collective conscience (consciousness)": the authority of a social group as a collective whole over its members. The most important part of the collective conscience is the system of social norms, which authoritatively regulates the behavior of the group members.

By "political authority" I mean exactly what Max Weber defined as *"legitime Herrschaft."* This term has had various translations in English, none of them wholly satisfactory. The term "authority" is often used and serves to convey the duality which I have already mentioned, of compulsion and inner acceptance. Authority relations, however, can pertain among equals (as with social authority), and Weber insisted that *legitime Herrschaft* was always a hierarchical relation—a relation between ruler and ruled. The ensuing discussion will I hope justify my translation of Weber's term as "political authority." I thus follow Weber in understanding political authority to be authority possessed by particular persons or institutions to govern group activity, that is, as governmental authority possessed by a government.

B. Authoritarianism and Collectivism

We are dealing here with polar types. In practice, actual systems of authority typically combine political and social authority. For example, Weber defined traditional authority in terms of two principles: the inviolability of traditional norms, which comprehensively dictate all social behavior (here we see social authority quietly entering Weber's theory, without any explicit treatment), and the absolute authority of the patriarchical ruler.[30] Theoretically the two principles stand opposed to each other, for if tradition dictates all behavior, then the area of discretion possessed by the ruler will vanish, while the unlimited discretion of the ruler must overthrow the traditional norms, but the latent contradiction usually does not emerge clearly in tribal organization. There the "absolute" discretion of the ruler is typically exercised only within boundaries defined by the traditional tribal law. He is supposed to uphold and enforce this law, and if he fails to do so or, worse, acts in violation of it, his authority will be undermined. Thus his political authority upholds the social authority of the law and the social authority of the law upholds his political authority. A similar integration is supposed to hold between social and political authority in the case of modern legal authority, where the acts of the political authorities must be pursuant to law, and the positive law is thought to rest on a broad normative consensus in society.

Psychologically speaking, such a relatively harmonious integration and mutual support between social and political authority rests on an integration of the two sets of identifications, parental and peer, within the superego. Within the mind, parents and children are reconciled. On the one hand, the authority system is the externalization (projective aspect) of a relatively integrated set of such identifications. On the other hand, the superego code is the internalization (introjective aspect) of a system which integrates social and political authority.

The two types of authority may however come into conflict. To continue Weber's account, when traditional authority is vested in large-scale systems of imperial domination, there is a tendency to pull in one of two directions, either toward feudalism, where the traditional practices hedge the ruler in and deprive him of his power, or sultanism, where the ruler breaks through and destroys the fabric of tradition, and rules in a wholly unrestrained way.[31] In the same way, modern legal authority tends to move either toward legal formalism, which handcuffs the political authorities, or toward Caesarism: a dictatorial rule which conceals itself behind the facade of a legal system whose real substance has been destroyed.

In sum, social and political authority may be regarded as polar types which are sometimes approached in practice, but which usually exist together, partly integrated and partly in conflict with each other. I will call systems where authority approaches the political pole "authoritarian," and those which approach the social pole "collectivistic." Sultanism, Caesarism, Fascism, and Leninism are all authoritarian. Relatively pure types of collectivism are harder to find. Where such communities crop up, they are uniformly anarchic in character.

C. Individualism, Collectivism, and Anarchism

We are at last in a position to state some of the major conclusions of this essay concerning the nature and interrelations of anarchism, collectivism, and individualism.

To reject all social and political authority is not anarchism or individualism; it is nihilism. The case of Stirner shows this clearly.

Individualism asserts that there ought to be an area of privacy where the individual is not regulated by social or political authority. This area itself must be defined and protected by social and especially political authority. Individualism stands for limited social and political authority, and its most appropriate ideology is therefore liberalism.

Modern (capitalistic) private property is an illustration. In capitalistic societies people (or at least the dominant classes) feel strongly that the use of one's property (especially one's capital) should not be interfered with or regulated by one's neighbors or one's government.

Now what is the basis of this individualistic right? Suppose that it has no existence in social or political authority, and is no more than a moral right, universally recognized as self-evident, or the dictate of reason. A number of arguments can be raised that this recognition would be an insufficient basis to define and support modern private property.

Psychologically, the situation cannot arise, as argued above. At the very least, the children in such a society would be no respecters of private property, since their parents would not have authoritatively advanced and enforced such rights.

Sociologically, a moral consensus always rests on and reflects the system of social norms. Even if such social norms did not exist, they would soon grow out of such a consensus. Therefore, if we say private property as a moral right we must also say private property as defined and defended by social authority. As we will see shortly, however, a system in which political authority is denied, and in which private property has a purely social basis, must by its own logic move away from individualism and private property, and toward collectivism and communal property.

Philosophically, if private property rests on moral principles, then these principles will also dictate the ways in which private property should and should not be used. Instead of being an area of free discretion, private property becomes hemmed in by the very principle which creats it. This point emerges with great clarity, for example, from an examination of the chapter on property in Locke's *Second Treatise*. Locke starts with private property as a natural (moral) right, but cannot get from there to capitalist private property. For example, he cannot justify accumulation of more property than one can personally use, or the right of inheritance, on the basis of natural law—two points which strike at the heart of capitalist accumulation. Hence Locke switches, and introduces modern private property as a convention: that is, as a positive, not a natural, right.

Modern private property is inherently a legal idea. It presupposes a state apparatus: a juridical system which creates, defines, and protects private property. If modern private property is not positive, it is nothing.

It is this issue more than any other which separates libertarians from anarchists. Libertarians believe strongly in modern private property and hence, if they think straight, favor a strong though limited political authority, to establish and maintain private property, as well as other individualistic principles such as the sanctity of contract and a free market. Anarchists wish to sweep away the state apparatus and, as we shall see, all positive law. They recognize that in so doing they will also sweep away private property.[32]

D. The Social System of Anarchy

The core of anarchism is the rejection of all political authority whatsoever. A thoroughgoing application of this principle will lead to all of its other main features. This process leads not to individualism but to collectivism. Of course we are dealing here with a polar type, which both theory and experience indicate is impossible of achievement in practice, at least for long. The point remains that a serious attempt to eliminate all political authority must lead in the following directions:

1. *The principle of unanimity.* In the face of the need for effective governmental decisions if viable social organization is to be maintained, the elimination of political authority requires the adoption of the principle of unanimity. For suppose that all save one favor a given measure. To adopt this measure as binding is to place this dissenter in a position of subordination to the rest, and political authority has been introduced. Hence the group must make governmental decisions by meeting and discussing until unanimity has been reached. Furthermore, no special persons can be appointed to administer or enforce governmental decisions, for to do so would also be to violate the principle of equality. True, such a person could be regarded as the agent of the unanimity, acting for it, but by the same token so should everyone else. To single out any person or persons other than the whole group to perform this task is to introduce political authority. These provisos—unanimity of decision and lack of any governmental structure—obviously place

extraordinary constraints on the governmental process. We can imagine such a system only in a very special kind of community.

2. *The community must be very small in size.* As the size of the group increases, unanimity becomes harder and harder to reach, and the need for a specialized governmental apparatus simply to carry out the process of reaching a decision grows. One hundred members would seem to be near or even more than the maximum feasible number.

3. *Technology must be simple.* Technological advancement, especially in the process of production, requires a complex coordination of behavior which can be achieved only by a specialized governmental apparatus, as in a factory.

4. *The division of labor must be minimized.* The division of labor produces social stratification, and social strata are always ranked into higher and lower, superior and subordinate.

5. *Social cohesion must be high.* The lack of political authority and the principle of unanimity require a strongly imbedded and pervasive set of social norms, producing a high degree of uniformity and desire to conform.

5. *Individualism must be low.* It is important to note that individualism, as defined here, is not the opposite of social cohesion. It is not anomic; on the contrary, it is defined, expressed by, and imbedded in, a system of authority. However, the authority takes a special form, defining a right of individual choice within a certain area.

Within this area we must expect diversity. Genuine autonomy does not produce uniformity, for example, by unanimous adherence to a philosophical doctrine. Rather we must expect several philosophical doctrines, each with its own adherents. Uniformity can only be the product of authoritarian prescription, or, failing that, it will *become* authoritatively prescribed. Uniformity is both the product and the producer of social authority. A group of individualists will have views which are both diverse and strongly held. The wider the degree of latitude the more difficult will be the achievement of unanimity.

In sum, an anarchic community must tend toward smallness, lack of differentiation, uniformity, conformism, and social solidarity. Its collectivism will embody in a pure form what Durkheim has called "mechanical solidarity." Some of the anarchic counterculture communes closely approach such a polar type of antiauthoritarian collectivism.

E. The Psychology of Anarchism

These sociological considerations put us in a position to understand the psychology of anarchism. At the psychological level, anarchism represents a revolt against, and rejection of, parental authority. This rejection is not that of the individualist, whose inner identifications with the parents, in an autonomous superego, form the basis of the (partial) rejection of external authority. The individualist frees himself or herself from the authority of the parents by becoming like them: that is, by growing up.

Above all, the anarchist does not want to be like his or her parents. The revolt against parental authority is expressed through peer solidarity: peer identifications which form the basis of a lateral peer authority which opposes the vertical parental authority. The psychological prototype of the anarchic community is an adolescent gang: equalitarian, leaderless (temporarily), rebellious, with its own fierce conformist code which it asserts on its members and against its elders.

VI. POLITICAL

Anarchy is a form of government that springs from a basic hositlity toward political authority. This leads anarchism to attempt to negate the whole realm of the political: the state apparatus, positive law, political power, and the political process. This conclusion emerges if we think through what is involved in attempting to establish a government based on the rule of unanimity and the absence of political authority.

Imagine the process of making governmental decisions as it will operate in the ideal-typical anarchic community described in the previous section. These decisions must emerge as a unanimous consensus in a discussion in which all group members participate. These meetings cannot occur as a result of anyone's direction, for that person would then have political authority. They must occur spontaneously, or in conformity to an informal custom, or (less likely) according to a general rule itself the product of a unanimous decision.

Decisions are reached via the formation of group consensus. When the community meets and starts discussing a problem, we may perhaps find a wide divergence of views, beginning with differences as to what the problem actually under discussion is. We should expect the deliberations to be lengthy even over minor matters, while important decisions might take months or even years. Gradually the differences between the divergent views will lessen, and a consensus or "sense of the group" will begin to emerge. The remaining dissenting individuals now find themselves opposed not by a diversity of individual views, but by the will of the community as a collective whole. At this point the psychological and social pressures toward conformity acting both on and within the dissenters generally become irrestible, and unanimity is achieved with relative speed.

This idea of a group consensus as something over and above the sum of similar or identical views held by a set of discrete individuals, which has been formulated as "the general will" by Rousseau, and "the group mind" by Durkheim and Freud, has often been attacked as vague and metaphysical, philosophically and empirically untenable, but such a consensus is readily observable and its unique force easily felt by anyone who has participated in lengthy and informally structured group discussions around some question or problem.

The key to the process is the formation of this consensus. Once it appears, dissenting individuals, even if they form a relatively large minority, will quickly fall into line. When carried through successfully, this process has the effect of strongly reinforcing group unity and cohesion. The more bitter and heated the debate, the more aggression is discharged, and the more solid the final unity.

The process can fail in two ways. First the consensus may not emerge. In that case, no action can be taken, and the effect will be further to weaken group cohesion, which presumably has already become undermined. More commonly, failure will occur when consensus forms around more than one point of focus: that is, the group becomes split into two or more subgroups, each with its *own* consensus. In that event the governmental process has a divisive, not a unifying, effect. It serves to bring out and focus an underlying split which probably was already nascent. The community often then splits in two, with part of it leaving to form its own community. When the group has grown beyond a certain size, such a fission may be the only way of preserving the anarchic form.

Something close to this ideal-typical account may be observed in some of the present day anarchic communes. Melville has described the process as follows:

> No action will be taken on a question until there is general agreement about it. And nearly all the larger communes have some sort of decision-making meeting in order to determine what the consensus is on important questions. Joined together in the first place by some common vision [indispensable, Melville feels, for the successful operation of such communities], most of the groups are able to resolve their problems in meetings and at the same time reinforce feelings of group unity. When this consensus-seeking process doesn't work, it often indicates lack of unity, and a sign that part of the group should leave to form another community.[33]

Rousseau's insight and vocabulary capture the inner nature of anarchic government. The emergent consensus is experienced as a general will—the will of the group as a moral unit and not as an aggregate of private wills. At first all that manifests itself in the consciousness of the participants is the interaction of private wills, expressing themselves, arguing, bargaining, maneuvering. As the consensus emerges, the underlying identifications are activated; the decision is felt to be the product of a collective will, and possesses therefore the same authority as the informal social norms which define the group character and identity.

At its inception this general will need not be unanimous. As Rousseau says, "what generalises the will is not so much the number of voices as the common interest which unites them." [34] Here we have Rousseau's distinction between the general will and the will of all.[35] Ideally, in the deliberative process each member advocates not his or her private will, but what it is thought the general will ought to be. If the consensus which actually emerges differs from this conception, then the individual is faced with a decision. If the general will is accepted as authoritative, then the original conception is abandoned as erroneous. The real general will is accorded precedence. In Rousseau's words,

When a law is proposed in the assembly of the people, what is asked of them is not exactly whether they approve the proposition or reject it, but whether it is conformable or not to the general will. When, therefore, the opinion opposed to my own prevails, that simply shows that I was mistaken, and that what I considered to be the general will was not so. Had my private opinion prevailed, I should have done something other than I wished.[36]

Once formed, the general will pulls the dissenters into its fold. Those who continue to hold out and dissent are now in opposition, not just to the particular measure, but to the social authority of the group itself. They are outlaws, no longer group members, and may rightfully be deprived of their status, for example, by ostracism, or for Rousseau, even with death. Either way, by sucking divergent wills in or by spitting them out, the general will always produces unanimity.

Ideally the whole process must be without any specialization of role in the making of decisions, their execution, or their enforcement. A governmental enactment differs from the ordinary social norms only in two respects: first it is the product of a deliberate decision, and second it may be a decision in a particular instance, instead of taking the form of a general rule. Even positive law cannot be allowed. At a minimum, positive law requires someone to write it down and make it public—a governmental officer. Anarchic decisions, like the informal social norms in which they nestle, should be written only in the minds of the members of the community.

The governance of anarchy is sharply to be distinguished from that of voluntary associations. Government in voluntary associations is sometimes thought to be nonauthoritative, but, as I have argued at length elsewhere, all stable cooperative group relations require authority.[37] One of the special things about the authority of voluntary associations is its limited nature, both social and political. Thus a voluntary association typically has the political authority to expel members for nonpayment of dues, but not to use force on them (only the state may do that). So also, they typically have the social authority to impose certain standards of behavior among the members, but these standards concern only group interaction, not the life of the individual as a whole.

Voluntary associations always have a governmental apparatus, and the persons who occupy the posts in this apparatus regularly find their authority to govern, though limited, an amply sufficient base on which to establish *de facto* control over the governmental process and the activity of the group. Being invested with political authority, the governmental apparatus gives rise to political power, which is unequally distributed. The governments of voluntary associations are thus far removed from anarchy.

Suppose, however, that the members of a voluntary association, out of a passion for equality, abolished the whole governmental apparatus and adopted the rule of unanimity. In order to render this viable, a substitute for the discarded political authority would have to be found. As I have argued earlier, this would have to be a strong and pervasive system of social authority. A voluntary association without political authority could survive only if it turned into an anarchy such as I have described.

Since anarchy lacks political authority, it also lacks political power. This is not to say that there would be no power at all, however. There will be differences in influence based on natural factors such as strength or intelligence, and social factors, such as esteem and affection. In addition, insofar as there is a division of labor, the different social roles will present different opportunities and limitations for the exercise of influence. The division of labor produces a division of social authority (rights and duties defined by status) and hence a division and inequality of power. However, compared with the amount and differences in power obtainable through political organization, these differences in power will pale into insignifigance, especially because, as we have seen, the division of labor in an anarchy must be rudimentary.

We are now in a position to summarise the political credo of anarchism. Its central feature is radical opposition to the whole realm of the political—the state apparatus, positive law, political authority, political power, and the political process—because politics involves the acceptance of the principle that some people may tell other people what to do. What is anathema is not inequality itself (although anarchism is strongly egalitarian), but the inequality that comes into being when there is an inner acceptance of the right of some people to govern.

Anarchism is not opposed to the state itself, if one understands the state to be a community which possesses the authority to govern, nor does it oppose the coercive enforcement of governmental decisions. What it does oppose is the state apparatus, in its most fundamental feature of the assignment of aspects of the governmental process (the making, execution, and enforcement of governmental decisions) to specific persons.

The principles of anarchic government are as follows:

1. To the extent possible, government should be minimized.
2. Governmental decisions must be unanimous.
3. Such decisions are authoritative (i.e., they are obligatory and may rightfully be enforced) not because each person has willed it, but because it is the will of the group as a collective whole.
4. There must be absolutely no role differentiation in the governmental process: in the making, execution, or enforcement of governmental decisions.

In short, anarchist political philosophy can be summed up in the phrase, "government without politics."

VII. CONCLUDING

The assertion made earlier, that anarchism rests on and expresses a psychologically less mature level than liberalism, was not meant as a judgement of the comparative political and social worth of the two ideologies. Just as there have been mature scoundrels and immature saints, so psychological maturity and political and social worth are separate things, despite reams that have been written to the contrary.

In fact, it can be argued that on the social and political level the situation is reversed. The central political and social fact of our time, in my opinion, is the growing oppressiveness of the modern state. This institution is becoming more and more authoritarian, not because it does not possess social authority, but because its social authority is more and more manufactured by its political authority, and does not have any independent, balancing existence. The state is swallowing society up.

Liberals of course are worried about this development. They seek to limit and contain the social and political power of the state in various ways and to various ends. However, they do not stand in opposition to the modern state itself. Liberalism has always believed in the modern state, as long as it is organized and run in certain ways. Accordingly, liberalism has by now become a conservative and even reactionary ideology. This has been true of political liberals for some time, and is now more and more true of social liberals. Both seek to turn the clock back without changing its nature; so even if they succeed, events will only march on again in the same direction as before.

In the main, political thought in the modern era has taken the modern state for granted. The debate has been over how its authority can be justified, how it should be organized and run, and to what ends. Only anarchism has consistently swum against this tide, opposing the modern state apparatus in all its forms and guises, as they have appeared one by one.[38] As the modern state begins to look worse and worse, anarchism begins to look better and better. If its psychological content is regressive, perhaps this represents what Kris has called "regression in the service of the ego."

Anarchism, however, is not for the individualist. It is inherently collectivistic. Those who have espoused anarchism on individualistic grounds are in error. Their views have not been internally coherent, or have rested on weak psychological or sociological grounds.

Modern individualism has found liberalism to be the most appropriate political expression of its underlying ethical and social views. With the bankruptcy of liberalism, it must look elsewhere. By its nature it must remain committed to authoritative political organization, but it would also do well to look elsewhere than to the modern state to supply such organization. It must ask: Are there alternative forms of political organization which can rest on and express the values of individualism? The fact that no such form seems to have appeared on the horizon may indicate that individualism itself must be rethought and reformulated, instead of being, as it usually is, the unexamined premise from which analysis proceeds.

The characteristic faults of anarchism are its tendencies toward factional squabbling and senseless violence. These tendencies cannot be wholly eliminated, because they spring from the nature of anarchism, especially its psychological basis, but they can be mitigated.

Actually, the tendency toward factionalism is not too great a handicap. The anarchic group is naturally small, and the constant splintering will keep it that way. The proclivity for violence is more serious, but we should not forget that there has been an important pacifistic strain throughout much of the history of anarchism. One may divide anarchist groups into two camps: those who struggle against the state and seek to sweep it aside, and those who try to ignore it to the extent possible. It is in the former groups that one sometimes finds the stereotyped "wild-eyed zealot brandishing a bomb."

The politically active anarchist would do well to avoid too romantic or grandiose a posture. By its nature and beliefs, anarchism is incapable of generating and employing any significant political power. As Michels said, "he who says organization says power," and it is precisely this route which is closed to anarchists. At the most they can arouse and articulate for brief periods of time such opposition to the state as already exists. As long as the modern state is strong, nothing they do can weaken it significantly, and if it should become weak and fall, it will probably do so whether or not the anarchists are pushing. The overinstrumentalism so characteristic of modern politics—the direction of all activity toward the desired goal without any other considerations coming into play—is especially inappropriate for anarchists. They should instead concentrate on doing what they think is intrinsically right, without worrying too much about the political effectiveness or ineffectiveness of such action.

NOTES

1. My thanks to Gordon Schochet for his helpful comments on a previous draft.
2. Donald McIntosh, *The Foundations of Human Society* (Chicago: University of Chicago Press, 1970) [hereafter abbreviated as *Foundations*]; "Power and Social Control," *American Political Science Review* 57 (September 1963), 619-31; "Weber and Freud: On the Nature and Sources of Authority," *American Sociological Review* 35 (October 1970), 901-11.
3. McIntosh, *Foundations,* chs. 7,8. Although I have classified social control as nondeliberate here, in a more extended sense it can be regarded as

deliberate. One way of looking at social norms is to see them as the product of a general will or collective consciousness (Rousseau, Hegel, Durkheim) which is not the resultant of the interaction of many wills but the expression of a will or purpose which pertains to the group as a collective whole. On this view, the general will governs society in a way which is "deliberate" in a more than metaphorical sense. See McIntosh, *Foundations,* ch. 9.

4.   This second form of nondeliberate government can also be regarded as deliberate in an extended or special sense. Thus in a famous passage Adam Smith speaks of the regulation of the economy by an "invisible hand." This phrase need not be taken metaphorically, for Smith was a convinced deist, and others since have viewed the laws of free enterprise as divinely ordained.

5.   Robert Nozick, *Anarchy, State and Utopia* (New York: Basic Books, 1974).

6.   John Locke, *Second Treatise of Civil Government,* par. 19.

7.   Locke, chs. 7, 8.

8.   Or, "deliberately," an invisible hand.

9.   Or, "deliberately," the general will.

10.   Hegel, *Reason in History (A General Introduction to the Philosophy of History)* (New York: Liberal Arts Press, 1953), pp. 53-58. The quotes below are from pp. 56-58.

11.   Hobbes, *Leviathan,* ch. 30, pars. 2,3. See ch. 21 for Hobbes's discussion of freedom (liberty) and its relation to political power.

12.   Such a case is made in Robert Paul Wolff, *In Defense of Anarchism* (Ann Arbor, Mich.: Torch Books, 1970). Space prohibits a treatment of Wolff's book, but I have it in mind in much of the following discussion of the relation of individualism to anarchism. I am in agreement, but on different grounds, with the view of Nozick that individualism logically leads to limited political authority, not anarchism. Nozick, *Anarchy, State and Utopia.*

13.   Max Weber, "Politics as a Vocation," in *From Max Weber,* ed., Gerth and Mills (New York: Oxford University Press, 1946), p. 78. I have argued elsewhere that both carrots and sticks are coercive. Donald McIntosh, "Coercion and International Politics; A Theoretical Analysis," in *Coercion: NOMOS XIV* (Chicago: Aldine-Atherton, 1972), pp. 243-71.

14.   Max Stirner, *The Ego and His Own* (New York; Harper and Row, 1971), p. 112.

15.   Hume, "Of the Original Contract," in *Hume's Moral and Political Philosophy* (New York: Haffner, 1941), pp. 356-72.

16.   The other is, under certain circumstances, being asked to risk his life in battle. Hobbes, *Leviathan,* ch. 21.

17.   Stirner, *The Ego and His Own.*

18. Ibid., p. 66.
19. Ibid., p. 132.
20. Ibid., pp. 60-86.
21. Ibid., p. 236.
22. Ibid., pp. 211-12.
23. Ronald William Keith Patterson, *The Nihilistic Egoist: Max Stirner* (London: Oxford University Press, 1971). See also the comments of John Carrol in his Introduction to Stirner's work. Stirner, *The Ego and His Own*, pp. 32-33.
24. Ibid., p. 258.
25. Plato, *The Republic*, iv, 435–439.
26. For our purposes, Freud's most important treatment of identification is in *Group Psychology and the Analysis of the Ego; Complete Psychological Works,* vol. 18 (London: Hogarth, 1955). My previous treatments of identification have not sufficiently emphasised the projective aspect.
27. George Woodcock, *Anarchism* (New York: World Publishing Co., 1962), p. 64.
28. Quoted in Woodcock, ibid., pp. 83-84.
29. Pierre Joseph Proudhon, *What is Property?* (New York: Howard Fertig, 1966), p. 234.
30. Max Weber, *Economy and Society* (New York: Bedminster Press, 1968), pp. 226-31.
31. Ibid., pp. 231-32, 271-75.
32. In the general case, libertarians sometimes argue the possibility of automatic government, based on general recognition of private property, the free contract, a free market, etc. But by extension of the above arguments, such an automatic government can exist only if its conditions are defined and protected by a system of positive law—as Adam Smith well knew.
33. Keith Melville, *Communes in the Counterculture* (New York: William Masson, 1972), p. 130.
34. Rousseau, *The Social Contract,* Bk. II, ch. 4, par. 7.
35. Ibid., bk. 2, ch.3.
36. Ibid., bk. IV, ch. 2, par. 8.
37. McIntosh, *Foundations,* esp. pp. 238-52.
38. Other movements have of course opposed the modern state. I am here emphasizing the duration, tenacity, consistency, and fundamental nature of the anarchistic opposition.

16

PHILOSOPHICAL ANARCHISM REVISITED

GRENVILLE WALL

Although anarchism in some form or other has had numerous defenders in the history of political thought, it is rare to find a contemporary analytical philosopher arguing a case for it. Therefore it was to be expected that Robert Paul Wolff's little book *In Defence of Anarchism* [1] should have caused a modest flurry of excitement sufficient to prompt at least two replies in the philosophical journals.[2] Indeed, his argument might have been expected to arouse more interest than it has done, especially in view of the fact that he appears to deduce what many people would regard as a totally unacceptable conclusion from an equally unexceptionable premise. Presumably many of his readers have concluded that the paradoxical character of his argument betokens a faulty deduction and not troubled themselves to pinpoint the fault. However, despite its blemishes, it seems to me that the importance of Wolff's defense of anarchism has not been properly appreciated and that consequently the challenge it represents has not been properly met. Although I shall maintain that his argument is unsound, his chief error, properly diagnosed, is instructive, not only in connection with his particular thesis, but for political philosophy more generally.

The assessment of Wolff's argument is complicated by the fact that he equivocates over the precise grounds on which he bases his anarchist conclusion. However, according to the most challenging and most consistent interpretation which can be put on his argument, his defence of anarchism rests on the philosophical contention that the concept of *de jure* authority (which is taken to be the defining mark of the state) is logically incompatible with the notion of moral autonomy (the hallmark of the responsible individual). Consequently, the responsible individual is bound to refuse to acknowledge the legitimacy of any state. Since it is clear that Wolff has an individualistic conception of moral autonomy (a point to which I shall return), it follows that no justificatory theory of the state which is premised on ethical individualism can hope to succeed.

If this interpretation of Wolff's argument is correct, then it is of some significance. Although Wolff's Kantian sympathies are evident and well known, the primacy which he attaches to *individual* practical judgement is a view shared by many other moral and political philosophers who would not want to call themselves Kantians, at least, not in any strong sense. This commitment to the primacy of individual practical judgement is also shared, for instance, by many philosophers whose roots lie firmly in the empiricist tradition, as well as by many nonphilosophical theorists and liberal moralists. The point I wish to stress is that if Wolff's main philosophical contention is correct (i.e., that the individualist conception of moral autonomy is indeed logically incompatible with the recognition of *de jure* authority), then he has succeeded in exposing a fundamental incoherence in Western liberal-individualist political thought, for although liberals are defenders of the minimal state they do not claim that the recognition of the authority of the state is in itself incompatible with man's moral nature. Indeed, many of them have argued that the existence of the liberal state is an empirical precondition of the flowering of our moral nature.

In what follows, I shall begin by arguing that Wolff has indeed succeeded (though falteringly) in deducing his anarchist conclusion from his major premise. I shall then go on to suggest that rather than construing the argument as a successful defense of anarchism, Wolff's conclusion should cause us to doubt the truth of his major premise as he and many others have interpreted it. More specifically, I shall argue that his assumption of the primacy of individual practical judgement is mistaken and that consequently any political theory which is based on this assumption is also mistaken. Thus the virtue of Wolff's book lies, not in the claim that it defends anarchism successfully, but in the fact that it points unwittingly to a *reductio ad absurdum* of persistent and widespread attempts to analyse the state, and politics itself, in individualistic terms.

I. WOLFF'S THESIS

In view of the fact that Wolff's arguments have been interpreted in different ways by his critics,[3] it is necessary to begin by making my own view of them quite clear. Wolff's problem is "how the moral autonomy of the individual can be made compatible with the legitimate authority of the state." [4] He maintains that "the defining mark of the state is authority" [5] and that "authority is the right to command, and correlatively, the right to be obeyed," [6] which, in turn, implies the obligation to obey on the part of those over whom authority is exercised. Wolff also maintains that "the fundamental assumption of moral philosophy is that men are responsible for their actions." [7] Our responsibility derives from our capacity to choose. He draws a distinction between *being* responsible and *taking* responsibility: "Taking responsibility involves attempting to determine what one ought to do, and that ... lays upon one the additional burdens of gaining knowledge, reflecting on motives, predicting outcomes, criticizing principles, and so forth." [8] Further, "every man who possesses free will and reason has an obligation to take responsibility for his actions," [9] this obligation deriving from our capacity to reason. A man who has free will and takes responsibility for his actions is autonomous. Such a man "may do what another tells him, but not *because* he has been told to do it." [10]

Wolff presents the conflict between authority and autonomy forcefully on two occasions in the final section of Chapter I. The explicitly political version reads as follows: "The dilemma which we have posed can be succinctly expressed in terms of the concept of the *de jure* state. If all men have a continuing obligation to achieve the highest degree of autonomy possible, then there would appear to be no state whose subjects have a moral obligation to obey its commands." [11] Thus, if no autonomous agent has a duty to obey a command as such, no one can have a right to command and therefore there can be no such thing as *de jure* political authority. The autonomy of man is *logically* incompatible with there being such a thing as the *de jure* state.

Having, in Chapter I, seemingly demonstrated that the concepts of authority and autonomy are irreconcilable, Wolff proceeds, in Chapter II, to argue that their reconciliation is theoretcally possible: "There is, in theory, a solution to the problem which has been posed. . . . The solution is a direct democracy . . . governed by a rule of unanimity. Under unanimous direct democracy, every member of society wills freely every law which is actually passed. Hence, he is only confronted as a citizen with laws to which he has consented. Since a man who is only constrained by the dictates of his own will is autonomous, it follows that under the directions of a unanimous direct democracy, men can harmonize the duty of autonomy with the commands of authority." [12]

This is the claim that poses the first problem concerning the interpretation of Wolff's argument. What is puzzling about the passage just quoted is that it expresses the view that unanimous direct democracy embodies a reconciliation of what has just previously been depicted as a *logically* irreconcilable conflict. Given Wolff's stand on moral autonomy one might have expected him to have argued that unanimous direct democracy abolishes the conflict by showing how social life could be collectively regulated without the exercise of authority as defined by him. Surely his previous argument should be construed as attempting to show that the notion of the *de jure* state has no application because it contains a latent contradiction, *namely,* that the autonomous man has a duty to act heteronomously in relation to such a state's commands. If this is so, then it follows that *no* state can embody a resolution to the conflict as Wolff conceives it.

Wolff is clearly a little uneasy about his "theoretical solution," for in the next paragraph he says: "It might be argued that even this limiting case is not genuine, since each man is obeying himself, and is not submitting to legitimate authority." [13] But this, according to Wolff, would be wrong: "However, the case is really different from the pre-political (or extra-political) case of self-determination, for the authority to which each individual submits is not that of himself simply, but that of the entire community taken collectively. The laws are issued in the name of the sovereign, which is to say the total population of the community." [14]

This reply to the objection is inadequate. If we accept Wolff's earlier argument, then an agent acts heteronomously if he obeys the laws *because* they are enacted by the whole community, or *because* of the supposed *de jure* authority of the assembly. If he is not self-determined, then he is not autonomous in Wolff's sense, for the autonomous man "may do what another tells him, but not because he has been told to do it." The unanimous collective decision of the assembly (to which the agent has contributed) either constitutes a moral ground for acting in the way it prescribes or it does not. If the agent thinks that it does, then in acting in the way prescribed the agent is acting heteronomously. Since he is also acting in that way because he, as an individual, judges it to be correct, he is acting autonomously. So in this case the agent is both autonomous and heteronomous! If, on the other hand, the agent refuses to acknowledge that the assembly's decision in itself constitutes a moral ground for acting in the ways it prescribes, thus adding nothing to the moral weight of his own private decision, the agent acts autonomously and refuses to recognise the authority of the assembly. It is true that if you regard the assembly as being invested with *de jure* authority (which Wolff's earlier argument seemed to show that you should not), then there can be no conflict of substance between the content of its commands and those of your own conscience because the principle of unanimity rules this out. This is indeed an attractive feature of unanimous direct democracy. But it must not be taken as a *reconciliation* of the concepts of autonomy and authority as Wolff conceives them. To do so is to confuse *what* a man wills with *his reason* for willing it. Whether a man acts autonomously or heteronomously depends on the sorts of reasons he has for acting as he does: in this case, whether he acts in a certain way because *he* thinks it is morally right to do so, or because he has been commanded by the assembly. Thus, given his premises, Wolff should have concluded that the *de jure* state is indeed logically impossible and that not even unanimous direct democracy resolves the conflict between authority and autonomy as he conceives these notions.[15]

If my criticism of Wolff's "resolution" is sound, it sheds some light on the equivocation that exists over his real grounds for defending anarchism. The argument that is most prominent, in the sense of having most space devoted to it, is that what he takes to be the theoretical solution to the conflict between autonomy and authority, namely, unanimous direct democracy cannot be expected to work for any length of time or on anything but a relatively small scale. Therefore, in view of the overriding importance that he attaches to autonomy, anarchism seems to be the only alternative. He says: "As soon as disagreement arises on important questions, unanimity is destroyed and the state must either cease to be *de jure* or else discover some means for settling disputed issues which does not deprive any member of his autonomy. Furthermore, when the society grows too large for convenience in calling regular assemblies, some way must be found to conduct the business without condemning most of its citizens to the status of voiceless subjects. The traditional solutions in democratic theory to these familiar problems are of course majority rule and representation." [16] Wolff examines these "solutions" and argues that they do not solve the problem.

We have here a good reason for supposing that Wolff's defense of anarchism rests on the claim that it is *factually* impossible to sustain unanimous direct democracy for any reasonable length of time or on any significant scale and not on the claim, made in Chapter I, that the concepts of autonomy and authority are logically irreconcilable. However, toward the end of the book, he reverts to the position of Chapter I: "The magnitude of our problem is indicated by our inability to solve the dilemma of autonomy and authority even for a a utopian society! By and large, political philosophers have supposed that utopia was logically possible, however much they may have doubted that it was even marginally probable. But the arguments of this essay suggest that the just state must be consigned to the category of the round square, the married bachelor, and the unsensed sense-datum." [17] Here, Wolff's memory of his earlier arguments seems to have been selective. In this passage, the argument of Chapter I seems to have been uppermost in his mind, for the concept of the legitimate state is held to be a contradiction in terms. The argument of Chapter II for the theoretical solution of unanimous direct democracy seems to have been forgotten—the problem of autonomy and authority cannot be solved even in a utopian society (one governed by unanimous direct democracy?).

In view of the character of Wolff's equivocation, I propose to treat the contention that unanimous direct democracy constitutes a theoretical solution to the conflict between autonomy and authority as an aberration in his argument. Consequently, I shall interpret Wolff's main thesis as being that the *de jure* state is *logically,* and not just *factually,* impossible. The defence of this interpretation rests on two grounds. First, it is this position which, given his premises, Wolff validly argues for in Chapter I, and it is this position which, in Chapter III, he thinks his earlier arguments have established.[18] The second ground for adopting this interpretation is my argument against Wolff's belief, as expressed in Chapter II, that unanimous direct democracy constitutes a theoretical solution to his problem.[19]

II. WOLFF'S INDIVIDUALISM

I have argued that Wolff's defence of anarchism rests on the following contention: that the belief in the possibility of the *de jure* state is logically incompatible with the belief that men should strive to be morally autonomous agents. Like Wolff's other critics, I find his defense of anarchism unacceptable. However, it seems to me that his error lies in something they do not dispute: his conception of moral autonomy. At the beginning of this paper, I suggested that Wolff adopts an individualistic interpretation of moral autonomy and I indicated that what this means is to be explained primarily in terms of the primacy that is attached to individual practical judgement. Individualism of this kind, which I shall call "ethical individualism," raises each individual's own practical judgement, his own conscience, to the position of sole possible arbiter of right conduct for him. Each individual is, if you like, his own moral authority. Furthermore, for the ethical individualist, each individual is the *only* possible moral authority for him. There can be no *public* arena in which his judgements and actions can be authoritatively assessed from a moral point of view. This is because the advice, recommendations, exhortations and even the commands of others always stand subject to the findings of the court of each individual's own conscience or his own practical judgement. And since, in judging, we aim to judge *well,* each individual's own practical judgement serves as the only standard he is prepared to recognise in terms of which his conduct can be assessed. It is for this reason that individualists insist that the autonomous agent is the only person who can authorize his own actions. Consequently, the idea that there could be an *external de jure* moral authority is rejected.

That Wolff does adopt this individualist conception of moral autonomy and practical judgement is amply confirmed by a glance at the second section of Chapter I. For instance, he says: "The responsible man is not capricious or anarchic, for he does acknowledge himself bound by moral constraints. But he insists that *he alone* is the judge of those constraints" [20] (my italics). Later, he says that the autonomous man is self-legislating [21] and stresses the point that we are under an obligation to make ourselves the authors of our own actions.[22] Furthermore, when introducing the idea of unanimous direct democracy, he says that a man who is only constrained by the dictates of his own will is autonomous.[23] There seems little doubt, then, that Wolff's account of moral autonomy implies a belief in the primacy of individual practical judgement, and thus, a commitment to ethical individualism.

If this is so, we must now subject ethical individualism to critical scrutiny if Wolff's argument for anarchism is to be defeated. Elsewhere,[24] I have argued that one form of ethical individualism derives from a metaphysical dualism between reason on the one hand and will, appetite, passion or desire on the other. Actions and practical judgements are taken to be, in essence, expressions of the nonrational will of the individual. Reason is confined to playing merely formal and instrumental roles in practical judgement. This view of human nature is to be found in Hobbes, but its most forceful expression is to be found in Hume's famous dictum: "Reason is, and ought only to be, the slave of the passions, and can never pretend to any other office than to serve and obey them." [25] For Hume, this dualism of reason and passion presupposes a strictly *theoretical* conception of reason, according to which "Reason is the discovery of truth and falsehood," [26] and not, it should be noted, the discovery of good and evil—hence Hume's version of the fact-value distinction. Reason by itself is inert and incapable of moving men to act, whereas the passions, though casually active, are nonrational.[27] In Hobbes's case, the appetites are depicted as being all ultimately self-regarding, whereas other philosophers, with different moral psychologies, allow some to be genuinely other-regarding. Nevertheless, what is characteristic of many individualists from Hobbes, through Hume, to contemporary moral philosophers such as R. M.

Hare, is the priority which is given to appetite or desire (conceived as nonrational) in practical judgement and the confinement of reason to a servile or a purely formal and instrumental role. For such philosophers, practical judgement is necessarily individual in character, for ultimately it is founded on the individual's own contingent appetites or desires.

A trace of this dualism of reason and will is to be found in Wolff's book. For instance, when discussing the concept of responsibility, he says: "The obligation to take responsibility for one's actions does not derive from man's freedom of will alone, for more is required in taking responsibility than freedom of choice. Only because man has the capacity to reason about his choices can he be said to stand under a continuing obligation to take responsibility for them." [28] Although Wolff asserts that men possess both free will and reason, he might be thought to concede, perhaps unwittingly, that it is possible to conceive of beings who have the capacity to reason but lack free will, and beings who have free will but lack the capacity to reason. He gives no indication that in his view the possession of reason and free will are necessarily connected.

However, it would be wrong to to make too much of this brief passage. In any case, it might be a mistake to attribute a straightforwardly Humean form of individualism to Wolff, especially in view of his Kantian sympathies. Kant tried to develop a much richer conception of practical reason than was possible in the context of Hume's philosophy. The centerpiece is, of course, the categorical imperative: "Act only on that maxim through which you can at the same time will that it should become a universal law." [29] For Kant, practical reason, properly so called, is universal, and not, as it was for Hume, merely a species of theoretical reason slavishly subservient to the passions of the individual. This is why the categorical imperative takes the form it does. But the residual individualism which is implicit in Kant's conception of duty is revealed by the fact that the universality of practical reason is only an *aspiration* of *individual* practical judgement. The test of whether or not a maxim of action is in accord with duty is still depicted as an individual affair: the individual has to ask *himself* whether *he* can will the maxim in its universal form. Admittedly, Kant thought that the appeal to the categorical imperative constituted an objective (i.e., supraindividual) test of the moral correctness of any proposed action. However, most philosophers regard this as too strong a claim on Kant's part. In a later work,[30] Wolff himself points out that in its first and second forms, the categorical imperative lays down only a negative criterion of practical rationality insofar as it rules out contradictory willing. What follows is that although the exercise of practical reason rules out policies that are internally inconsistent, it provides no way of distinguishing between self-consistent policies that are moral and those that are not. Even after the exercise of practical reason, one course of action may seem right to one individual and wrong to another. Each individual has no option but to put faith in his own judgement; hence the collapse into individualism. Therefore it is only to be expected that Wolff should say, as quoted earlier, that a man who is constrained only by the dictates of his own will is autonomous, for practical reason, in the form of the categorical imperative, cannot (despite Kant's claims) constrain the will in any substantial way.

If my account of the origins of Wolff's individualism is correct, it explains why the concepts of autonomy and authority must be conceived by him as being fundamentally opposed. The recognition of, and obedience to, authority can be seen only as submission to an alien will. To submit to the authority of another is either to submit to the nonrational desires of another, or to renounce one's highest formal duty (namely, to act in accordance with one's substantive duty as determined by oneself with the aid of the categorical imperative) in favor of another person's (possibly different) idea of one's substantive duty. What could be more absurd than this? The recognition of authority becomes, as it was for the leading figures of the French Enlightenment, the epitome of *un*reason. It is only to be expected that the possibility of the state's having *de jure* authority over the individual must be rejected, for if the practical judgement of the individual is sovereign then the state cannot be sovereign.

Now we reach the nub of the matter. In the paper to which I have just referred, I suggested that ethical individualism is just a special case of philosophical individualism. The latter is characterized by its giving logical priority to first person judgements. In many of the epistemological writings that followed Descartes, the authority for theoretical judgement was located in the individual—in the "clear and distinct ideas" of Descartes himself, in Locke's "ideas," in Hume's "impression," and in the "sense data" of more recent writers. We now know that great difficulties lie in this approach to epistemology. My contention here is that much moral and political philosophy has incorporated an analogous mistake—the mistake of locating the authority for practical judgement in the individual also. In the case of the empiricists, it is located in the appetites, passions, or desires, and in the case of Kant, in the Good Will.

If the conception of moral judgement implicit in ethical individualism were correct, each individual would have "privileged access" to the moral character of his own actions but no access to the moral character of the actions of others. That is to say, since each individual is the sole and final authority on the morality of his own actions, so another individual is the sole and final authority of the morality of *his* actions. This implies that we should have no basis on which to judge the morality of each other's actions, and this, in turn, implies that no sense could be given to the notion of moral disagreement. Furthermore, if there is no authoritative public arena in terms of which the moral conduct of an individual can be assessed, it is difficult to see how we could make sense of holding someone morally responsible, and possibly worthy of punishment, for what he has done. These difficulties are bad enough, but they are only symptomatic of a deeper difficulty: within the framework of ethical individualism it makes no sense to speak of moral *judgement* at all. If, in judging, we aim to judge correctly (which, surely, we do), then it is only possible to speak of "judgement" in contexts where correctness is possible and therefore only in contexts where mistakes are possible too. However, the necessarily private character of moral judgement, as seen by the ethical individualist, rules this out. The following thought is an appropriate one for the ethical individualist to entertain: "One would like to say: whatever is going to seem right to me is right." Wittgenstein's reply is, of course, "And that only means that here we can't talk about 'right.' "[31] Wittgenstein's argument against the possibility of a logically private language is also an argument against the possibility of logically private judgement; that is, judgement of a kind where the individual whose judgement it is, is logically the only possible authority on its correctness. It shows that it is only possible to employ the concept of judgement in contexts where there are public criteria of correctness. Where there are no such criteria, the concept of judgement has no application, and *a fortiori*, it is impossible to raise meaningfully the question of whether or not one's "judge-ments" are correct or mistaken. For ethical individualists there are no criteria of this kind: they are supposed to be freely chosen by the individual. Thus, if Wolff wishes to preserve the concept of moral judgement, he must reject his individualist view of it, and with it, his individualist conception of moral autonomy.

III. AUTONOMY AND AUTHORITY RECONSIDERED

If Wittgenstein's argument against the possibility of a logically private language is sound, it follows that ethical individualism is false and that Wolff's conception of moral autonomy is mistaken. The moral authorization of action cannot therefore lie with the private judgement or the conscience of the individual. But if this is so, what becomes of the concept of moral autonomy? For after all, it might be urged, moral autonomy is nothing if not conceived as the keystone of ethical individualism. Alternatively, perhaps it can be rescued and recast in such a way that the alleged conflict between autonomy and authority can be shown to be illusory.

According to Steven Lukes,[32] the concept of autonomy was first clearly formulated (after Aristotle) by Aquinas in opposition to the medieval doctrine that the order of a superior must be obeyed no matter whether it is just or not. Against this Aquinas maintained that every man must act in consonance with reason. What authorizes an action is not the fact that it is willed or commanded, not even when the command is issued by a superior. Only reason can authorize action. Thus autonomy can be conceived, not as the regulation of one's actions in accordance with the determination of one's *will*, no matter what this happens to be, but the striving to regulate one's conduct in accordance with *reason*. This conception of autonomy is antiauthori*tarian*, but not obviously antiauthority. It also clearly presupposes some fairly substantial form of practical reason. But if one adopts a rather more restricted view of reason, such as Hume's narrowly theoretical conception along with the related dualism of reason and passion, the concept begins to collapse. Its antiauthoritarianism remains, but in the absence of a theory of practical reason, authority and authoritarianism become indistinguishable, and the authorization of action is left to lie with the nonrational passions of the individual. Whereas the older conception of autonomy points to a contrast between action on the part of the agent that is authorized by reason and action that is not so authorized (whether willed by the agent himself or commanded by a superior), the newer, degenerate conception of autonomy points to a contrast between action willed by the agent himself (and therefore authorized) and action commanded by another person (and therefore not authorized).

Paralleling these two conceptions of autonomy are two conceptions of authority. First, the one that parallels the degenerate conception of autonomy, is conceived, as it is by Wolff, as an alien will demanding obedience and on which reason can, at best, only place formal constraints. Hence the seeming irrationality involved in the recognition of authority. For Hobbes, the problem of the authority of the sovereign is doubly acute. This is because not only is the submission to authority submission to another's will—in the last analysis, to his appetites—but since all wills are egotistical, it is the submission of one's own life to another's private good, for in Hobbes's view: "COMMAND is where a man saith, *Doe this,* or *Doe not this,* without expecting other reason than the Will of him that sayes it. From this it followeth manifestly, that he that Commandeth, pretendeth thereby his own Benefit: For the reason of his Command is his own Will onely, and the proper object of every mans Will, is some Good to himselfe."[33] If this is so, then the commands of the sovereign will have no significance to the subject, unless he has what Peter Winch calls "some ulterior reason"[34] for taking notice of them—that is to say, fear of the sovereign's power. Once established, the sovereign can confront the subject only as an external power—a force to be reckoned with. Hence Rousseau's comment: "Force is physical power, and I fail to see what moral effect it can have. To yield to force is an act of necessity, not of will—at the most, an act of prudence."[35]

Against this conception of authority according to which it is something essentially alien to the individual may be set another conception of authority that parallels the older view of autonomy. It presupposes that there is a right and a wrong way of doing things, established practices (which need not be inflexible), and that this way of doing things is not determined by the (possibly capricious) will of the individual, no matter what his rank in the hierarchy of authorities. The authority and the individual over whom authority is exercised participate in activities and forms of social interaction that are governed by established rules and criteria for determining the correct way of proceeding. Both parties (e.g., the priest and his parishoner, the parent and the child, the officer and the private soldier) owe their allegiance to the rules and criteria that are imbedded in, or are taken to be constitutive of, the practices in which they participate, because it is by reference to them—to what is taken to be reason in the relevant domain—that action is ultimately authorized. Therefore the authoritative character of the authority's commands or pronouncements derives from the fact that they are at least *claimed* to be in accordance with reason. Thus the individual over whom authority is exercised stands in what Winch [36] calls on "internal" relationship with that authority, one which is mediated by the rules of the activity or practice in which they both participate, rather than in the external or alienated relationship of the individualistic model.

The very existence of public rule-governed activities brings with it the notion of authority in relation to those activities, for as Winch observes, "The idea of such an established way of doing things . . . presupposes that the practices and pronouncements of a certain group of people shall be authoritative in connection with the activity in question." [37] If this were not so, how could we give any sense to the idea of *teaching* someone to do something—for example, teaching children how to play games, how to speak grammatically, or even how to think for themselves—not anyhow, but *well* about moral issues? [38] Sometimes the authorities will be widespread; sometimes they will be few in number, especially if the activity or practice is specialised or remote from daily life. Where there are rule-governed activities and practices, it is possible for one person to have a better grasp of them than another, greater expertise in applying the rules to particular cases, and so on. That is to say, it is possible for persons to be recognised as authorities in the relevant sphere. And since morality is a public practice, or a family of public practices, it follows that moral authority is possible. To deny this implies, in the end, that moral judgement is not possible.

The recognition of authority—even moral authority—is not the irrational business it is presented as being in Wolff's book. It is a necessary accompaniment of public rule-governed activites and practices—of social life itself. This does not imply that an individual or body of individuals, no matter how learned or wise, can claim absolute authority, in the sense that they can validly claim that *any* decision or pronouncement they make should be regarded as binding or correct. For one thing, no individual is infallible. For another, if a pronouncement departs too much or too obviously from the rules or principles of the activity or practice in question, it loses its authoritative character. For example, Winch has suggested that if the pope were to issue an encyclical denying the existence of God and advocating the practice of free love, it is doubtful if it would be recognised by the faithful as carrying papal authority.[39] Human fallibility does not undermine the concept of authority in the moral sphere any more than the fallibility of scientists undermines the concept of authority in science. Quite the contrary: it is the existence of human fallibility that makes human authority possible, for as Wittgenstein's argument shows, if incorrect judgement were not possible, correct judgement would not be possible either.

We can now see why the conflict between authority and autonomy is illusory. The recognition of authority is necessarily connected with the existence of public rule-governed activities and practices and public criteria of correctness in judgement. But it is precisely the existence of such criteria that makes judgement, and therefore autonomy, possible. Autonomy and authority are really just two sides of the same coin.[40]

IV. POLITICS AND INDIVIDUALISM

If, as I have argued, the concepts of autonomy and authority are not flatly incompatible, Wolff's defence of anarchism collapses. There is, however, another defect in his case for anarchism that is equally fundamental in character and perhaps symptomatic of other respects in which individualism is an inadequate framework in which to conduct social and political analysis. This defect is that the whole question of the *de jure* state is treated in a thoroughly *apolitical* manner. It is as if politics does not exist for Wolff, or is indistinguishable from morality in all important respects.

The apolitical character of Wolff's discussion of the *de jure* state can be brought out by noting features of two of his principal arguments. First, the *a priori* argument of Chapter I against the possibility of the *de jure* state is conducted on a purely *moral-philosophical* plane. No attempt is made to mark off the realm of the moral from the realm of the political. One of the consequences of this omission is that apart from such perfunctory remarks as "The defining mark of the state is the right to rule," there is no systematic attempt to analyse the concept of the state or to examine what it is that makes the state into a specifically *political* institution. Indeed, the remark just quoted does not rule out the possibility that Wolff thinks of the state as only purporting to be a moral institution. There is, for instance, no examination of the grounds that might be adduced by those opposed to anarchism to support the claim that the state can legitimately exercise *power* as well as authority and no examination of how moral authority might be distinguished from political authority.

Secondly, Wolff's apparent blindness to the category of the political is no more clearly revealed than in the contention of Chapter II, that anarchism is implied by the impracticability of unanimous direct democracy. Earlier, I suggested that it was surprising to find Wolff arguing that unanimous direct democracy would, if it were practicable, embody a reconciliation of the concepts of autonomy and authority, rather than constituting a mechanism of community self-regulation in which political authority is abolished. Surely, in one important sense of "politics," politics is unnecessary when agreement over common policies can be reached by an open and spontaneous discussion of their technical and moral merits and without resorting to or threatening, however indirectly, to resort to the exercise of power in some form or other. Politics enters the scene for any given community when this kind of open and spontaneous moral agreement cannot be reached and when the adoption of a common policy is necessary.[41] But it is precisely at this point that Wolff turns his face against politics and advocates anarchism. To a rough approximation, if politics, rather than the mere pursuit of self-interest, is the art of reconciling and conciliating conflicting interests within a framework of power relations so that a plurality of competing proposals for a common policy can be reduced to a single proposal, then the practice of politics is not only automatically in conflict with treating people as autonomous agents (as conceived by Wolff), it is unnecessary in a unanimous direct democracy—that is, unnecessary in what Wolff considers, in Chapter II, to be the only legitimate form of the state. Given my rather crude definition of politics, this implies that the state cannot be (morally) legitimate if it is a political institution. The oddity of this result should not go unremarked, for the nature of politics, one of the most important spheres of human activity, is left unexamined in a treatise on political philosophy. None of the most important philosophical questions about politics, such as its relation with morality, its connection with justice, its rationale, its necessity, and so on, is discussed. The case for politics, and *a fortiori*, the case for the political state, has not been found wanting, it has not even been examined.

What is beginning to emerge is that Wolff's individualism and his disregard of politics are more than accidentally connected. For instance, insofar as politics involves the exercise of power, whether institutionalized in representative assemblies or not, it is antithetical to treating people as autonomous agents in the way conceived by Wolff. This is hardly surprising, but I think it is symptomatic of deeper difficulties. At the beginning of this paper, I suggested that one of the merits of Wolff's book was that it unwittingly exposes an incoherence in liberal-individualist political thought. One aspect of this incoherence can be represented in the following way. Sometimes politics is depicted as a nasty business in which individuals grasp after power so that they can advance their own, or some sectional or class interest, usually at the expense of the interests of others. Either this is all there is to it, or there is something more. If there is something more to it, then it seems to me (though I shall not argue the case here) that the practice of politics, while recognising and arising from either genuine or merely apparent conflicts of interest, would be a pointless activity in which to engage sincerely if it were thought that even in an ideal world the just reconciliation of interests might turn out to be impossible. In other words, it is an *a priori* presupposition of political activity (as opposed to the mere pursuit of private or sectional interests) that justice a genuine community of interests are both possible. Consequently, if politics is to be a rational activity, the nature of practical reason must be such as to *guarantee* the possibility of justice and a genuine community of interests. But it is precisely this guarantee that ethical individualism is precluded from giving. This is because for individualists, judgements of interest, like moral judgements, are founded on the contingencies of *individual* consciousness.[42] If they were so founded, then even in a world that is in all other respects ideal, it might turn out that justice and a community of interests were not realizable owing to what are conceived to be legitimate and rationally irresolvable conflicts of interest. Thus if Wolff's position implies a rejection of this *a priori* presupposition of the practice of politics, then not just the concept of the *de jure* state but the *entire* vocabulary of politics lacks any proper application. Consequently, those who engage in political activity deceive themselves about the nature of that activity. Furthermore, those who study politics are also under a fundamental misapprehension about its true character. For Wolff and those who think like him, "politics" is just a name used to refer to what is really a species of immoral practice. However, it is far from clear that we could make sense of much of our social life without using the terms in our political vocabulary with their normal meaning. But one thing is clear: if we reject Wolff's implied political skepticism, then we must choose a framework other than that of ethical individualism in terms of which to conduct the philosophical analysis of political concepts.

NOTES

1. R. P. Wolff, *In Defence of Anarchism* (New York: Harper Torchbook, 1970).

2. Robert F. Ladenson, "Legitimate Authority," *American Philosophical Quarterly,* IX, 4 (October 1972), pp. 335-41, and Rex Martin, "Wolff's Defence of Philosophical Anarchism," *The Philosophical Quarterly,* XXIV, 95 (Spring 1974), pp. 140-49.

3. Ladenson takes the view that Wolff is arguing for a logical incompatibility between autonomy and authority, whereas Martin seems to think that Wolff's main contention is that the *de jure* state cannot be exemplified as a matter of fact. See note 19 below.

4. Wolff, *In Defence of Anarchism* p. vii.

5. Ibid., p. 18.

6. Ibid., p. 4.

7. Ibid., p. 12.

8. Ibid.

9. Ibid., p. 13.

10. Ibid., p. 14

11. Ibid., p. 19, In view of Wolff's later flirtation with the notion of unanimous direct democracy, which is the cause of the main problem of interpretation, it is worth quoting the version of the conflict as given in his paper "On Violence," *Journal of Philosophy* LXVI, 19 (2 October 1969), p. 607. He says: "Briefly, I think it can be shown that every man has a fundamental duty to be autonomous, in Kant's sense of the term. Each of us must make himself the author of his actions and take responsibility for them by refusing to act save on the basis of reasons he can see for himself to be good. Autonomy, thus understood, is in direct opposition to obedience, which is submission to the will of another, irrespective of reasons. Following Kant's usage, *political obedience is heteronomy of the will"* (my italics).

12. Wolff, *In Defence of Anarchism,* pp. 22-23.

13. Ibid., p. 23.

14. Ibid.

15. In this connection, see the passage quoted in note 11.

16. Ibid., p. 26.

17. Ibid., p. 71.

18. This is also the position taken in "On Violence." See note 11.

19. The two critics of Wolff to whom I made an earlier reference (see note 2) adopt opposing interpretations of his argument. Martin notices the inconsistency between Chapters I and II, but plumps for the view that Wolff should be taken as maintaining that the *de jure* state (in the form of unanimous direct democracy) can never be exemplified as a matter of fact. Nevertheless, he argues (rather implausibly, in my view) that the case of the philosophical anarchist, construed in this way, is inconclusive. Ladenson, on the other hand, takes Wolff's claim to be the stronger one that the concept of morally legitimate political authority is incoherent. However, he does not notice the discrepancy between the positions taken in Chapters I and II. He accepts Wolff's account of moral autonomy but goes on to suggest that Wolff's defence of anarchism rests on a confused response to the question: "Why does a citizen have a duty to obey the law even when he opposes it in conscience?" However, this is not Wolff's question, nor is it in any sense his starting point. The problem that lies behind *this* question is only a problem for someone who *already* acknowledges that he has a *prima facie* obligation to obey the law. But it is precisely the possibility of the autonomous man having *any* obligation to obey the law that the argument of Chapter I appears to rule out. In effect, Ladenson depicts Wolff's anarchist thesis as arising from a mistaken response to a certain kind of *moral* conflict, whereas in Chapter I Wolff depicts it as arising from a *logical* conflict within our system of moral concepts. Thus

Ladenson's attempt to defuse Wolff's argument is misconceived from the outset.

20. Wolff, *In Defence of Anarchism,* p. 13.

21. Ibid., p. 14.

22. Ibid., pp. 14-15. See also the passage quoted from "On Violence" in note 11 above.

23. Ibid., p. 23.

24. Grenville Wall, "Freedom Versus Reason: A Reply," *The Philosophical Quarterly,* XXV, 100 (July 1975), pp. 213-29.

25. D. Hume, *Treatise,* Bk. II, Pt. iii, Sec. 3.

26. Ibid., Bk. II, Pt. i, Sec. 1.

27. Graphically put by Hume in his infamous remark: "It is not contrary to reason to prefer the destruction of the whole world to the scratching of my finger." *(Treatise,* Bk. II, Pt. iii, Sec. 3).

28. Wolff, *In Defence of Anarchism,* p. 12.

29. I. Kant, *Groundwork of the Metaphysic of Morals,* translated by H. J. Paton as *The Moral Law* (London: Hutchinson's University Library, 1956), p. 58.

30. R. P. Wolff, *The Autonomy of Reason* (New York: Harper Torchbook, 1973), pp. 159-61.

31. L. Wittgenstein, *Philosophical Investigations* (Oxford: Blackwell, 1953), Part I, para. 258.

32. Steven Lukes, *Individualism* (Oxford: Blackwell, 1973), p. 52.

33. T. Hobbes, *Leviathan,* Pt. II, Ch. xxv.

34. Peter Winch, "Man and Society in Hobbes and Rousseau," in *Hobbes and Rousseau,* M. Cranston and R. S. Peters, eds. (New York: Anchor Books, 1972), p. 246.

35. J.-J. Rousseau, *The Social Contract,* Bk. I, Ch. 3.

36. Peter Winch, "Authority," in *Political Philosophy,* A. Quinton, ed. (London: Oxford University Press, 1967), p. 98.

37. Ibid., p. 100.

38. The difficulties involved in adopting an individualist approach to moral education and the necessity for reinstating the concept of moral authority in relation to moral education are discussed by the present author in "Moral Autonomy and the Liberal Theory of Moral Education," *Proceedings of the Philosophy of Education Society of Great Britain,* VIII, 2 (July 1974), pp. 222-36, and in "Moral Authority and Moral Education," *Journal of Moral Education,* IV, 2 (February 1975), pp. 95-99.

39. Winch, "Authority," p. 105.

40. This way of resolving the autonomy versus authority issue might be objected to on the grounds that it is either too conservative or involves

a commitment to moral relativism. It might be argued that my identification of practical reason with the rules and criteria for determining the correct way of proceeding within established practices and activities is conservative insofar as it neglects the fact that such practices and activities *change*. It would be foolish to deny that they do change and therefore I do not want to be saddled with the charge of conservativism. This then exposes me to the second charge: that I am a relativist, committed to the view that what constitutes reason is entirely relative to a particular culture or historical period within a culture. My response to this is to say that either a change in the criteria of practical rationality is only a *mere* change, or, in some circumstances a change can be regarded as constituting *progress* in the canons of practical reason. I reject the relativist implications of the first alternative. However, the defence of the view that there can be progress in practical reason would require a separate argument and is therefore beyond the scope of this paper.

41. I draw on the definition of the concept of a "political predicament" given by S. E. Finer in *Comparative Government* (Harmondsworth: Pelican Books, 1974), p. 8.

42. For a critique of the individualist analysis of the concept of "interest" see Grenville Wall, "The Concept of 'Interest' in Politics," *Politics and Society,* V, 4 (1975), pp. 487-510.

17

ON THE "KANTIAN" FOUNDATIONS OF ROBERT PAUL WOLFF'S ANARCHISM

PATRICK RILEY

I

In his *In Defense of Anarchism* what Robert Paul Wolff has done, while borrowing the "cloak" of Kant's "legitimacy," is to develop the notion that only a "unanimous direct democracy" in which everyone actually consents to everything is "legitimate" because only in such a scheme is everyone truly "autonomous"—"autonomy" not being preserved, on this view, by "tacit" consent, representative government, and majoritarianism: in short, by Lockean politics.[1] Wolff's political position, then, turns on the idea that autonomy is "the primary obligation of man"; that this autonomy can be politically preserved only in a unanimous direct democracy in which everyone "gives laws to himself"; that, failing the creation of such a democracy, one must come down in favor of philosophical anarchism.[2] This political theory might, Wolff says—"if I may steal a title from Kant (and thus perhaps wrap myself in the cloak of his legitimacy)"—be called *Groundwork of the Metaphysics of the State.*[3]

Now what is interesting here is that Robert Paul Wolff has turned "autonomy" into a substantive moral duty, into "the primary obligation of man," whereas Kant's argument (whose authority

294

Wolff would like to "steal") is that unless one considers man, from a hypothetical "point of view," as if he were "autonomous," then none of his substantive moral duties—summarized in the general notion of treating persons as "ends"—would be *conceivable*. Kant holds, that is, that while the objective reality of autonomy cannot be demonstrated, it must nevertheless be presupposed as the *conditio sine qua non* of conceiving oneself as responsible, good, or just; that a being which could not conceive itself as an autonomous "moral cause" could never imagine itself responsible or good or just. Autonomy, then, for Kant is a necessary point of view, or a necessary hypothesis, in explaining the possibility of the common moral concepts which we actually use; but autonomy is not *itself* a substantive moral duty. It is rather the hypothetical condition of being able to conceive *any* duties.[4] Since Kant would not say that we have a duty to be autonomous, he would not support Wolff's politics either; indeed, while Kant prefered "republicanism," he supported any legal order which creates a context for self-moralization by removing impediments to that process.[5]

It is perhaps serious enough that one borrow the "cloak" of Kant's legitimacy, only to subvert it; but even more serious is the problem of relating the common moral duties—such as refraining from murder—to Wolff's "primary obligation" of autonomy. Would one say, for example, that one acted "autonomously" by refraining from murder such that "refraining from murder" becomes an instance of "autonomous action"? Is the obligation, then, one of *not* murdering *(simpliciter)*, or is it one of not violating one's own autonomy by murdering? That is, if the primary obligation of man is autonomy, "the refusal to be ruled," are all obligations ultimately "obligations to oneself"? Along what lines, then, does one view "secondary" obligations to others? To say that everyone's autonomy is to be respected would take care of both "self-regarding" and "other-regarding" obligations; but this is not what Wolff argues— though Kant of course does.[6] Moreover, if one's "primary obligation" were to respect the autonomy of *everyone,* the anarchism which Wolff supports when "unanimous direct democracy" cannot be attained would not *irresistibly* follow: after all, one could say that respect for the autonomy of everyone necessitates a legal order insofar as "respect" is only an imperative rather than a fact; but if one's primary obligation is "autonomy, the refusal to be ruled," then anarchism appears to be more nearly inevitable, and perhaps more natural than "unanimous direct democracy" itself. Wolff may possibly think that having a "primary obligation" to be autonomous is equivalent to having an obligation to respect the autonomy of everyone, but this of course is not true. Thus he has not only transmogrified Kant, whose authority has been illegitimately borrowed; he has provided too convenient a foundation for his anarchism.

In what follows it will be argued that Robert Paul Wolff's treatment of autonomy as the "Kantian" primary obligation of man has the following consequences: (1) it leads to treating "autonomy" as a substantive duty, contrary both to Kant and to good sense; (2) this error leads to neglect of Kant's notion that the primary substantive moral duty of men is to treat other men as ends-in-themselves whose dignity ought to be respected [7] (i.e., to respect others' autonomy, not just one's own); and (3) this initial error leads to the further misfortune of suggesting (or at least implying) that anarchism is a "Kantian" doctrine necessitated by "autonomy" *qua* "the refusal to be ruled"—whereas in fact Kant argues that government is absolutely necessary to provide a context or environment within which one can pursue a good will (a will, that is, never to universalize maxims which would treat persons as mere means to arbitrary purposes [8]). Properly understood, Kantianism neither argues for "autonomy" as a substantive moral duty (still less as "the primary obligation of man"), nor urges that anarchism is necessitated by the "refusal to be ruled." It does indeed insist on moral autonomy (as the ground of the possibility of conceiving and having duties), but not just on *one's own* autonomy; nor does it ever argue that moral autonomy and government are incongruent. One cannot wrap the cloak of Kant's legitimacy around an anarchist argument which he would have thought illegitimate.

II

That Robert Paul Wolff has transmogrified and not just "applied" Kant's theory of autonomy is plain enough from an inspection of Kant's aims in the *Groundwork of the Metaphysics of Morals*.

Kant builds his moral philosophy on the notion of a good will as the only "unqualifiedly" good thing on earth: [9] that is, on the notion of a kind of moral "causality," itself undetermined by natural causes, which is the source of man's freedom and responsibility. (The content with which the good will strives to harmonize when it "universalizes" the "maxims" of its action—in Kant's case respect for the dignity of persons as "ends in themselves"—will be taken up in Section III of this paper.) Since, however, Kant's claim in the *Critique of Practical Reason* that "the autonomy of the will is the sole principle of all moral laws" [10] might appear to lend color to Wolff's "Kantian" claim that "the primary obligation of man is autonomy," it will be useful to look with some care at what Kant has to say about will, autonomy, and their relation to each other.

The history of the free-will controversy is notoriously thorny (and often acrimonious), but it is at least arguable that Kant was able to avoid most of the confusions over the notion of will which had introduced a degree of incoherence into the "voluntarist" tradition (as he inherited it from Hobbes, Locke, and Rousseau) [11] by defining the will as "a faculty of determining oneself to action in accordance with the conception of certain laws," as "a kind of causality belonging to living beings insofar as they are rational." [12] A being that is capable of acting according to the conception of laws, Kant suggests, is an intelligent or rational being, and "the causality of such a being according to this conception of laws is his will." [13] And freedom, he argues, is the capacity of this will *qua* causality to be "efficient"—to produce (so to speak) moral "effects"— independent of "foreign causes" determining that will.[14] The will, then, according to Kant, is a kind of "noumenal" or intelligent causality which is itself independent of natural causality, and a being possessed of this kind of "causality" is *autonomous*.

Setting aside for the moment all the difficulties involved in this position—the fact, for example, that freedom and will are only "necessary hypotheses" which explain our (merely) practical conviction that something could and ought to have been done by us, though it was not done, because we are in part *noumenal* beings belonging to a "world of intelligence" who can produce moral effects through our free "causality"; [15] that such a *noumenal* world may be only a point of view (but not a "constitutive" principle of "theoretical" reason) which we are obliged to adopt in order to explain our notions of freedom and duty [16]—waiving all this for present purposes, it seems that if Kant can make this concept of will intelligible and plausible, he is also able to avoid the reduction of will to Hobbesian "appetite" or to a Lockean "uneasiness of desire." [17] For Kant's definition of will insists on consciousness (on understanding the conception of a law), on determining oneself independent of external causes (such as sensations). On this view a notion such as moral responsibility at least begins to become intelligible: after all, if one is the "free cause" of something of whose character he was conscious, the "effect" can reasonably be imputed to him; whereas if his will is simply the "last appetite in deliberation" (in the manner of Hobbes), then he may be the *efficient* cause of an effect, but not (as it were) the moral cause of it.[18] By insisting on will as the undetermined causality of a rational being who understands the conception of the laws according to which he acts (whereas objects in physical nature indeed act *according to* laws, but not according to the *conception* of them), Kant is able to rescue a rational foundation for a distinction between morality and psychology—a distinction without which, in Kant's view, "autonomy" would be unintelligible.

One uses the word "rescue" in this connection because Nietzsche once said of Kant that he is "in the end an underhanded Christian"; [19] by this he meant that Kant had attempted to salvage the doctrines of free will, responsibility, autonomy, and the like, in an "underhanded" way—that is, by making those notions necessary but *hypothetical.* There is a certain truth in this charge, once one brackets out the elements of accusation and malice. For Kant does begin with what he takes to be the ordinary moral conceptions with which everyone operates ("criticism can and must begin with pure practical laws and their actual existence"), [20] and suggests that he is supplying, not "new" moral principles, but simple a "transcendental deduction" of common moral concepts—that is, an explanation of how those concepts are in principle possible, as distinguished from pleasure, utility, or legality.[21] In the explanation of the possibility of moral ideas, Kant does not feel entitled to use traditional ideas of freedom, will, and autonomy in traditional ways, as if those ideas were unproblematical and "constitutive" principles of theoretical reason having the same status as the principles of empiricism. As he says in the *Groundwork,* "freedom is only an idea of reason, and its objective reality in itself is doubtful; while nature is a concept of the understanding which proves, and must necessarily prove, its reality in examples of experience." [22] Since, however, if the idea of a free will as a *noumenal* or intelligent casuality is given up all morality will become "empirical," Kant argues that

> ... for practical purposes the narrow footpath of freedom is the only one on which it is possible to make use of reason in our conduct. ... Philosophy must then assume that no real contradiction will be found between freedom and physical necessity of the same human actions, for it cannot give up the conception of nature any more than that of freedom. [23]

Kant, then, proposes to rescue a nonempirical, non-"pathological" morality—in which men have autonomy because they shape their own conduct according to rules which they understand, and do not simply have Hobbesian "last appetites" which are determined by a causal chain the first link of which is in the hand of God [24]—by preserving some traditional moral ideas in a hypothetical form. His best-known version of this is to be found in the incomparable Part III of the *Groundwork,* where, after defining the will in terms of autonomy—that is, in terms of its capacity to give laws to itself, undetermined by "phenomenal" causes—Kant begins to introduce his hypothetical qualifications. Every being which "cannot act except under the *idea* of freedom," he says, is "in a practical point of view" really free, just as if a "theoretically conclusive" proof of free will were possible. [25] This freedom cannot be proved to be "actually a property of ourselves or of human nature," but it must be presupposed "if we would conceive a being as rational and conscious of its causality in respect of its actions, that is, as endowed with a will." [26]

If a rational being is to be possessed of a "causality" which is itself not causally determined, Kant urges, one must draw a distinction between "a world of sense and the world of understanding." With respect to "mere perception and receptivity of sensations," he argues, one must count himself as belonging to the "world of sense"; but insofar as he is capable of initiating rational "pure activity," he must count himself as belonging to "the intellectual world." [27]

> A rational being ... has two points of view from which he can regard himself, and recognize laws of the exercise of his

faculties . . . first, so far as he belongs to the world of sense, he finds himself subject to the laws of nature (heteronomy); secondly, as belonging to the intelligible world, under laws which, being independent of nature, have their foundation not in experience but in reason alone [autonomy].[28]

If one belonged solely to the world of understanding, Kant goes on, then all of his actions would conform to the principle of "autonomy of the free will"; if one were solely a creature of sense, then only a will determined by desires and inclinations would be possible. (Here one should take careful note of the phrase, "autonomy of the free will": autonomy is a hypothetical "property" or "attribute" of a free will, not a substantive moral duty.) Since beings such as men, who are partly rational, recognize themselves as "subject to the law of the world of understanding, that is, to reason," this law is an imperative for them. A semirational being has duties because his will ought to (and could) conform to reason, but is affected (though not determined) by desire and inclination. What makes categorical imperatives of morality possible, Kant insists, is that the idea of freedom "makes me a member of an intelligible world, in consequence of which, if I were nothing else, all my actions *would* conform to the autonomy of the will; but as I at the same time intuit myself as a member of the world of sense, they *ought* so conform." [29]

Kant ends his treatment of the "groundwork" of morality, however, by reaffirming the hypothetical (though necessary) character of a "world of understanding," of freedom, of a faculty of willing—a "world" in which men necessarily take themselves to be "autonomous." The conception of an intelligible or *noumenal* world is, he grants, only a "point of view which reason finds itself compelled to take outside the appearances [of the phenomenal world] in order to conceive itself as practical." [30] Freedom, too, is "a mere idea" which holds good "only as a necessary hypothesis of reason in a being that believes itself conscious of a will." [31] (Here, indeed, despite this cautiousness, Kant is going farther than in the *Critique of Pure Reason,* where he dares affirm only that freedom is not in principle impossible or contradictory, once one draws a distinction between a *noumenal* and a phenomenal world.) [32] But sometimes, as in the preface to the *Metaphysics of Morals,* he is willing to be less cautious, to say that in practice freedom and will *prove* their reality.

In the practical exercise of reason . . . the concept of freedom proves its reality through practical basis principles. As laws of a causality of pure reason, these principles determine the will independently of all empirical conditions . . . and prove the existence in us of a pure will in which moral concepts and laws have their origin.[33]

And the *autonomous* will, of course, is precisely that which determines itself through "practical basic principles . . . independently of all empirical conditions."

Now it seems clear enough that in his discussion of "autonomy," Kant has not treated that moral quality either as the "primary obligation" of man or as "the refusal to be ruled"—except perhaps in the wholly nonpolitical sense that the autonomous man refuses to be "ruled" by his own inclinations (which would constitute "heteronomy"). The autonomous being is one who refuses to allow himself to be determined by his "phenomenal" character, who shapes his own conduct in terms of what "practical reason" demands. But this autonomous being, *qua* free, rational moral agent, does not *display* his autonomy by "refusing to be ruled": he displays it in conforming his will to the dictates of practical reason. And for Kant practical reason points out an "end" quite other than a mere "refusal to be ruled"—namely, respect for the dignity of persons as ends-in-themselves. (Therefore in Kant one "gives" the moral law to himself only in the sense that one recognizes it and makes it the motive of his action. One does not "give" it in a quasi-existentialist sense of "creating" what was not "there.") [34]

Since respect for persons as "ends" constitutes the content of Kantian ethics—Hegel and J. S. Mill to the contrary notwithstanding [35]—one must now turn to the "ends" of Kant's moral philosophy, to the question of *what* the categorical imperative demands. One may think the notion of persons as "ends" unintelligible, or incoherent, or (at best) vague, but one cannot represent as *Kantian* a moral-political theory which leaves this notion out of account; still less can one substitute the "primary obligation" of refusing to be ruled for respect for the dignity of persons as ends-in-themselves.

III

The best-known version of Kant's argument that persons are ends-in-themselves is probably the one which comprises the whole middle section of the *Groundwork of the Metaphysics of Morals* (though, as will be shown in Section V, it is an argument which Robert Paul Wolff finds "difficult" and not persuasive). Kant begins with an argument about two kinds of ends: "relative" ones and "objective" ones. Ends generally, he urges, serve the will as the "objective ground of its self-determination": the arbitrary ends which a rational being proposes to himself "at pleasure" are only relative, since these ends change as his desires and interests change; but if there exists "something whose existence has *in itself* an absolute worth," something which, as an end-in-itself, can be a "source of definite laws," then *this* end could be the "source of a possible categorical imperative." [36] These reflections lead Kant to the claim that "man and generally any rational being exists as an end in himself, not merely as a means to be arbitrarily used by this or that will, but ... must be always regarded at the same time as an end." [37]

Kant begins to try to make good this claim by saying that if there is to be a categorical imperative, it must be one which "being drawn from the conception of that which is necessarily an end for everyone because it is *an end in itself,* constitutes an objective principle of the will." This principle, he goes on, must be built on the notion that "[a] rational nature exists as an end in itself." [38] Kant's proof of this is, strictly speaking, "intersubjective" rather than "objective": men necessarily (he says) conceive their own existence as an end-in-itself, but every other rational being regards its existence in the same way, "so that it is at the same time an objective principle from which as a supreme practical law all laws of the will must be capable of being deduced." [39] In view of this Kant reformulates the categorical imperative (which in its original version had insisted only on willing one's maxims as "universal" laws) [40] to read: "so act as to treat humanity, whether in thine own person or in that of any other, in every case as an end withal, never as means only." [41] (Even at this point, plainly enough, Wolff would have difficulty in representing as "Kantian" the notion that autonomy *qua* "the refusal to be ruled" is the primary obligation of man.)

After adducing a few examples, Kant goes on to say that the idea of men as ends-in-themselves is not merely derived from "experience" because it does not "present humanity" as an arbitrary and contingent end (self-proposed "at pleasure") which may or may not be adopted, but as the "supreme limiting condition of all our subjective ends." [42] He then introduces, however, a distinction between "objective" and "subjective" principles, which probably accounts for Wolff's ability to replace "objective ends" with "autonomy, the refusal to be ruled" as the "content" of Kant's ethics:

> The objective principle of all practical legislation lies . . . in the rule and its form of universality which makes it capable of being a law . . . ; but the subjective principle is in the end; now by the second principle, the subject of all ends is each rational being inasmuch as it is an end in itself. Hence follows the third practical principle of the will . . . the idea of the will of every rational being as a universally legislative will. [43]

This formulation appears to put the "objective principle" above the "subjective" one; since, however, it is the "subjective" *end* (men as ends-in-themselves) which provides universal maxims with a nonarbitrary "content," the "subjective" element of this formulation is essential if one is not to leave "ends" out of Kant's ethics and fall back on something else—for example, autonomy as the "primary obligation" of man. This difficulty, however, will be returned to shortly.

Kant next relates his argument to what he had said about the will. The reformulated categorical imperative is a "law of one's own giving," a law legislated by one's own will, but not in terms of a mere "interest" such as happiness. The moral laws to which a man is "subject," he urges, are given by his own will—a will which, however, is "designed by nature to give universal laws." A will which determines itself by laws which recognize objective ends is *autonomous,* Kant says, while one which makes merely contingent ends the maxims of its action is *heteronomous.*[44] (Here, as is evident, "autonomy" is *defined* in terms of willing a certain kind of end— namely, respect for persons *as* ends—and not in terms of refusing to be ruled.)

The idea of the will as universally legislative (in terms of objective ends) leads, Kant then suggests, to the concept of a "kingdom of ends." This "kingdom" or "realm" he defines as "a systematic union of rational beings by common objective laws." In language reminiscent of Rousseau, Kant argues that a rational being belongs to such a kingdom as a member when he is subject to its laws, and that he belongs to it as a "sovereign" when, "while giving laws, he is not subject to the will of any other." He goes on to show that in such a kingdom of ends, which is only an "ideal," everything has either a value or a dignity; whatever has mere value can be replaced by something of equivalent value, but that which is the condition of anything else's *having* a value—that is, man—has dignity.[45]

Following this Kant sums up his whole argument in a way which it is essential to examine, since it shows clearly why his critics (and even quasi-followers such as Wolff) have not always seen that Kantian ethics does involve an "end." All of the formulations of the categorical imperative, Kant insists, "are at bottom only so many formulae of the very same law." All maxims which follow the categorical imperative, he says, are characterized by

> 1. A *form,* consisting in universality; and in this view the formula of the moral imperative is expressed thus, that the maxims must be so chosen as if they were to serve as universal laws of nature.
> 2. A *matter,* namely, an end, and here the formula says that the rational being, as it is ... an end in itself, must in every maxim serve as the condition limiting all merely relative and arbitrary ends.
> 3. A *complete characterization* of all maxims by means of that formula, namely, that all maxims ought, by their own legislation, to harmonize with a possible kingdom of ends.[46]

Now the problem here is obvious: what Kant calls a "matter" in Part II. is at other times called "subjective"; and immediately below the very passage just quoted he says that while it is better to start from the "formula" of the categorical imperative (the principle of universality), it is "useful" to consider the other factors as well (that is, the matter or "end" of a maxim, and the complete characterization of all maxims) in order to bring the moral law "nearer to intuition." There are problems, then, in Kant, if one regards even *objective* ends-in-themselves as something introduced into the "higher" notion of formal universality merely in order to "gain entrance" for morality, intuitively conceived. And Kant himself sometimes seems to invite this, above all in the *Critique of Practical Reason,* where he insists that the moral law is simply formal and "abstracts as a determining principle from all matter—that is to say, from every object of volition." [47] (Given this, one can understand why Wolff might want to leave man *qua* "end" out of account, since an "end" would seem to be an "object of volition.") Since, however, Kant also insists on the notion of an "independently existing end" which one must "never act against," on the "dignity of man as a rational creature," [48] it is at least possible that the three elements of a moral maxim—the (universal) form, the matter (or end), and the "complete characterization"—are all *necessary,* and no one of them sufficient (e.g., the form alone). This interpretation, though far from irresistible, is supported by an important passage from Kant's *Tugendlehre:*

> Since there are free actions, there must also be ends to which, as objects, those actions are directed. But among these ends there must be some which are at the same time (i.e., by their very concept) duties. For if there were no such ends, and since no action can be without an end, all ends for practical reason would always be valid only as means to other ends, and a categorical imperative would be impossible. Thus the doctrine of morals would be destroyed. [49]

If this is the case—and it is Kant himself who is saying that morality would be *destroyed* if there were no objective ends to serve as the "object" of the categorical imperative—and if what is "subjective" in a maxim (the end) is not inferior to what is "objective" (the form), but is only a different and essential aspect of a completely characterized maxim, then Kant's moral philosophy is only somewhat problematical, but neither the piece of arid formalism that Hegel said it was nor a system in which autonomy *constitutes* the "end" of morality. Even though Kant's proof of the validity of an objective end-in-itself in the *Groundwork* is intersubjective rather than (as he hoped) objective—since it rests on everyone's having the same view of himself as an ultimate end—the argument is at least persuasive, if not as decisive as Kant may have imagined. H. J. Paton, in his splendid *The Categorical Imperative,* has perhaps given Kant's position its most forceful expression. After granting that Kant, in speaking of the idea of an end-in-itself, is "manifestly extending the meaning of the word 'end,' " Paton goes on to say that

> An objective and absolute end could not be a product of our will; for no mere product of our will can have absolute value. An end in itself must therefore be a self-existent end, not something to be produced by us. Since it has absolute value, we know already what it must be—namely, a good will. This good or rational will Kant takes to be present in every rational agent, and . . . hence . . . every rational agent as such, must be said to exist as an end in itself.[50]

This interpretation gains additional force when one notes that Kant says, in the *Groundwork,* that it is the fitness of a person's maxims for universal legislation which "distinguishes him as an end in itself," which gives him dignity as a willing sovereign in a kingdom of ends.[51] This serves to relate the good will (which was initially defined simply as an undetermined faculty of willing universally) to the notions of "dignity" and of "objective end": the good will has dignity because it is capable of willing the objective end, that is, the dignity of men as "independently existing" ends. Dignity is then both something the will *has,* and something it *respects* in its volitions.

It is not, however, only in the *Groundwork of the Metaphysics of Morals* that Kant tries to defend the notion of an end which is not derived from inclination, happiness, or utility. Indeed, his most subtle and imaginative defense of the idea of men as ends-in-themselves—a defense which shows plainly that for Kant autonomy *qua* the refusal to be ruled is *not* the "end" which gives us a "primary obligation"—is to be found in the *Critique of Judgment.* In Part II of this remarkable work, which is concerned *(inter alia)* with the possibility of purposiveness in an apparently "mechanical" world, with showing that while purposiveness cannot be shown actually to exist in a way that satisfies the "determinant" judgment, it can at least be presupposed by human "reflective" judgment in its effort to make the world intelligible to itself, Kant urges that while the "purposes" of things in the natural world (e.g., the "purposes" of plants or animals) are imputed by us to those things (which certainly cannot themselves conceive purposes), man is the ultimate purpose of creation on earth because "he is the only being upon it who can form a concept of purposes, and who can by his reason make out of an aggregate of purposively formed things a system of purposes." [52]

Now if Kant is right in believing that "lower" beings cannot conceive worth or purpose or final ends (let alone conceive of *themselves* as unconditioned ends), and that God is deduced out of the concept of moral perfection (rather than the reverse), then men as persons, as moral beings, will be the only "unconditioned" thing in nature, and will have to serve as ends-in-themselves if there is to be any such thing. This is why Kant can say, again in the *Critique of Judgment*, that it is not open to us, in the case of man as a moral agent, to ask the question, for what end does he exist? "His existence," Kant argues, "inherently involves the highest end." [53] This is true, he grants, only if nature is considered as a teleological system, in which one mounts from things which are conditioned (caused) to that which is unconditioned: everything in a purposive nature is caused, except man as a *noumenal* being, for his will is an uncaused causality and hence "qualifies him to be a final end to which all of nature is teleologically subordinated." [54] What this means is that for Kant not God but the moral law—which only men can certainly know and (sometimes) follow—is the "final cause" of creation considered as teleological; man would thus be an end-in-himself because he is the only being capable of conceiving and following the sole *unconditioned* end that can be known.

What is particularly impressive about this argument—which is at once the most bold and the most persuasive of Kant's arguments about men as ends-in-themselves—is that it is spun purely and simply out of the concept of purposiveness itself; that it relies on nothing more than asking *what* kind of concept "purpose" or "end" is, and *who* is able to conceive such a concept (and himself as the "subject" of the concept). It is the most beautifully economical argument one can imagine. And the reason that, in the end it is more persuasive than the argument of the *Groundwork* is that in that work Kant *begins* by arguing that a categorical imperative treating men as ends must be "drawn from the conception of that which is necessarily an end for everyone because it is an end in itself," but finishes by reversing the argument, such that the notion of men-as-ends is an end in itself *because* it is an end *for* everyone (since everyone conceives himself as an end). In the *Groundwork,* then, Kant's hoped-for "objective" principle is replaced by a kind of universal intersubjectivity. But in the *Critique of Judgment,* where the argument about men-as-ends arises directly out of the concept of an end, out of a consideration of what such a concept means and who could conceive it, Kant does not have to worry about universal intersubjectivity taking the place of objectivity—except of course in the sense that judgments about purposiveness are "reflective" and not "determinant."

The arguments for objective ends in the *Groundwork* and (above all) in the *Critique of Judgment* are certainly the most impressive ones that Kant produces; it is worth pointing out, however—particularly to those who would make autonomy a Kantian "primary obligation"—that in other important works he at least alludes to these arguments. In the late *Anthropology,* for example, he declares that man is "his own last [final] end"; [55] and in *Theory and Practice* he reënforces the view that he is trying to exclude only "empirical" ends (but not all ends) from his moral philosophy when he says that "not every end is moral (that of personal happiness, for example, is not); the end must be an unselfish one." [56] Perhaps, in the end (so to speak), Kant's whole position on the question of man as an end-in-himself, problematical as it is, is best summed up in his *Tugendlehre:*

> Man in the system of nature ... is a being of little significance and, along with the other animals, considered as products of the earth, has an ordinary value. ...
>
> But man as a person, i.e. as the subject of a morally practical reason, is exalted above all price. For as such a one *(homo noumenon)* he is not to be valued merely as a means to the ends of other people, or even to his own ends, but is to be prized as an end in himself.[57]

And this same *Tugendlehre* is of the greatest importance in showing that for Kant there are ends "which are at the same time (i.e., by their very concept) duties"—those duty-giving ends being "one's own perfection and the happiness of others." [58] While one cannot treat here Kant's detailed working out of these "ends which are duties," it is at least clear that *neither* of those dutiful ends involves "autonomy" *qua* "the refusal to be ruled"—except, again, in the wholly nonpolitical sense that one's own perfection would require that one not permit himself to be "ruled" by his inclinations. And since for Kant there are duty-giving ends which relate to *others*—here one thinks particularly of the duty to respect others and of the duty to promote "the happiness of others"—a truly Kantian ethics *cannot* fall into the Wolffian dilemma of treating one's own autonomy as "the primary obligation of man"; hence on an authentically Kantian view obligations to others cannot be merely "secondary," or intelligible only *in the light of* refusing to be ruled. For nowhere does Kant say that "autonomy, the refusal to be ruled" is an "end which is at the same time a duty."

IV

It should now be possible to treat quite briefly the claim made near the beginning of this paper—namely, that "one could say that respect for the autonomy of everyone necessitates a legal order insofar as 'respect' is only an imperative rather than a fact." Now Kant, indeed, does say something very much like this; there is no trace of anarchism in his political and legal theory.

The reason that one has a duty, for Kant, to enter into what he calls a "juridical state of affairs," is that moral freedom involves both the "negative" freedom of the will from "determination by sensible impulses," and the "positive" freedom of a will which is determined by reason itself (i.e., to respect the dignity of persons as ends-in-themselves); negative freedom is thus instrumental to (or the condition of) positive freedom.[59] If this is the case, and if "public legal justice" can remove or control some of the objects which can incline the human will to be shaped by "impulse"—if politics can control, for instance, a fear of violence which might lead one to violate the categorical imperative—then politics is supportive of morality because it advances negative freedom. This point is made best by Kant himself in the first Appendix to *Eternal Peace:* government, or public legal justice, he suggests, by putting an end to outbreaks of lawlessness, "genuinely makes it much easier for the moral capacities of men to develop into an immediate respect for right." For everyone believes, Kant goes on, that he would always conform his conduct to what is right if only he could be certain that everyone else would do likewise; and "the government in part guarantees this for him." By creating a coercive order of public legal justice, then, "a great step is taken *toward* morality (although this is still not the same as a moral step), towards a state where the concept of duty is recognized for its own sake." [60]

Kant reenforces these views—none of which seems to involve an endorsement of anarchism—in the *Anthropology,* in which he supplies what one might call a "psychology of government." The "mania for domination," he argues, "is intrinsically unjust and its manifestation provokes everyone to oppose it. Its origin, however, is fear of being dominated by others: it tries to avert this by getting a head start and dominating them." [61] (Surely this is a perfect instance of the "asocial" side of "asocial sociability" which Kant describes in his *Idea for a Universal History!)* [62] But domination, he goes on, "is a precarious and unjust means of using others for one's purposes: it is imprudent because it arouses their opposition, and it is *unjust* because it is contrary to freedom under law, to which everyone can lay claim." [63] Government, which provides "freedom under law," can *manage* this psychology: it can alleviate our desire to dominate others (out of fear that they will dominate us) by creating a system of public legal justice in which only law is coercive; thus both the *fact* of domination and the *fear* of domination can be (at least) moderated by government. And this may make it more nearly possible to exercise a good will, to respect the dignity of others as "ends."

These passages alone should make it clear enough that Kant, far from being an "anarchist" in virtue of his theory of autonomy, thought government and law to be essential as a context or environment for morality; but a few additional lines from *The Metaphysical Elements of Justice* will make this plainer still. Indeed in that work he declares flatly that it can be said "of the juridical state of affairs that all men ought to enter into it if they ever could (even involuntarily) come into a relationship with one another that involves mutual rights." [64] So clear did this "ought" seem to Kant that he even permitted himself to say—rather surprisingly—that "everyone may use violent means to compel another to enter into a juridical state of society." [65] And this is the case because "if legal justice perishes, then it is no longer worthwhile for men to remain alive on this earth." [66] Now this is not anarchism; and, indeed, one could sooner accuse Kant of putting up with *any* kind of legal order which provided the most *minimal* "context" for morality, than of being a partisan of anarchism.[67] The real question is not whether he was an anarchist—very plainly he was not—but whether he provided a political and legal theory adequate to serve as the instrument of (his own) morality. This question, however, cannot be pursued in a piece whose aim is simply to show that one cannot borrow the cloak of Kant's legitimacy as an ornament for Wolff's "groundwork."

V

It is *only* by conceiving autonomy as a substantive duty, as a "primary obligation" which requires that one "refuse to be ruled," that one could possibly represent a theory of anarchism based on autonomy as "Kantian." But this "Kantianism" vanishes when one unwraps the cloak of Kant's legitimacy from *In Defense of Anarchism* and sees that this conception is a misconception. Thus it is heartening to see that much of this misconception is either abandoned or moderated in Wolff's new and very instructive commentary on Kant's *Groundwork,* which he has entitled *The Autonomy of Reason.* With a refreshing and admirable candor which seems to be missing in the more dogmatic *In Defense of Anarchism,* Wolff says that "I find Kant's treatment of the principle of autonomy perplexing . . . my real problem is that . . . despite some very strong contrary indications, Kant turns out not to be saying what I personally want him to say." [68] Now what Wolff "wants" Kant to do is to stick to a particular definition of autonomy which he put forward in the *Groundwork*—a definition which Wolff takes to be "the classic explication of the concept of autonomy." [69] Wolff begins by citing Kant himself: "The will is therefore not merely subject to the law, but is so subject that it must be considered as also *making the law* for itself and *precisely on this account* as first of all subject to the law (of which it can regard itself as the author)." [70] And in his gloss on this passage Wolff urges that "the words which I have italicized in this passage are the heart of the concept of autonomy. From them, I believe, flow the most far-reaching consequences for politics as well as for ethics"—consequences which he thinks the reader will find in *In Defense of Anarchism,* which he cites in a footnote.[71] In representing the "Kantian" autonomous man as "making the law for himself"—a quasi-existentialist representation which leaves out of account the fact that Kant simply treated autonomy as a hypothetical "property" of a free will, and which ignores the fact that one cannot "make" moral law if it is already *there* (in the form of a duty to respect the dignity of others as ends-in-themselves)—Wolff acknowledges that he is insisting on what (he thinks) Kant *ought* to have said, rather than on what Kant actually did say. For if one looks at the next part of "the classic explication" of autonomy, Wolff says, "it becomes clear that acting only on laws that one has given to oneself and being bound by them only because one has so given them is not at all what Kant has in mind!" [72] Instead, he grants, the notion of autonomy, far from meaning *simply* "giving laws to oneself," seems merely to mean "legislating disinterestedly, that is to say, legislating independently of or in abstraction from the particular interests of the agent." [73] And Wolff finds this "unsettling" [74]—which indeed it is, if one thinks of autonomy as a "primary obligation" and as a capacity to "make" law, but which it is not if autonomy is simply a hypothetical property of the will and involves nothing more than recognizing (and applying to oneself and others) the single "objective end" which is "also a duty."

Since he finds it "unsettling" that Kant fails to define autonomy in the way that he "wants," and since he holds that autonomy must be seen as a "primary obligation" which involves "making" law and "refusing to be ruled," Wolff professes to find "two incompatible doctrines" at the heart of Kant's moral philosophy:

> On the one hand, he belives that there are objective, substantive, categorical moral principles which all rational agents ... acknowledge and obey. If this is true, then the notion of self-legislation seems vacuous. On the other hand, he believes (I think correctly) that rational agents are bound to substantive policies only insofar as they have freely chosen those policies. But if this is true, then one must give up the belief in objective substantive principles and recognize that the substance or content of moral principles derives from collective agreements to freely chosen ends.

Now this extreme "contractarian" interpretation of Kant's ethics is simply insupportable; even if Kant is *sometimes* a quasi-contractarian in his political theory, he is not in his moral philosophy.[76] Kant never says, with Rousseau, that "the engagements which bind us to the social body are obligatory only because they are mutual"; [77] on the contrary, his notion that the "objective end" of respect for the dignity of persons *as* ends constitutes everyone's duty is aptly summarized in his claim that among laws "those to which an obligation can be recognized *a priori* by reason are *natural laws*" [78]—that is, not laws "made" by "collective agreements."

Wolff could not think that autonomy and "objective moral principles" constitute "two incompatible doctrines" in Kant unless he first defined autonomy in terms of *making* law and of *refusing* to be ruled; but that of course is what he has done. And as a result he has represented as an inconsistency *in Kant* a "problem" which arises wholly out of the fact that Kant fails to say (by Wolff's own admission) what he "wants" Kant to say. Hence the misrepresentation of Kant as a contractarian in moral philosophy who believed that "men are bound by substantive policies only insofar as and only because they have legislated those policies themselves." [79] (This is not only an inaccurate account of Kant's ethics; it is even an inaccurate account of his quasi-contractarian politics, which does *sometimes* rely on the "Idea of the original contract." [80] It is an account which turns Kant into Rousseau.)

But it is "no accident" that Wolff is reduced to offering such a contractarian account of Kant's ethics; it is an inevitability, given Wolff's view of the (non)viability of the notion of "ends" in Kant's philosophy. "How," Wolff asks, "might Kant go about demonstrating the existence of an end in itself?" And the answer is that "strictly speaking, he offers no argument at all." [81] After citing Kant's injunction to "act in such a way that you always treat humanity, whether in your own person or in the person of any other, never simply as a means, but always at the same time as an end," Wolff observes that while Kant has "touched the very heart of morality," it is nonetheless "very difficult to tell what Kant means by the injunction to treat humanity as an end-in-itself." [82] Now there is no doubt that this *is* problematical, and that one must look outside the *Groundwork*—particularly to the *Critique of Judgment*—in trying to decide what Kant means by an end-in-itself; nonetheless in *The Autonomy of Reason* Wolff succeeds in making persons *qua* ends not merely a "difficult" notion, but a virtually unintelligible one. At one point he says the following:

> Presumably, what Kant means by treating humanity as an end-in-itself is that I must never fail to take account of the fact that I am dealing with rational moral agents rather than things. In short, I must keep in mind that *they* have purposes too. This in turn involves respecting their purposes, rather than ignoring them.
>
> Now, however true this injunction may be—and I believe it is the very bedrock of morality—we are still without the substantive criterion that Kant seeks. For consider: either respecting the purposes of other moral agents means making their purposes my own, in which case I am implicated in their pursuit of immoral ends; or it means making their *moral* purposes my own, and I am left to discover a criterion for distinguishing good from bad purposes.[83]

But Kant does not suggest that we take others' purposes *as our own;* he argues that we should respect others *as ends.* And that will involve not treating them as mere means to some arbitrary purpose: that is, not killing or robbing or deceiving others with a view to pleasure or convenience. It is not only not *difficult* to make this intelligible, it is one of the more straightforward tasks in interpreting Kant. If, for example, on entering one's box at the theater, one slaps the attendant across the face with a view to demonstrating one's social "superiority," one is treating him as a means to a "relative" end; but if one simply permits him to perform his normal functions, one treats him "at the same time" as an end. Admittedly the notion of treating others as ends is often "negative" in Kant: it involves not killing, not robbing, not deceiving, and so forth.[84] Even so, this is an intelligible moral "content," and one which is not so "difficult" that one needs to fall back on a contractarian interpretation of Kant, or to suggest that in Kantianism one might have to take others' immoral purposes as one's own.

Despite this "difficulty," *The Autonomy of Reason* is at least a wholly candid exposition of what Kant actually said—coupled with suggestions about what he "ought" to have said. It constitutes an advance on *In Defense of Anarchism* because it separates the real Kant from a reconstructed and improved Kant. And if one fixes his attention on what Kant actually said, it turns out that autonomy is a hypothetical property of a free will, not a substantive moral duty; that there is thus—at least on Kantian grounds—no "primary obligation" to be autonomous, to "refuse to be ruled"; that since there is no obligation to refuse to be ruled—to be an anarchist, when unanimous direct democracy is impossible—there is in fact an obligation to recognize government and law as providers of a "context" within which a good will is more nearly possible; that for Kant the substantive moral duty which is *not* constituted by autonomy *is* constituted by the duty to respect others as ends-in-themselves; that in view of this all duties *cannot* be "duties to oneself." If, in short, one removes the cloak of Kant's legitimacy from Wolff's groundwork, one finds that that cloak does not profit from being draped around something else—even a something else constructed by one who grants that Kant "correctly identified the principal problems of moral philosophy and . . . had some genuine insight into their solution." [85]

NOTES

1. Robert Paul Wolff, *In Defense of Anarchism* (New York, 1970), pp. 21 ff.
2. Ibid., pp. 18-19, 21ff.
3. Ibid., p. ix.
4. On this point cf., *inter alia,* the author's "On Kant as the Most Adequate of Social Contract Theorists," *Political Theory* (November 1973). In the present essay the author has drawn freely on this earlier work, particularly in sections II and III—not so much because the earlier work is unsurpassable, but because the author cannot presently surpass it.
5. Kant, *The Metaphysical Elements of Justice,* trans., John Ladd (Indianapolis, 1965), pp. 75 ff. For a full treatment of this point, cf. Section IV of this essay.
6. Wolff, *In Defense of Anarchism,* pp. 12-19; Kant, *Fundamental Principles of the Metaphysics of Morals,* trans. Abbott (Indianapolis, 1949), pp. 45-46. (Hereafter the Abbott translation of the *Grundlegung,* will be cited as *Groundwork,* ed. Abbott, in order to bring Abbott's terminology into line with Wolff's. Obviously one can render *Grundlegung* as *Groundwork, Fundamental Principles,* or *Foundations.*)
7. In his new *The Autonomy of Reason* (New York, 1973), which is a

commentary on Kant's *Groundwork,* Wolff makes it clear that he finds the notion of men as ends-in-themselves "difficult" (pp. 173 ff.). For a full treatment of this point, cf. Section V of this essay.

8. Cf. Section IV of this essay.

9. *Groundwork,* ed. Abbott, p. 11.

10. Kant, *Critique of Practical Reason,* trans. L. W. Beck (Indianapolis, 1956), p. 33.

11. Cf. the author's "How Coherent Is the Social Contract Tradition?" in *Journal of the History of Ideas* (September-December 1973); his "Will and Legitimacy in the Philosophy of Hobbes," in *Political Studies* (Oxford [December] 1973); his "Locke on 'Voluntary Agreement' and Political Power," in *Western Political Quarterly* (March 1976); and his "A Possible Explanation of Rousseau's General Will," *American Political Science Review* (March 1970).

12. *Groundwork,* ed. Abbott, pp. 44 and 63.

13. Kant, *Critique of Practical Reason,* trans. Abbott (London, 1923), p. 222.

14. *Groundwork,* ed. Abbott, p. 63.

15. Ibid., pp. 63 ff.

16. Ibid.

17. Cf. the pieces on Hobbes and Locke mentioned in note 11 above.

18. Cf. the piece above on Hobbes mentioned in note 11.

19. Nietzsche, *The Twilight of the Idols,* in *The Portable Nietzsche,* trans. W. Kaufmann (New York, 1954), p. 484.

20. Kant, *Critique of Practical Reason,* in *The Philosophy of Kant,* ed. C. J. Friedrich, (New York, 1949), p. 238.

21. *Groundwork,* ed. Abbott, pp. 5-8.

22. Ibid., p. 72.

23. Ibid., p. 73.

24. Hobbes, *Leviathan,* Ch. XXI: "Every act of man's will, and every desire, and inclination proceedeth from some cause, and that from another cause, in a continual chain, whose first link is in the hand of God the first of all causes." (Oakeshott ed., p. 138.)

25. *Groundwork,* ed. Abbott, pp. 64-65.

26. Ibid., p. 65.

27. Ibid., p. 68.

28. Ibid., p. 69.

29. Ibid., pp. 70-71.

30. Ibid., p. 75.

31. Ibid., p. 76.

32. Kant, *Critique of Practical Reason,* in *The Philosophy of Kant,* ed. Friedrich, p. 241.

33. Kant, *The Metaphysical Elements of Justice,* p. 22.

34. This, however, is how Wolff interprets Kant in *The Autonomy of Reason;* see Section V of this essay.

35. Cf. the author's article mentioned in note 4 above.

36. *Groundwork,* ed. Abbott, p. 45.

37. Ibid.

38. Ibid., p. 46.

39. Ibid.

40. Ibid., pp. 19-21. The various "stages" and "transitions" within the *Groundwork* are extremely well explained by Wolff in *The Autonomy of Reason,* pp. 24 ff.

41. *Groundwork,* ed. Abbott, p. 46.

42. Ibid., p. 48.

43. Ibid.

44. Ibid., pp. 49-50.

45. Ibid., p. 50.

46. Ibid., p. 53.

47. Kant, *Critique of Practical Reason,* trans. Abbott, p. 204.

48. *Groundwork,* ed. Abbott, pp. 53-55.

49. Kant, *Tugendlehre,* trans. J. Ellington as *The Metaphysical Principles of Virtue* (Indianapolis, 1964), pp. 42-43. For a discriminating discussion of the question whether Kant's ethics is "deontological" or "teleological," see John Atwell, "Objective Ends in in Kant's Ethics," in the *Archiv für Geschichte der Philosophie* (Berlin, 1974), Band 56, Heft 2.

50. H. J. Paton, *The Categorical Imperative* (London, 1947), pp. 168-69.

51. *Groundwork, ed. Abbott, p. 55.*

52. Kant, *Critique of Judgment,* in *The Philosophy of Kant,* ed. Friedrich, pp. 348-49; cf. Kant's *Uber den Gebrauch Teleologischer Prinzipien in der Philosophie,* in *Immanuel Kant: Werke in Sechs Bänden,* ed. W. Weischedel (Wiesbaden, 1957), Vol. V, pp. 165 ff.

53. Ibid. *(Judgment),* p. 354.

54. Ibid.

55. Kant, *Anthropologie in Pragmatischer Hinsicht,* 3d ed. (Königsberg 1820), Vorrede, p. iii: "Der Mensch . . . sein eigner letzter Zweck ist." (There is, finally, a fine translation of the *Anthropology,* done by Mary Gregor [the Hague, 1974]; cf. the author's review of this edition in *Political Theory,* 1976.)

56. Kant, *On the Common Saying: "This May be True in Theory, but it does not Apply in Practice,"* in *Kant's Political Writings,* ed. H. Reiss (Cambridge, 1970), p. 65 n.

57. Kant, *Tugendlehre,* trans. Ellington, pp. 96-97.

58. Ibid., p. 43.

59. Kant, *The Metaphysical Elements of Justice,* p. 13.

60. Kant, *Eternal Peace,* in *Kant's Political Writings,* p. 121 n.
61. Kant, *Anthropology from a Pragmatic Point of View,* trans. Gregor, p. 140.
62. Kant, *Idea for a Universal History with a Cosmopolitan Purpose,* in *Kant's Political Writings,* pp. 44-45.
63. Kant, *Anthropology,* p. 140.
64. Kant, *The Metaphysical Elements of Justice,* p. 70.
65. Ibid., pp. 76-77.
66. Ibid., p. 100.
67. On this point, cf. Kant's flat assertion in *Eternal Peace* that "any *legal* constitution, even if it is only in small measure *lawful,* is better than none at all, and the fate of a premature reform would be anarchy" (in *Kant's Political Writings,* p. 118 n). Here, as is evident, anarchism is not favorably treated by Kant.
68. Wolff, *The Autonomy of Reason,* p. 178.
69. Ibid.
70. Ibid.
71. Ibid.
72. Ibid. (The exclamation mark is Wolff's.)
73. Ibid., p. 179.
74. Ibid.,
75. Ibid., p. 181.
76. On this point cf. the author's article mentioned in note 4 above.
77. Rousseau, *The Social Contract,* in *Political Writings,* trans. F. Watkins (Edinburgh, 1953), p. 31.
78. Kant, *The Metaphysical Elements of Justice,* p. 26.
79. Wolff, *The Autonomy of Reason,* p. 181. Whether one should call this position contractarian or existentialist is not altogether clear.
80. Same as note 76 above.
81. Wolff, *The Autonomy of Reason,* p. 174.
82. Ibid., p. 175.
83. Ibid., pp. 175-76.
84. *Groundwork,* ed. Abbott, p. 54: "Since in the idea of a will that is absolutely good without being limited by any condition . . . we must abstract from every end *to be effected* (since this would make every will only relatively good), it follows that in this case the end must be conceived, not as an end to be effected, but as an *independently* existing end. Consequently it is conceived only negatively, that is, as that which we must never act against, and which, therefore, must never be regarded merely as means, but must in every volition be esteemed as an end likewise."
85. Wolff, *The Autonomy of Reason,* p. 4. In his article entitled "A Pseudo-Anarchist Belatedly Replies to Robert Paul Wolff" *(The Journal of*

Critical Analysis [July 1972], Donald Stewart concedes too much when he speaks of the Kantian tradition which Wolff has made his own," but is on sound ground when he speaks of Wolff's "grudging defense" of anarchism (as something recommendable only when unanimous direct democracy cannot be attained). And Stewart's closing observation is striking: "Wolff's insistence . . . upon moral autonomy as the *primary obligation* of man commits him to something very much more radical than mere anarchism; it commits him . . . to a morally aggressive state of nature from which there is no escape, [to a] *bellum morale omnium contra omnes.*"

18

ANARCHISM AND VIOLENCE

APRIL CARTER

The attitudes to violence within the anarchist tradition are complex and contradictory, and the issue remains contentious among anarchists today. In the past the advocates, or at least the defenders, of violence have predominated. There is, however, also an important strand of anarchist thought which has insisted on the intrinsic importance of nonviolence for anarchism. Tolstoy is its most impressive spokesman.[1] This essay is concerned with the question of whether anarchist beliefs logically require adherence to nonviolence, and whether anarchist commitments tend nevertheless to encourage celebration of violence. For the purposes of this discussion it is necessary to assume a minimum set of ideas which comprise the core of anarchist theory, despite the diverse interpretations and emphases of individual anarchist thinkers. Noviolence too has varying connotations, but it is taken here to mean simply a total renunciation of violence, whatever the circumstances.

There are three preliminary grounds for suggesting that anarchists are committed by their own beliefs to renounce violence: the necessary association of violence with the state; the close links between violence and authoritarianism; and the nonviolence implied by anarchist values.

The very concept of the state has violence built into it, as it is suggested by Weber's well-known and often adopted definition of the state as a body having a monopoly of legitimate force within a given territory. Since anarchists reject the notion of legitimacy in relation to the state, they are committed to oppose a monopoly of illegitimate force. The persuasiveness of the anarchist case against the state has been greatly increased by the scale of violence used by some modern states against their own people—the Stalinist terror compared with Tsarist repression, for example—and by the vastly increased capacity for destruction wielded by states as a result of modern science. "Atomic warfare makes anarchists of us all" is seen as a stock generalization by William O. Reichert writing in 1969.[2]

Secondly, anarchists who espouse an anti-authoritarian philosophy cannot ignore the sociological links between violence and authoritarianism. Armies, which are designed to perform certain types of violence, are exceptionally authoritarian and hierarchical types of organization, and if they seek political power are notoriously destructive of parliamentary and liberal regimes. The impact of war undermines civil liberties, and prolonged civil war may result in authoritarian and centralized rule. It can be persuasively argued that the civil war in Russia destroyed popular political energies and enthusiasm and provided the Bolsheviks with the excuse to eliminate all their rivals, so consolidating their dictatorship.

Thirdly, the libertarian and individualistic values of anarchism appear to be basically incompatible with the violent infliction of the most extreme wounds on an individual's body, mind, and spirit and the denial of life. Given a commitment to ensure that we all live life more abundantly, anarchists cannot denigrate the intrinsic value to be placed on life and health. Even Hobbes, the most rigorous philosopher of the necessity of state power, admitted the inherent and irreducible tendency of the "natural man" to resist the threat of chains and execution. Most anarchists are prepared to uphold the absolute rights of this natural man to life and freedom against the claims of conventionally understood social interest and political necessity. If they deny the right of execution to the state in any circumstances there are difficulties in arrogating this right to themselves. Yes!

There are therefore some immediate grounds to assume that anarchist beliefs entail repudiation of certain forms of violence in certain circumstances. Whether the anarchist is required, if consistent in his beliefs, to renounce all forms of violence is examined below. It is, however, necessary at this point to distinguish two different sets of circumstances in which anarchists must articulate their attitudes to violence. Like other minority groups, anarchists have often to decide whether or not they are prepared to give qualified support to political movements whose goals or methods they do not wholly approve, but who represent the cause of progress against racism, colonialism, capitalism, or dictatorship. At this level interesting questions of principle and tactics arise, but the issue of violence is only part of a broader dilemma. This essay does not therefore deal with the question of anarchist attitudes to violence by other organized political groups. Instead it concentrates on anarchist attitudes to violence initiated by anarchists, or violence in popular uprising, which anarchists can wholeheartedly support, although in the latter case complications inevitably arise because of the involvement of other political parties.

There are at least four lines of argument which anarchists might employ to escape the conclusion that they are logically obliged to renounce use of violence:

1. that anarchists oppose the state because it is the supreme embodiment of repression, not because they oppose state violence as such;
2. that the violence adopted by anarchists is different in kind from the violence of the state, and is not therefore inconsistent with anarchist values;
3. that revolutionary violence does not promote authoritiarianism;
4. that even if violence is in principle incompatible with anarchist values, its use is justifiable and inescapable in the pursuit of anarchist goals.

I. VIOLENCE AND REPRESSION

In order to consider the first argument, we need to look at the nature of political repression. There are two ways in which the state suppresses freedom: by indoctrination which "persuades" people to surrender their liberty, and by coercion, including violence, which forces them to do so. It is therefore possible to suggest the hypothetical case in which a repressive regime is maintained solely by brainwashing its citizens from the cradle to the grave, and to claim that anarchists would be as opposed to this regime as one which relied mainly on prison camps and firing squads. This extreme case is, however, both practically and logically impossible, since the total success of indoctrination depends upon the regime's ability to restrict by force any activity which might endanger belief: thus indoctrination requires strict censorship, restrictions on individual freedom of travel, and the forcible elimination of any unexpected eruption of individual rebelliousness, as envisaged in the totalitarian utopias of Zamyatin's *We* and of Orwell's *1984*. Unless the realm of thought and belief is totally closed, there is always the possibility that people will change their minds. If a regime allows people real freedom to alter their ideas it is not in any simple sense relying on indoctrination, nor is it wholly repressive. Indeed a commonsense criterion of the repressiveness of a regime is the degree of force it uses against those who dissent or rebel—this violence is not only a consequence of a repressive ideology, it is part of the meaning of repression. In fact, the anarchist who claims that the truly repressive nature of the state still exists in parliamentary regimes, but is masked by the prevailing ideology, has to point to the brutal violence used against those outside the political consensus—for example, rioting blacks, or to the violence used, when the state feels challenged, against demonstrators or strikers.

If we examine the question whether violence is intrinsic to repression from the standpoint of the individual seeking freedom, we reach the same conclusion. There are well-known difficulties in defining freedom, but it is reasonable to start from the basic assumption that an individual's freedom depends on the absence of immediate and hurtful physical constraints and of extreme sanctions: an individual is freer out of jail than in it; freer without the constant threat or arrest and torture; and freer if he is not in fear for his life. Thus freedom in general increases the more the powers of violence wielded by the state against the individual are restricted, and the more the use of these powers is restricted. Anarchists, instead of looking to the rule of law to maximize personal freedom, look to the total abolition of the organs of state violence.

A slightly different way of approaching the problems of whether anarchists are committed by the logic of their position to regard violence itself as an evil is to ask why anarchists oppose the state. The concept of the state entails three major institutions: bureaucracy, police, and the army. The administrative bureaucracy does not raise the question of violence directly, although it is arguable that the nature of bureaucracy may, by creating psychological remoteness, increase the inhumanity of a prison service, a ministry of the interior, or a defense department. But any critique of the police—although it may also focus on their vested interest in surveillance and control of the population and in restricting civil liberties—must entail a criticism of their methods, whether in suppressing demonstrations or extorting confessions, and on the ways in which the state punishes captured criminals. Violence is even more central to the role of the armed forces. Anarchists may hate war because they see it in Bourne's phrase as "the health of the state" and because wars are waged by powerful elites at the expense of the poor and powerless. However, war means killing and maiming enemy soldiers and civilians who are in the path of war, and destroying towns and villages; and modern war means mass and indiscriminate killing of civilians, if not of whole populations. It is indeed clear from the anarchists' own writings that they loathe the punitive violence of the state because of its barbarity, that they condemn the inhumanity of mass executions and deportations by regimes putting down revolt, and that they are appalled by the cruel and indiscriminate nature of war.[3] Anarchists are not alone in rejecting the more savage forms of punishment and warfare, but their rejection is more total because it is not mitigated by the orthodox justifications in political theory for rule by the sword and *raison d'etat,* and it is more passionate and consistent than criticisms of state violence by liberals and socialists.

It is therefore reasonable to conclude, both from the logic of their position and from the evidence of many anarchist writers, that anarchists believe violence is an evil *as* it is practiced by the state, and not only *because* it is practiced by the state and is used for repressive ends.

II. ANARCHIST VIOLENCE

When considering whether anarchists can claim that the nature of the violence used by their side is qualitatively different from that used by the state, several criteria present themselves: the type of violence used, the spirit in which it is used, the extent of violence used, and whom it is used against. It is of course easy to tilt the argument by contrasting the purest forms of anarchist violence with, for example, the worst atrocities of colonial regimes or the H-bomb, and there are clearly circumstances in which police or military forces do act with restraint and discrimination. Nevertheless, typical forms of anarchist violence can be contrasted with typical forms of state violence. The violence most associated with anarchists, and praised within the anarchist tradition, is the assassination attempt against the individual tyrant and the insurrectionary battle at the barricades, or its rural equivalent of the peasants marching on the local town.

Both types of anarchist violence rely on limited technology—a gun or homemade bomb in the first instance, any weapon which comes to hand in the second—as opposed to the arsenals of destruction available to the armed forces and even the police. Both are heroic forms of violence, involving direct risk to those who take part: the role of the individual assassin acting on his own initiative can be contrasted with the remoteness and corresponding lack of passion and personal responsibility felt by judges who order executions, or generals who order an attack. (This distinction would not of course apply to a conspiratorial organization with its own "generals.") Both can be limited in their extent and discriminate in their targets: assassination attempts are ideally directed against specific individuals who are in some sense guilty of injustice, or at least are in public and powerful positions and representative of a regime; insurrectionary fighting is limited to the forces of the state who attempt to suppress the rebels. They therefore contrast with the indiscriminate killing of most warfare. We have therefore instead of a pacifist philosophy of anarchism a kind of just war theory, in which violence is to be used discriminately for ends which are just.

The validity of anarchist violence must be judged, however, not only by the degree of violence used, but by its effectiveness, by its results (which may be unpredictable and lead to quite uncontrolled violence), and by its influence on the future actions of anarchists and other protesters.

The effectiveness of exemplary acts of violence must presumably be measured by their impact on public opinion, and in particular on the workers and peasants whom anarchists seek to arouse. Political effectiveness is always dependent on the specific context and the precise nature of an action, so simple generalization about the value of propaganda by deed is clearly impossible. Moreover, the opinions of both contemporaries and historians about the short-term or long-term efficacy of various anarchist campaigns of violence have differed—given the difficulties of finding clear evidence and criteria for denoting success or failure in these circumstances, there is a natural tendency to confirm personal predispositions toward or against this type of action. There are, however, certainly reasonable grounds to doubt, in most political contexts, whether an assassin's bomb or an abortive attempt to raise the barricades will further sympathy for the anarchist cause in general, or for specific social goals; and there is therefore even greater doubt whether such action will act as a clarion call to the oppressed to right their wrongs. In a debate about the moral justification for propaganda by deed the onus is clearly on its proponents to show convincingly that it will work.

It is possible to generalize more confidently about the probable repercussions of anarchist violence at the level of governmental response: it is extremely likely that it will be made a pretext for mass arrests, banning of radical movements, and quite possibly the execution of anarchist leaders—as happened frequently in response to anarchist violence in the last decades of the nineteenth century and early years of this century; or it may lead directly to the setting up of the apparatus of a police state, one result of the nihilist assassination campaign in Tsarist Russia.[4] At best it is likely to increase police harassment of radicals and to reduce civil liberties. The just-war doctrine included the principle that the likely benefits must outweigh the probable costs of war; in the case of exemplary anarchist violence the certain costs have usually greatly outweighed the problematic gains.

The greatest disadvantage of the doctrine of limited anarchist violence is that in practice it suffers from much the same weakness as the just war theory itself—that over time the goals tend to be exalted with ideological fervor to justify increasing the scope of violence, while all practical and moral restraints are removed from the actual means used. Thus the selective assassination attempt, directed with great personal risk at the individual tyrant, easily becomes in other hands—including anarchist hands—the bomb tossed into the crowded restaurant on the vague justification that it will mostly kill the bourgeoisie, or simply that it will create a stir. The anarchist campaign in the 1890s declined in this way into indiscriminate slaughter. This objection applies more strongly to the use of bombs than it does to attempts to start a local uprising— though the latter may involve unnecessary destruction. (In terms of contemporary relevance the latter is almost totally outmoded: barricades are only likely to be thrown up as defensive action against the police.) The likelihood of setting in train indiscriminate imitation of acts of exemplary violence is however a crucial objection to sanctioning an initial violent act, which purely in its own terms might claim considerable moral and political justification. It is easier to initiate a habit of violent protest than to limit it, as we are currently relearning.

There is therefore a case for renouncing exemplary forms of anarchist violence on grounds of prudence and of moral responsibility, even if violence is seen as justifiable in principle. A more fundamental objection can, however, be made to any attempt to justify anarchist violence: that anarchist values are inherently and necessarily incompatible with use of violence, given anarchist respect for the sovereignty of the individual and belief in the unqualified rights of each individual. No anarchist society would sanction one execution, let alone mass executions or wars on other societies. It can be urged that the standards of the ideal society cannot be applied to the struggle to realize that society. But anarchists have always rejected the idea that there are two sets of values, one to be applied now and the other reserved to the indefinite future. Anarchism is a creed to be demonstrated in practice. The central anarchist objection to Marxism is that Marxists underline the dichotomy between ends and means, and hence in practice have found endless "realistic" reasons for postponing their alleged goals. (This question is taken up in more detail later.)

Some anarchists might, however, be prepared to argue that the ruling classes of the existing society have forfeited the right to anarchist sympathies and are therefore morally in a separate category. There is a strain in anarchist thought which depicts execution of the oppressors as a positive revolutionary act, and which can be traced from Bakunin through the anarchist assassins to the Durutti column in the Spanish civil war. This tendency to group individuals into abstract social categories, and then to invest certain categories, like the workers, with supreme virtues and others, like the capitalists, with supreme evil is, however, contradictory to the central tenets of anarchist thought. It is true that Emile Henry is credited with the saying that "there are no innocent bourgeois"; but the attitude of mind which classifies groups of people under labels as a prelude to liquidating them can best be described as "totalitarian," in the sense Hannah Arendt intends in her discussion of the logic of totalitarian ideology,[5] not anarchist. The anarchist concern with the concrete individual, rejection of the rights of the majority over the minority, and condemnation of fictitious entities like "the people" used as a guise to take away individual rights, all suggest dislike of political labels. Anarchists also attack the Marxist dogmatism about social classes, which stands in the way of truly humanist and revolutionary attitudes—it is not accidental that Bakunin is also the most Marxist of anarchists, even though he too criticised the exclusiveness of the Marxist class theory. If anarchists distrust political fictions that justify the denial of actual freedoms, they must distrust more a style of thinking which justifies the most final denial of freedom—death. Moreover the logical connection between belief in revolutionary violence and this inhuman and abstract style of ideological thought suggests the danger for anarchists that violence will destroy the spirit of libertarianism.

III. VIOLENCE AND AUTHORITARIANISM

If it is true that the nature of anarchist values should preclude violence, then whether or not violence promotes authoritarianism is a purely secondary issue. It is, however, an issue important in its own right; and, given the primary stress of anarchist thought on freedom as the central value, it is clearly relevant to anarchists who insist on the need for violence. Three major questions can be raised about the connection between violence and authoritarianism: whether the nature of violence requires hierarchical organization; whether the prolonged experience of violence destroys the qualities of popular initiative and resistance upon which anarchists depend; and whether violence encourages authoritarian reactions. It is only possible here to sketch in possible answers.

The intrinsic link between organized violence and authoritarian organization is suggested by the nature of most armies. It is clear that the specifically anarchist forms of violence can escape the need for elaborate organization, and the initial stages of a popular uprising also avoid it, but the problem is directly relevant to civil war.

It is possible to challenge the necessity of military hierarchy for a popular army by suggesting that the traditional gap between officers and other ranks has reflected the divisions of a class society, and that authoritarian discipline is required to make regular soldiers and conscripts kill and risk being killed, whereas revolutionary armies are egalitarian and enthusiastic. Most guerrilla armies have, however, relied on hierarchical organization and have often exacted a discipline even stricter than that of regular armies. Even the anarchist columns in Spain accepted military commanders, although they insisted on democratic forms of decision-making. Whether this method of running an army was militarily efficient is still debatable. Obvious difficulties arose when anarchist columns refused to obey general battle orders, and some anarchists who supported merging the political militias into a regular army thought too much time was lost at the front in discussion. On the other hand George Orwell, as an officer in the POUM militia, was prepared to see the advantages of leadership by democratic persuasion because of the crucial importance to the revolutionary side of the morale and conviction of those fighting.[6]

Anarchists can make the more general point that it is mistaken in all forms of human activity to assume that a hierarchical style of organization will promote genuine efficiency, and they can cite the striking ineffectiveness of hidebound general staffs; for example, in World War I. Nevertheless this anarchist belief in spontaneous and cooperative organization is less persuasive in relation to military activity than it is in other spheres. In peacetime activities it is quite possible that temporary chaos, duplication of effort, and some lapses in organizational efficiency may be compensated for by greater enthusiasm and inventiveness; or, where the situation is more structured but based on democratic principles, that time lost in reaching agreement ensures greater cooperation afterward. But it can be fatal to lose a battle. Large-scale violence does suggest the need for leadership and discipline. So much for large-scale violence!

While the problem of authoritarian organization impinges on

those engaged in violence, the authoritarian tendencies which arise from the experience of violence concern a whole society. It is important to note, however, that wars may have a radicalizing as well as a conservative influence. War justifies concentration of power and suppression of civil liberties, but it has also unleashed revolutionary movements or promoted internal dissent. The radicalizing tendency may be due to the breakdown of old modes of life and disillusionment with the war and the effectiveness of the government—as in World War I. A civil war in its early stages is likely to unleash popular enthusiasm for rapid change, both when a revolutionary party is challenging the old order and when people are rising to the defense of a recent revolution. There is, however, a danger that in the long run war weariness, and the social problems created by war, will sap popular enthusiasm and initiative, promote a reaction away from revolutionary consciousness, and encourage Bonapartism. The demands of military necessity may also undermine original libertarian ideals—true of some of the anarchist leaders in the Spanish civil war.

Sporadic acts of violence are less likely to have any permanent results, though even isolated violent protests may encourage an authoritarian frame of mind, and an extended campaign of violence is certainly likely to encourage popular opinion to sanction destruction of civil liberties and favor savage measures of repression—both reactions have occurred in Britain in response to IRA attacks. The likelihood that anarchist or other political violence will encourage an authoritarian reaction by the government was raised earlier, but it is more important to stress here the impact on popular habits of mind. Anarchists might in tactical terms welcome government repression, but promoting authoritarian habits in society is directly contrary to anarchist goals. There is no absolute necessity that an act of violence will strengthen popular reliance on the state—in some circumstances it might be seen as a blow of deliverance from tyranny—but these circumstances are much rarer than anarchist theorists of violence have assumed.

It can be concluded that there is a tendency for violence to promote forms of authoritarianism for various sociological and psychological reasons, but there are exceptions to this tendency. In itself the connection between violence and authoritarianism is not a sufficient reason for anarchists to abjure all types of violence, though it has a bearing on the problem of ends and means.

IV. THE NECESSITY OF VIOLENCE

Even if violence does contravene anarchist values, many anarchists would be prepared to justify it as a regrettable necessity. Kropotkin is perhaps the most eminent representative of this point of view. The apparent necessity of violence stems from the anarchist commitment to revolution, which cannot be totally nonviolent.

Revolutions pose for anarchists unique opportunities and difficulties: they demonstrate the anarchist ideal of popular spontaneity, but they also require the most rigorous calculations of political necessity. Spontaneity is demonstrated in the actual outbreak of revolution, as in February 1917 in Russia or in Hungary in 1956, and in the creation of popular forms of self-government: factory councils, agricultural communes, or soviets. Political necessity is imposed by other organized political groups. Anarchists in both Russia and Spain found themselves being forced to decide whether or not to support specific political parties and policies. In addition they had to decide whether or not to cooperate with other parties to defend the gains of revolution against attack from the right. So the problem of using violence was compounded by other political compromises simultaneously being forced upon anarchists in the name of realism. Certainly there is considerable historical irony in the fact that many anarchists fought to secure the dictatorship of the Bolshevik party, which effectively crushed all libertarian groups within four years of having come to power; and that even during the Spanish civil war the anarchists were being ruthlessly suppressed by their allies.

The problem of violence in revolution arises at four stages: (1) the initial overthrow of the regime; (2) popular violence in accomplishing social revolution (for example, dispossessing landlords) or in exacting vengeance from hated representatives of the old regime; (3) organized violence against potential counterrevolutionaries; (4) civil war.

The violence used to overthrow a regime can be strongly justified in terms of ends and means when the regime has been very repressive and when the revolution commands such popular support, even in the police and armed forces, that the violence needed is minimal. The difficulty with this defense of revolutionary violence is that it is extremely unlikely that violence will end after this initial stage. If one takes into account the scale of violence which may be entailed in all four stages of the revolution then the destructive effects of the revolution seen as a whole may outweigh the benefits. (It is, of course, debatable whether counterrevolution is inevitable, but it is certainly extremely probable.)

The logic of this view would require anarchists to cease celebrating the glories of revolutionary achievement and to cease propaganda encouraging revolution, and some anarchists have preferred to seek gradual change through persuasion and example rather than rely on the uncertainties of mass action. But it is not possible to rest the argument here, for two reasons. One is that anarchists are correct in identifying the creative and libertarian elements in popular revolution and it is therefore consistent with their overall commitments that they should hope to realise in the future the positive promise of revolution and avoid its worst consequences. Secondly, anarchists are usually in no position to decide whether or not a revolution will occur. Instead they have to react to the new situation created by popular initiative, and their choice is whether to support and seek to influence a living movement or to stand aside in the name of dogmatic purity, because they do not totally approve of everything which has been done. If they give active support, whether or not they actually take up arms, they have some moral responsibility for the violence entailed. But if they stand aside they abandon the opportunity to influence in any way the course of events and to try to prevent violent excesses. It is clearly possible to give qualified support to a revolutionary movement while opposing instances of unnecessary violence or of authoritarianism.

The central problems for anarchists are posed not by spontaneous revolutionary violence but by deliberate and organized violence. Where this takes the form of executing or imprisoning enemies, or potential enemies, then it is the kind of punitive and quasi-judicial violence which anarchists condemned when undertaken by the state. Moreover, organs which become accustomed to meting out "revolutionary justice" are in danger of becoming as oppressive as the police and courts of the old regime—they may indeed be even more arbitrary and tyrannical. The only possible justification for organized violence against supporters of the previous regime is that such action is "necessary," either to appease popular anger or—more cogently—to neutralize potential counterrevolutionaries.

Raising a popular army to fight in a civil war also contains twin dangers: of re-creating in a new guise an instrument of state power, and of engaging in the kinds of violence characteristic of the state. It can of course be claimed that such a war is defensive, and that the case for abandoning overscrupulous concern for principle in the interests of solidarity and political realism is exceptionally strong in these circumstances, whether in Russia or in Spain. But the dilemma involved has already been briefly discussed: will a pro-longed, bloody and bitter civil war inevitably pervert the nature and goals of the revolution?

The argument from necessity raises the question of whether it is consistent for anarchists to justify forms of organized violence by the argument that the end justifies the means. Anarchists are logically precluded from simply adopting a Marxist view of the realistic necessity of violence because of their constant criticism of the Marxists for ignoring the means-end dimension in their strategy of revolution.

V. ENDS AND MEANS

Anarchists reject in principle (if not always in practice) the idea of political leadership, the idea of centralized organization, and the idea of political parties because they see them as corrupting influences, bringing authoritarianism, hierarchy, bureaucracy, and political power into the socialist movement, whose aim is to abolish these phenomena. They have also ever since Proudhon and Bakunin warned against the creation of a new state power after revolution, urging that such a state would inevitably grow into a new instrument of oppression. They are unmoved by arguments based on the political need for strong organization, for political compro-mises to win support, or for the necessity of state power to crush counterrevolution. In the realm of politics they are committed to a utopian stance not only with reference to ends but also to means, shunning contamination with politics in all its conventional forms, refusing to endorse even progressive parties or to take part in elections, however crucial the possible outcome. They therefore repudiate all arguments based on political responsibility, as usually understood, which requires the risk of some personal corruption for the social good, and they deny that it may be necessary to use some forms of political power in order to prevent gross abuses of power. When it comes to violence, however, many anarchists are prepared to use a little violence to prevent greater violence by the state, or even a lot of violence to try to achieve the anarchist vision of society. It would seem that the logic of this approach is that it is worse to cast a ballot than to fire a bullet, even if the ballot is intended to undermine the existing regime.

Anarchists' willingness to use violence whilst eschewing contamination from political power is particularly odd when one remembers that many thinkers have assumed that the most double-edged and dangerous element in political activity is the fact that it may often involve, directly or indirectly, use of violence. Weber, in his essay "Politics as a Vocation," commented that "The early Christians knew full well the world is governed by demons and that he who lets himself in for politics, that is, for power and force as means, contracts with diabolical powers. . . ."[7] Weber was arguing against the idea that the purity of means necessarily ensures the desired goal—but anarchists appear committed to the "ethic of ultimate ends" in their attitudes to conventional politics.

It is open to anarchists to try to show that compromise with political power is more damaging to anarchist ideals than compromise with violence, because for example one compromise with conventional politics leads to further compromises, whereas compromise with revolutionary violence is more finite; or because compromise with politics is more destructive of anarchist utopianism than the more heroic gestures of violence. But given the tendency of violence to lead to further violence and for prolonged violence to promote authoritarianism, it is hard to see how a transitional reliance on the state is regarded as a source of permanent corruption for a revolutionary movement, while a transitional reliance on violence is not. Nor is it clear why anarchists should feel free to make subtle discriminations about the nature of different types of violence and to invoke arguments based on political realism when they make a blanket condemnation of all forms of party and parliamentary politics and take an absolutist position against even temporary involvement in, for example, an election. The utopianism of anarchism logically entails also the utopianism of pacifism, in the sense of rejecting all forms of organized violence.

There are, however, two styles of utopian thinking: one which lays absolute stress on purity of means and excludes all concern with immediate results, and with calculations of political possibility and political gain and loss; and one which is centrally concerned with the relationship between means and ends, but is equally aware of the requirements of political responsibility. The first style of thinking is represented in both the anarchist and pacifist traditions by Tolstoy, whose utopianism depends explicitly on a religious faith. The second is represented by Kropotkin, with his creative ability to propose practical libertarian alternatives to the existing forms of economy and society, and by Gandhi, who developed the method of nonviolent action from an expression of individual conscientious objection into an effective means of mass struggle. This second approach involves some degree of compromise with political realities because it entails political involvement, but sets clear limits to this compromise.

The method of nonviolent action can be presented as a partial answer to the argument that violence is a necessity. It can certainly be argued that nonviolent methods can substitute for propaganda by deed, since civil disobedience, boycotts, strikes, and sit-ins provide means of rousing public attention, challenging the government, and demonstrating modes of action which could be undertaken on a mass scale. (Anarchists might argue that nonviolence can more easily be absorbed and neutralized by the establishment than violence, but this is a question of the tactics and style of protest rather than simply of violence or nonviolence; and nonviolence carries fewer tactical disadvantages precisely because it relies rather more on persuasion, and rather less on coercion and shock tactics.) It can also be argued that nonviolent action provides a *partial* alternative to revolutionary violence. The example of the Gandhian struggle for Indian independence demonstrates that violence is not always necessary to overthrow a regime, and the example of Norwegian resistance to the Nazi-backed Quisling regime suggests that nonviolent resistance can sometimes be used to defend social institutions and social values even if military defeat is acknowledged.[9] It cannot be claimed on the basis of historical experience so far that nonviolent methods can always be a substitute for violence—and even where the political case for nonviolence is strong the psychological case may be weak, since most people still

instinctively identify active resistance with violence. But it is
precisely at the point where the argument reverts to the demands of
realism that the anarchist, like the pacifist, is forced to be utopian
by the logic of his overall position.

VI. ANARCHISM AND PACIFISM

Both anarchism and pacifism are characterized by very similar
forms of utopian thinking, and both have similar strengths and
weaknesses. Their weaknesses are obvious in the inability of both to
speak directly to many immediate political problems and to engage
fully in the politics of responsibility. Their strengths lie in their
ability to challenge conventional and possibly false notions of
political realism, to open up the boundaries of what is possible, and
hence their potential to discover and experiment with alternatives
to authoritarian modes of organization or violent methods of protest
and struggle. The creativity of both the anarchist and nonviolent
traditions depends on their uncompromising absolutism and commitment to purity of means, because without this element of faith it
is difficult to resist the demands of realism. The pragmatic
revolutionary will decide that because a spontaneous movement
showed uncertainty about strategy the answer is to build a
centralized party, or because one civil-disobedience campaign was
unsuccessful that it is time to launch guerrilla warfare.

Given the convergence of views between pacifists and anarchists
on the nature of war, the responsibility of the state for war, and on
the horrors of penal violence, and given the similarity in styles of
thinking, it seems at first sight odd that there is not more overlap
between the pacifist and anarchist movements. The explanation lies
in part in the divergent historical background of the two movements. Woodcock points out that, like other nineteenth-century
radicals, anarchists inherited the image and example of revolutionary violence created by the American and French revolutions.
Secondly, the mainstream of anarchist thought has been closely
associated with the socialist movement, and anarchists have therefore tended to accept the standard Marxist view that pacifism is a
middle-class phenomenon, and a doctrine which by its very stress on
nonviolence objectively supports the status quo and condemns the

oppressed who take up arms. Thirdly, the anarchist epic within the Spanish civil war has made claim to anarchist loyalties and underlined the association between revolution and violence.

There have also been some substantive differences between the standard anarchist and pacifist approaches. Whereas anarchists have regarded governments as enemies to be resisted, pacifists have often put their faith in peace conferences or, in the case of the Quakers, sought to "speak truth to power." In the area of social reform the pacifist tendency has been toward good works, social work, and penal reform, whereas the anarchist has looked to self-help, communal independence, and the abolition of the penal system.

The gap in ideas and attitudes between many anarchists and pacifists narrowed considerably in Britain and the United States in the 1960s, when anarchists had become increasingly concerned with the warmaking capacities of the state, and many pacifists imbibed libertarian ideas and turned to direct action to resist military policies. The unity of the two movements was illustrated by Paul Goodman. This convergence of two traditions could also appeal to a common American inheritance of anarchism and nonviolence: Reichert's article (mentioned above) refers to Thoreau, Ballou, Tucker, Emerson, and Whitman.

The anarchist movement as a whole is, however, still unwilling to repudiate altogether its past associations with violent protest—anarchist-inclined groups have played a role, although relatively a very minor one, in the recent trend toward "guerrilla action"—and to renounce its more significant commitment to revolutionary violence. Although historical memories and myths from the past may partially account for this continuing support of violence, and anarchists are also no doubt open to the influences of the theorists of guerrilla warfare, there is a more substantive reason. Within anarchist thought and values there are elements which are peculiarly receptive to the appeals of violence. Those anarchists who believe, not that violence is an unfortunate necessity to be justified in some circumstances, but that violence carried out by revolutionaries is a positive and liberating act, are clearly immune to arguments in terms of ends and means. Indeed, the value of the violent act may be seen as independent of its results.

VII. THE ROMANCE OF VIOLENCE

It would be possible to explain the anarchist attraction to violence in Weberian terms: that it is the very utopianism of anarchism which encourages belief in the possibility of hastening in the age of gold in one burst of apocalyptic destruction. This view is almost certainly relevant, but it is a critique which extends beyond anarchists to other utopian theorists. There are in fact more specific reasons why anarchists are prone to exalt violence: its Dionysian quality, its associations with the spontaneity of revolution, and the romanticism of heroic violence. All these elements can be found in Bakunin's celebration of revolutionary violence.

The anarchist conception of human nature and of the ideal of human behavior is very varied, but there is an important tendency in anarchist thought—predominant among contemporary anarchists—to celebrate the instinctual and sensual nature of man, which means not only exalting sexual freedom but uninhibited Dionysian frenzy. Murray Bookchin, for example, writes of the Paris Commune "which floated on a sea of alcohol—for weeks everyone in the Belleville district was magnificently drunk," and he links this experience of literally intoxicating freedom to the abandon with which, when faced with defeat, they threw life away and burned down half of Paris fighting to the last.[10] It is inherent in the very nature of the Dionysian festival spirit—certainly when it is the result of casting off habitual repression—that it can promote a destructive as well as joyous passion. Thus spontaneous violence can be seen as a necessary and positive part of revolutionary liberation, not just in defending newly won freedom, but in creating it. A libertarian view of human nature need not be associated with belief in self-expression through violence—Alex Comfort, for example, tends to present sex as an alternative to the thrills of violence—but there is some psychological connection between belief in overthrowing the inhibitions of sex and the inhibitions of violence, especially where both are strictly condemned by "bourgeois morality."

The violence associated with revolution can also be seen as simply one aspect of the spontaneous popular activity generated, a natural prelude to the creative spirit of insurrection. From this perspective violence is a part of a total process, and the value placed on violence stems mainly from the value placed on the popular self-expression and self-organization characterisation of revolutionary outbursts. The importance of violence therefore derives from its historical and emotional associations with the image of popular revolution and as a facet of heroic drama.

There is, however, a sense in which violence quite specifically adds to the romanticism of revolution and to the sense of high drama. Violence is also an essential element in the tragedy of revolutions that have failed. The very concept of the barricades is a romantic and dramatic concept. But it is important to analyze why revolutionary violence is romantic whereas the violence of the state is not. Romantic violence is that of the young or the poor and virtually unarmed who pit their courage and idealism and desperation against the superior arms of the rich, powerful, and ruthless, and against the symbols of political and military might. Where it is successful it wins not because of superior force but for political and psychological reasons: the soldiers disobey their officers, or the government loses heart and gives in. The only real strength usually possessed by revolutionary crowds is that of numbers. Where revolutionary violence is defeated, the tragedy and heroism lie in the unequal nature of the odds: the youth hurling a stone at a tank, or the ill-fed and ragged army fighting against elite divisions and an air force. The epic is not so much of violence as of courage in combating the superior violence of the other side. Indeed violence is romantic in inverse proportion to its military efficiency.

Thus the continuing appeal of violence within the anarchist tradition (and indeed outside it) does not lie solely, or perhaps even primarily, in calculations of the efficiency and necessity of violence from a realistic standpoint. The attraction of Dionysian violence lies rather in the fact that it is spontaneous, reckless, and in a sense irrational, and that it is still seen as the archetypal form of human resistance to oppression and the medium through which heroic values can most fully be expressed. This feeling that there is a positive virtue in violence cannot easily be countered by moral reasoning, considerations of prudence, or the claims of moral and logical consistency, so although anarchist beliefs do require adherence to nonviolence, many anarchists are unlikely to be convinced.

NOTES

1. Tolstoy rejected the label "anarchist" because of its association with violence, but is generally regarded by anarchists as one of their major theorists.

2. William O. Reichert, "Anarchism, freedom, and power," *Anarchy*, 111 (May 1970); reprinted from *Ethics*.

3. See, for example, P. Kropotkin, *Law and Authority;* Emma Goldman, *Anarchism and Other Essays;* Herbert Read, *Anarchy and Order;* Alex Comfort, *Authority and Delinquency in the Modern State*.

4. See historical chapters in George Woodcock, *Anarchism* (London: Penguin, 1963); Irving L. Horowitz, ed, *The Anarchists,* (New York: Dell Publishing Co., 1964); and Richard Pipes, *Russia under the Old Regime* (London: Weidenfeld and Nicolson, 1974), pp. 297-302.

5. Hannah Arendt, *The Origins of Totalitarianism* (London: Allen and Unwin, 1958), pp. 468-74.

6. George Orwell, *Homage to Catalonia* (London: Penguin, 1964).

7. H. H. Gerth and C. Wright Mills, eds. *From Max Weber* (London: Routledge and Kegan Paul, 1964), p. 122.

8. "Utopianism" is used here in the sense of adherence to an ethic of ultimate ends, not in the sense of believing in specific blueprints for the future.

9. On nonviolent action and nonviolent resistance see for example: Joan Bondurant, *Conquest of Violence* (New York: Oxford University Press, 1958), and Gene Sharp, *The Politics of Nonviolent Action,* (Boston: Porter Sargent, 1973).

10. Murray Bookchin, *Post-Scarcity Anarchism* (Wildwood House, 1974), p. 277.

BIBLIOGRAPHY

ROBERT A. KOCIS

This list of works on, or concerning the philosophic issues raised by, anarchism cannot and does not attempt to be comprehensive and exhaustive. It has been compiled with the interests and needs of students of political theory and philosophy primarily in mind. Nicholas Walter's excellent bibliographic note, "Anarchism in Print: Yesterday and Today" in Apter and Joll's *Anarchism Today* (Garden City, N.Y.: Doubleday and Co., 1972), constitutes an important beginning for the researcher. The books listed in the first grouping contain bibliographies. This list attempts to avoid duplication of these works, with the exception of certain classic and primary materials.

I. BOOKS THAT CONTAIN BIBLIOGRAPHIES

Adamic, Louis. *Dynamite: The Story of Class Violence in America.* N.Y.: Chelsea House Publishers, 1968.

Avrich, Paul. *The Russian Anarchists.* Princeton: Princeton University Press, 1967.

Carlson, Andrew. *Anarchism in Germany.* Metuchen, N.J.: The Scarecrow Press, 1972.

Carr, E. H. *Michael Bakunin*. N.Y: Octagon Books, 1975.

Carter, April. *The Political Theory of Anarchism*. N.Y.: Harper and Row, 1971.

David, Henry. *The History of the Haymarket Affair*. N.Y.: Farrar and and Rinehart, 1936.

Guérin, Daniel. *Anarchism: From Theory to Practice*. N.Y.: Monthly Review Press, 1970.

Hoffman, Robert, ed. *Anarchism*. N.Y.: Atherton Press, 1970.

Joll, James. *The Anarchists*. Boston: Little, Brown, 1964.

Krimerman, Leonard, and Lewis Perry, eds. *Patterns of Anarchy*. Garden City, N.Y.: Doubleday, 1966.

Miller, Martin A., ed. *Selected Writings on Anarchism and Revolution: Peter Kropotkin*. Cambridge, Mass.: The M.I.T. Press, 1970.

Nozick, Robert. *Anarchy, State, and Utopia*. N.Y.: Basic Books, 1974.

Ridley, F. F. *Revolutionary Syndicalism in France*. Cambridge: Cambridge University Press, 1970.

Sargent, Lyman T. *New Left Thought: An Introduction*. Homewood, Ill.: The Dorsey Press, 1972.

Stafford, David. *From Anarchism to Reformism*. Toronto: University of Toronto Press, 1971.

Woodcock, George, and Ivan Avakumovic. *The Anarchist Prince: Peter Kropotkin*. N.Y.: Schocken Books, 1971.

II. THE SOCIAL AND CULTURAL CONTEXTS OF ANARCHISM

Arendt, Hannah. *On Revolution*. London: Faber & Faber, 1963.

———. *The Origins of Totalitarianism*. London: Allen & Unwin, 1958..

Aron, Raymond. *Progress and Disillusion: The Dialectics of Modern Society*. London: Pall Mall Press, 1968.

Avineri, Shlomo. *The Social and Political Thought of Karl Marx*. Cambridge: Cambridge University Press, 1968.

Barbu, Zevedei. *Problems of Historical Psychology*. London: Routledge and Kegan Paul, 1960.

Bennis, Warren G., and Philip E. Slater. *The Temporary Society*. N.Y.: Harper and Row, 1968.

Berman, Marshall. *The Politics of Authenticity: Radical Individualism and the Emergence of Modern Society*. N.Y.: Atheneum, 1970.

Bookchin, Murray. *Post-Scarcity Anarchism.* Berkeley: Ramparts Press, 1971.

Boudon, Raymond. *Education, Opportunity, and Social Inequality: Changing Prospects in Western Society.* N.Y.: John Wiley & Sons, 1973.

Bracan, Silvin. *The Dissolution of Power.* New York: Alfred A. Knopf, 1971.

Christie, Stuart, and Albert Meltzer. *The Floodgates of Anarchy.* London: Kahn & Averill, 1970.

Dahl, Robert A. *After the Revolution?: Authority in a Good Society.* New Haven: Yale University Press, 1970.

Ellenburg, Stephen. *Rousseau's Political Philosophy: An Interpretation from Within.* Ithaca: Cornell University Press, 1976.

Fromm, Erich. *The Sane Society.* N.Y.: Rinehart and Co., 1955.

Gellner, Ernest. "How to Live in Anarchy." In I. C. Jarvie and Joseph Agassi, eds., *Contemporary Thought and Politics.* London: Routledge and Kegan Paul, 1974.

Giddens, Anthony. *The Class Structure of Advanced Societies.* London: Hutchinson University Library, 1973.

Goldstene, Paul N. *The Collapse of Liberal Empire.* New Haven: Yale University Press, 1977.

Gurr, Ted Robert. *Why Men Rebel.* Princeton: Princeton University Press, 1970.

Hirsch, Fred. *Social Limits of Growth.* Cambridge, Mass.: Belknap Press, 1976.

Hobsbawm, Eric. *Bandits.* N.Y.: Dell Publishing Co., 1969.

———. *Primitive Rebels.* N.Y.: W. W. Norton, 1959.

———. *Revolutionaries: Contemporary Essays.* N.Y.: Pantheon Books, 1973.

Hoffer, Eric. *The True Believer.* N.Y.: Harper and Brothers, 1951.

Honderich, Ted. *Political Violence.* Ithaca: Cornell University Press, 1976.

Hyams, Edward. *Terrorists and Terrorism.* N.Y.: St. Martin's, 1975.

Joll, James. *The Anarchists.* Boston: Little, Brown, 1964.

Kaplan, Morton, A. *Alienation and Identification.* N.Y.: The Free Press, 1976.

Kelly, Aileen. "Good for the Populists," XXIV *The New York Review of Books* (23 June 1977), 10-15.

Krimerman, L. and L. Perry, eds. *Patterns of Anarchy.* Garden City, N.Y.: Doubleday & Co., 1966.

Lasky, Melvin J. *Utopia and Revolution*. Chicago: University of Chicago Press, 1977.

Lifton, Robert Jay. "The Protean Man" in *History and Human Survival*. N.Y.: Random House, 1968.

Marcuse, Herbert. *One-Dimensional Man: Studies in the Ideology of Advanced Industrial Society*. Boston: Beacon Press, 1964.

Mousnier, Roland. *Peasant Uprisings in Seventeeth-Century France, Russia, and China*. N.Y.: Harper and Row, 1967.

Nisbet, Robert. *Twilight of Authority*. N.Y.: Oxford University Press, 1975.

Nomad, Max. *Apostles of Revolution*. London: Secker and Warburg, 1939.

———. *Aspects of Revolt*. N.Y.: Burns & MacEachern, 1959.

———. *Dreamers, Dynamiters, and Demagogues*. N.Y.: Walden Press, 1964.

———. *Rebels and Renegades*. N.Y.: Macmillan, 1932.

Oakeshott, Michael. *On Human Conduct*. Oxford: Clarendon Press, 1975.

Passmore, John. *The Perfectibility of Man*. London: Gerald Duckworth, 1970.

Pawley, Martin. *The Private Future: Causes and Consequences of Community Collapse in the West*. London: Thames and Hudson, 1974.

Pennock, J. R., and J. W. Chapman, eds. *Participation in Politics: Nomos XVI*. N.Y.: Lieber-Atherton, 1975.

Plamenatz, John. *Democracy and Illusion*. London: Longman, 1973. (Esp. pp. 47-51.)

———. *Karl Marx's Philosophy of Man*. Oxford: Clarendon Press, 1975.

Schaar, John. "Equality of Opportunity and Beyond" in C. J. Friedrich and J. W. Chapman, eds., *Justice: Nomos IX*. N.Y.: Atherton, 1967.

Schwarz, Frederick. *The Three Faces of Revolution: Communism, Radicalism, and Anarchism*. Washington, D.C.: Capitol Hill Press, 1972.

Sennett, Richard. *Fall of Public Man*. N.Y.: Random House, 1977.

———. *The Uses of Disorder*. N.Y.: Knopf, 1970.

Servadio, Gaia. *Mafioso: A History of the Mafia from Its Origins to the Present Day*. N.Y.: Stein and Day, 1976.

Shklar, Judith. *After Utopia: The Decline of Political Faith*. Princeton: Princeton University Press, 1957.

———. *Freedom and Independence: A Study of the Political Ideas of Hegel's "Phenomenology of the Mind."* Cambridge: Cambridge University Press, 1976.

Talmon, J. L. *The Origins of Totalitarian Democracy.* London: Secker & Warburg, 1952.

———. *Political Messianism: The Romantic Phase.* London: Secker & Warburg, 1960.

Taylor, Charles. *Hegel.* Cambridge: Cambridge University Press, 1975.

Trilling, Lionel. *Sincerity and Authenticity.* Cambridge, Mass.: Harvard University Press, 1972.

Voegelin, Eric. *From Enlightenment to Revolution.* John H. Hallowell, ed. Durham: Duke University Press, 1975.

Watkins, Frederick. *The Political Tradition of the West.* Cambridge, Mass.: Harvard University Press, 1950.

Wiles, P. J. D. *Economic Institutions Compared.* N.Y.: John Wiley and Sons, 1977.

Wilson, Bryan. *The Noble Savages: The Primitive Origins of Charisma and Its Contemporary Survival.* Berkeley: University of California Press, 1975.

Wolf, Eric. *Peasant Wars of the Twentieth Century.* N.Y.: Harper and Row, 1968.

Wolin, Sheldon. "The Politics of Self-Disclosure" in *Political Theory,* Vol. 4, No. 3 (August 1976), pp. 321-34.

III. CLASSICAL ANARCHISTS: PRIMARY MATERIALS

A. European:

Anarchy. A monthly journal, Freedom Press, 84b Whitechapel High Street, London, E.1.

Bakunin, Michael. *Bakunin's Writings.* Guy Aldred, ed. N.Y.: Kraus Reprint Co., 1972.

———. *Michael Bakunin: Selected Writings.* Arthur Lehning, ed. N.Y.: Grove Press, 1975.

———. *On Anarchy.* Sam Dolgoff, ed. N.Y.: Random House, 1971.

———. *The "Confession" of Michael Bakunin.* Robert C. Howes, translator. Ithaca, N.Y.: Cornell University Press, 1977.

———. *God and State.* N.Y.: Mother Earth Publishing Assoc., 1915.

———. *The Knouto-Germanic Empire and the Social Revolution.* N.Y.: Mother Earth Publishing Assoc., 1916.

———. *Michel Bakounine et ses relotims slaves.* Annotated by Arthur Lehning. E. J. Brill, 1974.

Berman, Paul, ed. *Quotations from the Anarchists.* N.Y.: Praeger, 1972.

Freedom. A periodical founded and originally edited by Kropotkin. London: Freedom Press, since 1886.

Godwin, William. *Enquiry Concerning Political Justice.* I. Kramnich, ed. Harmondsworth: Penguin Books, 1976.

———. *Things as They Are: Or the Adventures of Caleb Williams.* David McCraken, ed. Oxford: Oxford University Press, 1970.

Grave, Jean. *Moribund Society and Anarchy.* San Francisco: Free Society Library, 1899.

Kropotkin, Peter. "Anarchism," *Encyclopaedia Britannica,* 11th Edition, 1910.

———. *Anarchism: Its Philosophy and Ideal.* London: Freedom Pamphlets, no. 10, 1897.

———. *Anarchist Communism: Its Basis and Principles.* London: Freedom Pamphlets, no. 4, 1891.

———. *The Conquest of Bread.* Edited and with an introduction by Paul Avrich. London: Penguin Press, 1972.

———. *The Essential Kropotkin.* Emile Capouya and Keith Thompkins, eds. N.Y.: Liveright, 1976.

———. *Fields, Factories, and Workshop.* Colin Ward, ed. N.Y.: Harper and Row, 1975.

———. *Kropotkin's Revolutionary Pamphlets.* Roger Baldwin, ed. N.Y.: Vanguard Press, 1927.

———. *Kropotkin: Selections from His Writings.* Herbert Read, ed. London; Freedom Press, 1942.

———. *Law and Authority.* London: Freedom Press, 1886.

———. *Memoirs of a Revolutionist.* N.Y.: Horizon Press, 1969.

———. *Mutual Aid, a Factor in Evolution.* London: Heinemann, 1902.

———. *Selected Writings on Anarchism and Revolution: P. A. Kropotkin.* Martin Miller, ed. Cambridge, Mass.: The M.I.T. Press, 1970.

———. *The State: Its Historic Role.* London, 1903.

———. *The Wage System.* London: Freedom Pamphlets, No. 1, 1899.

———. *War.* London: H. Seymour, 1886.

Proudhon, Pierre-Joseph. *General Idea of the Revolution in the Nineteenth Century.* London: Freedom Press, 1923.

———. *Selected Writings of Pierre-Joseph Proudhon.* Stewart Edwards, ed. London: Macmillan, 1970.

———. *Solution of the Social Problem.* N.Y.: Vanguard Press, 1927.

———. *What Is Property? An Inquiry into the Principle of Right and of Government.* N.Y.: H. Fertig, 1966.

Réclus, Elisée. *Correspondence 1850-1905.* 3 vols. Paris: 1911-1925.

———. *L'Evolution et Révolution.* Geneva: 1884.

Shatz, Marshall, ed. *The Essential Works of Anarchism.* N.Y.: Quadrangle Books, 1972.

Stirner, Max. *The Ego and His Own: The Case of the Individual Against Authority.* J. Carroll, ed. N.Y.: Harper and Row, 1971.

———. *The False Principle of Our Education.* Colorado Springs: R. Myles, 1967.

Tolstoy, Leo. *A Confession and What I Believe.* Oxford: World's Classics, 1921.

———. *The Kingdom of God Is Within You.* N.Y.: Bantam, 1971.

———. *The Law of Violence and the Law of Love.* N.Y.: Bantam, 1971.

———. *Tolstoy's Writings on Civil Disobedience and Non-Violence.* N.Y.: Signet Books, 1967.

———. *What Then Must We Do?* Oxford: Wold's Classics, 1921.

Woodcock, George, ed. *The Anarchist Reader.* Sussex: The Harvester Press, 1977.

B. American:

Berkman, Alexander. *A B C of Anarchism.* London: Freedom Press, 1964.

———. *The Bolshevik Myth.* N.Y.: Liveright, 1953.

———. "Kronstadt: the Final Act in Russian Anarchism," in Irving L. Horowitz, ed., *The Anarchists.* N.Y.: Dell, 1964.

———. *Prison Memoirs of an Anarchist.* Introduction by Paul Goodman. N.Y.: Schocken Books, 1976.

———. *The Russian Tragedy.* Berlin: Der Syndikalist, 1922.

———. *Nowhere at Home: Letters From Exile of Emma Goldman and Alexander Berkman.* Richard Drinnon and Anna Maria Drinnon, eds. N.Y.: Schocken Books, 1976.

Goldman, Emma. *Anarchism and Other Essays.* N.Y.: Mother Earth Publishing Assoc., 1910.

———. *Living My Life.* N.Y.: Knopf, 1931.

———. *Trotsky Protests Too Much.* N.Y.: 1938.

Rocker, Rudolph. *The London Years.* London: Robert Anscombe, 1956.

Spooner, Lysander. *The Collected Works of Lysander Spooner.* Weston, Mass.: M. and S Press, 1971.

———. *Natural Law.* Boston: Williams, 1882.

———. *No Treason: The Constitution of No Authority.* Larkspur, Col.: Pine Tree Press, 1966.

Tucker, Benjamin. *Individual Liberty.* N.Y.: Vanguard Press, 1926.

———. *Instead of a Book, By a Man Too Busy to Write One.* N.Y.: B. R. Tucker, 1893.

Warren, Josiah. *Modern Education.* N.Y., 1861.

———. *Practical Details in Equitable Commerce.* N.Y.: Fowler and Wells Publishers, 1852.

———. *True Civilization.* Boston: J. Warren, 1863.

IV. ANARCHISM AND MARXISM

Bakunin, Michael. *Marxism, Freedom, and the State.* London: Freedom Press, 1950.

Cranston, Maurice. *Political Dialogues.* N.Y.: Basic Books, 1968.

Engels, F. "The Bakuninists at Work." In *The Communist* (published monthly by the Communist Party of the U.S.A.), XVII (February 1938), pp. 143-57.

Gray, Alexander. *The Socialist Tradition: Moses to Lenin.* N.Y.: Harper and Row, 1968.

Horowitz, Irving Louis. "The Theory of Anarchism," in Gould, James, and Willis Truitt, eds., *Political Ideologies.* N.Y.: Macmillan, 1973.

Jackson, J. Hampden. *Marx, Proudhon, and European Socialism.* N.Y.: Macmillan, 1957.

Joll, James. *The Second International.* N.Y.: Praeger, 1956.

Kenafick, K. J. *Michael Bakunin and Karl Marx.* Melbourne, 1948; European distributors, Freedom Press, London.

Kropotkin, Peter. *The Place of Anarchism in Socialist Evolution.* London: W. Reeves, 1886.

Leibzon, Boris Moiseevich. *Anarchism, Trotskyism, Maoism.* Moscow, 1971.

Lenin, V. I. *State and Revolution.* N.Y.: International Publishers, 1932.

Lubac, Henri de. *The Un-Marxian Socialist: A Study of Proudhon.* London: Sheed, 1948.

Luxembourg, Rosa. *Accumulation of Capital.* London: Routledge & Kegan Paul, 1951.

————. *Reform and Revolution.* N.Y.: Three Arrows Press, 1937.

Marx, Engels, and Lenin. *Collected Works on Anarchism and Anarcho-Socialism.* N.Y.: International Publishers, 1972.

Plekhanov, Georgii. *Anarchism and Socialism.* Chicago: C. H. Kerr & Co., 1918.

Read, Herbert. *Existentialism, Marxism, and Anarchism.* London: Freedom Press, 1949.

Sorel, Georges. "The Decomposition of Marxism," in I. L. Horowitz, *Radicalism and the Revolt Against Reason: The Social Theories of Georges Sorel.* London: Routledge & Kegan Paul, 1961.

Stalin, Iosif. *Anarchism or Socialism?* Moscow: Foreign Languages Publishing House, 1951.

V. SOREL AND SYNDICALISM

Berlin, Sir Isaiah. "Georges Sorel." *Times Literary Supplement,* No. 3, 644; Friday, 31 December 1971; pp. 1617-22.

Brissenden, P. E. *The I.W.W.: A Study of American Syndicalism.* N.Y.: Russell and Russell, 1960.

Curtis, Michael. *Three Against the Third Republic: Sorel, Barrès, Maurras.* Princeton: Princeton University Press, 1959.

Horowitz, Irving L. *Radicalism and the Revolt Against Reason: The Theories of Georges Sorel.* London: Routledge, Humanities Press, 1961.

Ostergaard, Geoffrey. "The Relevance of Syndicalism," *Anarchy,* No. 28 (June 1963).

Rocker, Rudolph. *Anarcho-Syndicalism.* London: Secker & Warburg, 1938.

Russell, Bertrand. *Proposed Roads to Freedom: Socialism, Anarchism, and Syndicalism.* N.Y.: Barnes & Noble, 1966.

Sorel, Georges. *The Illusions of Progress.* Berkeley: University of California Press, 1969.

———. *Reflections on Violence*. London: Macmillan, 1961.

Stanley, John L., ed. *From George Sorel*. N.Y.: Oxford University Press, 1976.

Weisbord, Albert. *The Conquest of Power: Liberalism, Anarchism, Syndicalism, Socialism, Fascism, and Communism*. N.Y.: Covici-Friede, 1937.

VI. STUDIES AND BIOGRAPHIES

Basch, V. *L'Individualisme Anarchiste: Max Stirner*. Paris, 1904.

Berlin, Isaiah. *The Hedgehog and the Fox*. N.Y.: Simon & Schuster, 1966.

———. *Fathers and Sons*. Oxford: Clarendon Press, 1972.

Brailsford, H. N. *Shelley, Godwin, and Their Circle*. London: Home University Library, 1913.

Carr, E. H. *Michael Bakunin*. N.Y.: Octagon Books, 1975.

Coker, Francis W. *Recent Political Thought*. N.Y.: Appleton-Century-Crofts, Inc., 1934. Chapter VII, "The Anarchists," pp. 192-228.

Drinnon, Richard. *Rebel in Paradise, a Biography of Emma Goldman*. Chicago: University of Chicago Press, 1961.

Eltzbacher, Paul. *Anarchism*. London: A. C. Fifield, 1908.

Fleischer, David. *William Godwin: A Study in Liberalism*. London: Allen & Unwin, 1951.

Fishman, W. J. "Anarchism," in Maurice Cranston and Sanford Lakoff, eds., *A Glossary of Political Ideas*. N.Y.: Basic Books, 1969.

Hall, Bill. "The Economic Ideas of Josiah Warren, First American Anarchist," *History and Political Economy*. February, 1974; 6 (1), pp. 95-108.

Hoffman, Robert. *Anarchism*. N.Y.: Atherton Press, 1970.

Horowitz, Iving. *The Anarchists*. N.Y.: Dell Publishing Co., 1964.

Kedward, Harry. *The Anarchists: The Men Who Shocked an Era*. N.Y.: American Heritage Press, 1971.

Kelly, Aileen. "Lessons of Kropotkin," *The New York Review of Books*, October 28, 1976, pp. 40-44.

Krammick, Isaac. *The Politics of Political Philosophy, A Case Study: Godwin's Anarchism and Radical England*. New Haven, Conn.: Yale University Press, 1970.

Masters, Anthony. *Bakunin: The Father of Anarchism*. N.Y.: The Saturday Review Press, 1975.

Maximoff, G. P., ed. *The Political Philosophy of Bakunin: Scientific Anarchism.* Glencoe, Ill.: Free Press, 1953.

Miller, Martin A. *Kropotkin.* Chicago: University of Chicago Press, 1976.

Nomad, Max. "Johann Most" (six articles). *Modern Monthly,* IX-X. 1936-1938.

Novak, D. "The Place of Anarchism in the History of Political Thought." *The Review of Politics,* Vol. 20 (July 1958), pp. 307-329.

Parsons, Albert R. *Anarchism: Its Philosophical and Scientific Basics.* Chicago: Mrs. A. R. Parsons, 1887.

Paterson, R. W. K. *The Nihilist Egoist: Max Stirner.* London and N.Y.: Oxford University Press, 1971.

Pyziur, Eugene. *The Doctrine of Anarchism of Michael Bakunin.* Milwaukee: The Marquette University Press, 1955.

Redpath, Theodore. *Tolstoy.* London: Bowes, 1969.

Ritter, Alan. *The Political Thought of Pierre-Joseph Proudhon.* Princeton: Princeton University Press, 1969.

Simmons, Ernest. *Leo Tolstoy.* Boston: Atlantic Monthly Press, 1946.

Stafford, David. *From Anarchism to Reformism.* Toronto: University of Toronto Press, 1971.

Thompson, E. P. *William Morris: Romantic to Revolutionary.* London: Merlin Press, 1974.

Troyat, Henri. *Tolstoy.* Garden City, N.Y.: Doubleday, 1967.

Vizetelly, Ernest A. *The Anarchists: Their Faith and Their Record.* London, 1911.

Walter, Nicolas. "About Anarchism." *Anarchy,* No. 100, June 1969.

Wenley, Robert. *The Anarchist Ideal and Other Essays.* Boston: R. G. Badger, 1913.

Woodcock, George. *Anarchism: A History of Libertarian Ideas and Movements.* N.Y.: Meridian Books, 1962.

———. *New Life to the Land.* London: Freedom Press, 1942.

———. *Pierre-Joseph Proudhon.* London: Routledge & Kegan Paul, 1956.

———. *William Godwin: A Biographical Study.* London: Porcupine, 1946.

Zenker, Ernst Victor. *Anarchism: A Criticism and History of the Anarchist Theory.* London: Methuen, 1898.

VII. ANARCHIST MOVEMENTS (BY COUNTRY)

A. United States

Adamic, Louis. *Dynamite: The Story of Class Violence in America.* N.Y.: Chelsea House Publishers, 1968.

Bailie, William. *Josiah Warren—The First American Anarchist.* Boston: Small, Maynard, & Co., 1906.

David, Henry. *The History of the Haymarket Affair: A Study in the American Social-Revolution and Labor Movements.* N.Y.: Russell & Russell, 1958.

Foner, Philip Sheldon, ed. *The Autobiographies of the Haymarket Martyrs.* N.Y.: Humanities Press, 1969.

Hayden, Dolores. *Seven American Utopias: The Architecture of Communitarian Socialism, 1790-1975.* Cambridge, Mass.: The M.I.T. Press, 1976.

Jacker, Corinne. *The Black Flag of Anarchy: Anti-Statism in the U.S.* N.Y.: Scribner, 1968.

Kipnis, Ira. *The American Socialist Movement, 1897-1919.* N.Y.: Columbia University Press, 1952.

Martin, James J. *Men Against the State: The Expositors of Individualist Anarchism in America.* DeKalb, Ill.: Adrian Allen Assoc., 1953.

Maximoff, G. P. *Constructive Anarchism.* Chicago: Maximoff Memorial Publishing Co., 1952.

Perry, Lewis. *Radical Abolitionism: Anarchy and the Government of God in Antislavery Thought.* Ithaca: Cornell University Press, 1973.

Rocker, Rudolph. *Pioneers of American Freedom.* Los Angeles: Rocker Publications, 1949.

Schuster, Eunice M. *Native American Anarchism.* N.Y.: AMS Press, 1970.

Warren, Josiah. *Practical Applications of the Elementary Principles of "True Civilization."* Princeton, Mass.: B. R. Tucker, 1872.

B. Russia

Avrich, Paul. *The Anarchists in the Russian Revolution.* Ithaca: Cornell University Press, 1973.

———. *Kronstadt, 1921.* Princeton: Princeton University Press, 1970.

———. *The Russian Anarchists.* Princeton: Princeton University Press, 1967.

Carr, E.H. *The Romantic Exiles.* N.Y.: Frederick A. Stokes Co., 1933.

Edie, James et al., eds. *Russian Philosophy.* Chicago: Quadrangle Books, 1965.

Footman, David. *Civil War in Russia.* London: Faber, 1961.

Kropotkin, P. "The Constitutional Agitation in Russia." *Nineteenth Century,* 57, no. 335. January, 1905.

———. *Ideals and Realities in Russian Literature.* N.Y.: Knopf, 1915.

———. "The Present Crisis in Russia." *North America Review,* 172, 1901.

———. *The Terror in Russia.* London: Methuen, 1909.

Luxemburg, Rosa. *The Russian Revolution.* N.Y.C.: Worker's Age, 1940.

Makhno, Nestor. *La Revolution Russe en Ukraine.* Paris, 1927.

Maximoff, G. P. *The Guillotine at Work: Twenty Years of Terror in Russia.* Chicago: Alexander Berkman Fund, 1940.

Pipes, Richard. *Russia Under the Old Regime.* London: Weidenfeld & Nicolson, 1974.

Shatz, Marshall. "Anti-Intellectualism in the Russian Intelligentsia: Michael Bakunin, Peter Kropotkin, and Jan Waclaw Machajski," certificate essay, the Russian Institute, Columbia University, 1963.

Smirnov, Georgi. *Soviet Man: The Making of a Socialist Type of Personality.* Moscow: Progress Publishers, 1973.

Sorel, Georges. *Illusions of Progress.* Berkeley: University of California Press, 1969.

Ulam, Adam. *Ideologies and Illusions: Revolutionary Thought from Herzen to Solzhenitsyn.* Cambridge, Mass.: Harvard University Press, 1976.

———. *In the Name of the People.* N.Y.: Viking Press, 1977.

———. *The Unfinished Revolution.* N.Y.: Random House, 1960.

———. "The Uses of Revolution" in *Revolutionary Russia,* R. Pipes, ed. Cambridge: Harvard University Press, 1968.

Utechin, S. V. *Russian Political Thought: A Concise and Comprehensive History.* London: J. M. Dent, 1963. Chap. 8: "Regionalism, Anarchism, and Syndicalism."

Venturi, Franco. *Roots of Revolution.* Introduction by Isaiah Berlin. N.Y.: Grosset & Dunlap, 1966.

Voline. *Nineteen-Seventeen: The Russian Revolution Betrayed.* N.Y.: Lbertarian Book Club, 1954.

———. *The Unknown Revolution*. London: Freedom Press, 1955.

C. Spain

Bookchin, Murray. *The Spanish Anarchists: The Heroic Years 1868-1936*. New York: Free Life Editions, 1977.

Borkenau, Franz. *The Spanish Cockpit*. London: Faber, 1937.

Brennan, Gerald. *The Spanish Labyrinth*. Cambridge: Cambridge University Press, 1960.

Carr, Raymond. *Spain: 1808-1939*. Oxford: Oxford University Press, 1966.

———. "All or Nothing," *The New York Review of Books*. (13 October 1977, pp. 22 & 27.

Dolgoff, Sam, ed. *The Anarchist Collective: Workers Self-Management in the Spanish Revolution. 1936-1939*. New York: Free Life Editions, 1977.

Jellinek, Frank. *The Civil War in Spain*. N.Y.: H. Fertig, 1970.

Kaplan, Temma. *Anarchists of Andalusia, 1868-1903*. Princeton: Princeton University Press, 1977.

Meakes, Gerald H. *The Revolutionary Left in Spain, 1914-1923*. Stanford: Stanford University Press.

Orwell, George. *Homage to Catalonia*. London: Secker & Warburg, 1938.

Tellez, Antonio. *Sabate: Guerilla Extraordinary*. London: Davis-Poynter, 1974.

Thomas, Hugh. "Anarchist Agrarian Collectives in the Spanish Civil War," in Martin Gilbert, ed., *A Century of Conflict, 1850-1950*. N.Y.: Atheneum, 1966.

———. *The Spanish Civil War*. London: Harper, Ryerson Press, 1961.

D. France

Bakunin, M. *La Commune de Paris et la Notion de l'Etat*. Paris, 1871.

Booth, Arthur J. *Saint-Simon and Saint-Simonism: a Chapter in the History of Socialism in France*. London: Longmans, Green, Reade & Dyer, 1871.

Carr, Reginald. *Anarchism in France: The Case of Octave Mirbeau*. Manchester: University of Manchester Press, 1977.

Edwards, Stewart, ed. *The Communards of Paris, 1871.* London: Eyre & Spottiswoode, 1971.

Jellinek, Frank. *The Paris Commune of 1871.* N.Y.: Oxford University Press, 1967.

Kamenka, Eugene, ed. *Paradigm for Revolution? The Paris Commune: 1871-1971.* Canberra: Australian National University Press, 1972.

Kropotkin, P. *The Great French Revolution.* London: Heinemann, 1909.

Lefebvre, Henri. *La Proclamation de la Commune.* Paris, 1965.

Lissagary, P.O. *History of the Commune of 1871.* 1886; reprint, N.Y., 1967.

Maitron, Jean. *Histoire du Mouvement Anarchiste en France 1880-1914.* Paris, 1955.

Moss, Bernard H. *The Origins of the French Labor Movement: The Socialism of Skilled Workers, 1830-1914.* Berkeley: University of California Press, 1976.

Pierce, Roy. *Contemporary French Political Thought.* Chapter 4, "Simone Weil: Sociology, Utopia, and Faith." London: Oxford University Press, 1966.

Réclus, Elisée. *L'Evolution et Révolution.* Geneva, 1884.

Ridley, F. F. *Revolutionary Syndicalism in France.* Cambridge: Cambridge University Press, 1970.

Tuchman, Barbara. "Anarchism in France" in I. L. Horowitz, ed., *The Anarchists.* N.Y.: Dell Publishing Co., 1964.

E. Italy and Germany:

Carlson, Andrew. *Anarchism in Germany.* Methuen, N.J.: Scarecrow Press, 1972.

Holgate, P. *Malatesta.* London: Freedom Press, 1956.

Hostetter, Richard. *The Italian Socialaist Movement I: Origins (1860-1882).* Princeton, N.J., 1958.

Malatesta, Enrico. *Anarchy.* London: Freedom Press, 1942.

———. *A Talk About Anarchist Communism.* London; s.d.

Richards, Vernon, ed. *Errico Malatesta; His Life and Ideas.* London: Freedom Press, 1965.

F. Latin America

Bayer, Osvaldo. *Los Vengadores de la Patagonia Tragica.* 3 vols. Buenos Aires: Editorial Galerna, 1976.

Dulles, John W. F. *Anarchists and Communists in Brazil 1900-1935.* Austin: University of Texas Press, 1973.

Simon, S. Fanny. "Anarchism and Anarcho-Syndicalism in South America," *Hispanic American Historical Review,* XXVI (February 1946), pp. 38-59.

Womack, John. *Zapata and the Mexican Revolution.* N.Y.: Knopf, 1969.

G. India

Bandyopadhyaya, Jayantanuja. *Social and Political Thought of Gandhi.* Bombay, 1969.

Bhattacharyya, Buddhadeva. *Evolution of the Political Philosophy of Gandhi.* Calcutta, 1969.

Doctor, A. H. *Anarchist Thought in India.* Bombay: Asia Publishing House, 1964.

Erikson, Erik. *Gandhi's Truth: On the Origins of Militant Non-Violence.* N.Y.: W. W. Norton, 1969.

Gandhi, Mohandas. *Autobiography: The Story of My Experiments with Truth.* Washington, D.C.: Public Affairs Press, 1954.

———. *How Can India Become Free?* Lahore: Allied Indian Publishers, 1944.

———. *Non-Co-Operation.* Madras: Ganosh & Co., 1921.

———. *Satyagraha (Non-Violent Resistance).* Ahmedabad: Navajivan Publishing House, 1951.

Horsburgh, H. J. N. *Non-Violence and Aggression: A Short Study of Gandhi's Moral Equivalent of War.* London: Oxford University Press, 1968.

Iyer, R. *Moral and Political Thought of Mohandas Gandhi.* N.Y.: Oxford University Press, 1973.

Ostergaard, Geoffrey, and Melville Correll. *The Gentle Anarchists.* Oxford: Clarendon Press, 1973.

H. China

Lang, Olga. *Pa Chin and His Writings.* Cambridge, Mass.: Harvard University Press, 1967.

Scalapino, Robert. *The Chinese Anarchist Movement.* Berkeley: University of California Press, 1961.

VIII. CONTEMPORARY ANARCHISTS AND THEIR CRITICS

Apter, David E., and James Joll, eds. *Anarchism Today.* London: Macmillan, 1971.

Baldelli, Giovanni. *Social Anarchism.* Chicago: Aldine, Atherton, 1971.

Barber, Benjamin R. *The Death of Communal Liberty: The History of Freedom in a Swiss Mountain Canton.* Princeton: Princeton University Press, 1974.

Buchanan, James N. *The Limits of Liberty: Between Anarchy and Leviathan.* Chicago: University of Chicago Press, 1976.

———. "Review" of David Friedman's *The Machinery of Freedom,* in *Journal of Economic Literature,* Vol. XII, No. 3. September 1974. Pp. 914-15.

Carter, April. *The Political Theory of Anarchism.* N.Y.: Harper & Row, 1971.

———. *Direct Action and Liberal Democracy.* London: Routledge and Kegan Paul, 1973.

Chomsky, Noam. *American Power and the New Mandarins.* N.Y.: Pantheon Books, 1969.

———. Introduction to Daniel Guérin, *Anarchism: From Theory to Practice.* N.Y.: Monthly Review Press, 1970.

———. "Notes on Anarchism." *The New York Review of Books,* May 21, 1970.

———. *Problems of Knowledge and Freedom.* London: Barrie & Jenkins, 1972.

Coates, Ken, ed. *Essays on Socialist Humanism.* Notingham: Sokesman Books, 1972.

Friedman, David. *The Machinery of Freedom: Guide to a Radical Capitalism.* N.Y.: Harper and Row, 1973.

Goodman, Paul, and Percival. *Communitas: Means of Livelihood and Ways of Life.* N.Y.: Random House, 1960.

Goodman, Paul. *Drawing the Line.* N.Y.: Random House, 1962.

———. *Growing Up Absurd: Problems of Youth in the Organized System.* N.Y.: Random House, 1960.

———. *Like a Conquered Province.* N.Y.: Random House, 1967.

358 ROBERT A. KOCIS

——. *New Reformation: Notes of a Neolithic Conservative.* N.Y.: Random House, 1970.

——. *The Society I Live In Is Mine.* N.Y.: Horizon Press, 1963.

——. *Utopian Essays and Practical Proposals.* N.Y.: Random House, 1962.

Government and Opposition: A Journal of Comparative Politics. Issue: "Anarchism Today," Autumn 1970. Vol. V, No. 4.

Joll, James. *The Anarchists.* Boston: Little, Brown, 1964.

Marcuse, H. *Five Lectures: Psychoanalysis, Politics, and Utopia.* Boston: Beacon Press, 1970.

Marković, Mihailo. "Philosophical Foundations of Economic and Political Self-Management," in Ted Honderich, ed., *Social Ends and Political Means.* London: Routledge & Kegan Paul, 1976.

Newfield, John. *A Prophetic Minority.* N.Y.: New American Library, 1966.

Nozick, Robert. *Anarchy, State and Utopia.* N.Y.: Basic Books, 1974.

Perlin, Terry, ed. *Contemporary Anarchism.* Edison N.J.: Transaction Books, 1977.

Read, Herbert. *Anarchy and Order.* Boston: Beacon Press, 1971.

——. *The Cult of Sincerity.* London: Horizon Press, 1969.

——. *The Philosophy of Anarchism.* London: Freedom Press, 1940.

——. *The Politics of the Unpolitical.* London: Routledge & Kegan Paul, 1965.

Reiman, Jeffrey A. *In Defense of Political Philosophy: A Reply to R. P. Wolff's "In Defense of Anarchism."* N.Y.: Harpar and Row, 1972.

Rothbard, Murray. *For a New Liberty.* N.Y.: Macmillan, 1973.

——. *Man, Economy, and State.* Two volumes. Princeton: Van Nostrand, 1962.

——. *Power and Market.* Menlo Park, Cal.: Institute for Humane Studies, 1970.

Runkle, Gerald. *Anarchism: Old and New.* N.Y.: Delacort Press, 1972.

Sargent, Lyman T. *Contemporary Political Ideologies.* Homewood, Ill.: The Dorsey Press, 1972. Chapter 8, "Anarchism."

Sharp, Gene. *The Politics of Nonviolent Action.* Boston: Porter Sargent, 1973.

Ward, Colin. *Anarchy in Action.* London: Allen & Unwin, 1973.

——. "The State and Society," *Anarchy,* No. 14, April, 1962.

Wolff, R. P., Barrington Moore, and Herbert Marcuse. *A Critique of Pure Tolerance.* Boston: Beacon, 1970.

Wolff, R. P. *The Autonomy of Reason: A Commentary on Kant's Groundwork of the Metaphysic of Morals*. N.Y.: Harper Torchbook, 1973.

———. *In Defense of Anarchism*. N.Y.: Harper and Row, 1970.

———. "On Violence," *Journal of Philosophy*. LXVI, no. 19, 1969. Pp. 601-16.

———. *The Poverty of Liberalism*. Boston: Beacon Press, 1968.

———. *Understanding Rawls*. Princeton University Press, 1977.

Woodcock, George. "Anarchism Revisited," *Commentary,* August 1968.

———. *Anarchy or Chaos*. London: Freedom Press, 1944.

IX. INTERPRETATIONS OF EQUALITY, JUSTICE, AND POLITICAL AUTHORITY

Arendt, Hannah. "Truth and Politics," in Peter Laslett and W. G. Runciman, eds., *Philosophy, Politics and Society*. Third Series. Oxford: Basil Blackwell, 1967.

Barber, Benjamin R. *Superman and Common Men: Freedom, Anarchy, and the Revolution*. N.Y.: Praeger, 1971.

Bedau, Hugo. "Civil Disobedience and Personal Responsibility for Injustice," *The Monist,* October, 1970; pp. 517-35.

Berlin, Isaiah. "Equality," in Frederick Olafson, ed., *Justice and Social Policy*. Englewood Cliffs, N.J.: Prentice-Hall, 1961.

———. "Herzen and Bakunin on Individual Liberty,"; in Ernest Simmons, ed., *Continuity and Change in Russian and Soviet Thought*. Cambridge, Mass: Harvard University Press, 1955.

Cranston, Maurice. "Camus and Justice," in *The Mask of Politics and Other Essays,* London: Allen Lane, 1973.

Follett, Mary Parker. *Creative Experience*. N.Y.: Longmans, Green, 1924.

Hart, Herbert L. A. *The Concept of Law*. Oxford: Clarendon Press, 1961.

———. *Punishment and Responsibility*. Oxford: Oxford University Press, 1968.

Krader, Lawrence. *Formation of the State*. Englewood Cliffs, N.J.: Prentice-Hall, 1968.

Lakoff, Sanford A. *Equality in Political Philosophy*. Cambridge, Mass.: Harvard University Press, 1964.

Lukes, Stephen. *Individualism.* Oxford: Basil Blackwell, 1973.

Madariaga, Salvador. *Anarchy or Hierarchy?* N.Y.: Macmillan, 1937.

Marcuse, H. *Counter-Revolution and Revolt.* Boston: Beacon Press, 1972.

———. *An Essay on Liberation.* Boston: Beacon Press, 1969.

———. *Eros and Civilization: A Philosophical Inquiry into Freud.* Boston: Beacon Press, 1955.

Miller, David. *Social Justice.* Oxford: Clarendon Press, 1976.

Offe, Claus.*Industry and Inequality.* Trans. by James Wickham. London: Edward Arnold, 1976.

Pennock, J. Roland, and J. W. Chapman, eds. *Political and Legal Obligation: Nomos XII.* N.Y.: Atherton, 1970.

Schaar, John. "Notes on Authority," *New American Review,* Jan. 1970, No. 8, pp. 44-80.

Shils. Edward. "Deference," in J. A. Jackson, ed., *Social Stratification.* Cambridge: Cambridge University Press, 1968.

Tawney, R. H. *Equality.* London: Allen & Unwin, 1938.

Taylor, Michael, *Anarchy and Cooperation* (London and New York: Wiley, 1976).

Thomas, David. *Equality.* Cambridge: Cambridge University Press, 1949.

Thoreau, Henry. *Walden and "On the Duty of Civil Disobedience."* N.Y.: Airmont Publishing Co., 1964.

Wolin, Sheldon. *Politics and Vision.* Boston: Little, Brown, 1960.

Woodcook, G. *Anarchism and Morality.* London: Freedom Press, 1945.

X. EDUCATION AND THE ARTS

Binek, Horst. *Bakunin: An Invention.* London: Gollancz, 1976.

Conrad, Joseph. *The Secret Agent.* Garden City: Doubleday, 1907.

———. *A Set of Six.* Garden City: Doubleday, Page & Co., 1915.

Dostoevski, F. *The Possessed.* N.Y.: Macmillan, 1948.

Ellmann, Richard. "The Politics of Choice," *The New York Review of Books,* Vol. XXIV, June 9, 1977. pp 41-46.

Goodman, Paul. *Art and Social Nature.* N.Y.: Arts and Science Press, 1946.

———. *The Community of Scholars.* N.Y.: Random House, 1962.

———. *Compulsory Miseducation.* Harmondsworth: Penguin Books, 1971.

Hemmings, Ray. *Fifty Years of Freedom: A Study of the Development of the Ideas of A. S. Neill.* London: Allen & Unwin, 1972.

Herbert, Eugenia. *The Artist and Social Reform: France and Belgium, 1885-1898.* New Haven: Yale University Press, 1961.

Hoffman, Abbie. *Woodstock Nation: A Talk-Rock Album.* N.Y.: Vintage Books, 1969.

James, Henry. *The Princess Casamassima.* N.Y.: Macmillan, 1886.

Mackay, John Henry. *The Anarchists: A Picture of Civilization at the Close of the Nineteenth Century.* Boston, 1891.

Malamud, Bernard. *The Fixer.* N.Y.: Farrar, 1966.

Martin, David A., ed. *Anarchy and Culture: The Problem of the Contemporary University.* N.Y.: Columbia University Press, 1969.

Neill, A. S. *The Free Child.* London: Jenckins, 1953.

———. *Summerhill: A Radical Approach to Child Rearing.* N.Y.: Hart, 1960.

Read, Herbert. *Poetry and Anarchism.* N.Y.: Macmillan, 1939.

———. *To Hell with Culture.* London: Routledge & Kegan Paul, 1941.

Rocker, Rudolph. *Nationalism and Culture.* Los Angeles: McLeod, 1937.

Savage, Richard Henry. *The Anarchist: A Story of To-day.* Leipzig, 1894.

Spencer, Colin. *The Anarchy of Love.* N.Y.: Weybright & Talley, 1963.

Wolff, R.P. *The Ideal of the University.* Boston: Beacon Press, 1969.

Woodcock, G. *The Writer and Politics.* London: Porcupine Press, 1948.

XI. ANARCHISM AND EXISTENTIALISM

Aron, Raymond. *History and the Dialectic of Violence.* Oxford: Basil Blackwell, 1975.

———. *Marxism and the Existentialists.* N.Y.: Simon & Schuster, 1969.

Barrett, William. *Irrational Man: A Study in Existential Philosophy.* Garden City: Doubleday, 1958.

Burnier, Michel Antoine. *Choice of Action: The French Existentialists on the Political Front Line.* N.Y.: Random House, 1968.

Camus, Albert. *The Myth of Sisyphus and Other Essays.* N.Y.: Vintage Books, 1955.

———. *Neither Victims Nor Executioners.* Chicago: World Without War Publishers, 1972.

———. *The Rebel: An Essay on Man in Revolt.* N.Y.: Vintage Books, 1956.

———. *Resistance, Rebellion, and Death.* N.Y.: Knopf, 1960.

Cranston, Maurice. "Sartre and Violence," in *The Mask of Politics and Other Essays.* London: Allen Lane, 1973.

Hammarskjöld, Dag. *Markings.* N.Y.: Knopf, 1964.

Kaufmann, Walter. *Existentialism from Dostoevsky to Sartre.* N.Y.: World Publishing Co., 1964.

———. *Without Guilt or Justice: From Decidophobia to Autonomy.* N.Y.: Wyden, 1973.

Kierkegaard, Søren. *Journals.* N.Y.: Harper, 1959.

Molina, Fred, ed. *The Sources of Existentialism as Philosophy.* Englewood Cliffs, N.J.: Prentice-Hall, 1969.

Nietzsche, Friedrich. *Thus Spake Zarathustra.* N.Y.: Modern Library, 1917.

Oakeshott, Michael. "The Anarchist" (a review of Herbert Read). *The Spectator.* May 14, 1954.

Parker, Emmett. *Albert Camus: The Artist in the Arena.* Madison, Wisc.: University of Wisconsin Press, 1965.

Read, Herbert. *Existentialism, Marxism, and Anarchism: Chains of Freedom.* London: Freedom Press, 1949.

Sartre, Jean-Paul. *Being and Nothingness.* N.Y.: Philosophical Library, 1956.

———. *Existentialism.* N.Y.: Philosophical Library, 1947.

———. *The Flies.* London: H. Hamilton, 1946.

Willhoite, Fred. *Beyond Nihilism: Albert Camus's Contribution to Political Thought.* Baton Rouge: Louisiana State University Press, 1968.

XII. THE NEW LEFT AND STUDENT MOVEMENTS

Apter, David E., and James Joll. *Anarchism Today.* Garden City: Doubleday, 1972.

Aron, Raymond. *The Elusive Revolution: Anatomy of a Student Revolt.* Translated by Gordon Clough. London: Pall Mall Press, 1969.

Brown, Bernard. *Protest in Paris: An Anatomy of a Revolt.* Morristown, N.J.: General Learning Press, 1974.

Chapman, John W. "Personality and Privacy," in Pennock, J. Roland and J. W. Chapman, *Privacy: Nomos XIII.* N.Y.: Atherton Press, 1971.

Chicago Eight. *Conspiracy.* N.Y.: Dell Publishing Co., 1969.

Cohn-Bendit, Daniel. *Le Grand Bazar.* Paris: Belfound, 1976.

Cohn-Bendit, Daniel et al. *The French Student Revolt: The Leaders Speak.* Translated by B. R. Brewster. N.Y.: Hill and Wang, 1968.

Cohn-Bendit, Daniel and Gabriel. *Obsolete Communism: The Left-Wing Alternative.* Translated by Arnold Pomerans. N.Y.: McGraw-Hill, 1968.

Cranston, Maurice, ed. *The New Left: Six Critical Essays.* London: The Bodley Head, 1970.

Erikson, Erik. *Life History and the Historical Method.* Esp. "Reflections on the Revolt of Humanist Youth." N.Y.: W. W. Norton, 1975.

———. "Reflections on the Discontents of Contemporary Youth." *Daedalus,* Winter, 1970.

Feuer, Lewis. *The Conflict of Generations.* N.Y.: Basic Books, 1969.

Green, Gilbert. *The New Radicalism: Anarchist or Marxist?* N.Y.: International Publishers, 1971.

Gregor, A. James. *The Fascist Persuasion in Radical Politics.* Princeton: Princeton University Press, 1974.

Guérin, Daniel. *Anarchism: From Theory to Practice.* N.Y.: Monthly Review Press, 1970.

———. *Ni Dieu ni Maître.* Paris, 1967.

Hayden, Tom. *Rebellion and Repression.* N.Y.: Meridian Books, 1969.

———. *Trial.* N.Y.: Holt, Rinehart, & Winston, 1970.

Hoffman, Abbie. *Revolution for the Hell of It.* N.Y.: Dial, 1968.

———. *Steal This Book.* N.Y.: Grove Press, 1971.

Horowitz, Irving L. *Struggle Is the Message: The Anti-War Movement.* Berkeley: Glendessary Press, 1970.

Laing, R. D. *The Politics of Experience.* N.Y.: Ballantine Books, 1967.

Lipset, Seymour Martin, and Sheldon Wolin, eds. *The Berkeley Student Revolt: Facts and Interpretations.* Garden City, N.Y.: Doubleday, 1965.

Lipset, Seymour Martin, and Philip Altback, eds. *Students in Revolt.* Boston: Houghton Mifflin, 1969.

Long, Priscilla, ed. *The New Left: A Collection of Essays.* Boston: P. Sargent, 1969.

Marcuse, H. *Negations: Essays in Critical Theory.* Boston: Beacon Press, 1968.

Parsons, Talcott, and Gerald M. Platt. *The American University.* Cambridge, Mass.: Harvard University Press, 1973.

Rooke, Margaret Anne. *Anarchy and Apathy: Student Unrest 1968-1970.* London: Hamilton, 1971.

Roszak, Theodore. *The Making of a Counter-Culture: Reflections on the Technocratic Society and Its Youthful Opposition.* Garden City: Doubleday, 1969.

Rubin, Jerry. *Do It! Scenarios of the Revolution.* N.Y.: Simon & Schuster, 1970.

———. *We Are Everywhere.* N.Y.: Harper and Row, 1971.

Sargent, Lyman T. *New Left Thought: An Introduction.* Homewood, Ill.: The Dorsey Press, 1972.

Shils, Edward. *The Intellectuals and the Powers and Other Essays.* Chapter 13, "Plenitude and Scarcity: The Anatomy of an International Cultural Crisis." Chicago: University of Chicago Press, 1972.

Spender, Stephen. *The Year of the Young Rebels.* N.Y.: Random House, 1968.

Ulam, Adam. *The Fall of the American University.* N.Y.: The Library Press, 1972.

Wolfe, Tom. *The Electric Kool-Aid Acid Test.* N.Y.: Bantam Books, 1968.

Woodcock, George. "Anarchism Revisited," *Commentary,* August 1968, pp. 54-60.

XIII. DEFENSIVE COLLECTIVISM: PRESENT DISCONTENTS WITH HIERARCHY

Goodman, Paul. *People or Personnel: Decentralizing and the Mixed System.* N.Y.: Random House, 1965.

de Huszar, George B. *Practical Applications of Democracy.* N.Y.: Harper and Brothers, 1945.

Ioan, Bowen Rees. *Government by Community.* London: Charles Knight & Co., 1971.

Kontos, Alkis, ed. *Domination.* Toronto: University of Toronto Press, 1975.

Macpherson, C. B. *Democratic Theory: Essays in Retrieval.* Oxford: Clarendon Press, 1973.

Macrae, Norman. "The Coming Entrepreneurial Revolution: A Survey," *The Economist.* Vol. 261, No. 6956, pp. 41-65.

Manicas, Peter. *The Death of the State.* N.Y.: Putnam's, 1974. See Maurice Cranston's review, "Thoreau the Rascals Out," in *Washington Post,* January 19, 1975.

Meakin, David. *Man and Work: Literature and Culture in Industrial Society.* London: Methuen, 1976.

Rigby, Andrew. *Alternative Realities: A Study of Communes and Their Members.* London: Routledge & Kegan Paul, 1970.

Ritter, Alan. "Technology and Anarchism," paper delivered at the 1974 Annual Meeting of the Americal Political Science Association.

Sennett, Richard, and Jonathan Cobb. *The Hidden Injuries of Class.* N.Y.: Vintage Books, 1973.

Thayer, Frederick. *An End to Hierarchy! An End to Competition!* N.Y.: New Viewpoints, 1973.

Unger, Roberto Mangabeira. *Knowledge and Politics.* N.Y.: The Free Press, 1975.

INDEX